Hans H. Skei

William Faulkner: The Novelist as Short Story Writer

A Study of William Faulkner's
Short Fiction

Universitetsforlaget

Oslo – Bergen – Stavanger – Tromsø

PUBLICATIONS OF
THE AMERICAN INSTITUTE
UNIVERSITY OF OSLO

William Faulkner:
The Novelist as
Short Story Writer

'Old man', she said, 'have you lived so long and forgotten so much that you dont remember anything you ever knew or felt or even heard about love?'
– Faulkner, *Go Down, Moses*

© UNIVERSITETSFORLAGET AS 1985
ISBN 82-00-07303-3 (hardcover)
ISBN 82-00-07302-5 (paper back)

Distribution offices:

NORWAY
P.O. Box 2977 Tøyen
0608 Oslo 6, Norway

UNITED KINGDOM
Global Book Resources Ltd.
109 Great Russell Street
London WC1B 3NA

UNITED STATES and CANADA
Columbia University Press
136 South Broadway
Irvington-on-Hudson
New York 10533

Published with a grant from
The Norwegian Research Council
for Science and the Humanities

Cover:
The portrait on the cover is reproduced from Jack Cofield's book:
William Faulkner. The Cofield Collection, Yoknapatawapha Press,
Oxford, Mississippi 1978, with the kind permission of the author.

Printed in Norway by
Engers Boktrykkeri A/S, Otta

Contents

Works Cited

These 13. New York: Cape & Smith, 1931; London: Chatto & Windus, 1933.

Doctor Martino and Other Stories. New York: Smith & Haas, 1934. Referred to as *Doctor Martino.*

The Unvanquished. New York: Random House, 1938. Re-issue: Vintage Books, 1966, and later.

Go Down, Moses. New York: Random House, 1942. Re-issue: Vintage Books, 1973.

Knight's Gambit. New York: Random House, 1949. Re-issue: Vintage Books, 1978.

Collected Stories. New York: Random House, 1950. Re-issue: Vintage Books, 1977.

Early Prose and Poetry, edited by Carvel Collins. Boston: Little, Brown, 1962. Re-issue: London: Jonathan Cape, 1963.

New Orleans Sketches, edited by Carvel Collins. New York: Random House, 1968. Re-issue: London: Chatto & Windus, 1968.

Essays, Speeches and Public Letters, edited by James B. Meriwether. New York: Random House, 1966. Re-issue: London: Chatto & Windus, 1967.

Uncollected Stories of William Faulkner, edited by Joseph Blotner. New York: Random House, 1979.

References to these books are given parenthetically in the text, while references to all other books by Faulkner are given in the notes.

Preface

Faulkner's short fiction is still the most neglected area in Faulkner studies, although important basic work has been done. Joseph Blotner's biography of Faulkner and his editions of selected letters and uncollected stories shed light on Faulkner's short stories in general and on individual stories too. James B. Meriwether's *The Literary Career of William Faulkner* and 'The Short Fiction of William Faulkner: A Bibliography' must also be mentioned. My own study, *William Faulkner: The Short Story Career* (Oslo: Universitetsforlaget, 1981) is a bibliographical and textual study of Faulkner's short fiction. It forms a necessary basis for the present book, which gives an interpretation of Faulkner's total oeuvre as a short-story writer. My approach follows the chronology established in the *Career* book. The texts are discussed according to their place in the four periods of Faulkner's short story career: 'Apprenticeship Years, 1919–1927', 'The Major Period, 1928–1932', 'Short-Story Cycles and Stories for Novels, 1933–1941', and, 'Late Stories, 1942–1962'. Two chapters are devoted to the short stories in each of these periods, with varying emphasis on the formal aspects of the stories and their thematic significance.

An analysis of short stories, and of any narrative for that matter, must essentially deal with the relationship between the story recounted and the narrative discourse in which it is recounted. The shifting positions of the narrator in the narrative situation are of paramount importance in a study of Faulkner's short fiction, especially if the short stories are seen in relation to his novels.

To deal with all the short stories Faulkner ever wrote poses serious problems of structure. Basically, the stories are treated in chronological order in this book. Some kind of structure must be superimposed on the disparate and heterogeneous material, and the division into periods seems a workable solution.

Throughout the study the thematic interpretations are structured around certain themes that recur in Faulkner's short fiction. To ascertain that these themes are comparable and work on the same level, I have based them on similar sets of criteria (often socio-cultural or related to social psychology). In the discussions of formal elements much attention is given to the role of the narrator, with emphasis on his reliability, point of view, voice, etc. The relationship between the story recounted and the discourse in which it is told is also stressed, in an attempt to find characteristics of the novelist in the manner of narration or in the selection of material for the tales.

The title of this book indicates that Faulkner's short stories very often get their settings, characters and themes from what is mainly material for novels. This means that a great many stories are closely related to novels, either in progress, completed, or already published. The author's re-use of short stories in later novels, or the use of previously published stories to form a loosely joined novel, is well known. A different implication of the book's title seems more interesting, however:

Is it possible that a novelist writes stories different in nature from those an author who is foremost a short-story writer does? I ask the question, aware that the borderlines between the two fictional forms novel and short story fluctuate and can hardly be defined precisely. Yet Faulkner frequently chose material that appears to be outside the scope of the 'average' short story. He then condensed and contracted it to suit the demands of the form (and of the market). This practice may reveal something of the novelist behind the short stories. Narrative economy, condensation, ellipsis, allusions, summary are some terms that indicate the directions of an investigation of the relationship between short story and novel. Most of the stories that relate to one of Faulkner's novels represent a strong condensation of material that would normally extend beyond the limits of the traditional short story (and Faulkner in general wrote 'traditional' short stories). With the possible exception of the major years, Faulkner requires the longer and more epic form: there is a longing in him for the novel, with its wider perspective, its variety of destinies, its multiple point of views, and its wider implications.

A study of the novelist as a short-story writer must necessarily involve a discussion of narrative form. Nonetheless, the study of themes is also an important feature of this book. Faulkner's themes, whether defined in general or more specific terms, seem to remain stable over the years and are very similar in the short stories and in the novels. Accordingly, if Faulkner's short stories are a novelist's short stories in any sense, narrative concentration and the similarity of themes must be studied closely.

In the first chapter I pursue what I consider a minimal discussion of genre and of the problems encountered in the interpretation of a high number of short narratives. I also set forth some methodological qualifications. The aim of this book is not to discuss the short-story genre, using Faulkner's stories as empiric material, nor is it to offer a manual for the reading and interpretation of short stories. Yet narrative theory and short-story taxonomy are necessary parts of this study, since they provide a basis for the interpretive work in the book as a whole.

The inexhaustibility and multi-interpretability of Faulkner's short stories, together with the bulk of the material, make it impossible to reach anything at all like a final analysis. More than a neat conclusion and a unified thesis that finally is 'proved' to be right, the study of themes and narrative methods, the very *reading* of Faulkner's short stories, may be worth while. Interpretive rhetoric might have filled in some of the lacunae in this study, giving the appearance of answering all the questions now left unaccounted for. I hope to have avoided excessive use of such rhetoric.

Bibliographical Note

William Faulkner: The Novelist as Short Story Writer is closely related to my previous book, *William Faulkner: The Short Story Career,* which has a rather extensive bibliographical section. Since the *Career* book has been reprinted and made available at the time of the present book's publication, this book does not include a bibliography. A number of book-length studies of Faulkner have appeared since the bibliography in the *Career* book was completed (1981). For relatively complete and rather extensive presentations of Faulkner scholarship from the years 1980–2, the Faulkner Issues of the *Mississippi Quarterly* are recommended. The following list includes a selection of books from later years that have been used in the course of the final revision of my original manuscript (completed 1980) in 1984:

Bassett, John Earl. *Faulkner: An Annotated Checklist of Recent Criticism.* Kent, Ohio: Kent State University Press, 1983.

Bezzerides, A.I. *William Faulkner: A Life on Paper.* Jackson: University Press of Mississippi, 1980.

Bleikasten, André. *Parcours de Faulkner.* Paris: Editions Ophrys, 1982.

Brooks, Cleanth. *William Faulkner: First Encounters.* New Haven & London: Yale University Press, 1983.

Fowler, Doreen, and Abadie, Ann J., eds. *'A Cosmos of My Own'. Faulkner and Yoknapatawpha, 1980.* Jackson: University Press of Mississippi, 1981.

Fowler, Doreen, and Abadie, Ann J., eds. *Faulkner and the Southern Renaissance.* Jackson: University Press of Mississippi, 1982.

Gresset, Michel, and Samway, Patrick, eds. *Faulkner and Idealism: Perspectives from Paris.* Jackson: University Press of Mississippi, 1983.

Jenkins. Lee. *Faulkner and Black-White Relations: A Psychoanalytic Approach.* New York: Columbia University Press, 1981.

Minter, David. *Faulkner: His Life and Work.* Baltimore: University of Johns Hopkins Press, 1980.

Pilkington, John. *The Heart of Yoknapatawpha*. Jackson: University Press of Mississippi, 1981.

Strandberg, Victor. *A Faulkner Overview: Six Perspectives*. Port Washington, N.Y.: Kennikat Press, 1981.

Formerly unpublished Faulkner texts have also appeared in recent years. Among these must be mentioned the original text of *Sanctuary* (ed. by Noel Polk; New York: Random House, 1981); *Helen: A Courtship and Mississippi Poems* (Oxford, Mississippi and New Orleans: Yoknapatawpha Press & Tulane University, 1981); 'Father Abraham' (edited by James B. Meriwether, published in New York: The Red Ozier Press, 1983), and the unfinished novel *Elmer (Mississippi Quarterly,* 36 (Summer 1983)).

Recent articles (i.e., not listed in the *Career* book's bibliography) on individual short stories or on Faulkner's short-story achievement in general that have been used for the present study, are referred to in the notes.

I am grateful to Universitetsforlaget for their reprinting of *William Faulkner: The Short Story Career,* which has been out of print for some time.

Acknowledgements

Scholars and critics to whom I am indebted are referred to in the notes. Possible omissions are not intentional. I have, however, incurred a special debt of gratitude to Dr. James B. Meriwether, University of South Carolina, whose assistance has been of immeasurable importance to my work at all stages. For valuable suggestions, my thanks are also due to Dr. André Bleikasten, Dr. Jostein Børtnes, Dr. Jan W. Dietrichson, Dr. Arne Hannevik, University Lecturer Odd Inge Langholm, Dr. Noel Polk, Dr. Brita Seyersted, Dr. Per Seyersted, and University Lecturer Asbjørn Aarseth.

For permission to quote from unpublished material in their collections, I am indebted to Mrs. Paul D. Summers, executrix of the estate of William Faulkner, The William Faulkner Collections, University of Virginia Library. To the Henry W. and Albert A. Berg Collection, the New York Public Library, Astor, Lenox and Tilden Foundations and the manuscript department at the University of Texas at Austin, I am grateful for permission to read their Faulkner manuscripts and type-scripts.

I am also indebted to the following institutions: The Southern Studies Program at the University of South Carolina, the American Institute and the Department of Literature at the University of Oslo. The University of Oslo, and, above all, the Norwegian Research Council for Science and the Humanities have my warm thanks for scholarships and grants that have made this book possible.

Oslo, July 1984
H.H.S

1. William Faukner and the Short Story

...it is evidently equally foolish to accept probable reasoning from the mathematician and to demand from the rhetorician scientific proof.
– Aristotle, *Ethica Nicomachea*

I. The Short-Story Career

Faulkner's short stories form an important part of his complete *oeuvre*, and there is no reason whatsoever to give them only cursory treatment or mention them as interesting when or if they have any bearing upon his novels. His stories do not follow any of the rules of the formula stories[1] which flooded the market in the twenties and thirties as well as later; they are not typical or representative of the peculiar American branch of this genre, which a rich short story market gave rise to. Even though many of Faulkner's short stories are products of their time and place, Faulkner never learnt to write the well-rounded, slick, and perfect story with its almost mechanical progression through crises towards a point which was intended to come as a surprise and give a twist to the story told. Faulkner is probably fairly accurate in saying that he simply sought the best way of getting a story told, whenever he had a story to tell, and that he did not care which tastes or preferences he thereby offended or satisfied. Being an avid reader, not the least of short stories, he was of course influenced by various writers of his own time as well as of earlier days, but contrary to the many authors who reached a certain level of competency, and did not struggle to go beyond it once they had become successful, Faulkner never gave in to complacency.[2] It is more true of him than of any American writer of his generation, that he tried for the impossible, and when he, inevitably, failed to reach it, the failure was at least splendid and eloquent. Faulkner's self-image, his dream and his

15

dedication may, as Malcolm Cowley has suggested, have provided important incentives to growth. Cowley refers to Faulkner's reading as one of the manifestations of this self-image, which made Faulkner sacrifice almost anything to get his work done:

Very early in his career, Faulkner showed that he wanted to be not only a writer but among the greatest writers. Shakespeare, the Bible, Dostoevski, Conrad, Joyce: he read them all intensively. He had a spirit of emulation that kept driving him ahead to study and surpass his contemporaries, then to surpass himself. Some of his good stories became great stories only on revision, as note 'That Evening Sun' and *Sanctuary* and 'The Bear'.[3]

Hemingway admired Faulkner's courage in going ahead and doing things nobody else had dared, and he sensed that Faulkner had done the right thing when he 'tried for the impossible', even if the great craftsman Hemingway would have preferred greater lucidity and clarity of style. Hemingway's son, Gregory H. Hemingway, quotes his father about Faulkner: 'He's the best of us all – although he can't finish his novels and you have to wade through a lot of crap to get to his gold.' Hemingway is also quoted as having said that Faulkner lacked a 'literary conscience'.[4]

Faulkner published his first short story in 1919, a brief prose sketch called 'Landing in Luck', and his second piece of short fiction, 'The Hill', was published three years later. In the early twenties Faulkner also wrote intricate and overwrought stories, which were never published — 'Moonlight' and 'Love'. A story of adolescent love misinterpreted by an adult world, 'Adolescence', is much more competent and interesting, also because it foreshadows Faulkner's use of local background, of people he knew, and exploits themes that he would return to some years later. These stories are far less significant, however, than the sketches Faulkner wrote during his stay in New Orleans in the first half of 1925. The writing of these sketches, products of the influence of Sherwood Anderson and the author's intimacy with most of the literary bohemia of New Orleans at that time, gave Faulkner useful experience in the handling of narrative and in the presentation of character. Thematically the sketches and stories do not only emphasize the individual's alienation from the natural world, but also his search for communal ties, for participation and sharing with his fellow beings. Man's understanding of himself as being governed by some inexplicable but omnipresent and omnipotent destiny is also felt in these texts.

Europe of the postwar years and Faulkner's own 'lost generation' sentiments may have combined to strengthen his feeling of despair and loss, and did certainly add colours and contours to his bleak and sombre picture of the world as a wasteland in many stories which he probably began in 1926 or 1927, but which were not published till after 1930. More than before, and certainly more than ever later, these stories demonstrate the outrage of a potential believer; here is criticism of a stale and stifling social life, dissatisfaction with the loss of traditional values and with the ephemeral and materialistic values replacing them. In these stories one also senses a quiet despair over people's willingness to reject what might have been a good and decent life, partly because they lack the understanding of what life could be, but also because they are prisoners of rigid social systems of expectations, roles, and control, or because they fall prey to false myths. People see nothing wrong in using other people as objects to satisfy their own needs, whether for money, love, respect, or simple power, and people invariably choose the safe, static and certain, to any kind of uncertainty and change. Faulkner uses these elements, characters, and themes to show that change is inevitable because its only alternative is stasis and death.

Faulkner's most important short-story accomplishment took place over a short period of time, which I have chosen to call his 'major short-story period'. This is the period between early 1930 (when he sold his first short story to a national magazine) and the time when he first left for Hollywood (May 1932). Faulkner tried to sell many of the stories that were published in this period as early as 1928, and a good many of them originated between 1928 and 1930, so this period really begins in 1928.

In the years following this period, a few short stories of the same type as the average short story in the major period, were written. 'Uncle Willy', 'Golden Land', and 'Lo!' are examples of independent stories which do not relate significantly to any of Faulkner's novels. The period from 1932 and up to and including the publication of *Go Down, Moses,* is a period of novel writing *(Pylon, Absalom, Absalom!, The Wild Palms, The Hamlet),* which also means that a great number of stories were by-products of novels, and were used in novels, too. This is true for such stories as 'Wash', 'Evangeline',[5] 'Barn Burning', 'Mule in the Yard', and many others. Moreover, Faulkner ventured upon the writing of a series of stories, hoping to make much money by this writing of trash, as he himself described it, and though the Bayard-Ringo stories hardly deserve to be designated a 'pulp series',[6] they are distinctly different from the stories in the earlier period in many ways. The Bayard-Ringo Civil War stories were, with one exception, published as short stories in magazines. Then Faulkner revised most of the stories, and included the one he had written to finish the book and which had failed to sell,[7] in a book that must be regarded as either a cycle of short stories or a novel. Since there is little need to stick to rigid definitions of the novel, requiring unity, coherence, and an unbroken flow of narrative, *The Unvanquished* may certainly be defined as a novel. The stories which came to form *Go Down Moses* also belong to this period, and will be discussed from a similar point of view, since most of them occupy a middle position in Faulkner's short-story career: first they (with some notable exceptions) appeared in periodicals, then they were revised and used as chapters or parts of chapters in a published book, which the author insisted was to be regarded as s novel.[8]

Faulkner's few, not too successful and not too interesting, stories of detection, with Gavin Stevens as the ingenious knight who solves crimes and sees to it that justice is done, are short stories in their own right, and the collection of them, *Knight's Gambit,* must certainly be regarded as a short-story collection with a special kind of integrity. The fact that Faulkner for some time planned to include these stories in a collection of his, by then, uncollected stories also points to such an understanding.

In 1942 Faulkner made his last serious attempt to write short stories in order to make quick money and thus avoid going back to Hollywood, where he got little, if any, writing done. This attempt resulted in the last batch of short stories from Faulkner's hand, and even though some of these stories may have superficial relationships with some of his novels, they are self-contained, autonomous works of art. Needless to say, most of them were included in *Collected Stories.* The fact that these stories did not sell may in part be responsible for the steady decline in short-story production after 1942, and the stories written after this year may be described as 'chips from the novelist's bench'. Only in a few cases, when an article or a story was commissioned, would Faulkner write a short fictional piece which did not relate to a novel under way. He did not have to 'keep the pot boiling', he did not have to write short stories or to sell them, to make ends meet. After the sale of the movie rights to *Intruder in the Dust,* Faulkner's economy improved considerably, and the bare need, which had forced him to write short stories when he would rather have gone on with work on a novel, was no longer present to force him through the anguish, the agony, and the embarrassment of selling what he knew were first-rate stories, at a cheap price.[9]

II. What Is a Short Story?

Faulkner's contribution to the short-story genre has been considered to be relatively slight or of virtually no importance. Yet his use of 'mixed forms' – novels composed of joined stories, short-story cycles, fictional essays bordering on the short story – necessitates an introductory discussion of some of the characteristics of the short story. The main reason for discussing the borderlines between closely related literary genres is the help this can give the critic in the interpretations of individual stories and in the comparison of the novelist and the short-story writer William Faulkner. The presentation of some of the problems inherent in classification and definition of short fictional texts will thus also be a preliminary survey of the interpretive methods that are employed throughout this book.

It is hardly possible to define the short-story genre once and for all. A tentative, perhaps very general, definition of the short-story form, with emphasis on what appears to be the *differentia specificae* of the genre, must be reached before one goes on to describe and define the particular branch or brand of short stories at hand, according to historical period, national literature, the expectations and demands of the market and the literary institution in general. Faulkner's short fiction presents numerous problems in addition to the more basic ones related to the genre; his stories comprehend so many borderline cases that only the more general genre criteria can be used to show that these texts really belong within the same class of short fiction. There is little reason, however, to make one's definitions narrow and normative so that they exclude a number of texts that would certainly be included on the basis of common sense or general consensus about what a short story is, and I have tried to be both inclusive and flexible in the choice of material for this study.

There is a great variety of short-story forms, but they seem to have more in common than they have elements that could be used to distinguish between them. They all share intensity of vision, economy and precision in presentation, and they are generally rather concentrated or condensed so that they are short in length. These characteristics allow us to classify texts broadly as short stories. The abundant material prohibits all-inclusive definitions based on empiric data, while the innovation and experimentation within the form – frequent in Faulkner's early days – should warn critics not to prescribe what short stories should be or ought to be.[10] In Faulkner's case, one should be very careful not to overemphasize the difference between a short story in a magazine and a short story published originally in a book or even re-used in a novel. Publication information can but be a starting point for an inquiry into the distinctions that may exist between various short stories in the traditional short-story collections and those in a more coherent, structured book of short stories, such as, for instance, *The Unvanquished.* Individual short stories in a magazine, a collection, or a short-story cycle, are not necessarily different from one another in any deeper sense; it is rather the use they are put to in the various contexts that distinguishes between them. The functions of a short story within the larger whole (if there is such a larger framework) are more interesting than a comparison of individual stories independent of their context. There is every reason to follow Paul Hernadi's advice and 'focus on *the order of literature,* not on *borders between literary genres'.*[11] The function of a given text within its context (which does not have to be only inter-literary) is likely to yield more than the most ingenious attempts to classify it once and for all.

The problem of classification in literary studies may be formulated thus: How is it possible to define a genre, before one knows which works the definition must be based on, and how is it possible to know these works, not having defined the genre previously? This is the old problem of hermeneutics, and there is every reason to remind oneself that every reader has a kind of unreflected concept of genre which influences his evaluation of new texts he reads. The coercion of literary convention should not be underestimated, and the very practice of defining and classifying literary texts which we all follow, bears in itself testimony to this. We all seem to have a basic understanding of what a short story is. This understanding is hardly ever based on critical or analytical studies of a minimum of short-story material, but is a generalization from what often seems to be disparate and irreconcilable short-story texts read over the years.[12] On the other hand, empiric definitions will have to be based on such an enormous body of material that only to structure and classify it would be hopeless.

It is doubtful that genre-structure can be found through the interpretations of texts, no matter how broad the material for study is. The concept of genre is on a more abstract level and cannot be sought out on the basis of individual texts.[13] It may well be that narratives in general, whether long or short, are structures independent of any particular medium. What they have in common and what makes them narratives may well be the 'wholeness' or roundedness; that is, the way the narrative structure seems to maintain and close itself. Jean Piaget states the 'transformations inherent in a structure never lead beyond the system but always engender elements that belong to it and preserve its laws.'[14] Events in a narrative must somehow be related in a sequential composite, whereas random scenes, events, dialogue etc. compiled by chance cannot (or need not) be a narrative. Independent of the medium, narratives seem to require (or create their own) beginning, middle, and end. For a written narrative, the discourse does not have to follow what in a seemingly anthropological sense is the story's chronology, but may work through foreshadowing, retrospection, ellipsis, repetition etc., with the story-teller's, or artist's, disregard of simple causality, or greater understanding of the motivating forces behind a story.

Not only the random compilation of events and descriptions would fail as a narrative, and hence as a short story, if realized in the written medium in a limited length and with a certain intensity of vision and focus on a *Höhepunkt*. Also the single image or the single description would probably not be accepted as a story, as a narrative. The simple description of an event would perhaps be a borderline case, but somehow a movement, a development, a progression towards some end seem to be required. One of the chief characteristics of the short story, whether told orally to an audience or written, seems thus to be its end-orientation. In a sense the structure of the short story implies that it will be completed at its conclusion; tensions are resolved, crises have passed and led to happiness or grief, characters have gone through decisive experiences and lost or won; and all this has been implied from the very beginning of the story, because of its structure, because of its tradition, because of the coercive concept of 'short story' we have. Edgar Allan Poe's famous definition of a 'tale' may well be quoted at this point:

A skilful literary artist has constructed a tale. If wise, he has not fashioned his thoughts to accommodate his incidents; but having conceived, with deliberate care, a certain unique or single *effect* to be wrought out, he then invents such incidents – he then combines such

21

events as may best aid him in establishing this preconceived effect. If his very initial sentence tend not to the outbringing of this effect, then he has failed in his first step. In the whole composition there should be no word written, of which the tendency, direct or indirect, is not to the one preestablished design .... Undue brevity is just as exceptionable here as in the poem: but undue length is yet more to be avoided.[15]

Although it may be wrong to go as far as to maintain that the brevity of the short story is so significant in its structural consequences that Poe's normative definition is valid for short stories far outside the school or tradition he began, there is reason to suggest that the plotting of a short story leads intentionally to a conclusion. This conclusion may be called a denouement, a turning point, a crisis that leads to revelation or insight, and it may engender many questions from the listener or reader who lives in a world where something always follows the ending of a story. Still the short story, to be a short story and not a scene, a summary, an episode, an image, tends to give us a sense of an ending, of a conclusion to the events and people we have encountered in the narrative. The Russian formalist, Victor Shklovsky, distinguishes between two basic types of motivation that give us this sense of finality: either we experience in the short story opposition resolved or similarity revealed. In both cases Shklovsky sees a kind of circular movement that links the ending with the beginning, by comparison or by contrast, thus giving the feeling of wholeness and completeness.[16]

This end-orientation and this assumed feeling of completion are peculiar to the short narrative, whether told or written, and can thus be used to distinguish the short story from the novel when we think of the written literary forms of the narrative possibilities. The short story must keep within the limits established in its early parts and by the inherent motivations for the concluding paragraphs discernible there; the novel may conclude its main action long before the end, may then go on to tell new stories, reveal new destinies and new worlds, apparently in a way that would make it possible to extend the novel to any length. It is also barely possible to contend that the short story, despite its being a highly sophisticated literary form, susceptible to all kinds of experiments and never ceasing to surprise us in its inexhaustible resourcefulness and its ability to renew itself, is more closely related to the oral story telling than the modern novel is. The modern novel, whether we place its roots in England in the 1720's or not, is perhaps a more 'literary', a more bookish form than the short story in general has become. Thus the narrative voice, which is often so pervasively felt in many short stories even when they appear to be non-narrated (no explicit narrator and minimal narration), may be inherited from the original and genuine story-telling situation, with a teller and his audience. The many narrators, overt or covert, obtrusively felt or minimally present in Faulkner's fiction, are worth a close study when we look for distinctions that may prove the hypothesis that Faulkner's stories are a novelist's short stories. Of course, the narrator, the implied author, the point of view of the story telling, the narrative voice etc. are common property to the narrative discourse of story as well as of novel, although in our case it may be that the novels with the most extravagant use of a narrator (Suratt, or, Ratliff, e.g.) are often made up of revised versions of previously published short stories.

III. Why is a Short Story Short?

In a study of Faulkner's short stories with emphasis on their relationship to his novels, an understanding of what makes a short story *short,* even if its material is broad, is needed. The relative brevity of the narrative of a short story must accordingly be commented on. The brevity of a short story has structural consequences, and it seems likely that the short story is more end-oriented than the novel and that it gives the reader a sense of wholeness and completeness through resolved tensions or revealed similarities. But the short story is short in relation to what? The story may be narrated in a discourse that takes more time than the events of the story take, and still be relatively short. It may be narrated in a discourse that takes much less time (to read, to listen to) than the actual events of the story, and still be fairly long. Any discourse has the capacity to choose what it wants to present, to state, to imply, or to leave out completely. The discourse may thus be very selective or very inclusive, yet the different narrative discourses may nonetheless satisfy the requirements that we have for the short story. Likewise, any discourse may choose its order of presentation, its frequency of repetition, its duration of a certain scene, etc.

A short story can be short for various reasons, but it may be useful to distinguish at least between two fundamental reasons: the material is in itself brief, or, if the material is broader, the story may be short because the artist has cut and compressed his material to reach his goals in telling the story. This distinction between the object of representation and the manner of presentation was originally made by Norman Friedman, and he presents his project in these words:

We will . . . discuss the size of the action (which may be large or small, and is not to be confused with the size of the *story*, which may be short or long), and its static or dynamic structure; and then the number of its parts which may be included or omitted, the scale on which it may be shown, and the point of view from which it may be told. A story may be short in terms of any one of these factors or of any combination . . .'[17]

Friedman's most important point is that 'a short story may be short not because its action is inherently small, but rather because the author has chosen – in working with an episode or plot – to omit certain of its parts. In other words, an action may be large in size and still be short in the telling because not all of it is there.'[18] The short-story artist thus has a set of independent variables to deal with, and depending on which variables are used, a story becomes short although its material may not be of brief compass. Friedman is aware that what he calls a static story, normally is relatively short because so little change (if any) is involved, while a complex dynamic action, involving the protagonist's movement from one state to another, requires more space. It is of course tempting to answer Friedman's question 'What Makes a Short Story Short?' by asking 'Why is a Short Story Not Shorter?' if the business of handling independent narrative variables is the most crucial aspect of the writing of short stories. Yet Friedman's observation that an episode or an incident may be expanded to become a relatively long story, while a more comprehensive material may be shown on a 'contracted scale' in a relatively brief prose text, is revealing. Faulkner's short stories seem mostly to be of the second type: condensed stories where much material is left out or only alluded to, and where the contraction and condensation, whether the author intended it or not, help to maximize the artistic effect. This, then, may be used to show that Faulkner primarily is a novelist, whose observations of people and incidents required the longer form, in which he could reiterate his attempts to come to terms with his experiences, and where interpretations of events could be re-interpreted and looked at from different angles. Such an understanding would, however, also indicate the close affinity between Faulkner the novelist and Faulkner the short-story writer. In some of his best novels, Faulkner's material is not very broad in scope, and does not really require novel-length to be told, if the plot or the material in itself was most interesting. Faulkner deals with interpretation of events, understanding of character, and with change as a process altering our comprehension. This invariably goes beyond the scope of the short story. It is thus possible to maintain that Faulkner's short stories, possibly with the exception of the earliest stories and sketches, are a novelist's short stories in the sense that many of them may be regarded as condensed and concentrated material for novels. This does not imply that the short-story form was not the right one for this material; it only demonstrates that Faulkner's material – his immense array of unusual local characters, hunting stories, tall tales, the Southern legacy about the lost cause, slavery, the Civil War, the aristocratic families, etc. – was so rich and abundant that it often required the longer form. On the other hand, Faulkner's novels often seem to have started in a short story; that is, in a single image, a central episode, a good story: Lena Grove, barefoot and pregnant, getting around in the world, Caddy Compson in the tree, the idiot Snopes and the cow in the long summer days of Yoknapatawpha. Faulkner's deep insight into human nature, his desire to penetrate as deep as possible to see why and how people react in certain situations, his unrelenting scrutiny, his unflagging search for understanding, forced him to chain episode to episode to see if they cast light on one another, or to describe an event from a new angle, interpret a situation from another point of view, to see if new evidence could be found, or new insights achieved. Thus a story might grow into a novel, or related stories be combined into a unified work of a greater length. Often a short story could remain unchanged as a short story, self-contained and independent; or, in some cases, autonomous yet gaining support from numerous other stories and novels in the larger framework which is Faulkner's Yoknapatawpha fiction.[19]

IV. Short-Story Cycles

Faulkner is without doubt the greatest figure in Southern literature in the years after the First World War, and he is likewise an important figure in the new development of the short story in this period. His most important contribution to the short-story field or to the genre, where elements of form seem to be particularly significant, may well be his re-use of (revised) short stories in books which either are regarded as novels or as short-story composites. *The Unvanquished* and *Go Down, Moses* are the prime examples of this form. Moreover, Faulkner's interest in unity, coherence, and structure even in 'a mere collection' of short stories, is manifest very early in his career. He considered his New Orleans sketches to be a series, called 'Sinbad in New Orleans' and, later, 'The Mirror of Chartres Street'[20] and when publishing his first collection of short stories, he revised the stories that had been published previously, and grouped them in four sections so that the sum of the book's parts became greater than the individual stories put together. His strong awareness of structuring principles was not something Faulkner relied on only when he put together stories for a collection, or when he revised and rearranged stories to make a unified work out of them. The larger design and the structuring principles that had to be followed to create coherence and unity were in some cases present when individual stories were conceived, as if the author knew that he might re-use them in a new and different context.[21] In the case of *The Unvanquished,* this awareness seems obvious. Faulkner thought of the Bayard-Ringo stories as a series, but since he had written them for the *Saturday Evening Post* and thought of the early stories as pulp or trash, he had to recreate them so that they suited the more serious direction which his series took when he wrote the final piece, 'An Odor of Verbena'. This story was written to finish the book, to make it complete, to be the 'finale' of a unified work in which each unit works logically and consistently toward the final effect. *The Unvanquished* has been discussed as a brilliant example of a new literary genre, and although I am rather doubtful about this genre concept itself, a note on the 'short-story cycle' has to be included here.[22]

Forrest L. Ingram insists that he has discovered the short-story cycle, a new literary genre. The genre appears to be a modern one, since he works with cycles only from the twentieth century. It is possible to picture the range of short-story cycles as reaching from one extreme, which would be the mere collection of unconnected stories, while the other extreme would be the novel. Somewhere in between, then, is the short-story cycle. The short-story cycle's variety of forms may be illustrated by the terms 'arranged cycle' and 'completed cycle.' An arranged cycle is a series of stories that have been brought together by an editor or an author so that one feels that the stories throw light upon one another by association or simple juxtaposition. A cycle may also have been composed as a whole, in the way that an author has conceived of it as a series and created it according to some master plan. This is, to some extent, what Faulkner did in *The Unvanquished*. But he did more: he revised, expanded, redistributed emphasis, added one important story, so that the composed cycle became a completed cycle. Although I see no need for the terms themselves, Ingram's description of a completed cycle fits *The Unvanquished* very well:

> By completed cycle I mean sets of linked stories which are neither strictly composed nor merely arranged. They may have begun as independent dissociated stories. But soon their author became conscious of unifying strands which he may have, even subconsciously, woven into the action of the stories. Consciously, then, he completed the unifying task which he may have subconsciously begun.[23]

The problem of Ingram's 'new' genre concept is that it calls for organization and unity to such an extent that any book that satisfies his requirements might rightfully be called a novel, when or if the same characters, juxtapositions, and themes recur or are developed from story to story within the cycle. In all cycles of stories a balance between the individuality of each story and the demands of the larger unit must be sought. This balance is, indeed, a very precarious one, and Ingram may be right in his unqualified judgment that in such books as Faulkner's *The Hamlet* 'one feels that the necessities of the larger unit may have triumphed over the individuality of the independent stories', whereas Ingram feels that in *Go Down, Moses* the individuality of the stories 'demolishes the cohesion of the larger unit'.[24] Adherence to and compliance with a neat genre concept should not, however, be used to pass quality judgment on works of art. In Ingram's case this seems to happen rather often.

Important in a short-story cycle is the pattern of recurrence and of development, which operate concurrently. The pattern of recurrent development affects all aspects of the individual stories and contributes to the final significance of the whole.

Winesburg, Ohio, Dubliners, The Pastures of Heaven, and *The Unvanquished* are a few examples of modern short-story cycles. They may, indeed, seem to have little in common, and will not all qualify as 'short-story cycles' if Ingram's definition is used.[25] Yet they indicate a special interest in the form: a modern tendency to compose, arrange, or complete sets of individual stories in order to form a new whole. There is little doubt that Faulkner had what Ingram calls 'the cyclical habit of mind',[26] which he indicates may have some connection with 'mythic consciousness'. Faulkner did of course create his mythic kingdom, and very early in his career he superimposed a design on otherwise very different stories. Yet if *The Unvanquished* is Faulkner's best example of a short-story cycle, and I believe it is, it was by no means only his cyclical habit of mind that made him create the series and later reshape it into a tightly unified whole. *The Saturday Evening Post* and other magazines had discovered that readers enjoyed meeting the same characters and the same background again in new stories; furthermore, serialization of novels was often a great success. To create stories centred around the same character or placed in the same environment did not necessarily lead to the creation of a short-story cycle, but the best writers saw the further possibilities of the form. The popular series in the big magazines encouraged the more serious short-story artists to try the 'cyclical form', and some of these writers used the form with great success. Editors also often encouraged writers to use the same characters in new stories.

When Ingram hails *The Unvanquished* as a superb completed short-story cycle and states that *The Hamlet* and *Go Down, Moses* fail drastically to satisfy the demands of this new genre, a value judgment is obviously implied. A perfect short-story cycle may be a less impressive and important book than a book in which the stories retain so much of their individuality that they demolish the cohesion of the larger unit, to use Ingram's words. *The Unvanquished* and *Go Down, Moses* are excellent examples of this, since there can be little doubt that *Go Down, Moses* is superior to *The Unvanquished* in all respects, albeit it may lack the linear unity of a short-story cycle, by Ingram's definition.

V. Methodological Considerations

Every narrative can be described as a structure with a story expressed through the discourse. 'Story' would then refer to the contents of, in our case, a short story, while 'discourse' refers to the expression through narrative statements of different sorts, set forth in written language. In the following chapters this narrative dichotomy will be emphasized through the very analysis of many individual short stories, since the relationship between 'story' and 'discourse,' with particular attention being paid to the narrator's role, will be central throughout the study. I have not felt obliged to follow exactly the same method or approach in all of the interpretations: on the contrary, I have felt free to stress the thematic significance of certain stories at the expense of formal commentary, and vice versa. Basically, however, a balance has been sought.[27]

For my discussions of themes, I take for granted a certain knowledge of Faulkner's novels, and venture the proposition that his themes are very much the same in the short fiction, with minor modifications. It is not totally irrelevant to claim that the modern short story is very much concerned with the outsider, with people on the fringes of society, and that the voice of the narrator (if heard) is often a lonely and despairing voice. The narrators in Faulkner's short stories are very different people; some of them are audible, others are only felt to be present as a transmitting source, to help in the act of communication that goes on between the narrator and the reader. Faulkner's manipulation of the various parties that it takes to create a narrative is often revealed through the narrators: some of them are unreliable, others seem to represent the wisdom of the tribe, the common moral code of the small town, etc., and thus the distinction between the narrator and the implied author may either be very clear, irony often being the result, or the two may support one another so that the narrator's explicit comments and interpretations of actions and events correspond to the 'norm' of the implied author in the text.

In my discussions of the different narratives that are Faulkner's short stories, I rely on many theories about narrative structure, beginning with James and Lubbock in the first decades of this century, continuing through Wayne C. Booth's seminal study, *The Rhetoric of Fiction,* and, as far as this study is concerned, ending with Seymour Chatman's *Story and Discourse,* and, although used very sparingly, Gerald Genette's *Narrative Discourse [Figures 111,* 'Discours du récit'].[28] While Chatman investigates the narrative dichotomy in his theory, Genette works with three levels in the narrative discourse, adding to Chatman's two levels the level of narration, or narrating; i.e., the producing narrative action:

Story and narrating thus exist for me only by means of the intermediary of the narrative. But reciprocally the narrative (the narrated discourse) can only be such to the extent that it tells a story, without which it would not be narrative, ... and to the extent that it is uttered by someone, without which ... it would not in itself be discourse. As narrative, it lives by its relationship to the story that it recounts; as discourse, it lives by its relationship to the narrating that utters it.[29]

As indicated above, I discuss Genette's third level as a part of my interpretation of the narrative discourse, paying particular attention to the narrator's role; e.g. in the many stories in which Faulkner attempts to establish a traditional (oral) story-telling situation. Also, whenever point of view or voice (of the narrator or the implied author) is discussed, the relationship between story and narrating, as well as between discourse and the communication of that discourse, are discussed, whether I use Genette's term or not.[30] Moreover, this study is by no means an essay in method, but rather an attempt to read all the short stories written by one particular author, and then to report from the reading.

2. Short Stories 1919–1927
The Young Artist in Search of a Form

> I, too, am but a shapeless lump of moist earth risen
> from pain, to laugh and strive and weep, knowing no
> peace until the moisture has gone out of it, and it is
> once more of the original and eternal dust.
> – Faulkner, 'New Orleans'

Faulkner's early short stories are obviously not a novelist's short stories.
They are rather a poet's short stories, if such a term may be applied. This
implies that Faulkner basically must be regarded as a poet in the early
years of his career. When he arrived in New Orleans early in 1925, he
was a poet who had experimented with little success in the short story
and essay form; when he left New Orleans for travels in Europe in July
1925, he had, generally speaking, become a prose-fiction writer. The
sudden change brought about by the sojourn in New Orleans is therefore
of paramount importance in an investigation of Faulkner's growth as a
short-story writer. His primary interest lay in form and character, but he
soon found that a writer with real ability would find sufficient the
material he had to hand, no matter what it was. He did not, however, find
what he had to hand – his material and his particular methods of
handling it – till much later. In the early twenties he was constantly in
search of his material as well as of his form, looking in all directions. And
although one may maintain that he found a suitable form for the
depiction of the varied cast of New Orleans characters, his experimentation by no means ceased at this point. The New Orleans sketches may
be viewed as experiments on a small scale, with material that was so
limited that the formal experiments also became limited to the portrayal
of character, the handling of simple plots, and omniscient narration of
everyday scenes. Faulkner also made some interesting attempts at first-
person narration, using unreliable or highly limited narrators.
   In this chapter a presentation of Faulkner's earliest short fiction will
be given, with emphasis on theme as well as on form. Since Faulkner is

still uncertain as a literary artist in this period, and since it may be difficult to see the future master in any of the early stories, the stories require quite a close scrutiny, despite their rather poor quality. I have not found it worth while to deal at length with each and every story, or to study them all with special attention to the relationship short story/novel. A few foreshadowings of later works are mentioned, but there is reason to repeat that none of these stories can be regarded as a novelist's short stories, in the sense I have discussed in the Preface and in the introductory chapter. 1925 and the New Orleans writings represent an important change in Faulkner's career, finally leading him on to his material and, more slowly, to his form.

Some critics of Faulkner's early short fiction have found that his protagonists live in an isolated and fragmented environment, not knowing their own identity or their place in the world.[1] Other critics have seen in these early texts a struggle to balance the 'devastating unimportance of one's destiny' with the relative importance of one's life.[2] The solitary young men and women in Faulkner's apprenticeship prose fiction are often lonely and insecure and estranged even in a crowd, and inability to establish more than fleeting and ephemeral relationships is a typical trait. The human heart in conflict with itself is thus here from the very start; distorted relationships, deception, lies, and conceit are elements that are used in vain to establish some kind of belonging, some kind of meaningful existence. These attempts have an invariable tendency to backfire.

The estrangement from the social environment, from any kind of lasting and meaningful human relationship – love, forgiveness, understanding, sharing – is all too evident. The lack of human ties, the frailty of all bonds between people except, possibly, family ties, and the exclusiveness of the established societies in which the 'loners' live, are all elements that combine in various ways to depict most shadows and shades of human behaviour, human misery, and human greatness in Faulkner's later short fiction. Particularly typical of his short fiction of the early period (up to 1928) is loneliness: the private search, the desperate need for the touch of a human hand, for kindness, if not for love. Here are the quenched fire, the negated dreams, the unbroken inhibitions. Elementary human needs seem to be unwanted and despised and cursed by a cold, hostile and self-sufficient society of adjusted, conforming adults. An important element in Faulkner's early short fiction is the conflict between burning youth and the authority of the adult world. In a sense this conflict parallels the author's own insecurity and indecision as an artist and his search for a form in these early years. He had chosen to follow a vocation and a calling which would hardly be accepted as an occupation by his immediate environment. The great problem this created, even though Faulkner never doubted what he had to do, was that the local milieu – his postage stamp of native soil – had to be the warp and woof in the many-splendoured tapestry he wove over the years. He simply had to live where he lived to write what he wrote. He had to continue his quest, his search for a form. He had to create, regardless of what the world outside thought of it. So even the artist behind the creation of lonely figures in inhospitable if not hostile environments experienced some of the hostility and coldness and lack of understanding that he later would ascribe to his characters in the fictional world. The young artist's lonely search may also explain why many of the most dramatic conflicts in his short fiction have their basis in family situations, especially in the early years of the short-story career, while it is possible to see a development from the close-knit unity of the family to local problems and further to more universal conflicts in the short stories over the years.

Up to, and including, the composition of *The Sound and the Fury,* Faulkner's own striving and growth and vacillation may be said to correspond broadly to elements of his fiction, even though I would not suggest that autobiographical elements are especially significant in his writing of this period. The young man's dissatisfaction with what the world had come to, his fascination with poetry, and especially with the so-called 'decadent' poetry of the 1890's in which the world is weary, love and life brief, only death secure, and beauty withers so fast; all is clearly reflected in the early writings. Faulkner may have felt that he was different and that he, accordingly, did not have to adjust to normal standards of behaviour. One should not be surprised to find such attitudes more outspokenly in his fiction than in his poetry. In Faulkner's poems, where images and metaphors are often foreign or literary and where exactitude is what he aspires to, there is little room for individualization of conflicts and problems. Granted that some of these elements may be present in his poetry, but then rather as ideas, as *Weltanschauung*, as universal and eternal truths. In fiction they acquire a different sense of contemporaneity and actuality; in short, they become real problems of a real world; however fictional they are, they need not be fictitious.

The earliest of all known prose texts by Faulkner, 'Landing in Luck', is an amusing and mildly funny anecdote about a young cadet's first solo flight. Here the author unquestionably draws on experience from his training as an aviator in Toronto in 1918. The cadet, Thompson, who is angry with his officer and instructor because of his condescending attitude, wants to prove that he is 'no physical coward' *(Early Prose and Poetry,* p. 44). He makes an extremely bad take-off and strips a wheel off his plane. Miraculously, Thompson makes a perfect landing after circling about in the air to use up the petrol, and after having been placed 'on the laps of the Gods' *(Early Prose and Poetry,* p. 48) by the narrator.

It is possible to read 'Landing in Luck' as a thinly disguised self-confession, but one has to use very questionable biographical material even to do so. Anyhow, the story remains mainly funny and entertaining, and was probably meant to be so. It displays quite a measure of technical skill, especially in the handling of the shifts from ground to air and from straight narration to dialogue.

'Landing in Luck' works by means of irony, but this is an irony that is totally wasted on the characters in it, but which is implicit in the omniscient narrator's detached and distant voice and in the ironic fact that although cadet Thompson changes significantly through his experience, he does not *learn* anything from it. His behaviour is rather less in touch with reality than prior to the flight. Eagerness to show off, to pretend that one is better than one really is, may be the central 'idea' of this sketch, if indeed it need have one. The implications of this 'lightly amusing'[3] story should not be stretched too far, but it is permissible to mention that this text, despite its possible factual basis, is about a young man's flying and the fear he experiences while doing so. His nervousness and the ensuing danger is partly a result of the possibility of failure in the face of other cadets in one of the most exclusively male professions. Even if he is helped by fate so that he survives, he does in fact fail as a man, and quite predictably he cannot let this show.

'Landing in Luck' has some interest as the first Faulkner story about flying and flyers, but the story is inferior to all later such stories. It has been overlooked by most Faulkner critics, who instead have taken a special liking to 'The Hill'.[4] The very first Faulkner story deserves attention also because it is a clear and simple narration about a factual

34

event, while the other stories before the New Orleans period deal with the interactions of various characters, so that love and hope, lust and desire make for a less factual or concrete atmosphere than in 'Landing in Luck'.[5]

If the value and interest of Faulkner's early pieces of prose fiction are found to lie primarily in their relevance for his later and more mature work, then it becomes understandable that 'Landing in Luck' is by-passed and more attention is given to his second published sketch of the period, 'The Hill'. 'The Hill' was published three years after 'Landing in Luck', and Faulkner wrote at least two other short stories in between. If one is also interested in how Faulkner learnt his craft, it is of some significance that 'Landing in Luck' in all its simplicity demonstrates the relatively high level of competence Faulkner began on. His was, to begin with, an inborn talent, which needed practice in various genres to reach proficiency and perfection, but he probably needed less than many a writer who did not start off so well and who did not pick up the tricks of the writer's trade with equal ease and speed.[6]

'Moonlight' is Faulkner's second story chronologically, at least as far as we know. Since Faulkner tried to sell the story in 1928 as well as in 1935, it may well be that one of the two extant typescripts is from a later period than around 1920 when he remembered having written this story of youthful love.[7] The story nevertheless belongs in this early period, and despite the real possibility that one version stems from 1928 or later, Faulkner's revisions have been limited to improving and recasting the material of the older story. Both versions will be discussed here, because of the information this may yield as to Faulkner's early method of narration. 'Moonlight' is interesting also because it uses a small Southern town as the setting for the events, and it is typical of Faulkner in this period in its preoccupation with youthful love and unfulfilled dreams.

In the Southern town where 'Moonlight' is located, Saturday evening brings hopes of love and exciting experiences, but the rules for social behaviour, the standard code of conduct, and the expectations of boys and girls are incongruous. Robert and George pick up girls in a drug-store, simply because that is what boys are supposed to do, and when George is asked by Cecily if he loves her, even this question has a mechanical answer: 'He told her, in stereotyped phrases become a little glib.'[8] The boys' drinking of whiskey to gain courage, their brisk but not too serious attempts to 'make the girls', all this is presented in a very simple story. The plot is strictly chronological, and the actions and emotions involved are almost too clear and obvious. The strength of the story lies in the descriptive passages which Faulkner uses in order to create an atmosphere which underlines and empasizes the emotions at work among the characters. Faulkner draws pictures by using words; pictures reminiscent of his own drawings in this period; e.g. in *Marionettes*. Whole paragraphs are devoted to descriptions of the small Southern town this late August Saturday night:

> The stores were still open, since it was Saturday night, and the courthouse among its elms and fronted by the marble Confederate Soldier, was like a postcard. The elms in the blending of electricity and moonlight were a poisonous and illogical green and the courthouse with its eight columns had no depth whatever, for all the perspective of the spacious square.[9]

'Moon' and 'moonlight' are recurring words throughout the story, and darkness is used to contrast with the moonlight and to give a dreamlike and ghostly atmosphere in some of the scenes. The night becomes treacherous, because the foliage and the big houses cause parts of the streets to lie in complete darkness. The imagist poet paints the scene:

> The street was dark, arched over by the dusty foliage of late August, the pavement dappled with shadows of motionless leaves by the full moon of August. On either side the houses were darkened against the heat, and murmurs of talk came along the dead air from the porches . . .[10]

The moonlight and the heat and the mockingbird in the magnolia tree are all parts of a mystic pattern of imagery that Faulkner weaves into his story with great care. The story itself is not important or interesting enough to carry the weight of the descriptions, but the practice seems to have been a good one: in a story such as 'Dry September' Faulkner uses a similar pattern with great success and the 'light in August' we see painted here points forward to that novel more than ten years later.[11] It apparently took some time before Faulkner felt that he had mastered this kind of story-telling technique of blending dialogue and dramatic action with pure descriptive paragraphs that correlate with the story's theme and actions. In the revised version of 'Moonlight', the descriptions of climate and landscape have been kept down, while the male youth's dream of making love has been stressed more. The ambivalent attitude to sex and love-making shared by both sexes and to some extent explained by references to the expectations they have been conditioned to have, is still there. Faulkner has rid himself of the substantial and elaborate descriptions, but has chosen a more complicated narrative form. Even if the second version is basically chronological, a kind of flashback is used to allow the male protagonist to contemplate a note he has received from his girl-friend, providing information about the girl's family, his earlier meetings with the girl, Susan, and the resulting conflict with her uncle. This retrospective glance comes naturally in the story since 'he' does not have a friend to talk to about his problems, and because the whole drugstore part is left out of the second version. 'He' simply waits for Susan in the dark house, whiskey in his pocket, having been called there by her note. The most important elements of his thoughts and behaviour are related to his fear of being seen. This fear he shares with a number of young protagonists in Faulkner's short fiction, both in the twenties and thirties. He has more problems, however: even though he feels that he has reached 'that instant when desire and circumstance coincide' *(Uncollected Stories,* p. 495), he is ambivalent to what he looks forward to. He is afraid that he is too inexperienced, that he cannot live up to his own expectation. There is also the more experienced Skeet, who, like his other friends, has gone to Negro Hollow to be freed from innocence, while 'he' is even a scout! Susan, despite her note, acts in a way that apparently is meant to be typically feminine: she resists his attempts at seducing her, cries, fights, denies her note, and promises that – maybe tomorrow. His reaction to this not too unexpected turn is deftly described in the last paragraph ot the story:

'All right, all right.' He held her. He felt nothing at all now, no despair, no regret, not even surprise. He was thinking of himself and Skeet in the country, lying on a hill somewhere under the moon with the bottle between them, not even talking *(Uncollected Stories,* p. 503).

While the earliest version emphasizes the moonlight mood, the hot night and the hot blood and an insincere relationship become stereotype, only the stereotyped female character who acts her role with deliberate consideration – even to the point that her note is better than those in movies – remains as simple and shallow a character in the later version as in the early one. Some motivation and psychological explanation for the male character's conduct are given, and his desperate need to have Susan's body is not only the desire of the flesh of his sixteen-year-old body. He also wants to revenge himself on Susan's uncle, and he wants simply to *seduce* to get rid of his own virginity, his own inhibitions: in other words, to fulfil another of the expectations of the male role:

That's all I want, he thought. I just want to seduce her. I would even marry her afterward, even if I aint a marrying kind of man (Uncollected Stories, p. 500).

The male protagonist of the second version is more of a fully realized psychological character than George of the earlier version; his language is more sophisticated, even literary at times, and he questions his own motives for doing this and that. At the same time he is caught in a web made up of his own desires and dreams, which are also very clearly reflections of the rules and regulations of conduct and decent behaviour in the society he lives in.[12]

'Moonlight' anticipates elements in *Soldiers' Pay,* while a hammock scene foreshadows similar scenes in *The Sound and the Fury* as well as in *Sanctuary* and in some short stories, e.g. 'Elly'. The author seems to have taken a particular dislike to the innocent and ignorant young girl, even if he does not condemn her uncritically but places some of the responsibility on outside forces.

The story with the ambitious title, 'Love', is also concerned with love and its ramifications. Infatuation and jealousy are in point of fact more central in 'Love' than love itself, and the only lasting, serious, and genuine love is that which the oriental servant, Das, shows toward his master, Tuan, the Major. This love is based on gratitude: the Major has saved Das's life once. The love that may have led Beth to marry Jeyfus before the story opens can obviously be questioned, and Beth's interest in the Major is at best the curious and flirtatious young girl's infatuation with the older, expert seducer whose 'silver temples and ice-colored eyes' are irresistible.[13] The plot – or rather the plots – of this story are so complicated that it is futile to try to disentangle them, but a few remarks are needed. In the manuscript version the story is partly seen from the oriental servant's point of view, and centres round Beth, the Major, and the Italian maid. The maid is very passionate (she is Italian!) and believes that something is going on between Beth and the Major, whom she desires, and for whom she has prepared a love potion to arouse his feelings. The murderous scheme of giving poison instead of the love potion that the maid tries to work out, fails, because Das has been an apothecary assistant some time back in Indo-China.

This melodramatic and incredible plot, which is far more complicated than hinted at above, is reduced somewhat in the early typescript version. The emphasis is shifted from the love potion and poison game and the triangle to the Beth-Jeyfus sub-plot. Das's role is thus played down, and Beth becomes a more important character.[14] Her female fury is at the core of the story, and is seen in the opening lines:

In 1921 Beth came across the flagged terrace, her geranium colored dress taut with fury.[15]

The house guest in what amounts to being a haunted house, the Major, still plays the major role and he is still described as a 'cold man, with bronze skin and silver temples and ice-colored eyes . . . a challenge to women young and old.'[16]

The sub-plot is introduced in a dinner conversation and has to do with Jeyfus, Beth's 'air force', who is suspected of not having been through the war experiences he apparently has been bragging about. Jeyfus is to be put to a test to see if he really can fly a plane. When he does not want to try because his nerve is gone ('1916', he says, 'It's in the book'),[17] Beth immediately marries him and sends him off. She is later deceived into bringing him back, or perhaps she is convinced that the war-time experience had really taken place. The melodramatic intrigues involve the Italian maid, the footman Ernie, and the Major's servant, Das, in addition to the central characters, and they involve such things as arranging for Beth to see a notebook from the war, setting traps to fool and infuriate people, a knife-fight, etc. Faulkner allows himself everything in this story, but he ends up with an improbable story and a plot that is almost impossible to follow. A few extra typescript pages of what may be a later version of the story seem to indicate a different handling of the plot, possibly by concentrating on Beth and the Major and the maid, with Das as the faithful man-servant,[18] whom Beth feels could 'do murder for you [the Major]'.[19]

'Love' is not a successful story, nor is it a finished one, and Faulkner never found a way of handling the narrative complexities he encountered in this material. The material may best be described by referring to Faulkner's repeated attempts to make a synopsis or movie script out of the story; apparently he felt that this was a story of the kind Hollywood has told so many of.

'Love' is apprentice work, and even though Faulkner certainly became a better short-story writer later on, it is not certain that he learnt from his mistakes here. He simply had to shy away from this type of story, from the overcomplicated plots; otherwise he was likely to write very bad stories also late in his career.[20] There are some hints of things to come later, and some telling observations in 'Love'. The relationship between Das and the Major is one such element. The oriental is a 'slight man whom any wind might blow away, save that of destiny. To that he trimmed his sails with skill.. . .'[21] Here Das is obviously a representative of a different culture, because other characters seem to be preys to their destinies; not the least a number of characters in the New Orleans writings. Das's devotion to his master may remind us of Kipling's and Conrad's writings, and in the discussions of Western culture, which is here compared to the servant's background, Das appears to be a forerunner of the Subadar in 'Ad Astra'. The plane crash is likewise not unique in Faulkner's fiction. He would describe many such incidents later on, in stories such as 'Thrift', 'All the Dead Pilots', 'With Caution and Dispatch', and many others. Also, girls of Beth's calibre return in various disguises in later stories, as do rat-poison and jealousy. Faulkner was not ready for the technical complexities of such an elaborate story, and the story deservedly remains unpublished. 'Love' is not typical of the young Faulkner, but now and then he would mix himself up in complicated stories such as this one later in his career, and invariably these stories failed to sell.[22]

The loneliness and the lack of any deeper relationships with other human beings, be it love or something else, is very much at the centre of 'The Hill', Faulkner's most accomplished and most successful sketch from this early period. One should note, however, that even if 'The Hill' is a remarkable achievement, it may be regarded as a product of the *poet* more than of the short-story writer, and further that 'The Hill', despite its foreshadowings of numerous elements and ideas found again in later works, does not introduce an obvious and useful narrative technique which Faulkner could turn to in later short stories. 'The Hill' shows an author in complete command and control, knowing exactly what he wants to do and achieving exactly the effects he intends to achieve, but it is nevertheless the careful and artful prose narration of the contents and essence of a poem written prior to the sketch. Thus 'The Hill' as a short prose-fiction text demonstrates Faulkner's talent, perhaps even genius, as a writer, but the sketch is unique in his whole short-story career. The technique of the carefully balanced paragraphs of identical length, the use of only one character who is nobody and everybody, the ascension of the hill top, the pensive mood that prevails, and the solitary contemplation of life's drudgery and toil, could only be used in texts of this very special kind. In more elaborate and socially oriented pieces of writing these descriptive and philosophical passages had to be relegated to minor positions – to set the atmosphere or mood of a story or to accentuate its philosophical implications. So, for the artist in search of a form, 'Moonlight' and 'The Hill' represent two extremes of a necessary development, but neither of them would alone make possible the short-story achievement of the 1930's. Faulkner would have to find a middle way between the static prose sketch represented by 'The Hill', and the lyrical prose used in 'Moonlight'. He would also have to place his characters in a more specific social context and move them around before he could write better short stories. Yet 'The Hill' deserves extensive analysis in any study of Faulkner's short story achievement.

On the surface 'The Hill' is a very simple sketch. A nameless figure climbs a hill after a day of hard work, and when he reaches the crest of the hill he remains silent and immobile, till he slowly descends the hill in the last sentence of the story. Most of the story is a detailed description of the view from the hill-top and the solitary figure's reactions to the landscape.

The structure of the sketch is carefully planned. It consists of five paragraphs of approximately the same length, with the symmetry and style of a prose poem, as Michel Gresset has noted,[23] and, indeed, a prose poem it is. While the first paragraph takes the lone protagonist up on the hill so far that his shadow falls over the crest, the second paragraph gives a panoramic view over the valley now lying below the protagonist in the afternoon sun:

... The entire valley stretched beneath him, and his shadow, springing far out, lay across it, quiet and enormous. Here and there a thread of smoke balanced precariously upon a chimney. The hamlet slept, wrapped in peace and quiet beneath the evening sun, as it had slept for a century; waiting, invisibly honeycombed with joys and sorrows, hopes and despairs, for the end of time (*Early Prose and Poetry*, p. 91).

This eloquent and poetic description of the valley asleep is voiced by the omniscient narrator, but it is nonetheless scenery shaped and moulded through the protagonist's inner eye – the contemplated landscape is also the projected mental landscape of the he-figure.

By means of negation, telling what was *not* to be seen from the hill-top, the narrator gives a vivid picture of daily life and its burdens and hardships in the valley where the protagonist works but does not belong. Most of the sentences in the third paragraph are in the passive form, 'he' being used only once, but some of the negations are so qualified that they indicate the limited point of view of the spectator: 'no movement save'/'no sounds save' (*Early Prose and Poetry,* p. 91). The protagonist is the one who sees the smoke, and he is the one who hears the anvil breaking the silence.

In the fourth paragraph the narrative moves back to the lonely figure on the hilltop. He was briefly seen from the outside in the opening paragraph, but in paragraphs two and three the scenery and the few signs of people living in the valley are focal. Now the protagonist is seen from a short distance to allow for a better understanding of him. Moving from the twistings of his featureless face to the thoughts in his mind, we are led to see that he is incapable of comprehension. He is on the brink of experiencing something, of grasping some important connections, but it all eludes him. Alone on the hill, a valley at sunset stretched out beneath him, away from the daily strife for bread and clothing, he has been given a rare opportunity of communion, of transcendence, of spiritual elevation. He has been given a chance, unaware, to see his own life in a new perspective, figuratively speaking, but when the paragraph expires, he is only shaken by the force of spring in a valley at sunset. The possible epiphany never became an epiphany.[24]

What has happened to the young man is nevertheless 'something', and it seems to be explicitly stated in social terms in the fourth paragraph. What he has seen and understood and experienced – the 'something' – is also closely related to his admittedly vague understanding of what life is and not what it might be.

The sun sets in the last paragraph of the sketch, and the lone hill climber is released. In the twilight of the late spring afternoon 'nymphs and fauns might riot' (*Early Prose and Poetry,* p. 92), but these mythological visions, reminiscent of *The Marble Faun,*[25] do not touch the protagonist. The solitary dreamer has another and somewhat more concrete vision as he stands on one horizon and stares across at the other, 'far above a world of endless toil and troubled slumber; untouched,

42

untouchable; forgetting, for a space, that he must return' (*Early Prose and Poetry,* p. 92). Even though the protagonist must return to the valley, a dream of a different way of belonging is vaguely discernible in the concluding lines of the sketch.

The protagonist is nameless; he is only loosely placed in time and space, and he is *tieless*.[26] He is a working man whose face exhibits 'slow featureless mediocrity' (*Early Prose and Poetry,* p. 91) and who for some unknown reason ascends a hill.

It is hardly sufficient to say that 'The Hill' is 'another expression of Faulkner's vision of the Romanticist's idealized world', as one critic has put it.[27] The protagonist never really comes close to nature, and no real feeling of transcendence is achieved. In its universality and generality the sketch stresses the discrepancy between a world of beauty which can accommodate natural feelings and forces on one side and the sordidness of man's actual world on the other. The idealized world is not actively sought in the text, neither by the protagonist nor by the narrator, and the actual world, despite its tin cans and whipped vanities, also offers real and meaningful life in an organized society. This is suggested by the honeycomb image, and real life seems to be known by the antitheses of sorrow and joy, hope and despair.

A man climbing a hill in a literary text evokes allusions to Christian symbols. To seek a high point and to do it alone means to seek communion with God. But God, who is mentioned in the first paragraph of the text, is whimsical, and the church spire rises 'like [a] figure . . . rising in a dream' (*Early Prose and Poetry,* p. 90). God seems to be almost inaccessible, and religious controversy seems to be central in the society and its codes of conduct, but to the protagonist it appears to be a blind alley: *he* cannot be helped this way.

The hill-valley motif in a similar way evokes certain reactions in the experienced reader. The obvious one is to think of it in Freudian terms, thus emphasizing the sexual overtones that unquestionably are present in the text.[28] The other, not so obvious thought, may be that the protagonist who leaves the valley behind enters a level where the *artist* normally has found himself: isolated, estranged from his fellow beings, doomed to create. Thomas Wolfe also found that when the scouts had no use for the hermaphrodite, he had to climb Parnassus.

Thus the self-reflectiveness of Faulkner's work may be seen functioning here too.[29] Yet the very failure to grasp the meaning of what goes on, the failure to become inspired, may be regarded as an early description of what Faulkner repeatedly called 'the failed poet'–himself. This can only be so by way of implication, since the protagonist of 'The Hill' has to return: has to live in the mainstream of human life. He might have 'escaped' if he had been capable of understanding what he saw and felt, which we have seen that he was not.

The interpretations above can be further elaborated and supported by close readings of later works. The question of setting can thus be settled by demonstrating how scenes from *Light in August* are similar in setting and landscape to that of 'The Hill', and hence one can assume that what later became Jefferson is found in embryo here. A scene from *The Town*, referred to by a number of Faulkner critics and even supplying the title for an early book-length study of Faulkner,[30] is further evidence as to the setting. Yet this scene from the much later novel is more important for the significance of the hill climb in Faulkner's fictional world. Man has to walk up hills 'so that he can ride down' as Darl Bundren in *As I Lay Dying* puts it.[31] The hills provide man with a new perspective on the valleys where 'life was created' before it 'blew up onto the hills',[32] but also a new perspective on his own life and its relative importance in the life of men, in the history of the race:

> ... you to preside unanguished and immune above this miniature of man's passions and hopes and disasters – ambition and fear and lust and courage and abnegation and pity and honor and sin and pride – all bound, precarious and ramshackle, held together by the web, the iron-thin warp and woof of his rapacity but withal yet dedicated to his dreams.[33]

In 'The Hill' Faulkner created a 'tieless casual' and thereby gave a succinct picture of man in his struggle and in his dreams. The lonely figure on the hill is representative of many a Faulkner character in the early sketches, and in his later writings estranged and alienated figures would proliferate.

The old verities of the human heart seem to form a basis of Faulkner's more explicit and voiced outlook on the world around him, but he was not unappreciative of the functions of social and political and historical changes which might alter man's struggle and the human condition significantly. The apparent paradox between man's being basically the same and the necessity of change can be solved by referring to a vague distinction which Faulkner seems to maintain between individual man and man in the meaning Mankind: in the span of an individual's life-time there must be change, for without change there will be no growth and hence no life; but while this change seems important and vital to the individual, nothing in the field of human conflict, struggle, dreams, etc. is really changed. Old verities and old truths will be prevalent under all social conditions, and consequently one may expect that Faulkner's writings over the years will be variations of the same themes, repetitions of basically the same conflicts. This should not lead us to a *reductio ad absurdum*; the various individual manifestations of the enormous range of different conflicts are parts of what Faulkner depicts, and the not so insignificant problem of how ideas, dreams, conflicts, rapacity, misery, greatness are presented still deserves treatment.

If 'The Hill' embodies many of the important ideas and techniques of Faulkner's later writings, the expanded version of this sketch, 'Nympholepsy', is crucial to our understanding of Faulkner's growth as an artist in these years. This strange re-working of 'The Hill' was probably written in 1925.

In 'Nympholepsy' some of the phenomena one could only guess about in the earlier sketch are worked out with care, and because this is more of *a story* than its progenitor, 'Nympholepsy' pursues various themes further. This is in particular true of the theme of sexuality, which is only hinted at in 'The Hill'. It is one of the most central themes in 'Nympholepsy', however. Sexuality is elusive and escapes the protagonist, even though the whole story is strongly sensuous. Again Faulkner's poetry can be said to supply most of the imagery, and mythical beings are almost real in this story – at least as a projection of the protagonist's desire and lust.

The solitary labourer climbing the hill is a somewhat different person in this later story. He does not simply register the sound of an anvil; now the anvil's sound is 'like a call to vespers', and the invisible columns of the courthouse are transformed into 'pale Ionic columns': the courthouse itself is 'a dream dreamed by Thucydides' *(Uncollected Stories, p. 331)*. In 'The Hill' nymphs and fauns *might* riot in the dusk; in 'Nympholepsy' they *do* riot. Thus the theme of sexuality comes through much more strongly in the later text, and the protagonist dreams of 'a girl like defunctive music, moist with heat' *(Uncollected Stories, p. 331)*; a dream that is repeated near the end of the story after the futile chase of a nymph. There is a pervasive sexuality lingering all through the text.

Faulkner introduces a new element into his picture of the valley and

45

fills it with symbolic value: the river runs through the valley which is 'forever severed' (*Uncollected Stories*, p. 333).

When the protagonist, who feels himself ridiculed by the indifferent gods, runs swiftly towards home, he has to cross the river. He slips on a log crossing it, and 'He died time and again' before 'the water took him' (*Uncollected Stories*, p. 334). In the embrace of the water he has a vision of a woman, a dryad, who eludes him but whom he pursues through the silvery 'wheat beneath the impervious moon' (*Uncollected Stories*, p. 335) till she disappears and he throws himself 'flat upon the earth' (*Uncollected Stories*, p. 336).

After the chase the thoughts of tomorrow, of work and casual food and perhaps a casual girl to give comfort for a while, return. The experiences with the nymph and the 'death by water' lie behind; they will have to be adjusted to the reality he now faces.

Faulkner's symbolist imagery is still dominant in this piece, even if it was written as late as 1925. The imagery is not chosen because this is part of what Faulkner experimented with at this point in time, but because his material required it. The rather deliberate attempt at fusing mythic and realistic elements in a pastoral sketch is not too successful, and some of the shifts from one realm to the other account for comic effects. The use of 'Ionic columns' and 'cathedrals of trees' does not fit in too well with similes like the 'day draining from the world as a bath-tub drains, or a cracked bowl' (*Uncollected Stories*, p. 332-3). Otherwise the metaphors and similes and imagery at large are far more elaborate than in any of the earlier sketches, and they may at least indicate a writer on the move – even if it is in a direction he had to change away from later on.[34]

Loneliness, deprivation, and search for human contact – love, sex, friendship – are key-words in the early Faulkner texts. They are important also in the last of the pre-New Orleans prose-fiction texts, 'Adolescence', which was probably composed between the publication of 'The Hill' and the composition of 'Nympholepsy'. 'Adolescence' is in some ways unique among Faulkner's earliest stories in its being located to the Mississippi hills and in its having children and growth from innocent childhood to the harsh reality of the adult world as central elements. The story presents new and somewhat different indications of Faulkner's concerns in the early twenties, both as to technique and subject matter. The blending of poetic descriptive passages and straight prose narrative

46

is found here too, while the more sweeping, epic narrative comprising wide space and many years of development and change within one single paragraph, is new. This broad and epic narrative is a mark of Faulkner's short stories from 1927 and 1928, before he revised them to make them sell. The early versions of 'Victory' are typical of this epic, slow flow of narrative, as are also versions of the story about Elmer.

'Adolescence' deals with the problems of growing up and with the lack of love and understanding in the adult world. While the story is full of sexual if not erotic overtones, the erotic dreams and the hidden, subconscious sexual images are not those of the protagonists. They are rather something which misunderstanding adults project upon the young and innocent adolescents.

The story exhibits no mastery of plot or narration as it moves slowly along a chronological line, now and then taking wide and sweeping overviews. Slowly and convincingly there emerges from the descriptions of autumns, winters, springs, and summers, a picture of Juliet (Jule) Bunden, who lives with her grandmother because of her dislike of her stepmother. She spends most of her time out of doors and grows out of the bitter childhood together with a simple boy, Lee Hollowell. Their natural and innocent friendship is brutally destroyed when the grandmother discovers Jule and Lee sleeping naked together under a blanket. The youngsters only seek warmth and comfort and find it in their comfortable closeness under the blanket.

The stream where the two youths swim and the sandy nook where they rest, the 'rain gullied hills and fecund river bottoms' (*Uncollected Stories*, p. 460), resemble descriptions and images used in much of Faulkner's early writing. In the last paragraph of 'Adolescence' Jule descends a hill, approaching the pool where she 'stared into the water in a sensuous smooth despair' (*Uncollected Stories*, p. 473). Like the protagonist in 'Nympholepsy' she feels the earth strike through her clothes, and the narcissistic elements which so many critics have pointed to in Faulkner's writing, perhaps in particular before 1930, are present here too. Juliet, contrary to the protagonist in 'The Hill' and 'Nympholepsy' (and, for that matter, 'Landing in Luck'), seems to receive some message and grasp a little more of how life on earth must be:

She wondered dully and vaguely how she could ever have been wrought up over things, how anything could ever make her any way but like this: quiet, and a little sorrowful. Scarcely moving herself, it seemed as though the trees swam up slowly out of the dark and moved across above her head, drawing their top-most branches through star-filled waters that parted before them and joined together when they had passed, with never a ripple or change (*Uncollected Stories*, p. 473).

Central in 'Adolescence' is also the brother-sister relationship between Juliet and her youngest brother, Bud, who also runs away from the stepmother. In Jule's concern for the pathetic little figure there is an undercurrent of the futility and pointlessness of a life from which death would hardly be an escape. One slightly sentimental scene between Jule and Bud may well be the best single scene in the 26 page long story, which is quite interesting when we know how significant this kind of relationship would become in some of Faulkner's major works.[35] The incredibly wicked grandmother is of course also an early predecessor of similar characters in *The Sound and the Fury, Light in August,* and a number of short stories.[36] Her reason for treating Jule so harshly after her 'discovery' may be her fear of bad blood from the good-for-nothing Lee Hollowell, and another important element in numerous later Faulkner texts is thus introduced.

In a study of Faulkner's development as a prose-fiction writer the use of dialect in the dialogue parts of this story is interesting. Dialogue abounds here, and it is instrumental in creating the villainous figure of the grandmother. The local colour of the language is also deftly used to describe – through Lee's words in particular – the lazy summer days by the river in youth's 'happy time, so clear and untroubled' (*Uncollected Stories,* p. 462). The use of colloquialisms and the authentic setting of the Mississippi hills are used to set some dramatic action in motion, and this is a step forward for Faulkner. He had used a similar setting in 'The Hill' for a static story where no word was uttered, but in 'Adolescence' he has peopled this landscape and moved the people from within. Juliet experiences a number of situations where she must make a choice, and, tears in her eyes, she follows an inner conviction of what is right and decent. As many a strong young girl in Faulkner's short stories she can do little but throw herself on the ground, weeping in despair.

Faulkner's first short stories present a rather heterogeneous material, and the variety and experimentation is great, especially if one considers the narrative forms employed. The *poet* expectedly leaves his mark on all stories, except perhaps 'Landing in Luck'. In 'Moonlight', 'Adolescence', and, to some extent, 'Nympholepsy', Faulkner blends poetic description with dialogue, dramatic discourse, and slow but easy-flowing prose. The inclination for tableaux, for arresting motion in order to contemplate it, is another trade-mark of the young poet, and at times the opposition between motion and stasis is overdone.

To draw a conclusion about which direction Faulkner's prose fiction would take on the basis of these sketches is hardly possible – if the known result is not extrapolated into the material. During these formative years Faulkner also wrote some book reviews and voiced opinions as a literary critic. (Some of these essayistic writings will be discussed in the next chapter.) If Faulkner was still uncertain and insecure as an artist before his arrival in New Orleans, his acquaintance with Sherwood Anderson and his considerable success as a prose writer (the sketches and *Soldiers' Pay),* transformed him from a 'failed poet' to a budding fiction writer of great promise. If, indeed, one year should be singled out as the most important in Faulkner's development as an artist, 1925 would be *the* formative year. Within this one year Faulkner may be said to have made the transition from being a poet to becoming a fiction writer.

In Faulkner's early stories we can watch the young and uncertain artist in search of a form, but we also see that he did not find his form during these years. In fact, he had to find his *material* before be could find a form that was his own and that suited the material he had discovered. Yet his apprenticeship writing gave him good practice and prepared him for the more extensive narratives that he would write in the years immediately following. We may find some signs of the directions of Faulkner's short-story interests in the years ahead in the earliest texts. On the one hand we have the poetic stories, dealing with love and moonlight and mockingbirds, dense in symbolism and metaphors; on the other hand we have the more realistic depiction of everyday experiences. Here the author relies on experience and observation and relates his stories through personal narration in a discourse that by and large corresponds to the actual story, and where chronology is maintained. The local milieu is already used – in 'Adolescence' and 'Moonlight' – while the more philosophical texts ('The Hill') are only loosely related to this milieu. Otherwise the author has sought universality or, at least, trans-individuality. Most important in these early years is probably that Faulkner from the very beginning experimented in the fictional genres, and told stories in rather traditional narratives while he was still a poet and very much wanted to be a poet. Real experimentation is rare, yet

Faulkner struggled with his texts to find better ways of telling them, and this minimal experimentation is important. He would continue his quest till he found his material and his form; he would never settle for the average and ordinary. And when he came to New Orleans in 1925, new incentives to growth were offered.

3. Short Stories 1919–1927
Sinbad in New Orleans: The Artist's Discovery of His Material

> But to create! Which among ye who
> have not this fire, can know this joy,
> let it be ever so fleet?
> – Faulkner, 'New Orleans'

The so-called 'New Orleans Sketches'[1] represent William Faulkner's first concentrated and consistent performance as a prose-fiction writer. He must be considered mainly a poet when he arrived in New Orleans early in 1925. When he embarked for Europe in July 1925 he had, so to speak, completed a metamorphosis to become a writer of prose fiction. Off and on poetry, the highest form of literary art in which he felt himself to have failed, would still demand his attention. His second book of poems, *A Green Bough,* was published many years later.[2] But the poems for this book were written prior to the New Orleans visit, so the publication of the first collection of poetry, *The Marble Faun,*[3] may well be said to mark the end of Faulkner's career as a lyrical poet. 1925 is the first year in Faulkner's career devoted almost entirely to the writing of fiction. But one should stress that no full-fledged fiction writer took over from the poet; there was still a long, lonely, and strenuous road to go before a book like *The Sound and the Fury* could be written.[4]

Faulkner had by 1925 published 18 individual poems, written one extremely poetical play, and in December 1924 his book of verse, *The Marble Faun,* had been published.[5] A great number of manuscripts of poems – or fragments of manuscripts – also show that Faulkner up to 1925 wrote chiefly poetry and also worked constantly to improve his poems through numerous revisions. As many as ten typescripts of one single poem exist.[6] Against this enormous amount of poetry at various stages of completeness can be measured only two published brief prose sketches and the unpublished short-story attempts discussed in the preceding chapter. It is also evident that Faulkner thought of himself as a poet.[7] The brief residence in New Orleans thus seems to have been of crucial importance to Faulkner, because it marked a rather abrupt turning away from poetry to prose. In sharp contrast to earlier years, 1925 saw the publication of seventeen fictional pieces by Faulkner; the writing of *Soldiers' Pay* was undertaken; the transition was completed.[8]

How could he change so quickly? Faulkner must be said to have started out on a high level as a writer and he acquired new techniques with apparent ease. He had experimented with prose fiction since 1919. It is also interesting to note that Faulkner had expressed himself as a literary critic in *The Mississippian* as early as 1920,[9] and had voiced very clear opinions on what literary art ought to be, what the artist's concerns should be. Most revealingly, he had emphasized the artist's need for his local American background because the artist must be completely familiar with his characters and events to make believable, three-dimensional, self-motivated characters.[10]

Only one of these early review-essays deals with prose fiction, with the novel, and although Faulkner's view on poetry and the poet is identical with his view on the artist and literary art in general, he always seemed to maintain a clear distinction between the poet and the prose-writer. (The classical genre distinction is obvious and not discussed here.) In a review of three books by Joseph Hergesheimer, Faulkner writes that Hergesheimer's people

are never actuated from within; they do not create life about them; they are like puppets assuming graceful but meaningless postures in answer to the author's compulsions, and holding these attitudes until he arranges their limbs again in other gestures as graceful and as meaningless.[11]

In the same essay, Faulkner heavily attacks what he calls 'the literary colors of the day', criticizing Hergesheimer because 'Sinclair Lewis and the New York Times have corrupted him.' So although Hergesheimer knows 'the tricks of the trade', he had better describe 'trees or marble fountains, houses or cities', if he must write.[12]

Two other essays are relevant here. One is the essay on 'Books & Things: American Drama: Eugene O'Neill',[13] the other is also on American Drama, but with the subtitle 'Inhibitions'.[14] In the former essay the point made by Faulkner is that art is pre-eminently provincial, and he makes a brave assertion in the concluding paragraph about the qualities of the American writer's medium – his language:

It [a national literature] can, however, come from the strength of imaginative idiom which is understandable by all who read English. Nowhere to-day, saving in parts of Ireland, is the English language spoken with the same earthy strength as it is in the United States; though we are, as a nation, still inarticulate.[15]

In the latter essay, Faulkner repeats his opinion of the language, calling it 'One rainbow . . . on our dramatic horizon', and 'our logical savior'.[16] Moreover, Faulkner seems to have learnt that art is not only often provincial, but that the quantity or quality of the material is irrelevant to 'a man with real ability [who] finds sufficient what he has to hand.'[17] Faulkner's basic distrust in ideas for their own sake probably prevented him from anything approaching a serious study of literary theories, philosophical ideas, and the like. What he learnt was presumably mostly transferred to him through conversations with others and by listening; this seems particularly to have been the case during his sojourn in New Orleans. What Faulkner read and must have read with great awareness as to technique, style, and characterization were fiction and poetry – and Faulkner read the very best in both genres. Influence from a number of writers and critics is easily detectable in his early poetry as well as in his prose.[18] Phil Stone believes that W.H. Wright's *The Creative Will* represents 'one of the most important influences in Bill's whole literary career',[19] and this assumption has been developed further by some other critics later on.[20]

Critics generally agree that the principal interest in Faulkner's early sketches lies 'in their foreshadowings of what was to come in the later works'.[21] These foreshadowings are easily traced, especially on an elementary level, but if one, like Cleanth Brooks, is dissatisfied with the New Orleans sketches as such, the only excuse for discussing them seriously is their helpfulness in explaining later works. Brooks writes:

One has to be very charitable not to dismiss as mere hackwork the character sketches and short stories that Faulkner published in *The Double Dealer* and the New Orleans *Times-Picayune* in 1925. Furthermore, one can scarcely plead in extenuation of their awkwardness the youthfulness of the author, for Faulkner was writing his very promising first novel, *Soldier's Pay* [sic], during the very months that saw the publication of these *New Orleans Sketches. Soldier's Pay* was not in the least inept. It is in fact a quite remarkable piece of work and was regarded as such by most of those who reviewed it in 1926. By contrast, nearly all the short stories that the young writer contributed to the *Times-Picayune* are trivial, and the writing is forced and artificial where it is not simply hackneyed.[22]

Some of Brooks's criticism of the sketches may be to the point, but I think it would be fairer both to the New Orleans sketches and to Faulkner's novel if the former were judged as apprentice work, serious if not always successful, and the latter as a promising first novel with serious flaws and with a certain mannerism of language which it shares with most of the sketches.[23]

Carvel Collins in his very clear but sadly undocumented 'Introduction' to *New Orleans Sketches*[24] repeatedly talks about them as 'apprentice work', as does Philip Momberger, whose dissertation deals at length with the early sketches.[25] Momberger finds that local scenes, dialects and folkways are not described merely for their own sake. Local detail serves an explicit purpose: 'to render the quality and meaning of experience in the modern city',[26] and sees in this an attempt that Faulkner was often to renew.

In the New Orleans sketches we meet persons who are close relatives of the 'tieless casual' in 'The Hill' and who share his dreams and visions. It is hardly justifiable, however, to transport the hero from his hilltop to the iron-balcony of Chartres Street, and one had better study the New Orleans sketches themselves in an attempt to locate whatever unity or coherence there is between them and to assess their own quality and value. The primary interest of the literary narrative lies in the text itself, but the secondary interest – to follow and judge Faulkner's development as a writer of short fiction – will also be given close attention.

It is possible to see New Orleans as a kind of urban Faulknerian wasteland where human beings are estranged from everything which was an integrated part of their lives in the past: nature, God, and fellow men. It is also justifiable to see the various characters in the Vieux Carrée as drifters, foreigners, outsiders, who of their own free will have chosen New Orleans in a frantic attempt to regain contact with the American way of life, with the 'mainstream'. In such a line of thought, Faulkner's original title for the second series of sketches, 'Sinbad in New Orleans', proves helpful:

First of all, the original title points to a matter of considerable thematic importance – that of Destiny, or Fate, as opposed to the free will of the individual. In one of the series of tales in *The Thousand and One Nights* Sinbad himself makes a rather sharp distinction between these opposing forces. Once he has set out upon a voyage, and once some calamity has befallen him, he sees himself as a mere plaything in the hands of Fate, one whose only alternative is to submit himself in good Eastern fashion to the will of Allah. Without exception, however, the decision to undertake any given voyage is by Sinbad's admission, his own; and it is usually through his own ingenuity (an exertion of the will and of the imagination) that he escapes his various predicaments.[27]

The allusions given by the 'Sinbad' title imply that it is by their own willed actions and choice that the protagonists of the New Orleans sketches have placed themselves in the hands of Circumstance. The characters are always shown at a point where Circumstance has brought about some kind of crisis; either they are trying desperately but not too cleverly to cope with a hopeless situation or they are nostalgically dreaming of other times and places when the world was young and green. Some people, like Jean Baptiste in 'Home', reach the insight that they are themselves responsible for the course their Destiny has taken; that they have helped to 'forge the chain of circumstance' (*New Orleans Sketches,* p. 30) which they now blame for their pitiful situation.

This is only part of the truth, however. Although the conservative Faulkner in later years stated his lack of interest in *social* literature, much social criticism is implied in the New Orleans stories, and it is not only criticism of an inhuman urban environment. The unnatural urban life gets its fair share of the criticism, but accompanying this is a clear awareness of social injustice.

Something makes the old human vices come to the surface more frequently in the city. This is not so only *because* it is a city. A bustling, busy city like New Orleans is but an example, or a symptom, of the new era and the new civilization where Mammon is the only God and goal, and where competition makes the world go round. Faulkner's protagonists are often *losers* in the American pursuit of an elusive happiness; they are outsiders, and their own responsibility must not be stressed too heavily. Faulkner in point of fact does not do so in these texts, which may be one of the reasons why he has been accused of sentimentality.[28]

Faulkner's New Orleans sketches are portraits of characters, situations, milieus, and attitudes, but at the same time 'society' is here shown to produce losers. One should be very cautious not to accuse Faulkner of any kind of 'propaganda' writing – he would never have thought of it, even if outrage because of injustice is one of the characteristics of the young William Faulkner.

Some emphasis must be accorded to the organization of the sketches, since it is easy to over-emphasize their unity and coherence now that typescript evidence has revealed that Faulkner conceived of the sketches as a series.[29] These sketches can be compared, contrasted, and grouped together on the basis of various criteria; e.g. the use or non-use of a narrative persona. One can also easily imagine one group of characters or one kind of experience as being more central than others, in particular if the narrator's attitude to certain events and characters supports such a notion. A number of stories thus have to do with recent and unsettled immigrants in New Orleans, whereby a strong and efficient contrast between the new world and the one they have left is achieved. Other divisions can be superimposed on the more narrow divisions based on character and social environment. The overall picture of the city is finally, made up of all characters, all dreams, all longings and all defeats and shortcomings.

An introductory discussion of one sketch should provide an opportunity to single out some characteristics and elements which may prove to be typical or representative of the New Orleans writings in general. A natural choice of one story here is the opening text of the 'SINBAD IN NEW ORLEANS' typescript – as well as the 'Mirror of Chartres Street' typescript: the sketch 'Mirrors of Chartres Street'. This was also the first sketch published by the *Times-Picayune,* and it would thus also appear to give a title to the whole series, which in turn would give the impression that the following sketches were portraits – gossip, hearsay – from the familiar New Orleans street.

'Mirrors of Chartres Street' is told by an 'I' narrator who also participates in the story. He is a young man, proud of his appearance and clothing; a thinly disguised self-portrait of the young William Faulkner.[30] The 'I' figure notices a bum, a crippled alcoholic in the street who asks him for a quarter, and tries to soften the narrator by telling him that he himself may not always be so well off.

The bum is equipped with 'eyes as wild and soft as a faun's' (*New Orleans Sketches,* p. 15), and with his one leg and the crutch he uses, he enters in the story's second paragraph the very realm of myths and dreams in America: the movie theatre,

where was one of those million-dollar pictures of dukes and adultery and champagne and lots of girls in mosquito netting and lamp shades. Truly, his was an untrammelled spirit: his the same heaven-sent attribute for finding life good which enabled the Jews to give young Jesus of Nazareth with two stars in His eyes, sucking His mother's breast, and a fairy tale that has conquered the whole Western earth; which gave King Arthur to a dull world, and sent baron and knight and lads who had more than coronets to flap pennons in Syria, seeking a dream (*New Orleans Sketches,* p. 16).

The 'I' figure finds the cripple to be a typical representative of the dream-seeker, the imaginative spirit. Yet the narrator keeps at a distance from the bum, considering himself far too superior to be a prospective bum himself.

The detached view, the non-involvement, is typified when the 'I' narrator observes the city scene and comments on his last view of the beggar from a railed balcony. Now the cripple with his dreams is seen as he 'darted and spun on his crutch like a water beetle about a rock' (*New Orleans Sketches,* p. 16). The cripple has a long quarrel with a policeman and defends a number of rights which he claims to have as an American citizen, and he also asks a number of rhetorical questions. Being an outsider as a result of the lack of protection and pension for workers maimed on the job, the bum knows that he must accept his arrest, but his eloquent banalities *must* also be said. There is still some pride left in him so he has to conjure up a picture to himself, not deceiving anybody else, of a friend's car being sent for him when the police wagon arrives. On this basis it is possible to understand the observer's thoughts of 'Caesar mounting his Chariot' (p. 18). In a dreamer there is always a quality unbroken and undisturbed, leaving him invincible.

The role of the policeman in the sketch is very limited: he does of course represent law and justice, which is what the bum asks for, but has also 'Got a gov'ment job: thinks he can do whatever he wants' *(New Orleans Sketches,* p. 17). In the bum's accusation is vaguely implied that even if the cop does his little-envied job he might have shown some human concern.

The bum is a dreamer, an outsider, a loser in the competitive society, but foremost he is a bum and will so remain. The narrator, on the other hand, might learn something from his observation of this loser. He might have been able to understand that life really can fare so with an honest worker, and he might have understood that he is not guaranteed his health or well-being himself. Yet the bum becomes nothing but a picturesque figure whom he can invest with qualities he only dimly recognizes. The narrator is ready for pity and mercy and twenty-five cents, but his compassion stops there. Yet the spectator and observer of the story is not only and barely a watcher, preferring to travel light. Together with the bum, the cop, and the bystanders, he shares a dream which fails to bring understanding and human contact simply because these people inhabit separate levels on the social scale. 'I' has to remain detached, the bum must describe an imaginary rectangle around himself with the crutch, and the policeman *is* authority. The hint from the beggar that he and the narrator might be akin, carries a deeper meaning than the narrator is able to grasp.

This bum is of course no Sinbad figure who has made up his mind and chosen his Destiny. On the contrary, the can hardly be made responsible for having placed himself in the hands of whatever Fate or Circumstance he has been hit by. The text gives no reason to doubt the railroad accident in which the bum was maimed. One has to be careful not to condemn a man for lack of endurance under these circumstances, and an accident can befall anyone. The narrator fails to get as simple a message as this, as his narrative reveals very clearly.

The unnamed spectator climbing a summit to grasp a meaning, discover some universal law, transcend the routines of daily labour but failing to do so even to the extent that he fails to learn from his experience of spiritual failure, is a recurrent figure in Faulkner's early writings. In this first New Orleans sketch the experience and the failure are of less interest than in 'The Hill', because the story is much coarser and by no means so carefully structured as the former text.

Yet 'Mirrors of Chartres Street' exhibits many of Faulkner's qualities as a prose writer. Language is economically used, the many shifts from indirect narration to speech and from narrative to dramatic presentation (or from high to minimal narration) are deftly handled. The very problem of reaching what may be considered a valid interpretation of the text testifies to its richness, either directly or by way of implication. At any rate, 'Mirrors of Chartres Street' must have meant excellent practice to the young William Faulkner, and is a good piece of apprenticeship writing.

In this first sketch we have met no Sinbad directly, but the obvious choice for a Sinbad figure in this text and in a number of others is the narrator – the 'I' figure. The unnamed, tourist-like first-person narrator of some of the New Orleans sketches is not a native of the French Quarter, and hence he is on some journey when he is there. The narrator who has set out on this journey must let himself become involved – directly or indirectly – if adventures are to happen, if Fate shall be given an opportunity to play with him. Fate, on the other hand, seems to be central in the lives of some of the characters described by the narrator, and some of them are indeed on a long voyage. In a broader and more general sense all the characters in the New Orleans sketches are on a voyage, the destination of which is unknown but certain. This certainty is not taken into account when people act and behave, and the brevity of their stay is rather used as an excuse for being self-centred and egotistic. The young narrator in these sketches, behind whom is the young writer William Faulkner, often complained that people did not appreciate the good life better,[31] but the streets of New Orleans were perhaps not a place where positive human values could prosper.

The sketch that Faulkner intended to be the first in either of the series he envisaged is representative of the New Orleans writings, in so far as it makes use of a first-person narrator and describes one of the losers in the competitive and unfriendly urban environment.

Variety and unevenness are two terms that may be used to describe most of the New Orleans sketches. Faulkner seems to be most interested in the characters he has observed, and he presents them in different ways. In some cases this means that a varying degree of detachment and distance between the narrator and the characters denotes the significance given to the characters, while in other cases no narrator is present in the text, so that dramatic presentation and dialogue (non-narration or minimal narration) must render the experience there is. The narratives of 'Mirrors of Chartres Street' and 'Damon and Pythias, Unlimited' could thus be grouped together on the basis of the use of a first-person narrator, while stories like 'Home' and 'Jealousy' have no such narrator and rely rather heavily on dialogue, although the implied author is easily detectable in these stories.

Basically, the New Orleans sketches are just sketches: i.e., they are quick and direct and uncomplicated descriptions in relatively few words of an incident, a character, an episode – some of which are given added significance by having some bearing on the spectator-narrator, whether he is a first-person narrator or only implied in the text. The first-person narrator who reacts to whatever happens in 'Mirrors of Chartres Street' and 'Damon and Pythias, Unlimited', is also present in the more elaborate sketches, 'Out of Nazareth' and 'Episode', and in the brief sketch, 'Peter'. In the three last-mentioned texts he is not alone, even if 'I' narrates the episodes. His friend the painter, Spratling, accompanies him, and especially in 'Out of Nazareth' this is aptly done so that David's behaviour and writing leave an impression on both of the friends and the narrator can record this. In Faulkner's development, the 'I/Spratling' stories are progenitors of the 'I/Don' stories later in Faulkner's career; e.g. 'Mistral'. 'Out of Nazareth' is an important experiment on Faulkner's part also because it applies the frame device; that is, the presentation of David and the narrator's reactions to him work as a frame for the story that David has written and gives to the friends when he leaves. Faulkner would use the device again numerous times, and in 'Country Mice' one can see how he does this with greater ease and less artificiality than in 'Out of Nazareth'.

Most of the New Orleans sketches are told in the third person with a strong element either of dialogue or of a combination of dialogue and monologue. Certain attitudes may be detected to reveal an implied author who is, predictably, not too different from the first person, participating narrator of other sketches. One could say that the narrator is dramatized in the former group of sketches, whereas he keeps at varying distance from his characters and observations in the latter group. One should also keep in mind that it does not really make much of a difference whether first or third person narration is chosen.[32] At the same time one should remember that there are at least two distinctly different types of first-person narration in the New Orleans writings: one might use Booth's distinction between self-conscious narrators and the more simple narrators or observers who are unaware that they tell a story, produce a literary work. The first type includes sketches like 'Damon and Pythias, Unlimited' and 'Out of Nazareth', while the second type includes 'Cheest'. 'Country Mice' can be seen as a rather elaborate combination of these two types of narrative stance: the self-conscious narrator relays his part of the story in the frame, the simple narrator renders his boot-legging experience in the story proper. This technical device with the elaborate use of a frame (either in one or in two parts) may have something to do with Faulkner's familiarity with Southwestern humour, with the tall tale, and with oral narratives in general. He would employ this technique, time and again later in his career, too. The use of covert first-person narration, or first-person plural narration without ever disclosing the 'I' who speaks for the group or the community is not yet attempted by Faulkner, and the setting of the scene and the ensuing slow and detailed story of an event in the community or in somebody's life by an observer and an acknowledged story teller, still lies in the future. The stories that are told by an 'I' who is not the self-conscious artist-figure in the New Orleans period are close to being monologues or soliloquies. The narrators are highly unreliable, and we feel the presence of the implied author strongly through the very design of the monologues. It may well be that the dramatic monologues used in a number of the sketches are Faulkner's most important achievement and the single most important step forward in his development as a story teller in this period. Granted that 'The Hill' in a sense works as if it were a monologue, it is nevertheless told from the outside by someone who understands more than the mind he follows in its gropings. The significance of the monologues in the New Orleans period is self-evident: they are Faulkner's first elementary experiments in a type of personal, inside narration that would be used with great success and enormous impact in major works like *The Sound and the Fury* and *As I Lay Dying*.[33] The fact that the monologues are at this point already those of thwarted, suffering, unadjusted individuals is also telling. They often include longing and self-pity, but also stoic and stubborn endurance and a quiet acceptance of one's fate. 'The Cobbler' is of this last-mentioned type, while 'The Priest' is more of an interior monologue where psychological and personal problems, a struggle with alternative possibilities, and a debilitating ambivalence are rendered in the tormented religious person's own idiom. Both the cobbler and the priest have their sub-narratives in 'New Orleans', together with a number of other representative figures of the great city of New Orleans.

There is reason to look more closely at the monologues among these texts, since broad classifications are handy and time-saving, but tend to lack in precision what they gain in simplicity. 'New Orleans' is the text that lends itself best to such a scrutiny. This is a composite of eleven sub-narratives, all of which are interior monologues or soliloquies,[34] in a language carefully handled to give each character individuality. Through the functioning of irony we are allowed to share an opinion of the speakers with the arranging (implied) author. Through the technique of the monologue the speakers in all their thwarted misinterpretations of life expose themselves to us, because of a norm imparted by the implied author to the readers.[35]

In most collections of the New Orleans material, 'New Orleans' is regarded as a kind of overture to the whole series. This is based on the misunderstanding that the chronology of the appearances of the *Times-Picayune* sketches and this *Double Dealer* contribution corresponds to the author's intended chronology, which it by no means does. The scattered critical remarks on the New Orleans writings all seem to take it for granted that 'New Orleans' is meant to open the 'series' of sketches. One should perhaps judge it as a kind of summing-up before Faulkner again takes us to the Vieux Carré in the successive pieces, but some problems as to its singularity still remain unsolved. Even if we disregard the non-authorial emphasis on the sub-titles, which tend to break up what was probably meant to be a rather smooth flow of narrative prose,[36] 'New Orleans' is likely to linger in our minds as the very introduction to the urban scene created by Faulkner in all these sketches. This is not only so because earlier acquaintance with 'New Orleans' printed as *the* introduction to the sketches has biased us, but also because 'New Orleans' serves so well as a presentation of the characters in the city. These characters function through their internal monologues as the very voice of the city itself. Richard P. Adams comments on the relation between 'New Orleans' on the one hand and the *Times-Picayune* sketches on the other:

> The monologues in *The Double Dealer* are character sketches in which the language is archaically stiff and the characters remain abstract. There is little in the way of setting or event, and the effect is missed because there is not enough potential energy of motion to make a stop impressive. What the speakers contemplate seems almost as static as the artificial moment of contemplation itself.
>
> The *Times-Picayune* sketches are longer, more various, and more narrative. All are at least anecdotes, and ten of the sixteen are cast in more or less recognizable short-story forms. Two are expansions of themes which had been less fully developed in the *Double Dealer* group.[37]

Even if one, like Adams, is dissatisfied with 'New Orleans' because of the static artificiality of the individual monologues, one may maintain that 'New Orleans' gives a varied and complex mosaic of characters and destinies in a city you either love or leave, and that this complex picture is further diversified through the delineation of events in the subsequent sketches.

In the quotation from Adams he refers to two short stories that are 'expansions of themes which had been less fully developed' in 'New Orleans'. One of these is 'The Cobbler', while Adams sees 'The Kid Learns' as an expansion of the 'Frankie and Johnny' sub-narrative, a claim that may be doubtful, since another much more elaborate and consistent expansion of this sub-narrative also exists ('Frankie and

Johnny', *Uncollected Stories,* pp. 338–47). But 'The Cobbler' is definitively a recasting of the elements in the similarly titled sub-narrative in 'New Orleans'. The old cobbler is contemplating his life and has enough potential energy and wisdom to fill this role, since he is vested with some of the insight and understanding we readily believe old people to be in possession of. The story is limited to the cobbler's point of view and is consistently told in his words – as a monologue. It opens and ends on his receiving shoes for repair, and he promises the customer to get the shoes back later the same day. A question or an assumption from the customer as to where he comes from, makes the cobbler give the long monologue about his background and his life, and there is thus given a probable reason and a factual setting for the monologue – both of which Adams felt were missing in the shorter pieces in 'New Orleans'. Faulkner takes us inside the mind of a character and lets us follow his thoughts as they wind about. Occasionally we are even allowed to listen in on direct speech, set apart in the text by quotation marks.[38]

Faulkner's early mastery of language and his unusual sensitivity to the local and personal idiom all assert themselves here. In 'The Cobbler' the pictures of the landscape where the cobbler grew up are reminiscent of Poe's 'Eleonora',[39] and serve superbly to relay a youthful experience of a goat herder 'among the sun-swelled rocks' *(New Orleans Sketches,* p. 66). Despite the private nature of this monologue, despite the romantic tale it weaves, despite the fairy-tale atmosphere of it, reality and realism are allowed to intrude: the cobbler's girl married the 'grand signor'. This realistic touch to the extremely romantic and nostalgic tale is necessary; if things had worked out differently the cobbler would not have had his dreams, and together with his yellow rose they would have been withered and gone a long time ago. Only loss can possibly be sustained and kept alive for such a long period. The cobbler can turn to a romanticized past for sustenance and comfort, but his attempt to arrest motion – keeping youth forever in a yellow rose – is doomed from the beginning.

Faulkner expanded one more of the sub-narratives into a longer sketch, which remained unpublished until 1976; viz. 'The Priest'.[40] This monologue is a lyrical prayer by a character who is torn between wordly lusts and heavenly pleasures, and who is unable to choose between them. In his understanding, they cannot possibly live side by side. Contrary to the cobbler who had accepted his 'destiny', the priest remains pathetically motionless and desperate in his ambivalence; in a frenzy he mingles Ave

Marias with sexuality – which of course tells something about the implied understanding of celibacy and priesthood in this brief narrative.

Faulkner's experimentation here is very important in any study of his growing sophistication as an artist. But it is perhaps more interesting in a study of the technical experimentation that led to the writing of the major novels than in a study of narrative technique employed in the later short stories. The monologue never plays an important part in Faulkner's short-story telling.[41]

'The Kingdom of God' is one of the first of Faulkner's stories – the earliest among the New Orleans sketches – that relies on a plot or an intrigue, and accordingly it is more of a *story* in the traditional sense of the term than the sketches we have dealt with so far. The story opens with the description of a car speeding down a New Orleans street; two men alight while a third remains seated in the car. This is the idiot, the brother of one of the bootleggers who left the car, and he is with them on this business trip because he is 'a kind of luck piece, anyway' *(New Orleans Sketches,* p. 56). The story is told by an omniscient narrator, and what is most interesting here, in addition to the handling of the plot, are the many detailed and varied descriptions of the idiot brother. The initial description is of course, as Charles D. Peavy has shown, 'an early casting of Benjy.'[42]

The face of the sitting man was vague and dull and loose-lipped, and his eyes were clear and blue as cornflowers, and utterly vacant of thought; he sat a shapeless, dirty lump, life without mind, an organism without intellect. Yet always in his slobbering, vacuous face were his two eyes of a heart-shaking blue, and gripped tightly in one fist was a narcissus *(New Orleans Sketches,* p. 55).

Elaborate and varied descriptions of the idiot's eyes follow these initial ones, and they are supplemented by the descriptions of the other characters' reactions to him. One bootlegger talks about the 'good homes for his kind' *(New Orleans Sketches,* p. 56; cf. Jason in *The Sound and the Fury)*; the policeman asks if he is a 'mad cow', and also if the whole zoo has broken out *(New Orleans Sketches,* p. 58–9). The use of such animal metaphors may be indicative of the failure to love one of these poor people who belong in the Kingdom of God, and it also says something about the general quality of human relationship in New Orleans.

An even more conscientiously elaborated short story than 'The Kingdom of God' or any of the other sketches preceding it, is 'Out of Nazareth'. It is appropriately regarded as one of the most important texts in the whole series, both for its own merits and because it contains numerous prefigurations of work to come.

The title of this story, as well as its principal character, David, direct us to look for parallels with Christ – as does also the fact that the story was printed in the *Times-Picayune* on Easter Day 1925. Technically the story is simple enough. The I-figure, again presumably a thinly disguised self-portrait of the author himself,[43] and his friend Spratling are taking a walk in Jackson park. The thoughts of the narrator, the dialogue with his friend and their later encounter with a youth and their dinner with him, form the first part of the *frame* wherein the youth's manuscript piece is contained; the frame's last part is the first-person narrator's comments on the story by David and a concluding note on the impression the youth has left upon the two friends, both of whom are artists themselves.

The first scene of the story is given in imagery of the kind Faulkner used so often in his poetry: 'in terrific arrested motion' *(New Orleans Sketches,* p. 46), 'narcissi and hyacinths like poised dancers' *(New Orleans Sketches,* p. 46), 'a vague Diana in tortuous escape from marble draperies' *(New Orleans Sketches,* p. 47). The artificiality of this language and the elevated thoughts of the narrator are forcefully contrasted with the simple, natural David and his story. By including David's manuscript in his story, Faulkner achieves an ironic dimension which he makes only scant use of, but the apparent reluctance to comment or to mock the young talent is in itself a revealing commentary. A few direct comments on the young man's art are given, and the narrator finds it to be 'blundering and childish and "arty" ' *(New Orleans Sketches,* p. 53), but cannot denounce it because he senses some creative impulse behind it – perhaps the same impulse that makes him relay the encounter with David himself?

By commenting on David's text, the narrator, and consequently the author himself, is able to say something about an artist and what he can be and do. Adams may indeed be right when he finds that it is not far from the 1925-expressions in 'Out of Nazareth' to the Nobel prize speech in 1950:[44]

But seeing him in his sorry clothes, with his clean young face and his beautiful faith that life, the world, the race, is somewhere good and sound and beautiful, is good to see *(New Orleans Sketches,* p. 54).

'Sunset' and 'Country Mice' are the final stories that will be commented upon in connection with Faulkner's story-telling techniques in the New Orleans sketches. 'Sunset' does not need sustained commentary on this level: it is an occasional piece of writing, triggered off by a note in a newspaper about a black desperado who has slain three people before he has killed himself. Faulkner makes his own, rather moving, at times hilariously funny but finally saddening, story out of this material. Interesting on the technical plane is Faulkner's use of nature as a foil of human character, or the use of nature to assist and emphasize a development in a story. The hiding scenes and the dying of the Negro are accompanied by clear and vivid imagery from nature; including lengthy descriptions of the changing day and weather. Now and then nature and man merge:

Here was a wind coming up: the branches and bushes about him whipped suddenly to a gale fiercer than any yet; flattened and screamed, and melted away under it. And he, too, was a tree caught in that same wind: he felt the dull blows of it, and the rivening of himself into tattered and broken leaves (New Orleans Sketches, p. 85).

'Country Mice' is a story of its time and day, the first story where Faulkner manages to handle a plot that is close to being overburdened and too complicated, and the first story where attempts at using detective-story techniques may be found.

Only in its setting of the narrative frame is this story located in New Orleans, since the bootlegger-protagonist is representative of the gallery of New Orleans characters already exposed in the preceding sketches and stories. He is also the first-person narrator of the story proper, after the *real* first-person narrator has set the scene, which includes a presentation of the 'take-over narrator'.

The narrative technique in this story is unique among all the New Orleans stories. It resembles, as mentioned, the technique employed in 'Out of Nazareth', but there the story within the frame is said to have been written by somebody else [David] and then given to the first-person narrator of the frame. In 'Country Mice' the story proper is told to the frame narrator during one of the two friends' 'airing off' trips by car. The story is based on a common theme in the tradition of Southwestern humour: a bargain involving the swindling of supposedly sophisticated city people by an unexpected shrewd country hick. The modernization of the tall tale by using cars and aeroplanes allows for an even 'taller'

66

treatment of the theme of the story. In his relationship to the bootlegger the frame narrator reveals step by step what the bootlegger stands for, and much criticism of materialism is thus exposed. The bootlegger's story also pursues the theme of the significance of experience – provided you learn anything from it. The bootlegger has learned that he had better drive slowly – i.e. within the speed limit – through small country towns, which is not very important knowledge, at least not outside his illegal racket.

With confidence and ease Faulkner sets the scene, and the transition to the bootlegger's taking over of the narration is smooth and fluent. When the bootlegger has assumed the burden of narration, the rest of the story is entirely and almost exclusively his – the first-person narrator interrupts only a few times and only at the outset of the story. This enables the bootlegger (or rather the first-person narrator who in point of fact is the one who recounts what the bootlegger relayed to him) to use dialogue, direct speech, the pronouns 'I' and 'he' without any risk of confusion with the same pronouns in the frame. The tall tale about how a whole load of whiskey was swindled from the bootlegger allows Faulkner to introduce an aeroplane, and he thus returned to an element not used since his first story, 'Landing in Luck'.[45] But 'Country Mice' also points forward, to a story like ' "Once Aboard the Lugger - - " ' and more generally to other stories where the frame device is applied.

Even if Faulkner's main interest while working out the series of sketches commonly known under the somewhat misleading 'New Orleans Sketches' was *form* and character, there is more to these stories than just that – especially since both form and character in themselves contribute to a description of New Orleans, of a modern urban scene. Furthermore, many characters in these sketches share some shortcomings, beliefs, hopes, and dreams, and there is thus every conceivable reason to comment on the modern city, city life, and the ideas and attitudes prevalent in these sketches.

Faulkner's early title 'Sinbad in New Orleans' may of course be taken to point to the importance of destiny and fate, and one may use this title as a vantage point for a search for references to Destiny and Fate. If one finds a high number of such references, there is reason to form a hypothesis that Faulkner chose the title because so many of his characters felt that they were victims of some unappeasable destiny, and it does not really matter in this context whether the characters themselves are –

partially or fully – responsible for bringing themselves into positions where they are subject to the workings of some obscure fate. To prove the validity of the hypothesis one would have to prove that the number of references to Destiny and Fate was much higher than in Faulkner's other writings of approximately the same period, or in general. I find it likely that this is so, but not drastically so, and accordingly the title would in my view rather indicate the type of relation in which Faulkner (and his first-person narrator and the implied author of the sketches) felt he stood to New Orleans and its inhabitants. *He* might indeed think that Fate had something to do with his encounter with Spratling, Sherwood Anderson, and the literary bohemia of New Orleans, who together proved to be so crucial in his development as a fiction writer. Fate is also in the texts linked with character, and very often the conception of Destiny is nothing but a convenient excuse for being unable to adjust, for bad luck, for losing in the fierce competition that makes a city like New Orleans go round. To blame destiny for whatever disasters you suffer, and to see the workings of some unknown and inexplicable Fate in whatever places you at a disadvantage, is nothing but an apology, an attempt to relieve oneself of responsibility for one's own doings. It may, of course, also be seen as an acceptance of defeat, or simply as defeatism. If fate rules, everything may just as well be left in the hands of fate, man can do so little anyway. Many of the characters in the New Orleans texts blame destiny or fate for their various predicaments, simply because it is a normal thing to do. Faulkner's understanding of his own characters would support such an understanding; to refer to Destiny would just be one among many banalities that the characters on the streets of New Orleans use freely.

A few characters would nevertheless qualify for the 'Sinbad' figure, and they seem to have an understanding of fate and circumstance and their own power to shape their lives which closely resembles the one held by Sinbad of old. Jean-Baptiste of 'Home' is one such character, and he discusses with himself the extent to which a man may affect his Destiny through assertion of his own will: 'Who are you, to assume charge of a vessel, the destiny of which you cannot know' *(New Orleans Sketches,* p. 31); but despite the obvious negative answer implied in the very question, Jean-Baptiste breaks the chain of destiny – *art* being instrumental in saving him from becoming a criminal. He listens in on a tune that reminds him of his youth and of his dreams of a better life, and this in turn prevents him from committing the crime he has been planning.

Jean-Baptiste is one of the very few characters in the New Orleans sketches who is able to transcend the baseness and debauchery of his life, and who seems to have a fair chance of breaking the chain of destiny. He can do this, because he does not try to escape from his problem, while other characters avoid facing their problems where they really are (Antonio in 'Jealousy', Johnny in 'The Kid Learns', most of the characters in 'New Orleans', etc.).

The 'technical' use of destiny should also be mentioned; i.e. destiny functioning as *deus ex machina* to bring a story forward, bring about a change in the plot, or the like. One could for instance easily maintain that destiny steps in and strikes Antonio the final blow in 'Jealousy' when the old pistol in the curiosity shop suddenly fires. This is a different type of destiny, however, and all in all only a few characters – notably those with a religious background (Jewish, Catholic) – seem to have a clear understanding of what Destiny means. The Jew in 'New Orleans' has accepted a nearly fatalistic *Weltanschauung,* and he sees his life as insignificant in itself but important as a link in the everlasting chain of his race.

'Destiny' is not only a household word for some of the characters met in the New Orleans sketches; the word is also used regularly by the narrator, whatever position he chooses to stand in in relation to the story he tells. Perhaps a brief note on this use of 'destiny' in 'Sunset' can demonstrate this. The Negro character of this story has been convinced that his roots are in Africa, and is now on his way there, without the faintest idea of where Africa is. White men deceive him into giving away the little money he has and to work for his fare on the ferry, and he is cursed by everybody all the time. Once the idea of Africa has fastened in his mind he is confident in his faith and allows 'destiny to carry him along the river front' *(New Orleans Sketches,* p. 78). Destiny is here used simply to indicate a firm belief, an undeviating faith, a one-track mind: when all is insecure and uncertain, you may choose to let your boat drift, but if that is to let Destiny take over, then Destiny always takes over whatever you do or do not do, and the whole term becomes meaningless.[46] The Negro's 'Destiny' is nothing but the result of human frailty, social injustice, unbelievable avarice and meanness, in short, racial prejudice, inequality as an important and cherished principle of social life; the jungle law with the survival of the fittest as a guide line for much human interaction.

Faulkner's many-coloured picture of New Orleans is a country-man's description of a modern urban society as a human wasteland. Through the sub-narratives of 'New Orleans' we meet different but presumably representative characters. Together they form a sort of choir, which ultimately becomes the city itself speaking. The city comes to life through the rising and falling, hopeful and despairing voices of 'New Orleans'. It is a city full of unadjusted and misplaced persons whose lack of human contact and communication in general is typical. One might say that New Orleans is a city full of destinies, but the important fact is that these destinies are *produced* by the city. A heterogeneous sample of human beings, flotsam on the flood of life, has a rendezvous in the big city: *is* the city. Hope and despair, joy and sorrow, satisfaction and longing, deferred hopes and defunct dreams, brutality and inhumanity, competition and lust for money and sex, life appearing to be only food and sleep (and little enough of both), or life being a dream and a fire, being to *create* something out of despair and misery – all this is part of 'New Orleans'.

The girl on the street selling her body asks if there was love once, if there was grief once; now she is selling her body to get 'the bright things' (p. 13) so greatly appreciated in modern society. To her, as to most of the people in Faulkner's New Orleans, love and grief seem to be something which they experienced a long time ago, in another and different social context. The old verities of the human heart are not unfamiliar to the people in New Orleans, but in an urban environment there seems to be no room for them. True, the voices of New Orleans reveal that love and grief are still felt, but the very form these voices are given signifies that love and grief are private matters which are rarely shared, and probably not considered shareable in the modern wasteland of the urban setting. The tourist, who sees the city from the outside, recognizes its ability to court and spellbind people because it offers so much in terms of worldly goods.

New Orleans is hostile, alien, and destructive to the immigrants in particular: people like Jean-Baptiste, Antonio, the Cobbler, the Negro of 'Sunset', and others. Jean-Baptiste finds New Orleans to be 'an open coffin' *(New Orleans Sketches,* p. 28) under the cold, cold stars that watch indifferently from above. No reciprocal understanding can be achieved in a fragmented society where nobody ever really listens to anybody. A number of the sketches illustrate the failure of speech, or the failure to communicate at all, so that commands like 'listen' and 'say' recur frequently. A number of stories also epitomize the necessity for bragging and lying about oneself, as a means of keeping one's dignity and self-respect, or simply as a means of survival. In 'Damon and Pythias, Unlimited' this is seen very clearly:

'Listen, mister, I been a chentleman all my life. You think I would put anything over on another chentleman? Listen, you got me wrong. Listen, you give me that money and I'll. . .' *(New Orleans Sketches,* p. 25).

The reference to the truce between Damon and Pythias in the title is, of course, ironic. No deals, no reciprocal respect, can be achieved between the two con men of the story or between the narrator-actor and one of them. What has brought about this failure to communicate, can be debated. Faulkner introduces a set of myths and dreams which together might be tentatively called 'the American dream' or the incessant striving to get into what one is led to believe is 'the mainstream' of American life. Some of these myths are of the religious kind (cf. 'The Priest'); they are important in the lives of a society of churchgoers, and the validity of these myths is questioned in a number of the texts. The most obvious myths are those that perpetuate the value of ambition and competition. In 'The Kid Learns' the American dream is cast in terms of competition and material success, and the story gives a drastic example of what can happen when the positive dream of doing a good job, winning a fair share of recognition and admiration, is transformed into something totally different in the utterly competitive urban society. The story of Johnny Gray's brief success as a small gangster opens on a *credo,* which not only applies to Johnny's line of business but to free enterprise as such. At the same time this credo adds to the picture of New Orleans as a money-ridden, competitive society, where human qualities like love and kindness are reduced to becoming virtually of no importance whatsoever:

Competition is everywhere: competition makes the world go round. Not love, as some say. Who would want a woman nobody else wanted? Not me. And not you. And not Johnny. Same way about money. If nobody wanted the stuff, it wouldn't be worth fighting for *(New Orleans Sketches,* p. 86).

Ironically enough, Johnny forgets his own materialistic philosophy of competition for the sake of a woman, and this ultimately causes his

71

death. Johnny is extremely single-minded, believing that his own quasi-philosophy based on an authoritarian belief in the survival of the fittest is the only possible one to live by, but his desire for a girl destroys all his dreams and his attempt to bring his life into business-like order is thwarted. Johnny knows that the way society is organized, he must bide his time even to take over in the world of gangsters, but when the Wop puts his hand on the arm of a young girl, Johnny acts foolishly and knocks the Wop down. The story's credo, quoted above, introduced the competition for a woman, and this philosophy now works its own fatal way.

Johnny advocates the American dream in its most materialistic, misunderstood sense in this story: he believes sincerely in his own interpretation of the dream, and he acts according to it. The demands of his philosophy of competition are neglected when he chooses to play the role of chivalric hero – even though he acts in accordance with the principle of wanting what a competitor wants. The myth drawn upon here clearly incorporates the hero's willingness to die, if possible honourably, for the lady of his choice, so Johnny's engagement with 'Mary' is also a death wish acted out subconsciously. On the conscious level Johnny is doing what he should not do: fight a superior enemy. What makes him do this is not the longing of his youth, nor his desire for a woman, but the fact that he has adopted a social philosophy where you *fight* for things your competitors want (e.g. a woman to *own:* 'I've got a girl now'. [*New Orleans Sketches*, p. 91] Johnny thinks). Johnny is thus caught in a web of perverted dreams, myths, or assumptions of what life is and what interrelations between people should be like.

Contrary to what is the case with many other New Orleans dwellers, Johnny is at ease in New Orleans, in love with the smells and sounds of the big city. Most characters are rather isolated and alienated, living their own secluded lives, longing for a past which is getting more beautiful each day, or for the touch of a human hand. The bums of the streets of New Orleans glare at each other if they do not shout, the priest in his chamber struggles with a life become too complex for him, the cobbler in his shop tries to arrest motion and keep youth forever in a yellow rose, dreaming of his Tuscany landscape of long ago. Some of the nostalgic dreams of 'home' and 'them good times' may serve as a norm against which the bareness of the urban scene can be gauged. This is not only so because Faulkner finds the countryside to be much preferable to the city, but also because old times are preferable to modern times. He is nevertheless aware that the past cannot be recaptured, and that man has to adjust to the ever-changing present.

Many stories deal with a feeling of some kind of bereavement, of loss, but at the same time the acquisition of success and money is questioned. The social fragmentation visible in New Orleans erects invisible but insurmountable walls between people: 'the usual mode of human relationship is the predatory assault of aggressor on victim', as Momberger puts it.[47]

Not all persons are tieless and alone: The married couple in 'Jealousy' have relatives and friends to discuss their problems with. It does not help much, but it leads to a shift in emphasis so that Antonio becomes a victim of his own emotional instability. His behaviour is not a result of non-belonging, and he does not indulge in reveries about what life has in store for him. Accordingly, one should be aware that not all problems, not every crisis in the fictional world of Faulkner's New Orleans can be referred to the urban scene and its effect on the people living in the city.

Many characters dream of a lost world, of 'the good old days', but they also dream of a better world in terms of social justice and humane relations. The dream they share may be said to be a regression to a lost childhood, a nostalgic longing for a rural home where communication existed, and again the Negro of 'Sunset' may serve as an illustration. His feverish dreams of escape make him long for childhood and for a freedom he never really has had:

Again it was dawn. The sun rose, became hot, and marched above his head. He was at home, working in the fields; he was asleep, fighting his way from out a nightmare; he was a child again – no, he was a bird, a big one like a buzzard, drawing endless black circles on a blue sky (*New Orleans Sketches*, p. 84).

The Negro will never draw circles on a blue sky: with his body on the muddy earth, only his eyes can be turned toward the sky and 'the cold, cold stars' (*New Orleans Sketches*, p. 85) watching him from above. Beneath these stars, *sub specie aeternitatis*, his life and his destiny mattered so little, and nothing came of his dreams.

'. . .to gain a part of that beauty which shall not pass from the earth, of companionship, of love, perhaps – who knows?' (*New Orleans Sketches*, p. 31) was Jean-Baptiste's dream. On the personal level more than on the social level hope can indeed be found in Faulkner's New Orleans:

73

the love between the idiot and his bootlegger brother is one example, and the youthful love between Frankie and Johnny is a particular instance of human contact, described in metaphors of childhood experiences and nature images which give evidence of the value of the relationship and the feeling called love which Jean-Baptiste dreamt of.

There is hope for the future in New Orleans because a few characters break out of their isolation; or because they are strong enough to endure it if necessary. Frankie in the untitled short story about Frankie and Johnny of the sub-narrative of 'New Orleans',[48] is the strongest, most persevering and self-sufficient character among all the New Orleans figures. In this respect she not only differs from the many lonely, estranged characters in the New Orleans pieces, but also from most other women in Faulkner's early fiction. Frankie refuses to play the accepted game between the sexes, using her body and virginity as the main assets ('a liberty bond' she calls it), and she is likewise reluctant to conform to please her whining mother. Frankie is at the same time presented as the eternal mother, the fecund ground for which it is only natural to give life, and she accepts this when she finds herself pregnant: to give birth to new life is an important and natural process, and no rules or expectations imposed on her by a sobbing mother and a lover 'worse than a movie' (*Uncollected Stories,* p. 345) can make her change her mind. Being much better equipped to voice her opinions and describe the role she fills, Frankie is a more intelligent forerunner of that nature's child, Lena Grove, in *Light in August.*

Contrary to most of the sketches, this story expresses happiness, however brief and transient, between the black walls in the blind streets of the city; and when the love relationship breaks up, Frankie is a much stronger and more determined character than the average inhabitant of Faulkner's New Orleans. The moments of happiness challenge Faulkner to write some of his most affirmative lines in this part of his career, and metaphors of nature are the vehicles to carry the emotions:

They looked at each other and a soft wind blew over flowers and through trees and the street was no longer blind and mean and filthy. Their lips touched, and a blond morning came on hills brave in a clean dawn *(Uncollected Stories,* p. 340).

When Frankie is able to reaffirm her personal integrity, forgetting about other people's thoughts and relying on her own power and ability alone, this is how Faulkner describes her emotional status:

74

She felt as impersonal as the earth itself: she was a strip of fecund seeded ground lying under the moon and wind and stars of the four seasons, lying beneath grey and sunny weather since before time was measured; and that now was sleeping away a dark winter waiting for her own spring with all the pain and passion of its inescapable ends to a beauty which shall not pass from the earth *(Uncollected Stories,* p. 347).

Frankie is strong and self-confident because she is a healthy, normal young girl who has a simple understanding of nature and her own worth. She has discovered some of the hollowness and pretence in human relations as they appear in New Orleans. The hope we can discern in her character relies to some extent on a nature myth, while the strongest and most persuasive sign of hope in New Orleans is found in the liberating and healing powers of *art* – not only for the artist but also for those who experience the beauty and truth and understanding of good art. In 'Home' Faulkner places a violin-player with a saw and a bow on the curb in an introductory paragraph, and this 'violinist' is instrumental in Jean-Baptiste's change of plans. Listening to the violinist, a nostalgic vision of the land of his youth comes to him. Contrary to most other characters in New Orleans who may share similar dreams, Jean-Baptiste reaches a kind of self-recognition:

He saw the cottage where he was born, and ate and slept, sharp in the sun; he saw the wheeling candle light soft in a golden dusk beneath a single star like a yellow rose. He saw all this and knew that he had pursued a phantom into a far land; that destiny had taken him across seas so that he might see with a clear eye that thing which his heedless youth had obscured from him, which three years in the mud of Artois and Champagne could not make him see *(New Orleans Sketches,* p. 33.).

Jean-Baptiste rises after this experience, and he goes away, towards dawn and a new day. He leaves whatever friends he may have had, since he has discovered the phantom he pursued (definitely materialistic and related to that elusive American dream), and there is some hope that he may ultimately find some of the beauty which he knows shall never pass from the earth. Jean-Baptiste has recognized that he has journeyed to a country foreign to his nature to find what his *home* was like, and a *tune* reminded him. The capability of art to bring about self-recognition, to communicate, and to transcend the ugliness and the boredom of New Orleans, is something rare and new in this fictional world – otherwise so filled with clangs and shouts and all kinds of noise.

A young boy whom 'I' and Spratling meet one day, Peter, also gives hope for the future, provided that the environmental influences do not change Peter into one of the small-time gangsters on the streets of New Orleans. Actually, it is most likely that this will happen, but the innocent, open, and faithful young boy inspires confidence that he may become one of the few who rise above the drab and desolate city streets and get away from the debased and unworthy life his mother leads. Circumstances may have forced her to choose her profession – she entertains men as Frankie's mother in a more elegant fashion did; she is described as a 'decayed lily' *(Uncollected Stories,* p. 493), and she treats her son harshly. Peter has unusual recuperative powers, and is still too young and innocent to suffer. The story about Peter ends on a note of hope, even if it is only Peter's hope that he will be able to spin his top next time the two artists visit him:

... Here was spring in a paved street, between walls, and
here was Peter, his sorrow forgotten, in a window, saying:
   'When you come next time I bet I can spit that top'
(Uncollected Stories, p. 494).

One sketch among the New Orleans material introduces a possible saviour; the young man called David in 'Out of Nazareth'.

Many factors point to David as a Christ figure. This is not so much due to the character himself as to the narrator's (and Spratling's) presentation of him, based on a first impression. He may have come from anywhere, according to the two friends: 'He was eternal, of the earth itself' *(New Orleans Sketches,* p. 47). His animal-like qualities, his peacefulness, his uneducatedness, and his preference for hay as a bed to sleep on, all combine to emphasize his closeness to nature. The only direct impression we get of David is through his own story, and the narrator's propensity for posture and artificiality, displayed not least in his own language in this sketch, makes him a highly unreliable narrator in this case.[49]

The sketch suggests David's true communion with nature and his easy ways with other rootless, vagabonding people, but this does not make him a Christ or a Saviour. He is certainly not Christ-like in his lack of any deeper contact with other people, or in his unwillingness to involve himself in the destinies of his fellow-men. This early and young Faulknerian Christ is no saviour; he has no disciples, makes no speeches to convert people, and whatever wonders he might be capable of, lie in the eyes of the taken-in beholders. David actually talks with himself and prefers solitude to company. If he were an early Christ-figure in Faulkner's fiction, or even just a young Christ, not yet ready for his harvest work in the Lord's vineyard, he should have been less reluctant to care for and serve others. The fact that he is eager to leave New Orleans does not signify 'the lack of any divine presence in New Orleans'[50] – David is always on the move.

The narrator's encounter with David leads to a renewed belief in goodness to be found somewhere, but it leads to no redemption, not even to a change as far as the readers are allowed to see. This is so common in the New Orleans writings, however, that one should not be surprised. The story of David only demonstrates that a lonely star may light up the dark firmament above the coffin-like city, but being of a natural kind, it must immediately return to more natural surroundings.

Faulkner's achievement in the New Orleans sketches may well be described by the tourist's reaction to the city itself: 'artificial but not brilliant' (*New Orleans Sketches,* p. 14). There is reason not to let the New Orleans writings stand alone as a single, homogeneous performance. Variety is on the contrary an important feature of the stories. There are nevertheless some themes, elements, interests, and techniques that dominate.

Faulkner's chief concern, and his most significant accomplishment in the New Orleans period, has to do with *form* and *character.* He always stressed his preoccupation with character, but in these early sketches form is what he worked hard and conscientiously with. The New Orleans pieces nevertheless remain minor, compared to what he managed to do shortly afterwards.

Faulkner's method in the art of story telling differs considerably from one story to another. He uses an omniscient narrator in some texts; he lets the characters of 'New Orleans' and a few other sketches speak in soliloquies or internal monologues, even using stream of consciousness technique at a fairly simple level; he introduces a frame narrator who lets another person function as narrator of the story comprised in the frame; he uses an 'I' narrator who seems to be the author himself in disguise. The first-person narrator is sometimes hidden very ingeniously, e.g. in 'The Kid Learns'; and often the complexity of a story stems from the author's play with points of view.

It is also fairly obvious that the first-person narrator's significance differs from text to text: his degree of detachment varies from the spectator/observer role in 'Mirrors of Chartres Street' to the critical understanding and implied admiration of the bootlegger in 'Country Mice' or the young poet in 'Out of Nazareth'. The bums of 'Damon and Pythias, Unlimited' do not take him in, as does, however, the posing, toothless Mona Lisa of 'Episode'. Humour and irony are also employed to reveal and uncover habits and deceits and deception; both are used with a deft hand in an otherwise not too interesting story, 'Don Giovanni'.[51]

Faulkner came to experiment more than most writers in a generation when experimentation was more the rule than the exception. Although the experiments in the New Orleans period never go further than an imitation of Joseph Conrad and Sherwood Anderson, the variety of angles used to approach the material from points forward to the technical complexities and brilliance of *The Sound and the Fury* and the multiple point of view of *As I Lay Dying*.

Faulkner's New Orleans texts present a city in its broad and many-coloured richness and variety. The treatment of peculiar American myths shows how discontented the artist is with the way of the world of his time. Criticism of false dreams, of delusions, of a system where money-making and status are of paramount significance also becomes criticism of a place and a way of life where human relationship have but a poor chance to thrive. People are invariably used by the strongest in a moral anarchy where the only norm is a very variable one given or implied by the narrator in each story.

What is there to do then, if a human being is but a lump of moist earth in the hands of God? Faulkner offers no ready answer, and there is no such answer. To say that the bleak world portrayed in the New Orleans pieces is an urban society and that the implied criticism accordingly is limited to this type of society, is hardly valid either. Its counterpart may be found in a living community in the countryside, but this is doubtful, as Faulkner would make clear through a number of stories later on. The agrarian dream is just a dream, which no post-capitalistic society can make come true and at the same time meet its needs and wants. The dreams of an arcadia as we see it in 'The Cobbler' and 'Home', to mention only two examples, are hardly realistic in terms of a possible retreat from an inhuman city life. The people of New Orleans must fight where they are, beneath the cold stars and in the eyes of an indifferent

God, keep their hopes of a golden day in the future when they have grown and matured enough to respect and love each other – but the hope for such a day is rather illusory in Faulkner's New Orleans.

Victory in all its possible meanings seems to be an illusion, and to the degree that the stories of this period reflect Faulkner's artistic capability, he is a loser himself. At this point, his first great attempt at using his art as a vehicle for conveying a message of understanding, love, and compassion to his readers, and to himself, failed. Perhaps it had to fail to be worth being repeated, and was a necessary 'failure' in Faulkner's steady growth and maturation as a short-story writer.[52]

Faulkner had journeyed from Oxford, Mississippi, to New Orleans, Louisiana, and would soon embark upon a longer voyage, for Europe. He may have come to think of himself as a Sinbad figure, a man of the world travelling hopefully, always on the lookout for the exciting, peculiar, bizarre, and interesting, always ready to participate and share experiences and adventures but also with a serious need to contemplate whatever passed, put it into perspective, look for a deeper significance. This somewhat modified and modernized Sinbad did not sever his ties with the town and the countryside he had left and to which he planned to return. Accordingly, nothing would be more natural than to tell a story from a background he knew much more profoundly and loved with a deep and lasting dedication. 'The Liar' is such a story, and together with the Conradian 'Yo Ho and Two Bottles of Rum', it hardly belongs to the *New Orleans Sketches* despite the fact that it was printed in the *Times-Picayune,* as was also 'Yo Ho and Two Bottles of Rum'.

'The Liar' has been given some undue praise as Faulkner's first published story with the rural setting so much of his later fiction came to rely heavily on.[53] 'The Hill', 'Adolescence', and, to a minor degree, 'Moonlight' make use of Faulkner's native country, of the region he knew best, but only 'Adolescence' makes use of country people in a way that resembles 'The Liar'. There is, nonetheless, some truth in statements considering 'The Liar' as first in more than one respect. The story is not set in or close to the 'village' as 'The Hill' is; it is removed to the back country of *The Hamlet* – far from the French Quarter and Chartres Street. The story is told by an acknowledged liar, named Ek, who is sitting in front of the unpainted store of Gibson. The narrator has lived the first twenty years of his life in the hill region. It seems as if Faulkner here, both in setting the scene and in his presentation of the characters, deals with something he knows very well; with 'everything he had absorbed about the hill regions of Lafayette County and North Mississippi'.[54] He had, indeed, begun to locate his little postage stamp of native soil.

The part of the story coming before Ek's tale displays Faulkner's interest in the omniscient frame narrator and in his listeners. Ek has four listeners, plus a stranger listening from a distance. Their simplicity, ignorance, childishness, and their admiration for imaginative ability are made clear; first by the brief narrative about how some hill people made for the woods when they saw a train, and then by an explicit statement:

His audience laughed too, enjoying the humor, but tolerantly, as one laughs at a child. His fabling was well known. And though like all peoples who live close to the soil, they were by nature veracious, they condoned his unlimited imagination for the sake of the humor he achieved and which they understood (New Orleans Sketches, p. 93).

Ek is the born story-teller, or *liar,* to whom 'silence was unbearable' *(New Orleans Sketches,* p. 95), and he accordingly sets out to tell a story claiming that for once his story is true: 'something cur'ous that reely happened' *(New Orleans Sketches,* p. 94). He cannot help digressing into a comic tale about the first pair of shoes he got at the age of twenty-one, and at this point of the story even the mysterious and sinister stranger joins in the laughter.

Lafe, who is one of the listeners, interrupts Ek twice in the early phase of the story, but after these incidents the narrator (Ek) is allowed to go on without further interruption from the listeners all the way up to the point when Ek tells about the murder he has witnessed and a rhetorical pause is necessary. This pause gives the frame narrator an opportunity to describe the listeners' reaction and give the clues that serve to explain what happens later on:

Their eyes were enraptured on his face, the hot black gaze of the stranger seemed like a blade spitting him against the wall, like a pinned moth (New Orleans Sketches, pp. 100–01).

The stranger's reaction, and Ek's attitude to him, are emphasized before Ek continues and brings his story to a conclusion:

He drew his gaze from the stranger's by an effort of will, and found that the pleasant May morning was suddenly chill. For some reason he did not want to continue (New Orleans Sketches, p.101).

Ek, the proverbial story-teller, is caught in the web of his own tale, and he must continue. Describing a murder in great detail, he reveals that he has been the only eye-witness to it; and suddenly the stranger ceases to be a stranger who keeps at a distance; a shot is heard, and while Ek is wounded, the stranger jumps on the train and the listeners remain seated, with the exception of Lafe. Faulkner had prepared the escape by mentioning the whistle in the only break in Ek's long story. In the setting of the stage, the railroad is important, and it comes as no surprise when it provides the author with a possibility of escape and a solution to the story as such.

Ek's story for once brings him no good. He is blamed by his listeners for telling the truth, and being stupid enough to do it in front of a murderer. Ek claims in his defence that he has told a lie, but he cannot help feeling that 'his veracity as a liar was gone for ever' *(New Orleans Sketches.* p. 103).

The story itself not only makes it likely that Ek's story is true, that the events narrated really have taken place; his 'yarn' must have been true to elicit a response like the stranger's. Comments suggesting that Faulkner here implies that the liar (i.e., the artist) may attain some truth through the telling of lies (i.e., fiction, and the tall tale in particular) seem to be beside the point.

'The Liar' may be considered a standard formula story of detection,[55] but yet it is more than that. The setting of the story in the back country, the colloquial speech used so abundantly, the dramatic love-murder conflict resulting in death, point to recurrent elements in Faulkner's later short fiction. The apparent detachment or distance between the frame narrator and the 'liar' and his listeners does not hide a deep and genuine interest both in the possibilities of the oral story-telling techniques and in the local characters portrayed here.

'The Liar' may have been written aboard the *West Ivis,* and it is probable that Faulkner's last story to appear in the *Times-Picayune,* 'Yo Ho and Two Bottles of Rum' was also written aboard the Europe-bound ship. Travestying the great sea-story teller Robert Louis Stevenson's pirate shanty (in *Treasure Island),* Faulkner had chosen his rather queer title, and the story deserves its title: the Chinese mess-boy Yo Ho pervades the whole tale, and if rum is not drunk, whiskey is a useful substitute, and this liquid eventually supplies the narrator with his grotesque turn in the last part of the funeral wake at the end of the story.

Being much more than a 'juvenile exercise in irony', [56] the story draws heavily on Faulkner's reading of Conrad, and, as Blotner remarks, the third person is here 'pure Conrad'.[57] With Faulkner using a ship and an Eastern harbour as his setting, and narrating the story through the voices of a better-knowing, vaguely ironic omniscient author, Conrad's influence must be acknowledged. There is more to the story than the Conradian elements, and the accidental killing (whose only significance has to do with the *burial* of the corpse) is treated so callously and the white men's reactions are so shallow and indifferent that the narrator's comments fail to convince. The contrasting of the crew and the officers can add only mock-ironic comments on cultural differences, and the narrator has prepared himself for comments of this type from the very outset of his story. A great deal of humour, both of the innocent and more morbid and grotesque kind, makes 'Yo Ho and Two Bottles of Rum' a story that points forward to particular scenes and effects and preferences in his later works. It might, indeed, be deemed very Faulknerian to let a ship race towards the nearest harbour to put the dead Yo Ho in his grave while the corpse is rotting in its coffin. The flippant, ironic tone maintained by the narrator in his presentation of the ship and her crew is Faulkner's own, and the explicit reference to 'destiny' could be used to link this story with the New Orleans sketches published earlier in the same paper.

Apart from the ironic tone and the distance thus kept by the narrator, he may be accused of prejudice against various nationalities. The typical British, Welsh, and Scottish qualities seem to be deliberately sought in this story, while the peculiar qualities of the Chinese contrast with the spirit and attitudes of the white men:

There is something eternal in the East, something resilient and yet rocklike, against which the Westerner's brief thunder, his passionate, efficient methods, are as wind *(New Orleans Sketches,* p. 126).

The cultural differences, to some degree based on misconceptions and prejudice, in point of fact *make* and carry the whole story. The narrator succeeds in convincing us that in the ability to endure, to face death, and to adjust to unusual circumstances, the Eastern race is by no means inferior:

82

But against that wall of contemplative Oriental calm, of preoccupation with something far, far older than Mr. Ayers the mate and his mushroom civilization of a short yesterday, he knew again a sense of irritating inferiority and uncertainty *(New Orleans Sketches,* p. 127).

The prevailing sense of gruesome and grotesque and implacable destiny, of mysteries as impenetrable as the woods themselves, changes the story in its latter half into a tale of horror and oppression. Yo Ho's body is more present now that he is dead, and the absolute demand from the crew to have him buried in the earth gives the narrator an excellent opportunity to use a description of the landscape through which the coffin is carried to create a situation where fear, superstition, and nightmarish thoughts seem to suffocate the white men:

The sun was red and implacable as a furnace mouth; once the beach was behind and they were among great impenetrable trees the heat became terrific. Mr. Ayers looked back at the calm, unsweating Chinese with envy and exasperation, mopping his florid face *(New Orleans Sketches,* p. 128).

Some of Faulkner's favourite words of the period are used time and again in 'Yo Ho and Two Bottles of Rum', but the very outrageous idea that ends the story is a trick which he fortunately did not turn to very often. Whiskey is part of the lives of the officers, and when they discover that whiskey is sent with the corpse to accompany the dead in his grave, the officers naturally drink it. Logically, if not humanely, they then decide to do away with a few more Yellows to procure more whiskey, but the Chinese disappear while the story slowly winds towards its end with the return of the men to the ship on the following morning.

The nightmarish landscape and its seeming hostility to the persons penetrating it would return later in Faulkner's short fiction, as would the whiskey and, of course, the hunt-motif used in 'Yo Ho and Two Bottles of Rum' and touched upon also in 'The Liar'.

'The Liar' and 'Yo Ho and Two Bottles of Rum' represent two distinctly different types of stories, and Faulkner would develop his short-story writing along both lines in the years ahead. 'The Liar' is thus an early 'country' story in which elements like love and hatred and violence are central in an otherwise humorously told tall tale, told to a public of ordinary men outside a store. The story thus obviously qualifies as a progenitor of the stories about Faulkner's townspeople and country people – those he mentions in a letter to Horace Liveright in 1927.[58] 'Yo

Ho and Two Bottles of Rum' is an early Faulkner story with an international cast of characters; each nationality is characterized on the basis of some proverbial idea of what is typically British, Chinese, etc. The story strongly emphasizes the stoic complacence and endurance of the Eastern race, and also introduces the hunt-motif – and it is important to notice that the hunt is for other human beings. It seems fair to suggest that these two texts form a kind of transition between the New Orleans period and the stories that Faulkner would write in the months immediately ahead, partly on the basis of his experience in Europe, partly on the basis of the new perspective his travels had given him on his native land. He would write a number of stories in the years up to 1930; either of the type suggested by 'The Liar' or with an international setting and cast and with elements reminiscent of the grotesquery of 'Yo Ho and Two Bottles of Rum'. He would be fairly successful in both types of stories, even though his best stories certainly are of the first kind.

By the time 'The Liar' and 'Yo Ho and Two Bottles of Rum' were published, Sinbad had long since taken leave of New Orleans and headed for new experiences, if not his own, then observations and vicarious experiences which would lead to later creation.

Faulkner had voiced the opinion that sound art 'does not depend on the quality or quantity of available material: a man with real ability finds sufficient what he has to hand'.[59] Very early in the twenties Faulkner tried out various forms of material that he possessed, and the New Orleans period enabled him to single out those types of material which might prove most valuable to him as an artist. It may well be that Faulkner found that parts of what he 'had to hand' were not substantial enough to be used in a novel, and that a number of minor incidents, anecdotes, observations and ideas lent themselves more readily to short stories. He had been a poet, and some of the beauty, artificiality, passion, lyricism and symbolism previously used in poems now had to be expressed in prose. A few stories, which may be described as allegories and which are distinctly different from all other Faulkner prose fiction, were written in 1926 and 1927. Beside allegorical short stories like 'Mayday' and, to a lesser degree, 'The Wishing Tree', Faulkner also relied on realistic descriptions of familiar things and observed experiences in unfinished stories like 'A Portrait of Elmer' and 'Christmas Tree'.[60] Perhaps Faulkner's real 'discovery' of what he 'had to hand' and his conscious and extensive use of it happened on a full scale in this period.

The immediate effects of his discovery of what he had to hand are seen in the novels, and it may well be that for some time his work on the novels left so little time for short fiction that the effects are visible in this genre only later.

Only two of the five stories written after the New Orleans period and before 1928 seem to have been brought to a satisfactory conclusion. These two stories were written for a special purpose. 'Mayday', the earliest of them, was hand-lettered and illustrated and bound and presented to Helen Baird as a gift booklet. As Carvel Collins has shown,[61] Faulkner was deeply in love with Helen Baird at this time and troubled by the fact that his love was not returned. Helen would shortly marry, and for the second time Faulkner experienced this kind of bereavement: Estelle Oldham had done the same thing a few years before. It is not surprising that Faulkner's feelings of transience and disillusionment went into the story 'Mayday'.

The second completed story was 'The Wishing Tree', which the author typed and bound and presented as a birthday gift to his step-daughter to be, Victoria Franklin, on 5 February 1927. But there exist two distinctly different versions of this story, and it is probable that the longer version is the older one, and Faulkner gave a copy of this to Margaret Brown, apparently on 11 February 1927.[62] Faulkner's own memory of how this story was invented indicates that this version is indeed the original story, and that he created the story to comfort a small girl slowly dying of cancer:

'I invented this story' . . . 'for Mrs Brown's daughter, about ten at the time, who was dying of cancer. I put it on paper and gave it to her so her family could read it when she wanted to hear it. This I did as a gesture of pity and compassion for a doomed child. . . .'[63]

The Victoria Franklin version of the story is the one that was published after Faulkner's death, both in the *Saturday Evening Post* and as a book.

In 1925 Faulkner put in a lot of work on a novel entitled 'Elmer', which eventually came to nothing. Apparently in a last attempt to salvage some of the material in this novel, he wrote a story of 57 typed pages, entitled 'A Portrait of Elmer', and despite various other fragments of stories that Faulkner experimented with on the basis of this material, the more coherent and complete typescript, now available in *Uncollected*

Stories of William Faulkner, will be used here.[64] The story fragment, 'And Now What's To Do', interesting as it may be because of its rather extensive use of autobiographical material, will be given only brief notice here. Finally, the material available for 'The Devil Beats His Wife' and 'Christmas Tree' makes it rather doubtful that much can be gleaned from a scrutiny of them. 'Christmas Tree' is a very poor story, the only interest of which may lie in the situation it sets up (the young married couple, almost haunted by their female relatives) and in its use of a marital conflict for what might have become a dramatic story.

One of the most important elements these stories have in common is the quest, the search, the journey set out upon to gain some of the beauty that so many Faulkner characters believe 'shall not pass from the earth'. Since many of these groping and uncertain attempts at understanding the human dilemma, the transience of love, the scarcity of friendship, and the vanity and vainglory of dreams and hopes seem to reflect the artist's own struggle to create, at least parts of them may be seen as psychological autobiographies. 'And Now What's To Do' is definitely based upon autobiographical material, upon elements that can be proved to be parts of Faulkner's own background and upbringing.[65] Elements of this text deal with the longings and compulsions of puberty, and the boy's inability to talk to girls. Later, when the boy is more grown up, girls are still an important part of his thoughts and his life, but going after them is 'Like going after something you wanted, and getting into a nest of spider webs.'[66] The lonely dreamer in 'The Hill' is vaguely discernible here, and when the protagonist moves about the country to get away from a girl whom he got into trouble, the resemblance to 'A Portrait of Elmer' is obvious. Elmer has a bastard son in Houston, and even though the boy's mother, Ethel, simply states that she is to marry somebody else, Elmer leaves, touring through a number of states, going north all the time just like the 'he' in 'And Now What's To Do'. The complicated and not really finished story about Elmer is also a story about the artist as a young man; a man who believes, despite his own experience with numerous girls and with being a soldier in the war, that experience can be replaced by art: 'But who wants experience when he can get any kind of substitute? To hell with experience, . . . since all reality is unbearable' *(Uncollected Stories,* p. 612).

'A Portrait of Elmer' includes a number of elements which Faulkner exploited and exhausted in his later fiction and which he might have felt reluctant to use if any of the Elmer material had been published in the late twenties. Elmer has a sister who is very kind and of whom he is very fond, Jo. She is the last one of the children who leaves the family, which is constantly on the move. There is also the episode with Velma in the barn, and the strange relationship to his 40-year-old spinster teacher, as well as the fire that destroys the family's house, and the wounded soldier reconvalescing from war. All these elements are central in Faulkner's early novels in slightly or substantially revised form; in novels as different as *The Sound and the Fury, As I Lay Dying,* and *The Hamlet.* The wounded soldiers had of course also been at the centre of Faulkner's first novel, *Soldiers' Pay.*

That Elmer has such problems in adjusting to a world that seems to offer nothing save money and work is understandable and forgivable; that he is unable to adjust at all and never knows what to make of his life nor of his art, is worse. It is also indicative of the conditioning he has been subjected to and the environment he lives in. It is, furthermore, revealing as to the myths he lives by. Elmer's sister, Jo, had told him 'when you want to do anything, you do it, do you hear? Dont let nobody stop you' *(Uncollected Stories,* p. 621). Yet Elmer dreams more about having a name than he really cares about his art; he dreams of '*Fame perhaps. Hodge, the painter' (Uncollected Stories,* p. 622), and he even envisages himself – in French – as the papers are likely to present him when he has become famous.

'A Portrait of Elmer' is so vague, and consists of so many disparate and disjointed elements never brought to a final and satisfactory unity, that a closer study of the short story would reveal numerous ambiguities and unsolved problems. The Elmer material in general would come to function as an arsenal of characters, incidents, relationships, and attitudes which the author could return to and draw upon in his later fiction. As a short story, 'A Portrait of Elmer' does not really point forward, and it is unrepresentative of Faulkner's capacity at the time he wrote it. The story has obvious relationships with later Faulkner stories, but these relationships are not very close and are also of the superficial kind.

Faulkner thus failed to finish his portrait of the artist as a young man – the complications presented by the Elmer material appear to have been beyond his grasp at the time. Undigested borrowings from Eliot and Joyce make the story uneven, and even the final typescript reads like a draft.

Written in 1926 and judged to be 'the most significant unpublished Faulkner story in existence' and 'Faulkner's finest piece of writing before *The Sound and the Fury*',[67] 'Father Abraham' was published in a limited edition in 1983, but it has not been possible to include this story here.

The complexity of Faulkner's writing at this time is seen in 'Mayday' and in 'The Wishing Tree'. These long short stories are far away from the realism of most of Faulkner's narratives: 'Mayday' is an allegory where a Medieval Knight on his quest through a forest is accompanied by Hunger and Pain; 'The Wishing Tree' is a children's fairy-tale where anything may happen, and, indeed, happens – even though the fantastic tale is set in a realistic frame and is proved to be a dream. But *in* the dream, the young girl, accompanied by a little red-haired fairy boy, Maurice, undertakes a journey through a forest in search of the wishing tree, and finally she meets with Saint Francis and learns an important moral lesson. The final images and the atmosphere of the two stories are very different, but this is not surprising: 'Mayday' is a story with strong sexual overtones, 'The Wishing Tree' is a story of hope and comfort and belief in some ultimate goodness somewhere in the world – goodness which anyone can contribute significantly to.

A number of foreshadowings and early attempts with characters and events in *The Sound and the Fury* can be found in 'Mayday' and – to a lesser extent – in 'The Wishing Tree'.[68] The most significant of these foreshadowings have been rather fully explained by other critics, and there should hence be no need to give a detailed examination here. These critics – despite the hypothetical nature of many of their assumptions – have done a fair job of establishing the complex, sustained, and fascinating development in Faulkner's career which led to the writing of *The Sound and the Fury*.[69]

In 'The Wishing Tree' Faulkner employs the conventional framework of a fairy-tale and gives comical treatment to numerous themes that would occur in much of his later writing. The little girl who *remembers* to 'get into bed left foot first and to turn the pillow over before she went to sleep'[70] shares some characteristic traits with Caddy Compson of *The Sound and the Fury*; adventurousness, avoidance of unpleasant experiences if possible,[71] and the way she [Dulcie; in the longer version she is called Daphne] is associated with trees also makes her akin to Caddy. The fact that she has a young brother who acts very unwisely and is utterly selfish also indicates some of the relationships between the two works. It may be correct to maintain that 'The Wishing Tree' occupies an intermediate position between 'Mayday' and the novel.

In 'The Wishing Tree' the children, accompanied by the Negro maid, Alice, and an old poor white, Egbert, and – later – a returned soldier, search for the wishing tree. On their way they are unable to recognize it when they see it, and when they finally find something that might be the tree they are looking for, it proves to be Saint Francis, who relays some moral wisdom to them. He tells them that if they and many other children each took a leaf from the wishing tree, there would soon be none left for those who came later. So Saint Francis gives the children a bird each in exchange for the leaves they had taken from the mellomax tree (which, indeed, was the wishing tree),[72] giving them this simple lesson:

' . . .if you'll feed it [the bird] and care for it, you'll never make a selfish wish, because people who care for and protect helpless things cannot have selfish wishes . . .'[73]

In 'Mayday' Sir Galwyn, constantly accompanied by the shadowy figures of Pain and Hunger, also sees a tree covered with 'bright never-still leaves',[74] and the tree is the very same one that the children saw and spoke to in 'The Wishing Tree':

The tree was an old man with a long shining beard like a silver cuirass and the leaves were birds of a thousand kinds and colors.[75]

The tree *is* simply Saint Francis again, but it is not yet time for him to answer any questions from the Knight: he has not yet been through his ordeal, he has not set out upon his journey. He is almost stopped short before the quest is begun; a girl in the stream running near the tree stretches out her arms to him, and had it not been for Pain and Hunger drawing him in opposite directions, he might have sought peace and slumber in the arms of what we later get to know as Little Sister Death. Still Sir Galwyn must go through some experience with his companions Pain and Hunger, and his situation while he waits for day to set upon his journey is described a couple of times in words that are so general and ripe with meaning that they seem to serve as an apt description of the human predicament: 'he was as one kneeling on a stone floor in a dark place, waiting for day.'[76] With Hunger and Pain waiting at his side all the time, it may seem reasonable that Sir Galwyn is tempted to seek death by water, to take a short cut to Eternity, as Quentin Compson would later do when he found no quiet, secluded, and absolutely safe place where he and Caddy could live innocently for eternal time. On the other hand, Hunger and Pain are the very reasons why Sir Galwyn enters the dark forest and sets out upon the quest, where he encounters, among other allegorical characters, Time. Time asks Sir Galwyn's two companions to tell the knight what 'this thing calling itself Sir Galwyn of Arthgyl' is. And they answer together:

'He is but a handful of damp clay which we draw hither and yon at will until the moisture is gone completely out of him, as two adverse winds toy with a feather, and when the moisture is all gone out of him he will be as any other pinch of dust, and we will not be concerned with him any longer.'

Later on, after the quest, Sir Galwyn is unable to explain how he knows that he is not only a shadow, but what he seeks is Experience, satisfaction of his hunger, release from his pains; and he does so by searching for a girl who reminds him of 'young hyacinths in spring, and honey and sunlight'.[78] The brave and faithful Sir Galwyn slays the defenders of virginity and innocence when needed in order to get to the beautiful ladies he encounters during his quest: Yseult, Princess Elys, and Princess Aelia. Briefly but urgently he falls in love with them, makes love to them, and leaves them with a sigh of relief. They may not quite have satisfied his dream image of young hyacinths in spring, they may have lacked some of the honey and sunlight, and they were not too different from other girls he had known. But more than this,

' . . . It occurs to me', young Sir Galwyn continued profoundly, 'that it is not the thing itself that man wants, so much as the wanting of it. But ah, it is sharper than swords to know that she who is fairer than music could not content me for even a day'.[79]

Sir Galwyn is on the brink of discovering what Shakespeare formulated centuries before Faulkner, that 'All things that are, are with more spirit chased than enjoyed'. The attempt to rid oneself of the hunger and the urge for experience, pleasure, excitement, self-gratification, and admi-

90

ration in all its varying forms, is doomed from the very beginning. To live is to be accompanied by insatiable hunger and pain and longing for something to happen to make life endurable. Hunger gives an apt description of what Man is, using Sir Galwyn as his example:

' ... You have known the bride of a king before even her husband looked upon her, you have possessed, in the persons of the daughters of the two most important minor princes in Christendom, the morning and the evening stars, and yet you have gained nothing save a hunger which gives you no ease. I remember to have remarked once that man is a buzzing insect blundering through a strange world, seeking something he can neither name nor recognize, and probably will not want. I think now that I shall refine this aphorism to: Man is a buzzing fly beneath the inverted glass tumbler of his illusions.'[80]

None of the insights revealed in the quotation above are radically new, even though Faulkner has had a happy hand in phrasing them. Hunger's description indicates that Sir Galwyn's quest is also for a kind of self-recognition, for his own identity. Who am I? and Where do I go? and what is there to do with one's life if man is nothing but a 'lump of moist clay' in the hands of some indifferent God? Sir Galwyn, who finally meets the Lord of Sleep, chooses forgetfulness, oblivion, and the Big Sleep through the embrace with Little Sister Death, the shining image of the girl of the Knight's dreams in the dark running water. Hunger and Pain close in on Sir Galwyn, and the image in the water reminds him of hyacinths in spring, promising a 'soft and bottomless sleep'.[81] When the water touches him, Hunger and Pain leave him, but only then does the good Saint Francis reveal that the only girl who can give comfort and sleep and relieve one of hunger and pain, is Little Sister Death.

Death comes as a relief, as something setting Sir Galwyn free from the pains and wants of human life, but pain is all through 'Mayday' associated with sex, and Sir Galwyn's suicide is depicted in images of sexual embrace. Sir Galwyn has engaged in sexual activities before, with some of the most attractive women of this world, without getting any real satisfaction. His various relationships have been preparations for the final sexual intercourse: with death.[82]

Galwyn seeks death by water, commits suicide, because he finds life and life's values unbearable. Being self-sufficient and self-confident, fighting for the things he wants and taking them, the odds he has to face are indeed insurmountable for the person who relies on himself alone and seeks help or support from nobody else. Galwyn apparently also finds the quest completely void of meaning or value, and at least his companion, Hunger, who has a propensity for aphorisms, might have told him that in the very quest itself lies its value. Even if love cannot transcend all hunger and pain and give oblivion and complete satisfaction, one should not be too troubled by the fact that all things are transient and cannot last. One may ask time to bide, or wish to go out of time, but one has to accept the limited consolation of love and kindness, and be satisfied with however little of a permanent and lasting value there is in life. Sir Galwyn never realizes that his all-time companions, Hunger and Pain, are his allies and are inevitable travel companions on the journey through life. By this inability to accept the necessity and inevitability of pain and hunger, Sir Galwyn in point of fact denies life itself and is never able to live. Hunger and Pain are allegorical figures, so one should of course also realize that Sir Galwyn is a lonely figure; his relationships with other people are brief and shallow, and leave him even more lonely and estranged. In this respect he embodies most of the characteristics of the solitary dreamer, but if his world is hostile, the world is not so much to blame as the dreamer himself, who is in charge of his own destiny to a limited but significant degree.

'Mayday' is more interesting for its relationship to some of Faulkner's novels, notably *The Sound and the Fury,* than for its possible kinship with other Faulkner short stories. Even if the more general thematic implications one finds in this story are applicable to many a short story, more specific connections and influences are difficult to pin down. There is, indeed, reason to stress the uniqueness of this story in Faulkner's short-story production, and maintain that 'The Wishing Tree', in spite of obvious significant differences, is the story that comes closest to 'Mayday' in terms of imagery, structure, and theme. The function of the good Saint Francis in the two stories is distinctly different. In Faulkner's later short-story career, certain themes in 'The Wishing Tree' are developed further and treated more seriously. These themes are associated with the Negro and his ability to live one day at a time and hence his capacity for endurance and perseverance; with the Poor White (white trash) and the perception of this representative of the white race by the Negro. The theme of the returned soldier, already developed far in Faulkner's first novel, *Soldiers' Pay,* is also found in 'The Wishing Tree', where the question of how we perceive, understand, and react to our human and social environment is also central. While the children accept all the magic around them without question and the old poor white has resigned all hope of change and environment, Alice views the world as accessible and understandable, something you can handle and come to grips with. She is always able to put things in their proper and sensible perspective, even though she may use explanations and excuses for this and that which are completely out of place. The Negro woman's solid and unchanging realism makes for much fun and laughter in 'The Wishing Tree', but nonetheless she prefigures that marvellous Negro character in *The Sound and the Fury,* Dilsey, and numerous other Negroes who are treated with respect and admiration in Faulkner's later works.

Such a Negro character is also found in the unfinished and rather sketchy manuscript 'The Devil Beats His Wife', where the Negro woman, Della, works for Doris and Harry who are married, and does whatever she can to keep the marriage together, even though she is wise enough to know that 'white folks takes marrying too important.[83] The importance given to Della as a character in this earliest version of a story that would take ten years and at least two more revisions before it was published, is reduced to almost nothing in 'Christmas Tree' (the second version of it), where Ruby is the one who sees to it that Doris's husband is sent for when the girl gets pregnant. The only interest in this extremely bad story may lie in its being a story of a marriage and the conflicts arising because the individuals are unwilling to give away any of their personal freedom or to accept any kind of new responsibility.

At this point in Faulkner's short-story career we can take leave of the dreamer, if not exactly of the hostile world. This is definitely a result of Faulkner's discovery of his local background, of the material he 'had to hand', and which he deemed would last him for a lifetime. Now that the background for the characters is there, the dreamer, the hero, the loser, and all kinds of ordinary people can be placed within a social context and act in a real world – to the extent that any fictional world is 'real'. This, however, also requires a narrative form that Faulkner has not really found yet, although it is vaguely detectable among the many experiments he made during the New Orleans period and after.

Many of the short stories in the New Orleans periods, and in the years immediately following, relate to Faulkner's novels in significant ways. Since the short stories were written first, most of these relationships may be viewed as foreshadowings of elements that would be developed further in later novels. This would be true for elements of 'The Hill', 'The Kingdom of God', 'Mayday', 'The Wishing Tree', and other stories. Most of these stories are rather unique in Faulkner's short-story career, they are preparatory and preliminary exercises on a small scale. They meant excellent practice for the author, who experimented with the position of the narrator, with the voice of the implied author, with a kind of double-narration and use of the frame device. Blending descriptive passages and dialogue, shifting smoothly from one to the other while adjusting the distance to the characters, Faulkner little by little came to master the more sophisticated narrative structures.

During these final formative years of the apprenticeship period we do not encounter the novelist as short-story writer any more than we did in the years before the New Orleans period. A characteristic of the novelist, or perhaps of the novelist and short-story writer as one, can be found in Faulkner's plans for two different yet similar series of New Orleans sketches. Both 'Sinbad in New Orleans' and 'The Mirror of Chartres Street' give a first sign of Faulkner's cyclical habit of mind, his strong tendency to re-use short stories in series to make loosely joined novels. Moreover, the short story about Elmer proves that material for a novel might become a short story, or vice versa. By this time, Faulkner had, of course, written his first novel, too.

It is very difficult to find a story in the early part of Faulkner's career in which he has material of such a scope and range that he has to compress it to suit the limited scale of the short story. Discourse-time is always as long as story-time, if not longer, although we should bear in mind that 'discourse-time' is a kind of pseudo-time, a convenient term that will be used in the discussions of the relationship between the novelist and the short-story writer.

'The Liar' and 'Yo Ho and Two Bottles of Rum' are two important stories in a study of Faulkner's development as a short-story writer. They indicate the directions in which his short-story art might develop, and, indeed, does develop, with the qualification that the former type little by little becomes all-important and is responsible for most of Faulkner's stories, and for his best stories.

Faulkner's 'postage stamp of native soil' is the discovery that more than anything else, theme or technique, moulds his short stories in the years ahead. From now on the stories that are located in Yoknapatawpha will, basically, be a novelist's short stories, not the least because any choice of characters, setting or story from this mythological kingdom will, by implication, induce so much that a short tale can only comprise it through strong narrative concentration. In Faulkner's major short-story period a high number of stories were written (or rewritten) between the writing of some of the author's major novels. This alone would be likely to leave its mark on the short stories, as we shall see that it does.

4. Short Stories 1928–1932
The Human Heart in Conflict With Itself

> You write a story to tell about people, man in his
> constant struggle with his own heart, with the hearts
> of others, or with his environment. It's man in the
> ageless, eternal struggles which we inherit and we go
> through as though they'd never happened before,
> shown for a moment in a dramatic instant of the
> furious motion of being alive, that's all any story is.
> You catch the fluidity which is human life and you
> focus a light on it and you stop it long enough for
> people to be able to see it.
>
> *-Faulkner in the University*

In this chapter the interest centres on short stories that deal with the
overprotected and deprived characters, mostly females, who are so
frequent in the author's stories from about 1930. Also, Faulkner's stories
about dreamers and artists, often living on the fringes of an increasingly
materialistic society, are discussed here. From a thematic point of view
the interpretations focus on the deprivation and despair many of these
characters experience, but also on the ensuing reactions: rebellion or
frustration, frequently with tragic results. But the weak and frustrated
share a dream of a better world, a different society, a meaningful
existence, with the artists and drifters we encounter in other stories.
Their aspirations and hopes are basically identical. This is not very
surprising, since all these characters must be judged outcasts in a world
where adjustment and respectability are keywords.

Formally these stories differ considerably, although those with a
female character as the victim of a rigid moral code are as a rule told by
a narrator, who either figures as a narrative persona in the text (being a
passive agent or watcher), or a covert or effaced narrator whose voice we
often hear and whose point of view very often determines the distribution
of sympathy in the story. The narrator may hide behind a 'we', and we
experience what has been called 'the community's point of view', although, as we shall see, this is a rather misleading term. Many of
Faulkner's narrators, and he relies on narrators, overt and covert, to a

very high degree, are highly unreliable, and the implied author, whose norms and attitudes we acquire through the narrative discourse itself, is often at odds with the narrators.

Since the Yoknapatawpha stories and those from the outside world are different in most respects, it comes as no surprise that they also differ considerably as to the narrative structure: the type of narrator or narrative voice, the degree of narration. The implied author's attitudes are less clearly in conflict with the narrator in the stories about artistic creation, for instance, or in the Beyond stories. Here the narrator's presentation of the story and its implications is more in accord with the norm of the narrative as a totality.

Faulkner's short stories in this period are often autonomous stories, independent in all respects of his novels. Yet they are at the same time a novelist's short stories, since they often sweep very wide to include more than a short story normally would contain. Only by means of an unusual narrative concentration – relying on very conscious selection of elements for narration, ellipsis, pause, etc. – do they become narratives of short-story length. The fact that few stories are non-narrated, or minimally narrated, but rely rather heavily on a narrator's presence and presentation (be he covert or overt), contributes to this narrative concentration. Discourse-time becomes shorter than story-time, and this makes it possible for the author to comprise very much in rather brief tales.

The more obvious relationship between a story and a novel will of course be given some notice, but the discussion of the short stories as a novelist's short stories will be taken up only at the end of the second of the two chapters dealing with this period. I have found it convenient to structure my interpretations of the more than forty stories from this period in two separate chapters, on the basis of themes, but also with formal considerations in mind.

Of the forty odd short stories that Faulkner wrote or completed between 1928 and 1932, a very high number are located in Yoknapatawpha – either in Jefferson or in its immediate surroundings.[1] For a number of stories set outside Yoknapatawpha, the principal characters are somehow related to this area. Almost all stories with an American setting are located in the South; in addition to Yoknapatawpha, the Virginia Mountains and the Tennessee Mountains are given as the settings for one story each, while unspecified Southern settings are used in stories such as 'Doctor Martino' and ' "Once Aboard the Lugger - - -" ' This is all rather predictable and applies to the whole of Faulkner's short-story career. The World War I stories, notably 'Victory', 'Crevasse', and 'Thrift' have a European setting and European characters, while stories set in post-war Europe – 'Mistral', 'Divorce in Naples', – have clear relations with an American experience and background despite their foreign setting. This is also true of 'Carcassonne', which is located in a Latin-American town but otherwise seems to exist outside time and space.

These short stories cover a wide range of subjects, and a number of related but nevertheless distinctly different themes may be found. Faulkner writes about his country and his village, about his South, and he writes about the people living there, moving from the Indians who originally owned the land to the Negroes who slave on it and from the poor whites who barely eke out a living to the well-to-do business men and plantation owners. *Race* may be said to be one of his subjects, *war* is another one, and *sex* might well be said to be a third, even though it is interlinked with many others and should not be over-emphasized. It is of course also possible to divide Faulkner's short stories in these years on the basis of what he himself said that it was the writer's duty to write about: love, compassion, pride, pity, and sacrifice.[2]

If one on the basis of a complete reading of all the short stories from this period, published as well as unpublished, finished as well as unfinished, wants to single out some central themes, a few themes are self-evident. One such theme might be described as estrangement, the loss of identity or of social belonging. In more general terms one might describe this as a conflict between the individual and the community,[3] and a search for the various solutions Faulkner's characters find to the problem of adjustment and conformity. Since the city people – especially those from a big city and with a certain ability for money-making – seem to have a different set of values and live by other social laws and morals than the people from the countryside in Yoknapatawpha, the contrast between culture on the one hand and nature on the other is well worth scrutiny. This contrast is further developed and given much more sophisticated treatment by Faulkner in *Go Down, Moses*. The richness and variety of Faulkner's short-story accomplishment in these years might also prompt one to discuss other pairs of contrasts; e.g. truth vs. illusion, interpretation or perception of reality vs. reality itself; progress vs. regression, and so on. Since Faulkner time and again stressed his preoccupation with character and with *people,* and with a sweeping gesture said that he always wrote about man's injustice to man, about the basest things in the life of men,[4] this alone might lead us to a thematic discussion where people's relations to other people, their *interaction* in a society of human beings is focal. The stories themselves bear out and support such an approach: a systematic grouping of the stories in this period based on what we might call socio-psychological criteria seems to be the least reductive and emphasizes Faulkner's central concerns in the short stories of this period.

A division of the stories between 1928 and 1932 on the basis of theme should not conceal the fact that most of the stories have something in common, especially from a general point of view. They all have something to say about man's role in a changing world, his capacity for adjustment, his adaptability. Generally speaking, 'man' in Faulkner's stories is rather adaptable and tries, by varying means, to make the best of life, either by bending and comforming or by breaking loose in rebellion and protest, or simply by sticking to a set of inherited traditional values. A systematic discussion of the stories on the basis of social interaction must also take into account that the stories cover a very long period of time; i.e. the historical dimension. Broadly speaking, the stories take place in three periods of time: the Past, which includes the early days of the Indian tribes, the Civil War and the undisturbed and unchanging rural Yoknapatawpha Country; the Recent Past, which includes the First World War and the years immediately following it. The third period would be the Immediate Past; Yoknapatawpha and Beyond in the late twenties and early thirties. Inevitably the stories cluster around certain peak periods in the history of the author's imaginary kingdom: the Civil War, the First World War, the drab years of uncertainty and industrialization and modernization in the 1920's and early 1930's. However, the short stories written around 1930 almost exclusively deal with the recent or immediate past – with the noteworthy exception of 'Red Leaves' and 'A Justice'.[5] Only later would Faulkner use the Civil War in a series of stories, and the very old times in Yoknapatawpha would form the background for many later stories, even if few of them are placed in historical time older than the Civil War.[6] Retrospective glances abound in the 1930 stories, to add background and motivation to the events on the now-level, and to underline the feeling of tradition in the midst of change and rootlessness, which at times pervade the stories. Faulkner very clearly saw the need for change and adjustment, but not simply because change always and unequivocally is for the better. Man was by definition always in motion; otherwise he would live in a stasis, which means that he would not be alive, since he would not grow or develop. The ability to re-adjust to the changing world while maintaining the accumulated wisdom and experience and knowledge of one's own generation and of earlier generations is a measure of man's success as a living human being among other human beings. The theme of change, or of the inevitability of change, finds various forms and expressions in Faulkner's short fiction.

One does not have to generalize about the short stories to find common elements. Three fourths of the stories have violent and sudden death in common; either a murder, a killing, or an accidental death, which should have been avoided. This is indicative of Faulkner's understanding of human relationships, yet one should add that love and sexuality also play important parts, often in the stories of violent and sudden death.

In all of Faulkner's stories of this period – and, to a lesser extent, in all his short-story career – there are people who vainly and desperately and incessantly try to ascertain that they are *alive,* that they are living, now, here, and that this after all is the only important fact in a world where so much is uncertain and heartbreaking and transient. The way in which they do this is an important part of Faulkner's writing: man seems to be something of an inscrutable wonder for the author, but he never relinquishes the hope of understanding and explaining, and, as a result, forgiving. By compassionate and careful observation of human behaviour, by scrupulous and unrelenting analysis of the forces underlying man's injustice to man, Faulkner added important insights to his life-long record of man. Around 1930 his belief in some kind of ultimate goodness and in the progress of man was not very strong; his short stories may well be said to express the outrage of a potential believer.[7]

One of the recurrent characters in Faulkner's short stories is the overprotected, controlled, and frustrated youth; primarily of the female sex, but not exclusively so. Obviously the weak and deprived characters, which means children and females of all ages, are subject to this protection and vigilance by those who know better and who profit from being in control. A harsh and loveless upbringing, with little if any freedom of choice and with severely limited social life, invariably brings frustration in its wake. This frustration is then misinterpreted by the grown-ups who are in control of the bereft and lonely characters, so that

100

new and more drastic measures are taken to ensure conformity and adjustment to the established code of behaviour. Frustration is no solution to any problem; it is inevitable as a reaction to immediate problems, but it is followed by more serious problems, or by attempts to break loose and start anew on one's own terms.

The trapped females, especially the very young ones, are found very early in Faulkner's short-story career, and the imprisonment is both a result of biological factors *and* of social expectations. Some of Faulkner's narrators share a rather queer and unwarranted understanding of what girls and women are like; examples can be found in 'Mistral', 'Black Music', 'Hair', 'Honor', and a good many other stories. This kind of misunderstanding and condescending attitude on the part of male protagonists in Faulkner's early stories is revealing, since it gives an indication of how deep-rooted this view of women is in the particular society and time Faulkner presents in his short fiction. The very masculine character of the world of Yoknapatawpha with its traditional treatment of women as either something to exhibit and admire and worship or something to use and discard, may account for some of the problems that the female characters face. Change is involved here too, and the most domineering and repressive characters generally belong to the older generations. It should also be remembered that older women more than anyone else represent tradition and the old code of behaviour. The grandmothers and mothers and aunts and, in a few cases, the mothers-in-law, see to it that the young people keep within the boundaries they know are the right and best ones. Even though some of the traditional elements of the female role may be biologically determined and thus cannot be changed, and even if the society in which Faulkner grew up and lived most of his life had strong and rigid convictions about what appears to be a universal understanding of what a woman's chief obligations and qualities are,[8] Faulkner approaches his female characters with understanding and is unexpectedly critical in his descriptions of the lives women are allowed to live. It is easy to misread Faulkner here, and it has been done more than once – primarily to support one's own notion of what the right and proper place for a woman is. Faulkner does not condemn his fictional female characters, even when he describes them as being corrupt or utterly bad, and he is very clearly aware that there are forces outside these women that condition them. The recurrent juxtaposition of the tradition-bearers and a society that cherishes virginity and innocence to maintain control over the upcoming generation indicates Faulkner's interest in the motivating forces behind the 'bad' behaviour of some girls and women. One could hardly talk of a person being condemned for not adjusting to her alleged role, when this role is described in very negative terms. The basic misreading of the Faulkner stories in which women figure prominently is thus to condemn these women, simply because they do not fulfil their functions as females, and to take for granted that the implied author also does so.[9]

In general terms the conflict may be described as a conflict between the individual on one side and the community and its laws, regulations, and expectations on the other. This is too general a view to be interesting, and it can only lead to vague and approximate descriptions of what Faulkner tries to show in his stories. The individual in this conflict is invariably a *weak* person who is dependent on somebody else for protection and support. Children and women are prime examples of this group, which might include larger groups or classes or even races: the poor whites, the Negroes, the Indians. We have then moved on to a different level of conflict, which is central in some of Faulkner's stories but which is virtually unimportant in the stories where individual conflicts and personal problems are focal. One should note, however, that the individual frustrations and the resulting madness or rebellion seem to be limited to what might be described as the upper classes in Jefferson or outside. People with less leisurely lives do not experience these problems, at least not to the same degree, and it may also be that the females of the lower classes are so burdened down by work and childbirth that luxury problems like their personal well-being are not contemplated at all. On the other hand, they may also live a more natural life and participate more meaningfully in work and social life than do their sisters in the cities.

Dreams are a central concept in Faulkner's short fiction, but the dreams and the dreamers are of many kinds. Typical for most of Faulkner's dreamers is that they are *outsiders* or *losers* in the competitive society they live in, so that they either see their dreams shattered or crushed by a harsh reality, or they create new dreams to live on, hoping that some beautiful morning. . . . Faulkner's short stories present a special group of characters who suddenly found that they had a very special opportunity to see their dreams of fame, admiration, and experience come true: the young men who went to the First World War, in particular the pilots. The validity of their dreams and the question whether any of them came true can be answered by a description of how Faulkner contrast their dreams with (1) the reality of war and (2) the reality of post-war America. The soldiers and pilots of World War I, as we meet them in what are commonly known as Faulkner's World War I stories, are not the only characters with a war experience who have problems in adjusting to peace-time reality. In some stories only brief comments or flashbacks show that the characters have participated in the war, yet the wartime experience has been just as decisive for those as for the characters we watch in action. 'Death Drag' and 'Honor' are examples of such stories.

There are, moreover, at least two more significant types of dreams in Faulkner's short fiction. Some characters dream of a better world beyond this one; that is, they flee the drudgery and hardships of reality by conjuring up a less sordid life beyond the gate of death, and they hope to make up for some of their shortcomings and losses in this world in the Hereafter.

Dreams may obviously be used to avoid the pressure of reality, in order to escape a situation or a condition which it is hard to cope with. To some extent this may be true of some of the dreams and dreamers in Faulkner's short fiction, but the more escapist dreams are treated as a solution in its own right later on. More often, however, the dreams are real enough, in the sense that they represent hopes and longings for something new and different in the characters' lives. Also, they have a basis in reality in the sense that they are reactions or responses to existing myths about freedom, opportunity for all, equality – the American Dream. In point of fact, it appears that those who have materialistic dreams, or no dreams at all, are better off than the 'dreamers', because materialistic success seems possible, and with few dreams come few disappointments. Faulkner, himself apparently something of a dreamer, seems to have taken a strong liking to the dreamers, be they pathetic and helpless like the girl in 'A Mountain Victory' or reckless and courageous and death-defying like the Sartoris twins. Also, the dream of transcending reality, through artistic creation, is a recurrent one in Faulkner's fiction, although it is at the core of only a couple of short stories: 'Artist at Home' and, especially, 'Carcassonne'.

Having presented some of Faulkner's central concerns in the short stories from about 1930, we now proceed to a more extensive discussion of the themes of overprotection and rebellion, individual and community, and dreamers vs. losers in the competitive society. In numerous short stories originally composed before 1930 – 'Miss Zilphia Gant', 'Elly', 'A Rose for Emily', 'Dry September', – the author presents similar conflicts, involving a young girl or woman and stifling parental authority. This conflict is found as early as in 'Adolescence' and in *Soldiers' Pay*. It appears to be one of the most central oppositions in the stories of the major period. Faulkner had apparently taken a special interest in a kind of extreme juxtaposition of the young and burning desire and the traditional society which is always so anxious to 'protect' youth.

'Miss Zilphia Gant' presents two generations of deprived and mis- treated women, and also indicates that life will not be much different for the third generation of females in this family, since she is brought up in the same cold and repressive atmosphere as her mother was. The oldest generation, Mrs. Gant, is betrayed by her husband who takes a 'youngish woman with cold eyes' (*Uncollected Stories,* p. 368) with him and disappears, sending his half-wit partner to break the news to his wife and their two-year-old daughter, Zilphia. Mrs. Gant revenges herself on her husband; apparently she kills both husband and mistress, and returns from her deadly mission, 'her face cold, satiate and chaste' (*Uncollected Stories,* p. 370). The narrator stresses Mrs. Gant's growing masculinity, yet lets her retain her 'female intuition' (*Uncollected Stories,* p. 370).

Let down by her husband and left to provide for herself and her daughter, Mrs. Gant develops a hatred of everything having the faintest hint of male, and makes up her mind to protect her daughter from the opposite sex. Zilphia and her mother live in a single room for twenty- three years, and for seven years farmers coming to town can see young Zilphia's face behind a barred window. Had it been up to her mother alone, Zilphia would have remained caged – in a double sense.[10] Zilphia must go to school, however, and her mother tries to keep all danger away from her by walking her to school. This overprotection continues long after school-hours, and Mrs. Gant takes every precaution to keep Zilphia away from males of all ages; to the extent that Zilphia in her desperate loneliness gets ill. Mrs. Gant is forced to slacken her grip a bit, but the fear and hatred of sexuality is still present, and Zilphia's body is examined before she is instructed about 'it' – sex, while her mother in a kind of bodily protest against her predicament as a woman becomes more and more masculine.

104

Zilphia's imprisonment lasts, and her mother's vigilance and spying never ceases. After Zilphia and a boy are discovered wrapped together in a blanket,[11] Zilphia is taken into the bondage of the sewing business and is seen sitting behind the same window for twelve years.

Zilphia is thus effectively shut in from all dangers of the outer world, since her profession as a seamstress entrenches her even more in a female and feminine world, where all customers are probably ladies. One day an itinerant painter discovers Zilphia; the town starts talking about Zilphia's beau, and with this male threat present, Mrs. Gant takes Zilphia home to the bungalow they now live in. Vacation and idleness bring Mrs. Gant to bed, and having watched her mother for three days, Zilphia finds the key, looks up her beau, and gets married. Her mother's hold on her is too strong, and Zilphia feels that she has got to go back to her. So her dreams of pot and brush are not to come true; behind locked doors, a shotgun in her lap, Mrs. Gant keeps watch till the painter leaves. Then, and only then, she feels safe to die in her chair.

Faulkner's description of Zilphia's situation and the reasons behind it gives a bleak picture of the relations between man and woman, and it is evident that he has tried to portray the growth from childhood to youth of a girl in an unusually difficult position. Zilphia has been subject to overprotection all her life, she has been taught to stay away from men, and she has been deprived of all the fun and games, friends and innocent affairs, that a normal girl would experience. Her natural development has been thwarted, and the fear of sex which her mother plants in her leads to sexual dreams and longings which bring shame with them, the same way that she is ashamed of her own body.

Faulkner has arranged 'Miss Zilphia Gant' in five parts and told the story strictly chronologically, apart from the mentioning of future events without specifying them in order to build up suspense. This use of anticipation, or the delayed specification of detail, is common in many Faulkner stories. If we look at it with the relationship between story and discourse in mind, we may describe it as discordance between these two temporal orders, and for this rather frequent device, Genette has designated the term 'prolepsis'.[13] The opposite relationship between story and narrative; i.e. that an event is mentioned, referred to, evoked later in the discourse than the point in time of the story when it actually took place, is called 'analepsis', and is, of course, an even more common device in Faulkner's short stories. Anachrony is almost as frequent as chronology, yet one should not forget that Faulkner often halts his narratives to introduce capsule stories that might be described by the term 'analepsis', but somehow seem to stand apart from the main part of the narrative and constitute its own temporal order.

The first version of 'Miss Zilphia Gant' was narrated by an omniscient narrator, but in the typescript and in the printed version the narration is more limited, it is almost personal, and the narrator's presence and voice are strongly felt in the text. Still we may describe the narration as covert, since there is no narrative persona explicitly present in the text. What is told in the story is what 'they' or 'the town' tells, but it is a misunderstanding to think that the narrator is a stranger to the town, who, accidentally, hears about Zilphia and looks into her story and then relates it to the readers.[13]

The story is sifted through the conscious mind of a person sufficiently interested in Miss Zilphia Gant to care to follow her destiny and interpret it. The narrator's relationship to Jefferson is not revealed till the last page where he uses 'our town'. The narrator is not an anonymous 'I' who inquires into things, as in 'Hair', nor is he a spokesman for the town of Jefferson or a community at large. Our knowledge of Miss Zilphia becomes, in spite of the narrator we sense behind the story, the public knowledge. A few 'I's' or 'me's' would only have changed our terms in describing the narrative technique, and they would not have changed the story's impact on the reader significantly. The first-person narrator is simply *felt* to be there, long before he loses his disguise and uses 'our'.

In the first part of the story, the narration is completely omniscient. The Gants live outside Jefferson, and a vague use of what 'they' (the Bend people) tell, reduces viewpoints and knowledge to a minor extent in the early parts of the story. When the protagonists settle down in Jefferson – to spend twenty-three years in a single room – a community 'they' might have been established to help the narration. Instead, what 'they' and 'the town' learn about the Gants is told to a narrator who then goes on to tell the whole story. The careful elaboration of the narrative position, probably to enhance credibility and add moral weight to the story, is not very successful, since the story rests poorly on incredible coincidences and neglects.

The story of Mrs. and Miss Gant has been told by the townspeople, 'they', to the anonymous somebody behind the story, who is also a

Jeffersonian. Faulkner has struggled to find the correct distance and to create the atmosphere of entrapment and enclosure in this story. To tell the pathetic and almost tragic story of a domineering mother and her effect upon a young daughter who longs for life and love, he has relied heavily on Freudian symbolism, and depicted prejudiced people with sneering contempt, although never directly. The narrative seems inconsistent, the story's symbolism heavy-handed and too overt, and all in all 'Miss Zilphia Gant' may be seen as an example of the author's early attempts to render a community's (faulty) understanding of an outsider through a community point of view. Thus 'Miss Zilphia Gant' is not only important because of its many foreshadowings of later works on the thematic level, but also as an early attempt at a narrative handling which Faulkner later would use with easy mastery.

Before we take a closer look at Zilphia's *reactions* to her situation, we shall look at various kinds of protection and suffering and deprivation and despair experienced by other characters in Faulkner's short stories of this period. Elly in the short story of that name is very much akin to Miss Zilphia, even though the factors responsible for conditioning her behaviour are of a totally different kind. Elly is also protected and sheltered, but not because of a mother with an abnormal hatred or fear of men. Elly's parents are both alive, and seem to be of the upper class in Jefferson. They appear to be well-adjusted, decent and rather boring people, so that to Elly her world is void of any meaning, any challenge, any worth-while experience. Within the story Elly is not set directly up against her parents as representatives of the greater outside society. Rather, she is set up against her grandmother, who represents tradition, authority, and an old-fashioned, rigid female role or code of behaviour. This conflict is the most salient feature of the overall conflict of the story, but Elly's real opponents are her parents and a society which, in her opinion, has nothing to offer her.

Elly is a young girl who experiences great difficulties while passing from childhood to womanhood. She is unable to cope with an adult world where one's freedom of choice is severely curtailed by traditions and expectations, and by social and sexual taboos. Elly is discovered with a man who is suspected of being part Negro, and the grandmother who discovers Elly uses her knowledge as a means of controlling and ruling Elly. The grandmother is an old, implacable woman, but Elly's outbursts are not so much directed against her as they demonstrate her own frustration and the immediate causes she finds for her unbearable situation:

'What else can I do, in this little dead, hopeless town? I'll work. I don't want to be idle. Just find me a job – anything, anywhere, so that it's so far away that I'll never have to hear the word Jefferson again' (*Doctor Martino*, p. 248).

This is, then, the basic conflict of the story: a conflict between a young girl who naturally expects and hopes for more in life than what she has found her family and Jefferson can give, and, on the other side, a non-permissive society, which is depicted as injurious if not destructive to a number of young women in Faulkner's short fiction. Elly lives in a big house, with 'a deep veranda with screening vines and no lights' (*Doctor Martino*, p. 243), and she feels trapped in this dark and isolated dwelling, where her grandmother's incessant vigilance adds to the feeling of imprisonment. Elly has most certainly magnified her grandmother's antagonism and watch-keeping, and her reactions also reflect personal insecurity and are projections of her own hatred. Elly's reactions to the conflict will be discussed below. It should be mentioned at this point that Elly over-reacts by becoming sexually promiscuous – a typical 'flapper'.[14] Only when Elly is having an affair with a man who *may* have Negro blood in him does the antagonism become paramount, and some sort of solution must be found.

'Elly' is in part located in Jefferson, but Faulkner refrains from using a community point of view – a first-person narrator who is more or less a spokesman for the town – as he does in a number of stories set in his imaginary town. 'Elly' is narrated by an omniscient narrator, but the angle of vision is mostly with Elly herself, so that we get very few unbiased portraits and interpretations of other characters in the story. The voice of the narrator is heard throughout the story, and if point of view (perceptual) and narrative voice are not mixed up, one should avoid making the mistakes in understanding the short story 'Elly' and its protagonist.

Elly is protected, and refuses to be so. She is deprived of a number of what she feels are her obvious rights, and revenges herself on her parental authorities by becoming sexually active and choosing her own partners. Her older sister in Faulkner's short fiction, Miss Emily Grierson, is also protected, and as in the case with Zilphia Gant but even more directly, her suitors are kept away; in her case by a strong father. Emily also misses what ordinary girls have, and her father's hold on her (or, rather, her father-binding) is so strong that this may account for her problems with men after his death.

When Miss Emily Grierson died, 'our whole town' went to her funeral. During the long years of isolation and what one might think would be oblivion, the town has remembered Miss Emily. She has become a 'tradition, a duty, and a care' (*These 13,* pp. 167–8). These types of responsibility may indicate the attitudes to Miss Emily of three consecutive generations in Jefferson.[15] Although Miss Emily has been 'a sort of hereditary obligation upon the town' (*These 13,* p. 168) from 1894, when Colonel Sartoris remitted her taxes, there are too many changes in personal pronouns throughout the story to accept 'our whole town' or a representative spokesman for the town, as *the* narrator of the story. There is reason to believe that the question of narration – or even of narrative distance or point of view – is too complicated to be explained fully, but it is necessary to stress that the voice of the community in 'A Rose for Emily' only applies to portions of the story. Since our total understanding and appreciation of the story largely depend upon the thematic subtleties which a close study of the narrator's role may yield, the structure of the narrative must be discussed at some length.

'A Rose for Emily' is divided into five parts, the first four of which differ little in length, while the fifth part is shorter. The basic elements of the story are told in fragments, a little at a time, with a confusing sequence of events, typical of much of Faulkner's writing of this period. The chronology is, after all, not too confusing, if we do not insist on pinning every event down to an exact date, as some critics have done with extraordinary results.[16]

The reason for telling the story is the very fact that Miss Emily has died; this is the first information that is given in the story, and it is the starting point for a story to which episodes and incidents are added as they, by way of association, implication, or closeness to the narrator, come to his mind. All this is of course an illusion, but it is an extremely carefully and skilfully arranged illusion. The deceptive casualness with which the story is told should not be allowed to deceive us into believing that this is a straightforward reminiscence about a lady who has just passed away.

The intriguing shifting of pronouns in 'A Rose for Emily' raises many questions, and there is some reason to venture the guess that Faulkner did not care too much about accuracy or exactitude here. This assumption offers no solutions to the narrative problems, and the very fact that Faulkner carefully revised the story, omitting some material from the final parts of it, indicates a great degree of control of the narrative. Nevertheless there seem to be clear distinctions between the 'we' of parts II and III and V, and the 'they' (various ones in part II) of the story, while the 'we' in part VI is the introductory 'we' implied in the term 'our whole town'. What 'they' do in part III is later done by 'we' in part IV (e.g., saying 'Poor Emily' behind the curtains, spying on her). If, for a moment, we test the validity of the first person ('we') narrator, he has much of his information from general gossip around the town, and some from first-hand observation. But he must be exceptionally well-informed to know what a special meeting of the board of aldermen discussed, or to describe the paper and handwriting of Miss Emily's letter to the Mayor. Furthermore, we are allowed to see Miss Emily open the bottle of poison at her home and read the label on it. This may of course only be dramatic presentation, but the question remains: how does the 'we' know this? The point of view is rather limited, and the narrator must have access to what appears to be relatively secret information. Does he (the single mind behind the 'we') know this through the druggist who sold the poison, and then speculate on what it was like when Emily arrived home? Are we forced to resort to the explanation that an omniscient author is at work in certain specific cases, while the verisimilitude or factuality is maintained when, e.g. the Baptist minister's experience with Miss Emily is never divulged? Or should we assume that the spokesman behind the 'we' is a close friend of the druggist? This may sound far-fetched, but is not altogether impossible. Then the same spokesman would have to be closely related to the presumably young man on the Board of Aldermen, and he must be one of the smaller 'we' group in parts II, III, and V, with an intimate knowledge of Miss Emily (having been a suitor?); and he must belong to her generation and share many of the then dominant attitudes about chivalry, the protection of ladies, aristocratic codes of behaviour, and so forth. This explanation may find some support in the fact that the same 'we' presents Emily and her father, and it is this 'we' that best understands Emily's refusal to let her father be buried:

We had long thought of them as a tableau: Miss Emily a slender figure in white in the background, her father a spraddled silhouette in the foreground, his back to her and

110

clutching a horsewhip, the two of them framed by the back-flung front door. So when she got to be thirty and was still single, we were not pleased exactly, but vindicated; even with insanity in the family she wouldn't have turned down all of her chances if they really materialized (*These 13*, pp. 172–3).

And further:

We did not say she was crazy then. We believed she had to do that. We remembered all the young men her father had driven away, and we knew that with nothing left, she would have to cling to that which had robbed her, as people will (*These 13*, p. 173).

Here it looks as if the 'we' is at a distance to the young men Emily's father had driven away, but his knowledge and understanding of Emily and her father is so intimate that this may just be a narrative stance. The paragraph does not leave much doubt about his being a representative of the average opinion of the townspeople, yet the 'we' figure knows more than 'they' do:

Already *we* knew that there was one room in that region above stairs which no one had seen in forty years, and which would have to be forced. *They* waited until Miss Emily was decently in the ground before they opened it (*These 13*, p. 181; my emphasis).

The many ambiguities and the added mystery resulting from this bewildering use of personal pronouns in 'A Rose for Emily' are *in* the text we study, and accordingly we have to come as close to an understanding of their effect as possible.

If we bring in the 'anonymous voice' which so many critics have found in Faulkner's fiction, this voice is heard clearly in many of the village stories. This voice may, indeed, be 'the author seeing himself distanced as one more perspective on the scene, one more legitimate but not conclusive point of view', to use Olga Vickery's apt description of this narrative device.[17] In Faulkner, Vickery says, 'authorial exclusion is replaced by authorial transcendence'.[18] Faulkner had plans for a book about his 'townspeople' as early as 1927,[19] and in 'A Rose for Emily' and many other village stories, he appears to be watching these people in some crucial moments of their lives, arresting their motion for a moment to create a tableau and showing them in all their struggle and despair, without comments, but with a pervasive voice, which ultimately distributes sympathy and antipathy, and conspires with the reader in creating the artifice that he chooses to construct.

111

'A Rose for Emily' is a gothic tale in the sense that it creates a doom-laden atmosphere where an old spinster who is totally shut out from the teeming outside world lives in a decaying mansion with one of the floors closed. Emily apparently refuses to accept the passing of time, or change in any sense. In contrast to most gothic fiction, Emily and her house are very much in and of this world, although she has felt compelled to end all association with her fellow men. Faulkner has been said to write about events that were expected to happen but never actually took place, yet it has been contended that he based his story on an actual couple.[20] In answer to a question whether the story came from his imagination, Faulkner said that it did, but maintained that 'the fact that young girls dream of someone to love' exists *a priori*.[21]

Emily's situation is to begin with that she lives with a strong father who lets her know her position but also that she is too good for the suitors who pay visits to her. He drives them off, and accordingly, by what Faulkner regards as some law of nature, she clings to her father. Her father then dies, and she is left to fend for herself, and has her first and only opportunity to meet a man, fall in love, be young and joyful. She has experienced how things wither and pass away, how loss and loneliness are what you are left with, and accordingly she tries to resist change. She finds a new way of keeping a lover forever, and is in fact capable of shutting herself out from the outside world to the extent that she conceals everything. Part of Emily's tragic situation stems from the fact that she is unable to adjust to a world almost completely transformed during her lifetime. She is able to keep her untenable position only by seclusion from the ordinary world, and she has to resort to introversion and a number of defence mechanisms to survive when social pressure threatens to destroy her position. Emily is capable of doing so, because she has a reality of her own. Emily's feeling of loss and deprivation and her fear of change – change that may take away what little she has left – account for some of her reactions. Emily is, however, also acting out what she has reason to believe is her alleged role as a woman, no matter how misunderstood it is. She only does 'as people will' (*These 13*, p. 173), but she is compulsively possessive and is clearly a case of abnormal psychology. Within the story, Emily very rarely acts out of character; the only time is perhaps when she has to let her father be buried.

Miss Minnie Cooper in 'Dry September' is the female character in Faulkner's short fiction who compares most nicely with Miss Emily

Grierson, and Minnie is presented in a retrospective capsule story, where her family background, social life, sexual experiences, and position in the town are given.

'Dry September' opens on an extended description of drought, violence and death. The dry weather has created an unrest bordering on despair, and when a rumour about a rape of a white woman reaches the receptive audience in the barber's shop, it is like fire being set to the grass after two rainless months. Behind the rumour is Minnie Cooper, who has experienced spiritual and sexual drought for a long time now, and who has reached her twilight zone, her dry September. Her situation has altered over the years; once she rode 'upon the crest of the town's social life', (*These 13*, p. 269). *How* empty her days were, can be seen from this description:

She was thirty-eight or thirty-nine. She lived in a small frame house with her invalid mother and a thin, sallow, unflagging aunt, where each morning between ten and eleven she would appear on the porch in a lace-trimmed boudoir cap, to sit swinging in the porch swing until noon. After dinner she lay down for a while, until the afternoon began to cool. Then, in one of the three or four new voile dresses which she had each summer, she would go downtown to spend the afternoon in the stores with the other ladies, where they would handle the goods and haggle over the prices in cold, immediate voices, without any intention of buying (*These 13*, p. 267).

Minnie has had her one love affair, with a bank cashier, and has consequently been reduced to an adulteress in the eyes of the town. Now, however, no men care to watch her on the streets, and she is filled with unrest and despair so that to her, as to the men in the barber's shop, something must happen. Her season of drought has lasted more than the sixty days without rain, and when nothing happens to change her situation, she is compelled to do something herself. Her fantasies, even the tragic one about rape, are created by her own understanding of what people expect; that is, she tries to live up to the expectations she believes the town has of her, even though she is most of all a parasite on this society. Minnie is an anachronism, yet the secluded and protected but ultimately worthless life she leads is not limited to her. The text shows that other *ladies* in Jefferson, possibly even married ones, have to fill their days with meaningless activities. Minnie's situation is both a result of her social position and of the rigid and stereotyped role a woman is supposed to fill and is prepared for through her upbringing. Minnie sees

113

life go past her without her participation, and she is not yet ready to accept the role that her mother and aunt seem to find sufficient. She has reached her twilight zone, but there may still be time and opportunity to postpone the descent of final darkness.

'Dry September' is told in the third person by an omniscient narrator, who changes point of view and manner of narration freely. Thus the readers are allowed to follow more than one string of events as they unfold, but always in chronological order. The narrative strategy allows the author to leave one chain of events for more important incidents elsewhere, and to return to it at a later point in time. This technique allows the author to avoid a direct description of the murder, because the story is then with Hawkshaw after he jumps out of the car. Allusions and metaphors leave no doubt about Will's fate, however, and the separate strings of events are closely related so that what happens on one level, bears upon the events on another level. More important, the tone and the setting of the story are powerfully symbolical of the ensuing action. The very confident use of third-person narration to control the distance, and to distribute sympathy, combines with the use of metaphors of dust and drought to create a stale and barren landscape. The metaphors suggest that the drought also applies to human beings and to the relationships between people. There are even indications of a causal connection between climate, landscape, and social conditions, and the terror and death which follow. Images of terror and death and descriptions of the barren and dry landscape are juxtaposed. It may thus be that terror and death, action at any cost, are not only given metaphorical emphasis by the nature-images but are rather results of the complete drought in the lives of the characters involved. At any rate, Faulkner's narrative strategy in this story functions exceptionally well, so that although close scrutiny may reveal how rigidly controlled the story is, the execution of his master plan for the story is hardly noticeable. As Joseph Reed puts it, here the narrative control moves 'beyond simple question of where to stand or empathetic attachment into a combination of almost Aeschylean artistry, involving distance, control, compulsion, dissective objectivity'.[22]

Zilphia, Elly, Emily, and Minnie share the fate of being women in what is definitely a man's world, and what is also a very class-conscious, snobbish, gossiping small town. They are all let down by the men they have close relationships with, and they all feel uneasy about the limitations put upon a woman's life by tradition, expectation, and common

114

consent. Faulkner goes beyond Jefferson and shows that women in other social classes and different environments also suffer because of their position in relation to *men*, and because of the pressure put upon them by the older generation; notably their mothers or some other representative of parental authority. He is careful, however, to stay within the limits of the area and people he *knows*; that is, even when a story is located outside Jefferson or Yoknapatawpha County, the characters are Southern and more or less conditioned by the peculiarities of their Southern background and upbringing. This is the case in stories such as 'Fox Hunt' and 'Doctor Martino'. 'Doctor Martino' presents a love triangle of a very peculiar kind, and it is related to the stories discussed above in the way a domineering mother determines the fate of the triangle. This dominant mother, carrying all parental authority in one single person, is found both in 'Adolescence' and in 'Miss Zilphia Gant', and the destructive force of this character should not be underestimated. In 'Doctor Martino' we thus again meet a principle that we have encountered in a number of stories: the principle of choking parental authority and dominance. The strange relationship between the old and sick Dr. Martino and the young and vivacious Louise King has developed from the girl's early childhood into what it is at the opening of the story, now that the girl is old enough to marry. The relationship reminds one of the patient and unusual relationship between a 'bad girl', Susan Reed, and Henry Stribling [Hawkshaw] in 'Hair'. Yet the resemblance between Susan Reed and Louise King on the one side, and between Hawkshaw and Dr. Jules Martino on the other, is not so close as one might think. Louise is in no way the wanton, teasing, sexually overt girl Susan is shown to be, and Hawkshaw does not share any of Dr. Martino's reasons for binding a young girl to him.

Mrs. King has brought Louise up to be what the proprietress at the summer resort where they spend their summer hollidays calls 'a wife to be proud of', and the atmosphere of the resort has apparently been the right one for Mrs. King in her attempts to form and mould her daughter. Louise's situation is somewhat different from those of the female characters we have discussed so far. She too is overprotected and prepared for her functions as a wife and mother, and her mother is very anxious that Louise does not throw herself away without getting the proper market value. That is why the doctor is such a nuisance to Alvina and to Louise's fiancé, the Yale man and oil man, Hubert Jarrod. Dr. Martino has told Louise that it takes courage and initiative and risks to stay alive and to prove to yourself that you are living, and she has done whatever he has suggested to prove to him and to herself that she could do it. She is, in other words, able to transcend her traditional role, and accordingly her mother and Hubert find that she is making a fool of herself. Whether the protests and the assertion of self-importance will be brought to an end and Louise forced to adjust, depends on her mother's ability to deceive and force people by playing them against each other. What Louise knows too well is that her position is a fragile one; she feels that everyone except Dr. Martino has let her down, and would gladly do so again to make her conform.

'Doctor Martino' is not only about Louise King and her strong mother and the situation this has led to for the young girl; it is also a story that presents a philosophy of life, some very bad psychological understanding of how young girls tend to behave,[24] and in its many thematic subtleties the story is close to 'Fox Hunt' where the love triangle and the manipulations reappear. 'Fox Hunt' is preoccupied with man-woman relations and with sex, more outspokenly than in most Faulkner stories, and a strong mother-figure looms in the background. Manipulations and deceptions are willingly accepted as a means of gaining control of other people, and the loser or victim is a young woman, Mrs. Harrison Blair. The marriage between Harrison Blair and his wife, now in the Carolina fields on her chestnut mare, has been a most unlucky and unhappy one from the very beginning. Their marriage is in reality a matching of two strong oddities by a mother who does not care about the feelings of her daughter or her son-in-law. The mother is nevertheless more on the husband's side, and wants her daughter to satisfy her husband's many whims, since this is her duty as a married woman. The domineering mother in 'Fox Hunt' surpasses all mothers in Faulkner's short fiction in viciousness and destructiveness because she has suddenly become rich. Money, evidently, has improved her social position and also given her self-confidence and power that she is eager to try out on somebody. Mrs. Blair becomes the victim. She has Southern roots and does not originally belong among the moneyed people, but little by little she is changed by money, by her mother, by her husband, and, finally, by the intrigues of the husband's valet and Steve Gawtrey. The valet outlines Mrs. Blair's growth and development under a protection that had to stifle her, and later he describes her plight in a marriage to a man whose lack of understanding and sympathy could make a more mature and self-secure person become desperate. The valet is nevertheless totally unscrupulous in his attempt to make Mrs. Blair a prey to Mr. Gawtrey who once did him 'a little favor' (*Doctor Martino*, p. 43). The valet furnishes the crucial clue to a final interpretation of the double hunt in the story (for the vixen and for the woman), when he concludes his tale and thereby ends the retrospective background for the events taking place on a *now* level.

'... You take a woman with long hair like she's got, long as she keeps her hair up, it's all right. But once you catch her with her hair down, it's just been too bad' (*Doctor Martino*, p. 47).

Whether Mrs. Blair will indeed be caught with her hair down, is a question we shall have to return to later, but the fact remains that she is an easy and pitiable victim for those who play their games for personal profit with human beings and feelings at stake. That the different observers of the hunt perceive and interpret what they see in different ways, widens the perspective of the story so that it contrasts at least three worlds, three outlooks on life, three modes of understanding. The business-like attitude to life and the little significance attached to adultery or seduction seem to be typical of city people, while the Southern farmers who watch the hunt are bewildered by the absurdities of this world of gentlemen.

The theme of overprotection and deprivation is typical in some of Faulkner's most interesting and convincing stories. The women, and, in a few instances, the *men*, who are so well taken care of as to become insecure and at times dangerous, have one thing in common with numerous other Faulkner characters who accept their situation without protest: they have the *dream* in common; a dream of a better world, in social terms, in terms of love and understanding, and they believe that this world *exists* and that it should be attainable some day, somewhere, somehow. How urgent the dream is, or how soon they expect improvement to take place, differs from character to character, from situation to situation.

The dream need not be materialistic, it need not have anything to do with what is commonly known as the American dream, even though numerous Faulkner characters live and suffer because of their firm belief in the myths of opportunity and social mobility. The dream may indeed be very modest, and in its simplicity and limitation, it demonstrates better than any narrative how naked and cruel life can be for some people. The young girl in 'A Mountain Victory' is one of the most moving examples of this. Her situation is by far worse than those experienced by the female characters in the stories we have discussed so far, in materialistic terms as well as in psychological ones. She is, together with her mother, who is beyond all hopes and all dreams, the weakest character in a white-trash family who live in a dilapidated log-cabin in the Tennessee mountains, where Major Saucier Weddel halts one night on his way back from fighting in Virginia during the Civil War. With her youngest brother, the girl shares a dream of a less harsh, less barren world than the one they seem doomed to live in forever – a world where girls wear shoes; and this dream in itself adds a touch of human frailty, helplessness, and desire to the story.

In the unpublished and not too interesting short story 'A Letter', Faulkner presents a woman who is left by her husband, who apparently has eloped with a girl to Mexico. She cannot do much about this, except wait for him to return; she is afraid of her mother-in-law and cannot ask her for help because she lives on the monthly allowance sent by her. This very typical situation for a woman who is tied down by children and who cannot renew herself and be interesting and exciting all the time is not used often by Faulkner in his portraits of trapped females. It is used, however, with a peculiar and unusual twist in 'The Brooch', where the husband is the one left alone when his wife reacts to the situation in the marriage by going to dances and dating other men. In this story, the male character is the overprotected and spoiled one, destroyed by a mother who never stops her guidance and guardianship. The strong, possessive, overprotective mother has a devastating effect on her son, and the bonds between them cannot be severed because so much is invested in the parent-child relationship. All new relationships, even marriage, have to yield to the pressure of the established and 'natural' parent-child association. This is in part so because the mother-child relationship is stable, solid, and secure, as opposed to the novelty, insecurity, and inherent danger in a new relationship. In 'The Brooch' the parental figure has attained ideal dimensions, and no new person can substitute and take the place of this person. Revolt against such a figure is almost inevitable, but it is seldom carried out with any conscious deliberation and is hardly ever successful. Ambivalence is what characterizes a person in such a situation, and Howard in 'The Brooch' is definitely imprisoned and thwarted in his development. Radical measures will be needed to solve his overwhelming problems of adjustment, but with the strong ties to his mother the result is likely to be disastrous. Howard's strange relationship to his mother may be explained by a reference to the early loss of his father. Miss Zilphia Gant, by the way, experiences the same loss. Since 'The Brooch' features a mother-son twosome (before Howard gets married), the mother's consistent and incessant attempts to curtail her son's freedom, may also be seen as an instance of a deserted and betrayed woman trying to gain control at least over *one male* and never lose him to another female. Howard's only possibility to escape his mother's vigilant maternity is to seek and establish sexual freedom and personal freedom in a natural relationship to another woman. The influence of his mother in the shaping of his character and behaviour makes this extremely difficult. In point of fact he acts in a fashion similar to his mother's when he more or less publicly claims *ownership* of Amy, who, surprisingly enough, agrees to marry him.

Howard's mother, the daughter of a small-town merchant, married a travelling salesman, who soon moved into her house to lead an easy life, but who abruptly left because he could not bear 'to lie in bed at night and watch her rolling onto empty spools the string saved from parcels from the stores' *(Collected Stories,* pp. 647–8). Her father dies shortly after, and the only male figure in her life is Howard, who gets all her affection and also all her protection to guard him from life's more sordid aspects. She attempts to enclose her son within the rigid limits of her world, protecting him from other children, then, later, from the opposite sex. Returning after Howard's education is finished to the Mississippi hamlet, she keeps Howard in a state of permanent and complete bondage through unflagging custody, helped and strengthened by a stroke that makes her immobile.

Within the frame of the story, the stroke may be seen as an act of God to set Howard free. It is at any rate a liberating event, or, more accurately, the event that promises liberation for Howard if he himself is able to act to break some of the ties that bind him to his mother. The question is, then, whether there is any chance for a person whose life so far has been controlled and determined by his mother to establish an existence on his own terms, in a new relationship.

Two more stories must be briefly mentioned before we turn to the reactions and consequences of the many tragic cases of protection and deprivation discussed above: the stories are 'Mistral' and 'Divorce in

119

Naples'. Basically these stories centre on experience and growth and maturation, with 'human tempering',[25] but they include characters and situations related to the problems discussed here. In 'Mistral' the two young men feel 'the secret nostalgic sense of frustration' (*These 13*, p. 329), partly because of their inexperience, but also because of what they learn about a young girl, a soldier, a priest and a series of mysterious events taking place in the small Italian village.

The girl in 'Mistral' lost her father in the war and her mother became a prostitute. The priest has therefore fetched her and kept her and raised her, thinking that 'she would be for the church'. (*These 13*, p. 289). She grows up to be 'the brightest and loudest and most tireless in the dances', (*These 13*, p. 289), and when the priest finds that she probably will not be for the Church after all, he decides to marry her off to a rich man, in spite of the fact that she has a boy-friend, who is perhaps her lover even.

The narrator's description of the girl is very typical, since numerous girls in Faulkner's early short stories are invested with similar qualities by the men, young and old, who watch them:

She was all in white, coatless, walking slender and supple. I didn't feel like anything any more, watching her white dress aswift in the twilight, carrying her somewhere or she carrying it somewhere: anyway, it was going too, moving when she moved and because she moved, losing her when she would be lost because it moved when she moved and went with her to the instant for loss *(These 13*, p. 319).

'Divorce in Naples' deserves mention here simply because this story deals with a tender and gossamer relationship of such a kind that everything in the social system around it will try and break it. Despite the frailty of the relationship, the tenderness and the genuine quality of the men's feelings should not be doubted. For the relationship is a homosexual one, and even though strange attitudes toward sex may be detected in this story, the relationship as such works, through crises, and the narrator appears to be very favourable to Carl and George and their rather bizarre union. Here, then, are two men trapped in an unaccepted relationship, and they will have to stand all kinds of jokes and antagonism and prejudice if the alliance shall survive. Knowing the chances of success (in social terms) of more 'normal' relationships, there is no reason to be particularly optimistic about the future of Carl and George.

The young girls and women in Faulkner's short stories have to find a way out of their situation, if only so that they can avoid or evade the threats from their parental authorities. A silent acquiescence to what the persons in power require is typical for many of the characters, but their reconciliation with the prescribed role is often only apparent, and rebellion is not ruled out as a possibility. A few of the female characters direct their revenge outward; Elly is the most outspoken also in this respect, and she retaliates by killing her grandmother even when this leads to the death of her lover and of herself.

Miss Zilphia Gant breaks out from her prison with her mother in the bungalow, but her rebellion, even if it includes a hasty marriage, is very short-lived. She returns to her mother, who succeeds in driving Zilphia's beau (her husband now) away at rifle point before she dies. Zilphia is alone; bereft of her one and only love; she awaits his return for six months, in vain. Her sexual dreams recur, strong and violent, and she seems to be in a permanent state of frustration. This feeling of frustration is not only a result of her being deprived of husband and lover; it is also a result of her understanding of what the normal life of a woman is; and her inability to give birth drives her almost insane. She hires a detective agency to spy on her husband, who has remarried, and she in her turn lives his marriage vicariously. Miss Zilphia's sexual frustration is of course conditioned by her mother's hatred of males, and peace cannot come to Zilphia till her sexuality eventually dies out.

Zilphia leaves town on the day the painter's wife is expected to have a baby (the detective agency has told her all this), but the wife dies giving birth to a daughter and her husband is killed in a car accident the very same day. Zilphia stays away for three years, and returns in mourning with a child who is placed behind a barred window, just as Zilphia herself grew up in such a room. The town has to accept that she is a widowed mother, but in the eyes of the town she still remains *Miss* Zilphia, growing plump in the wrong places, chatting with people when taking little Zilphia to school. History seems to repeat itself, and Miss Zilphia has learnt nothing from the harsh and loveless upbringing she was subject to. She finds nothing wrong about keeping little Zilphia behind the barred window, protecting her from evil but also from experience, or in depriving her of the most ordinary things in a child's life – friends, parties, outdoor play.

Zilphia's rebellion when she left her mother and married the painter was a short-lived one; she was unable to sever the ties that bound them together, and returned in a few days. Part of Zilphia's trouble arose from the fact that her understanding of the female role was combined with the fear and hatred of men which her mother had lectured her about from the days of infancy. The two attitudes are necessarily incompatible, but Zilphia finally finds a solution which is so special that it cannot possibly be transposed to other, similar situations.

Elly's reactions to the protection and the boredom she feels, include sexual experimentation, but only to a rather moderate degree. Only with Paul does Elly become serious: here she senses a possibility of getting away from Jefferson, but Paul is not a marrying man. Because of this, and because of the strong hold her grandmother has on her after having discovered Elly and Paul on the lawn, Elly for a period relinquishes all hope of change and improvement. Like Zilphia, who became a seamstress and settled down to a dull life after her mother had found her and the boy under the blanket, Elly accepts an armistice as she 'passed the *monotonous* rounds of her days in a kind of *dull* peace' (my emphasis; *Doctor Martino,* p. 250). She submits to becoming engaged to Philip, assistant cashier in a bank, 'a grave, sober young man of impeccable character and habits' *(Doctor Martino,* p. 250), who in allowing Elly to let Paul drive her to fetch her grandmother, who is visiting in Mills City, demonstrates male stupidity as well as an admirable trust in his fiancée.

Elly has chosen Paul as driver on this trip because she still hopes that he will marry her and take her away from Jefferson, and when he refuses to do so, her solution is to kill him and to kill her grandmother, who has made the relationship to Paul impossible as Elly judges it. Elly unquestionably wants to get rid of her grandmother in some way or other, but it is Paul's final refusal to marry her that makes her force the car off the road. Marriage to a man of 'impeccable character' and a dull, suburban life is a future so unbearable to Elly that she apparently feels she can sentence other people to death if they will not help her to escape. She *is* trapped, but she cannot break loose in a meaningful and positive sense by striking back blindly. By presenting women in similar situations in a number of other stories, Faulkner has indirectly shown that Elly's predicament is by no means unique, but nothing in the story indicates that Elly is aware of this. Her attempt to break loose and establish a better life for herself is therefore an individual's isolated attempt to fight a whole social system, and the attempt is doomed to failure.

In 'Elly' Faulkner presents a young girl in an ordinary white family in Jefferson who feels suffocated because of the limitations her social position and the fact that she is a woman put upon her. She reacts strongly and violently to this situation, and her position as well as her rebellion can be understood and described. With Miss Emily Grierson things are a little different. Emily reacts to a series of crises throughout her life. She carries her head high in all situations. She does not yield an inch to any modern demands about taxation or the like, and she keeps her pride and strong will as kind of bulwark against an unbearable, hostile outer world where, little by little, new generations with modern ideas take over the leadership. Emily may be a monument in the small town, but she is a fallen monument, and in the daily life of the community she is nothing but a living dead person – even though the narrator may have some strange reason for perpetuating the memory of her long after general interest has shifted from her and the lifestyle she is characteristic of, to the building of a better world outside and around the anachronistic and aristocratic lady in her decaying mansion.[26]

Emily has always insisted on doing things her own way; she never accepts or concedes to behaviour considered normal by the townspeople. Perhaps the town grudgingly accepts and even admires Emily because of her ability to be herself – they do not learn of the horrible murder she has committed till after she is dead. The monumental old lady passes respectfully and respected into the town's history. She

had gone to join the representatives of those august names where they lay in the cedar-bemused cemetery among the ranked and anonymous graves of Union and Confederate soldiers who fell at the battle of Jefferson (*These 13*, p. 167).

The inference that Emily has been *brought back* to the age she always lived in – some fifty or sixty years back – can be made.

Emily does 'what people will' – she clings to the few certain things there are in her life, and she refuses to accept change. With madness in the family, the murder by poison and concealment of the corpse are explicable acts, despite their horror. Her tragedy is not motivated only in her protected and sheltered upbringing or in an oedipal binding to her strong father. This may account for her relationship to Homer Barron, whom she decided to 'keep' because she had reason to think he would leave her. Much of her behaviour is also a result of her being out of touch with reality. She does not change, while the outside world changes rapidly. Emily becomes isolated in her mansion, in her world, because she has chosen seclusion, but also because time and change leave her behind. Emily's problems are rooted in her social status, her protected upbringing, and a father who drove her suitors away, and her solution is to destroy not to be betrayed, to conceal not to be discovered, to withdraw to be let alone with her memories and problems.[27] Her 'solution' is not a workable one; isolation and withdrawal may help her survive, but she is nevertheless very much a living dead.

The town, 'we' or 'they', say 'poor Emily' and 'poor Zilphia' as they spy and gossip on these pitiable females, and Miss Minnie Cooper is also thought of as 'poor Minnie'. Minnie has also had her 'beau', a widower and a cashier in a bank, but this was twelve years ago, and Minnie seems to have settled down to a quiet, uneventful life with her aunt and mother, sleeping her days away in complete leisure. Apparently, her withdrawal from life has not been so complete or so successful as Miss Emily's, and after sixty days of drought and heat, Milly falls victim to her own sexual dreams and fantasies. She conjures up a rape to make up for the complete disinterest men show her on the streets now. Minnie starts a rumour, which in its turn leads to action and finally to murder. She is not, however, *directly* responsible for the murder. The weather and climate have been used to explain the men's willingness to do something, at any price, but it is only within a rather peculiar social system that all thoughts of justice and truth would be set aside so quickly and easily. Beneath the pervading dust of 'Dry September' is a social system where one class is superior, and the other class, although not being slaves, still is considered inferior on all levels.[28] The two chief hangmen, McLendon and Butch, are more than willing to '...take a white woman's word before a nigger's' (*These 13*, p. 262). One should be careful not to charge only a few racists in the town with the slaying of the Negro, since nobody, with the exception of Hawkshaw, does anything to prevent the murder.[29]

Why, then, did Minnie tell her lie about the rape? The reference to the weather and to Minnie's own 'dry September', meaning that her fertility and sexuality are coming to an end, is not a satisfactory explanation. Minnie may well feel that something *must happen* to make life bearable, but she is also dissatisfied and hence prone to react rather arbitrarily, because the ideal life she misses appears to be the glamorous and exciting life created and beautified by the myth-makers in Hollywood. On the day of the rumour and the killing of Will, Minnie goes to a picture show:

124

The lights flicked away; the screen glowed silver, and soon life began to unfold, beautiful and passionate and sad, while still the young men and girls entered, scented and sibilant in the half dark, their paired backs in silhouette delicate and sleek, their slim, quick bodies awkward, divinely young, while beyond them the silver dream accumulated, inevitably on and on. She began to laugh. In trying to suppress it, it made more noise than ever; heads began to turn. Still laughing, her friends raised her and led her out, and she stood at the curb, laughing on a high, sustained note, until the taxi came up and they helped her in (*These 13*, p. 278).

Minnie obviously experiences a fit of hysteria, and her friends speculate whether the rape had taken place at all. Behind Minnie's desperate laughter and high screams is not only her failure in the social life of the small town, or her belief in the impossible dream-world made up in Hollywood, but most significantly her strong sense of failure because she is single. Minnie would not have despaired of being single if twosomes were not the accepted and normal, institutionalized practice; she would not have despaired of growing old and losing hold on men if being young and popular and admired by men was not the ideal induced in her and her sisters, not least by the Hollywood pictures.

'Poor Zilphia', 'poor Emily', and 'poor Minnie' have something in common in their inability to keep their 'beaus', and in the way they relate to the community they are members of. Elly has something in common with these older ladies too, especially in her background and upbringing, but she never suffers like they do over a long period of time because she acts so early in her life, and as we have seen, her action is fatal. Louise King in 'Doctor Martino' is also young and kept at heel by her mother, but she has found a reason for life and something to believe in so that her rebellion is a weak and guarded one. In fact, it is almost impossible for Louise to retaliate because the persons around her are so strong and powerful, and she does not fully grasp the intricacies of the scheming done by her mother and fiancé to liberate her from the spell Dr. Martino holds over her.

It may be fair to say that Louise remains enigmatic throughout the story, and it is possible that she was so to the author, too. He has to resort to general suppositions about how young girls are in a certain phase of their lives, and the narrator at one point seeks assistance from an instructor in psychology at Yale in an attempt to verify 'that strange, mysterious phase in which they [young girls] live for a while' *(Doctor Martino*, p. 5). Louise's behaviour is not condoned by her mother nor by Hubert Jarrod, and they find that much of what she does is done in direct opposition to their wishes. Louise's conduct – her braveness, vivacity, and problematical understanding of what life is all about – is given a twofold explanation in the text: In the first place she simply enacts what girls in a particular phase of their lives are likely to be and do, and in the second place she is explained as a product of her environment – her protective mother, the summer resorts, the early meetings with Dr. Martino. She is thus clearly seen as having been subject to a special kind of conditioning, due to the strange will-power and autokinetic abilities of the doctor. The implied author seems to be willing to settle for an explanation where the fact that Louise is a young girl, susceptible to evil, victim and victimizer at one time, is the most decisive factor. If we look at young girls elsewhere in Faulkner's short fiction, this is not very surprising.[30]

Louise rightfully feels that everyone but Doctor Martino lets her down; her mother lets her down, her fiancé does not care much for deeper feelings. Louise's life is strangely and closely connected to the aging figure of Dr. Martino. He has given her the vague ideas she tries to fight for about life being something more than what her mother and her rich and spoiled fiancé imagine. She cannot withstand their intrigues, which eventually lead to the death of the doctor and to Louise's marriage to Hubert. So the young and sleek man with his 'aura of oil wells and Yale' (*Doctor Martino,* p. 1) can continue to 'play around. . .with. . .[his] swamp angel' (*Doctor Martino,* p. 1), while Louise never again will test her capacity and endurance or swim any more rivers to prove that she is alive.

Mrs. Blair in 'Fox Hunt' suffers the same fate as the vixen her husband hunts down; there is no way she can escape the intrigues played by the men around her to satisfy the male egotism of a cynic who has set his eyes upon her and found that seduction might be worthwhile. Mrs. Blair has been commanded and forced by others all her life, and little resistance seems to be left in her, albeit she appears to be the incarnation of femininity, innocence, and beauty to the young farmer who watches her from a distance. She has become more or less of a doll, whose prime function is to satisfy the whims of her husband – even her mother persuades her to do so; and she has also become a plaything for the rich and leisurely gentlemen whose world she now belongs to.

Under such circumstances, Mrs. Blair cannot be expected to 'keep her hair up'; that is, remain untainted, faithful, innocent. The youth's description of Mrs. Blair after the hunt is significant: '*"She's got her hair down*. It looks like the sun on a spring branch'" *(Doctor Martino,* p. 49, my emphasis). To the valet this would only mean that he had delivered to Mr. Gawtrey what he had promised to deliver; to the youth, however, the scene has a rare beauty and purity which gives him a feeling of awe.

The final scene or tableau in 'Fox Hunt' is a pastoral idyll after the fall, and even if it has little to do with Mrs. Blair's situation, the kind of experience the young observer has is important. In a morning-quiet nature where the intruders have come and gone, he experiences unfaithfulness and adultery but tries to forget it at once. 'Look back' is repeated three times in connection with the last scene, and the inexperienced and innocent youth looks back, toward Mrs. Blair;

toward that remote and inaccessible she, trying to encompass the vain and inarticulate instant of division and despair which, being young, was very like rage: rage at the lost woman, despair of the man in whose shape there walked the tragic and inescapable earth her ruin *(Doctor Martino,* p. 51).

Mrs. Blair is thus another 'lost' woman, who perforce has to accept a different kind of life from that which she probably would have preferred herself. Her position is somewhat different from that of the other female characters we have discussed above, and her conflict is more vague and undefined than the other conflicts because she is not shown in her normal environment. Moreover, her background is not the class conscious, snobbish and narrow small-town environment in Jefferson, Yoknapatawpha. Since she suffers considerable strain and hardships and mistreatment outside Jefferson, in the world of gentlemen, Faulkner may have intended to show that frustrated and misused women by no means exist only within the boundaries of his kingdom.

In some way or other all these female characters try to break loose, and none of them succeed in doing so. Elly *protests* violently at the age of eighteen, with disastrous consequences. Emily Grierson does not protest overtly, but the consequences are at least comparable to those of Elly's action. Nor does Minnie Cooper protest, and yet she indirectly causes the murder of an innocent person. Among all these overprotected women in Faulkner's early short stories, Miss Zilphia may well be the most grotesque example, albeit she commits or triggers no crime. What she does is to perpetuate the enslavement and boredom of a woman's life by bringing up her 'daughter' in the same way as she was brought up herself. Louise King and Mrs. Blair are other examples of dependent, overprotected women who are deeply troubled because of the demands of the conventional role that they have to succumb to.

Faulkner's female protagonists in these stories seem to require a new and different social pattern to make life endurable. Despite the author's admiration for the strong women who survived the war, kept families together, and carried with them traditional values to new generations (Miss Jenny in 'There Was a Queen' is the most obvious example of such a woman, as we shall see), he also seems to understand that this ideal woman was conditioned by rather peculiar circumstances and can hardly be transplanted into a modern, urban society. In his more critical writings, as demonstrated by a number of short stories in the early thirties, his ideal is a social order where women are allowed to become useful, respected, full members of society. From generalizations about 'how women are', Faulkner revised his stories to give his female characters individuality, and he also related their destinies to their backgrounds and environments rather than to some vague notion of what is typically female.

Faulkner's women have been described as treacherous, mischievous, dangerous, and destructive, representing some kind of inborn female quality of evil.[31] A few of them may be described with these adjectives, but one should be careful not to make generalizations. A grouping of Faulkner's female characters into sexual versus a-sexual[32] is so gross an oversimplification that it can be overlooked. Further, to contend that Faulkner is troubled by sexually active women, or that only those beyond the menopause are understood by him, is even worse. One had better be cautious with what is attributed to the author and given as his opinions; furthermore, all his female characters, whether earth-goddesses, sexually warped 'flappers', or pillars of an old society, should be seen in their social context to be more fully realized and understood. They must, of course, also be discussed in their fictional context, so that the narrative techniques employed are examined to see how the author distributes sympathy and antipathy, and to see *who* reacts in what ways to the different women.

The only really overprotected and totally helpless *male* who compares nicely with the women characters so much in trouble, is Howard Bond in 'The Brooch'. He claimed possession of a girl, Amy, and married her. Howard's attempts at 'liberation' are doomed to fail because he apparently tries to find a girl who is the very opposite of his mother, a woman

128

who in no respects will satisfy the wishes his mother certainly will express, apart from the fact that she hardly wanted to see her son married. Amy is clearly the very antithesis of Howard's mother; she has a bad reputation, she is easygoing and vivacious. The information about the 'bad reputation' is rendered so that it becomes something of positive value, because Amy's name is 'a light word, especially among the older women, daughters of decaying old houses like this in which her future husband had been born' (*Collected Stories,* pp. 648-9), and the judgment of these ladies should, indeed, not be taken at face value.

Howard has to choose a girl very different from his mother in order not to jeopardize his unconscious binding to her. He tries to keep his courtship of Amy a secret, and after the marriage he tries to avoid his mother if possible. At the same time he virtually refuses to establish an independent life with Amy – he does not care to get a job, he does not want to move to another house. Amy's situation is not an easy one, but a kind of armistice seems to work for some time between the three people in the old house. A child is born, only to die a year later. Howard suggests that Amy may go out dancing again, and thus begins a bizarre play of secrecy and fear of detection. The worst Howard can imagine is that his mother will become aware of Amy's going out. When this eventually happens, Howard finds no better solution than to kill himself.

Howard feels the need for revenge, and the only possible one is, as he understands it, to abandon his mother. He could not give her up in preference to somebody or something else, but by killing himself he would not only rid himself of his mother's vigilance and power but also put an end to his own impotence and despair. The elaborate preparations for Howard's suicide leave no doubt about what he unconsciously tries to obtain.

Freudian psychology seems to have been used deliberately in the descriptions of Howard's ambivalence and fear, and the story is thus different from most other stories in which individual psychology is used much less directly and in less detail. 'The Brooch' very clearly demonstrates the old idea that childhood is an important formative period in everybody's life. Dependence, insecurity, and frustration all result from overprotection and enclosure in childhood, and in Faulkner's fictional world chances are small that an individual on his own can break the ties and go on to live a life as a free, whole human being.

The overprotected characters experience a non-life, and their attempts to flee it are futile. In Faulkner's short stories about the pilots from the First World War, a different pattern emerges. These characters have participated actively in life, at least for a short time, and in condensed narratives this period of life lived to the full is looked back upon, often with a touch of nostalgia, by a frame narrator who laments the losses of this 'doomed' generation. In the stories about the reckless pilots from World War I we encounter the dream of glory and fame, a dream that we shall later compare to the dreams of those select few who dream of artistic creation in some rather atypical short stories. 'Ad Astra' and 'All the Dead Pilots' are representative of their author, who once dreamt about becoming a hero in the war, but who, thirteen years later,[33] has achieved a kind of insight and wisdom that the youth of 1917 or 1918 did not possess. The narrators of these stories are still ambivalent in their attitudes to war and in particular to the young pilots, but the World War I stories as a group leave no doubt about the horrors of war.[34] Compared to the non-life the reckless heroes have to succumb to in America of the post-war years, a violent and sudden death in action may be preferable; this is at least what the narrator of 'All the Dead Pilots' voices as his opinion.

'Ad Astra' gives a concentrated, static, almost painful image of loss and decay, of broken dreams and hopes, of the very futility and waste of war. The soldiers who drink, talk, get drunk, quarrel, and fight over a German prisoner-of-war on the night of Armistice day, 11 November 1918, came to the R.F.C. full of spirit and high hopes. The Southerners in the group have come to fight in the war full of 'your goddamn twaddle about glory and gentlemen' (*These 13*, p. 62), and even the other soldiers have come to fight for their country, taking it for granted that glory and adventure and fame awaited them. Even instantaneous death would in some respects be the fulfilment of their dream, since this is regarded as the ultimate proof of life lived to the full. The soldiers feel that they belong to a generation doomed to 'walk the earth a spirit' (*These 13*, p. 79), and there is little hope for the pilots to be able to adjust themselves and find a new world after the war. They could realize their dream of adventure and glory by fighting in the war, but even if war itself may have given them opportunity to prove their courage and recklessness, the soldiers are also described as 'too young to have ever lived' (*These 13*, p. 51).

Believing that they are a doomed race, a lost generation, doomed to be spirits forever, they cannot flee their 'inescapable selves' (*These 13*, p. 51), albeit they try to drown themselves in a 'maelstrom of alcohol' (*These 13*, p. 51) and find some temporary relief in their alcoholic Nirvana.

'Ad Astra' as a title is blatantly ironic; it gives an indication of the kind of dream and hope the pilots brought with them to the war, and then the story itself demonstrates rather convincingly what has happened to the dream. The pilots have lost themselves completely, and there seems to be little hope that they will find themselves again – find their identities, establish themselves as ordinary, useful citizens – after the war. The sentiment that those who survived the war are just as dead as those who died in the trenches in France is repeated a number of times, and the title 'All the Dead Pilots' does in fact refer to pilots who survived the war, but who, in the narrator's opinion, have suffered a symbolic death. In 'Ad Astra' it is the turbaned Indian mystic, the Subadar, who voices all opinions on the theme of death and the loss befallen the soldiers because the war has come to an end. Some of his statements are at best platitudes. The Subadar and the German prisoner-of-war share a dream of a new and different future, hoping that defeat may prove beneficial to art, music, and the relations between men.

In 'Ad Astra' the pilots are losers, but their losses are limited to the war itself. Only by way of implication do we get a notion of the difficulties they are likely to encounter in a world at peace. In 'All the Dead Pilots' a frame narrator comments on the war and the pilots who had to live on after the short time of bravery had come to an end, and in this story the problems of post-war adjustment and the lost generation sentiments are more direct and precise. The philosophical statement that 'we are all dead' in 'Ad Astra' is here exemplified so that the practical consequences of this kind of death come through very distinctly:

But they are all dead now. They are thick men now, a little thick about the waist from sitting behind desks, and maybe not so good at it, with wives and children in suburban homes almost paid out... (*These 13*, p. 82).

The symbolic death not only implies a lost youth, dreams that failed, a problematic period of adjustment after the war; the dead pilots are dead *because they have adjusted* to a quiet, bourgeois life. These men have once seen and proved 'what the race could bear and become' (*These 13*, p. 82), and the story proper in 'All the Dead Pilots' should accordingly exemplify the period of real life, when the pilots lived out all the possibilities inherent in them. Yet the humorous story about John Sartoris and Spoomer and Spoomer's dog and the mad competition between them about girls none of them actually care about, can hardly prove anything about man's courage or cowardice.[35] The story demonstrates fighting skill, unbelievable recklessness, and a complete indifference to danger, which, in the narrator's understanding, seem to be examples of life lived to the full, of the capabilities of the human race. In comparison with the invulnerable British officer from Sandhurst, to whom war is nothing much but a nuisance, Sartoris is a loser; 'utterly without self-consciousness, utterly without shame of his childish business' (*These 13*, p. 90). Nevertheless, Sartoris is the one who really makes the most of the 'instant between dark and dark' (*These 13*, p. 82), which is also described as 'the instant of sublimation' (*These 13*, p. 109) before darkness settles again. Sartoris could not possibly die slowly, by degrees:

November 11, 1918, couldn't kill him, couldn't leave him growing a little thicker each year behind an office desk ... a little baffled, and betrayed, because by that day he had been dead almost six months (*These 13*, p. 95).

'All the Dead Pilots' nonetheless shows that the pilots have no real choice between a meaningless immediate death and an absurd non-life after the war. In the last analysis, whatever happens to them is outside their reach and their conscious choice. Since the narrator is so negative in his attitude to the post-war destinies of the war heroes, one should not forget that Faulkner's war stories in themselves show that suburban life in all its hollowness and emptiness is preferable to that brief flicker of glory and bravery when life was lived to the full. 'Real life' as the narrator apparently understands it, is impossible save for very brief moments. In point of fact, he himself states that this kind of life is 'too strong for a steady diet' (*These 13*, p. 109), and even though he is dissatisfied with post-war America, his central thoughts and the implied criticism remain ambiguous and evasive. What the narrator – and his story – shows, is that the dream could only be realized in the war by dying a hero's death, and further that none of the hopes and dreams cherished before the war have come true in the post-war era.

'All the Dead Pilots' is told by a first-person narrator with an artificial leg, who, because of his disablement, has access to first-hand information about many soldiers. John Sartoris is the most interesting character in the story, and it is therefore important that the narrator seems to be alien to Southern habits and language – he gives the impression of being British himself. The episodes selected by the narrator, humorous, now and then pathetic, do little to explain the old pilots' loss and death on 11 November, 1918. The story rather becomes a reminiscence, a sheltered memory cherished and brought to life through pictures of the heroes of the war and set up against what the narrator interprets as non-life.

The narrator's attitudes are crucial to an understanding of the story's significance. The lack of personal involvement on the part of the narrator and the distance in time makes this a more romantic story, in the sense that it gives another distorted impression of what the pilots were like, seen in retrospect thirteen years later.

The generalizations about the sad and undeserved fate of the soldiers who served their countries, are made concrete in the description of Alec Gray's destiny in 'Victory', which in many respects is Faulkner's most successful World War I story.

Alec Gray does not go to the war because of a dream, and the career he makes as a soldier and officer is not a dream coming true. He is fighting in somebody else's war, but his story may well be taken as a concretization of the more general ideas and presumptions about war in 'Ad Astra' and 'All the Dead Pilots'. Alec Gray is a Scottish shipwright; his family has built ships for 200 years, and family pride is extremely strong. Alec has followed the Gray family pattern, which is close to patriarchal, without any protests, but war opens his eyes for a world outside the Scottish fiords. Being mistreated and sent to the penal battalion, Gray makes up his mind to revenge himself on his Sergeant-major. He commits a bestial and premeditated murder, which in turn puts him in a position to lead a charge. He is decorated and chosen for officer training.

Somewhere along this chain of incidents, Gray has taken leave of his old world, and begins to dream about a new and different one. Alec no longer pays any attention to parental advice, which in this Scottish clan is the wisdom of tradition, the wisdom of the tribe: he has given up God, and he has taken company with those with whom he has very little in common save on a superficial level. He is caught in the spider-web of his new life, and suffers a rapid downfall after the war; at least as rapid as his rise during the war. England has little to offer her sons and lovers who return disabled from the war.

The God-fearing young Scot of 'Victory' has 'blunder[ed] blindly into valor' (*These 13*, p. 35) through his stolid dullness and because he has had a vision of a new life. Whatever his individual tragedy is, in relation to the other World War I stories he proves that not only Sartorises or other people of more or less aristocratic birth are lost and condemned: also the humble people who during a war rise to a pseudo-aristocracy (the officer class) will ultimately fall. The tragic results of Alec's break with his family and the traditional values it represents may also indicate that the plain people's values are normative: they set a standard against which other characters' actions and ideals may be measured.[36]

In 'Victory' the Europe of reconstruction is pictured in dark colours; 'a village of harsh new brick and sheet iron and tarred paper roofs made in America' (*These 13*, p. 4), and the room Gray rents for a night is described in images of death and decay. Words like 'tomb', 'death', 'cheap', 'cold' and 'sluggish' are used. Lack of communication makes people shout to each other, and those who have not suffered directly from the war pretend that they also suffer by illuding stoic acceptance of the common lot.

There is reason to suggest that the nameless soldiers and officers in 'Crevasse' are Scottish, and it would be possible to guess that Alec Gray is among them; especially because 'Crevasse' originally was a part of 'Victory'. In this story whatever dream the men may have had about war has become a nightmare. A small infantry patrol marches over a battlefield where the stillness is complete; the grass is 'dead-looking' and 'gorselike', forming 'bayonets' which 'saber' the men's legs (*These 13*, pp. 113—14). The stillness is profound and ominous, and in this ghostly nightmare of a landscape the earth suddenly begins to move and the whole patrol disappears underground. Twelve men die instantly, and the fourteen who are alive move through a valley of death, and search desperately for an exit. When the men try to dig a tunnel to get out of the trap, they 'burrow furiously, with whimpering cries like dogs' (*These 13*, p. 122), reduced to animals with only the instinct to survive left. The captain, the last one to leave the cave, repeats to himself that 'soon it will be summer' (*These 13*, p. 123),[37] but this hope is contradicted by everything else in the story. Even religious ceremony cannot function as a defence against the horrors of war. War is shown as demoralizing, dehumanizing, and the last note struck in this intense story of horror and desolation is one of meaninglessness and sombre despair.[38]

134

In 'Crevasse' the world of the living outside the cave cannot offer any hope of rebirth; and if the soldiers have any dreams they are dreams of survival. The war-scorched landscape is moribund, and summer seems far away. This picture of the wasteland of war demonstrates better than the sentimentality, lost-generation gibberish, and quasi-philosophical assumptions of 'Ad Astra' and 'All the Dead Pilots' what kind of reality the dreams had to be tested against. In 'Victory' the waste, futility, and cruelty of war are accompanied by prolonged descriptions of post-war Europe, where unemployment and dishonour face those who helped win the war, to maintain at least one dream, the most important of them all: the dream of peace in our time.

Faulkner wrote three more stories from the First World War, yet these stories are distinctly different in attitude and approach from the stories we have discussed above and which formed the opening section of Faulkner's first short-story collection, *These 13*. In 'With Caution and Dispatch', a story in two distinctly different versions, one of them even in two parts, written at about the time of 'Turn About', John Sartoris is the protagonist. He is with the English R.F.C, where he is rather harshly treated by his Flight Commander, and where he has to listen to a General briefing the pilots. To the British some of the myths and dreams of traditional British supremacy are evoked in the General's speech when he refers to 'Waterloo and the playing fields of Eton and here a spot which is forever England' (*Uncollected Stories,* p. 643). In the early version of the story, Sartoris's wild nature, his indifference, and his affairs with women are important elements, but the story does little more than show the recklessness and death-defiance of a wild youth who, tired of life and England, pays no heed to his officers nor to red tape. His only interest is to fly, but also this is done with insouciance and furious indifference that can lead to only one thing: a crash.

One paragraph of the early version of 'With Caution and Dispatch' indicates that Faulkner tried to incorporate some of the mood and philosophy of 'All the Dead Pilots' in this story. This is a description of the relationship between John Sartoris and a Major he has flown with earlier:

And that was all. They had existed, breathed breath and been aware of the hot and living blood, within the same intricate frail web of wire and blood and linen supported coherent and intact in the high vacancy of air [...] not by any strength but by inherent velocity alone; now they would part (it was England, in the spring of 1918) perhaps forever.

Actually it was to be forever, because on the sixth of the following July [. . .] a Canadian bugler would blow Last Post for Sartoris in a little cemetary [sic] behind Rozieres.[39]

In the two-part version of the story, received by Harold Ober in 1940, the story is condensed so that everything but the flying business is left out. The story is then carried on beyond the point where it abruptly broke off in the early version, so that Sartoris gets to France and to the scene of battle. The story is more humorous than it is tragic, and being Faulkner's purest flying story, it does not have much to say about the war itself or the men who fight in it. The author's firm knowledge of flying and of planes is used in minute descriptions of the 'Camels'. Sartoris belly-lands on the deck of a trawler, which is in fact a disguised ship for naval espionage, and this fact opens up for a rather mild criticism of the methods and morals of modern warfare. There are many things going on in a war of which the privates and the lower officers are not informed, and the generals are fond of playing hide-and-seek and of words like 'duty', 'patriotism', and 'glory'. John Sartoris does not care too much; he seems predestined for a violent and sudden death, and his behaviour indicates that he is aware of this himself. The distance between the higher officers and the private soldiers suggests that even if the soldiers – and the ordinary civilians – win this war by sacrificing millions of lives, the established class distinctions are taken well care of even during a war. If anyone ever believed that war might do away with some of the differences between social classes simply by forcing people to fight jointly for the same cause, Faulkner's World War I stories would force one to reconsider this belief. In 'Turn About' the criticism of the leaders is very strong, provided that one accepts the last paragraph of the story as an integrated part of it and not as an 'afterthought' which has little to do with the rest of the story.[40] The American pilot, Bogart, dives his bomber down onto a chateau in a desperate attempt to kill the generals who sat at lunch, and Faulkner himself has given a thirty years' delayed 'manual' to this story where he stresses the significance of the last paragraph:

. . . I think that when he [Bogart] dove his bomber down on the roofs of that chateau, it was a gesture of revolt against all the brassbound stupidity of the generals and admirals that sit safe in the dugouts and tell the young men to go there and do that . . . .[41]

This gesture of revolt is in fact what differentiates 'Turn About' from the conventional magazine story, since it makes the story end on a note of outrage and despair, elicited in the American pilot by the loss of someone too innocent to be wasted in the cause of the leaders who never risk anything themselves. Otherwise 'Turn About' seems to be a story relying on the myths about courage and loyalty and honour as essential qualities displayed in a war. All through the story laughter, youthful courage, honourable behaviour, and even patriotism replace the extremely negative tone in the earlier stories; except for the final paragraphs where Faulkner's more genuine moral concerns slip into the story. War is, after all, not the exciting challenge it appears to be for some time, but to the young English boy, Hope, war gives excitement and adventure in an otherwise dreary and dull life. The nonchalance of Hope, his *insouciance*,[42] may well be the cover for a fear and a fright that otherwise would have made it impossible to carry on the extremely dangerous work he and his older companion, Ronny, have undertaken. They have made the Channel their playground. Using a small vessel they launch torpedoes at German ships, but with death lurking around the corner, they seem to be primarily concerned with a private competition as to who is the first to spot ships with basket masts. Hope does not reveal the dangers of his work to Bogart, who understands it only when he accompanies the two Britons on one of their missions. It thus seems that Hope's laissez-faire attitude is a means of survival – but only till his time comes. There is in 'Turn About' a feeling that the war eventually will get Hope, and that he who should have gone to school and who fondly remembers his tour to Wales with his tutor, is doomed. When Hope is killed, Bogart's violent hatred is demonstrated in his mad act of heroic folly. The only hope left is that a calmer, more calculating mind survives to make the hopes of peace come true, to the extent that this is possible in a world where generals, princes, and kings always have the final say.

One of Faulkner's soldiers in World War I organizes his participation in what is not his country's war to make as much profit as possible. One might say that Willy [Wully] MacWyrglinchbeath of 'Thrift' has a very materialistic dream and that he is willing to go to any lengths to see this dream come true; i.e., to earn as much money as possible. It is hardly fair, however, to call his attitude a dream, and Mac is by no means a dreamer. He is rather one of the most realistic and rapacious characters in Faulkner's short fiction, but in a good-humoured way. The fact that Willy is a Scotsman is apparently meant to explain his greed and miserliness.[43] He always figures out what the best possible ratio between profit and riskiness is, trying to find a middle way between what is most profitable and at the same time gives him a reasonable chance to survive. At the same time, Mac just tries to wear the war out until the time comes when he may return home to the Highlands, where his neighbour is taking care of his house and cow and the money Mac sends him on a regular basis. MacWyrglinchbeath is honest, industrious, and economical. He is able to endure the hardships of war and survive without any apparent trouble, mainly because he is used to a struggle for life in the barren Highlands. He has been taught to be satisfied with the bare necessities of life, and for him the value of money is known by the amount of hard work it takes to earn it.

'Thrift' is a humorous story which may be seen as an antithesis to most of the credos about war set forth in the other war stories. Faulkner never collected or re-used this story, which would have been detrimental to what he tried to say in his other World War I stories. Together his stories about the soldiers in the First World War leave no doubt about the waste, folly, and stupidity of war. Here is rendered a war-time experience that makes credible the otherwise strange reactions of the returned soliders which we meet in other stories. The maladjustment, the reluctance to accept a peaceful life behind office-desks, the dread of suburbia, all become understandable on the basis of these stories. The story that has the closest relationship to these World War I stories is unquestionably 'Honor'. The principal character in 'Honor' is also an important figure in 'Ad Astra'.[44] Buck Monaghan refuses to become 'suburban' or chained behind a desk, and it is possible that he does so because he is unable to adjust to the rules and regulations of society. One may also see Buck's behaviour as an attempt to maintain his honour and self-respect, which is about the only thing left after a long war that wasted his youth and prevented him from learning a trade or anything useful and meaningful. Buck has once lived life fully, and he probably feels that his country and his countrymen owe him some gratitude and respect. Unable to stick to any job for more than a week or two and unable to find what he considers suitable work, he has obviously turned sour, blaming society and his fellowmen for his own failure to cope with difficult situations. One should keep in mind that the story is rendered as Monaghan's thoughts and reflections when he is in the office of his boss, Reinhardt, to quit a job as automobile salesman. The motivational and explanatory information is all given by Buck himself, and he is definitely an unreliable narrator. There is reason to think that he exaggerates his own bad luck and blames circumstance and the war when some of the blame really ought to be his own responsibility. Nevertheless, war has made a 'drifter' of Buck, and the most crucial experience in his past is the suicide of 'a fellow named White' *(Doctor Martino,* p. 356), who committed suicide because of his debt to Buck.

Buck has at any rate been unable to settle down after the war, and even though he says that he has become 'a civ again', the only thing he knows how to do well is flying and the things connected with this activity. He therefore takes up a job as wing-walker with a man named Rogers, gets into a love-relationship with Rogers's wife, and tries desperately to restore his integrity and conscience by letting Rogers get his revenge. In the scenes with Buck and Rogers up in the air, 'where it was cold and hard and quiet' *(Doctor Martino,* p. 364), Rogers saves Buck from the suicide he has staged and thereby gets a more refined revenge than even Buck has imagined. What it leads to is Buck's leaving town, never to return, and an even more rigid understanding on Buck's part of the qualities of a man's world. Women are a nuisance, all they always try to do is keep you down, annihilate your dreams, reduce the dimensions of your life. More important than love and hate and the man-woman relationship are other human qualities which Buck has experienced during the war, and which Rogers's behaviour reminds him of: honour, self-respect, and loyalty, which prevent men from letting down even their enemies in a dangerous situation.

Buck even escaped the housewife who aroused his sexuality because she combined so many of the qualities he considered feminine, and he takes the consequences of this rather narrow escape. His fear of being 'caught', of settling down, is very strong and account for his inability to keep a job for more than a few weeks. Buck has been strongly conditioned by a man's world during the war and during his time with the flying circuses, and his whole story proves that his attitude to women is superficial and prejudiced. His choice to be a drifter, to move from one job to another, is in part the result of his decision to avoid women.

Buck Monaghan is one of the soldiers who 'died' on 11 November 1918, but who has refused to become one of the dead soldiers in post-war America, at least if we use the definition of 'dead soldiers' given by the narrator of 'All the Dead Pilots'. He has not settled down, he is probably not a little thick about the waist after too many days behind an office-desk. The question is if he is a more admirable charcter than the adjusted soldiers who have settled down? The drifting, poor, but honourable Buck Monaghan understands himself as a product of the war which deprived him of so many opportunities, and he is at the same time very dissatisfied with the post-war world, where his personal qualities seem to count very little. He has refused to become debased, he has refused to give up his dream, but in the meantime he has gone sour. Buck might have been able to adjust a little, if only to make life easier for himself, and he might still have retained some of his admirable qualities which he now applies awkwardly and inadequately. Buck's opposite, his boss Reinhardt, is a money-making, successful businesman, and Buck's scorn for him is in many ways appropriate. Yet Buck's contempt for the greed and avarice of the contemporary scene and his honour and self-respect can be reduced to *selfishness* in the last analysis. Buck's honour solves no problems for anybody, and the way he describes how he narrowly escaped a woman and later is on the run to avoid women in general shows a narcissistic approach to life.

The pilots of the First World War had a very special opportunity of participating in the steadily expanding civil use of aeroplanes, but in the early days of flying, barn-storming air shows seem to have been more tempting. In addition to Buck's adventures in 'Honor', 'Death Drag' gives the most complete and elaborate picture of an air circus of the late twenties or early thirties in Faulkner's short fiction.[45] Even if the story may be found to be less about air-circuses of its period than about another instance of man's injustice to man, of people in conflict with their environment and hence with themselves, the story also demonstrates the same lack of firm ground to stand on as 'Honor' did. The flying men's apparent inability to form a realistic appreciation and evaluation of life and themselves seems to be typical of the generation of pilots who survived the war but could not adjust to a normal life afterwards. Wing-walking and stunt-flying give them an opportunity to keep some of their dreams alive, despite the fact that the flyers in 'Death Drag' are losers in all other respects.

The startling, almost grotesque, description of the men in the flying machines is a projection in time of destinies hinted at in the earlier war stories, e.g. 'All the Dead Pilots', where the introductory frame is the narrator's contemplation and lamentation of the 'non-life' of the aviators from World War I. The 'death-defying' show is an event characteristic of

140

the time and place, in the way it represents an unlimited belief in progress, in the vast possibilities of creating a better world through technical innovations. Two dreams are thus inherent in the show: the dream of the easy, free life which the flyers are anxious to keep alive, and the dream of progress and prosperity shared by all inhabitants of the small town.

The flyers are *intruders* in the 'little dead clotting ... of human life' *(Doctor Martino,* p. 88), and there is a definite clash between worlds of totally separate qualities when the airplane arrives and lands.[46] Yet there are certain elements in common between the two worlds and their inhabitants, and these elements are related to the dream of greater freedom, mobility, communication, and prosperity; in short, the dream of a better future. The modern world of air-travel and other conveniences, as represented by the visitors, seems to be accompanied by lies, deceit, illegalities, human misery, and death. This tragic inference can be made on the basis of the destinies shown in 'Death Drag', but it is more than likely that the three men here, in particular the one in command, cannot be taken as representative of the men who little by little will bring modern times even to all the 'dead clottings' about the land. Ginsfarb and Jock and Jake are rather left-overs from aviation's infancy. Due to bad luck (Jock), incompetent government (Ginsfarb), and certainly also personal problems not revealed in the story, they cling to a wretched aeroplane in order to make a living (defy death) and escape detection, since what they do is highly illegal.

Most of the characters in these stories are drifters of the post-war world, disillusioned veterans of the lost generation, who by various means try to make their situation bearable but who still refuse to adjust or to escape. In 'Pennsylvania Station' we meet a somewhat different loser, a man from skid-row who spends his days on a bench at Pennsylvania Station in New York, but who tells long and intricate stories to establish his own importance and to prove that nothing but bad luck and a combination of strange coincidences and circumstance have brought him to his present situation. The need to tell, the almost desperate urge to spin a tale, which in part is fabricated by his own imagination, the unwavering insistence on his nephew's being a good boy with a decent job, all these elements reveal a man who tries to deceive himself as a means of survival. He tries to conjure up a picture of himself and his family background in order to explain and excuse his present sojourn in skid-row. Only subconsciously does it slip through that the old man's nephew, Danny, probably is responsible for the present status of his uncle. The old man is more or less lost in his dreams of a past that he distorts to make it acceptable, and even though the intricate story about his sister, his nephew and the money paid down on his sister's coffin, is interesting as such, the lonely, suffering, poor old man and his false dreams are what really matter. Furthermore, the old man and his tragic situation is not anything unique. He tells his story to a companion, who is young but already in a similar position, and they are not the only ones:

While they stood there three other men came . . . with faces and garments that seemed to give off that same effluvium of soup kitchens and Salvation Army homes (*Collected Stories*, pp. 609–10).

One could easily draw a moral lesson on the basis of this story; it might even be helpful to do so, but it seems to be too vague and general to say that these men are losers because they have been mistreated or taken advantage of by the upcoming generation that has displaced them and made them obsolete. There is little doubt, however, that Faulkner's picture of the big city in this story offers a partial explanation of why many people must become losers:

Then they both looked up the ramp and through the arcade, toward the doors on Seventh Avenue. Beyond the doors lay a thick, moribund light that seemed to fill the arcade with the smell of snow and of cold, so that for a while longer they seemed to stand in the grip of a dreadful reluctance and inertia (*Collected Stories*, p. 624).

Contrary to the more human world of the countryside and even the village in Yoknapatawpha County, the world of 'Pennsylvania Station' is inhuman, cold, dreary, implacable, monotonous. It takes more to retain a dream in such an alien and hostile environment, but if the dream is all you have, it seems to be the only thing that can sustain you and help you survive in skid-row.

The dream of moving upwards in society is cherished by many Faulkner characters, and since this is a materialistic dream in a world becoming more and more interested in money and materialistic success, a large number of these characters succeed. One of the most successful of these characters is Martin, the Big Shot, in the two versions of the same story, entitled 'The Big Shot' and 'Dull Tale'.[47] Dal Martin has

142

worked his way up from being a tenant farmer's youngest son to becoming the man who runs and owns a whole town. He has made a fortune as a contractor, and now lives in a huge bungalow with his sixteen-year-old daughter. Most of his dreams seem to have come true, but there is one goal that is harder to achieve than the others, even if bribes are used. Martin has dreamt about sending his daughter to the debutante ball which the Chickasaw Guards give each December. This very old and prestigious society stems from the early days of the Civil War and is run by Gavin Blount, who refuses to be bribed into letting someone without the appropriate social status attend his ball. In the version of the story called 'The Big Shot', an episode with Popeye, a gangster, and illegal whiskey peddling is included, and this sub-plot also furnishes the tragic and wryly ironic conclusion of the story. Gavin Blount, who also has some dreams, accepts Martin's offer to build an armoury in Blount's grandfather's name;[48] later he tries to nullify the agreement. When Martin turns him down, he commits suicide. Martin's daughter, who is running out all night and spends much time with the sons of the old and rich families and whose road to top social status seems open because of the ball, is accidentally killed by Popeye – her father's hired man. The father has stretched himself beyond his reach: there appear to be certain things in life that money cannot buy, and his unlimited vanity gets its tragic reward.

'Dull Tale' does not include the Popeye episodes, but otherwise the story is basically identical with 'The Big Shot'. Gavin Blount is also here the leader of the Guards, but they are named the Nonconnah Guards, and in 'Rose of Lebanon' and its later version, 'A Return', this position becomes even more important than in 'The Big Shot'/'Dull Tale'. To be a Flag-Corporal – the highest officer – in the Nonconnah Guards is in many ways Blount's dream come true. A great-uncle and namesake had been chairman of the 1861 ball, and through his fate (he was killed at Chickamauga) the war has become very personal to Gavin. One lady in particular embodies everything glorious and feminine and beautiful: Lewis Randolph. She came from Mississippi to the Nonconnah Guards' ball in 1862, to be the date of Charles Gordon. She married Charles shortly after the last ball and before he went to the war, in which he was killed during a raid on a henhouse,[49] and she bore a son, Randolph [Ran] Gordon, who has become a millionaire in Memphis while his mother refuses to move, no matter how rich her son becomes. Gavin Blount is a doctor, who has 'inherited from his father a practise which, by twenty odd years of unflagging endeavour he had reduced to the absolute minimum',[50] and he is a bachelor. He has not married because nobody can match his image of the ideal woman – Lewis Randolph. Gavin Blount asks Randolph Gordon if he knows why he has never married, and gives the answer himself: 'Because I was born too late. All the ladies are dead; there's nothing left now but women.'[51] Living in a dream world, peopled with ghosts and filled with myths of a glorious past, Gavin does his best to live in both worlds; to live now and then. Randolp Gordon is the 'I' of the following conversation with Gavin:

'You cant live then and now too,' I said.
He looked at me then. 'I can die trying'.
He didn't look away now. 'You mean, you will die trying,' I said.
'What if I do? No one will suffer.'[52]

Gavin Blount has not married because there were no more ladies left, or because the only one left, Lewis Randolph, turned him down:

. . .he sat quietly, not looking at me· 'She wouldn't have me.'
'Who wouldn't have you?'
'Lewis Randolph.'
Lewis Randolph is my mother, She is 82 years old.[53]

Gavin Blount lives in a past full of shadows and is unwilling to give up his futile dreams of recapturing it: living now the way they did some sixty-five years ago. The old, irrevocable days have been replaced by the new and modern days and ways, and in his eyes the Old South with its traditional values is disappearing: Chicago and New York patterns are introduced in the Southern towns, and Jews in fine clothes reap their lawful profits. Gavin Blount is perhaps an anachronism, and he refuses to change because of his infatuation with a dream; yet, at the same time his refusal is based on an understanding of what the new world and life in general is coming to, and he cannot accept that. The dream of the Old South, the dream of a pleasant agrarian paradise where solidarity and humanity were important and where people knew exactly where they belonged, recurs in Faulkner's fiction: Gavin Blount is in many respects a prefiguration of Hightower in *Light in August,* as Millgate has shown.[54]

144

If a character finds it problematic, not to say impossible, to adjust to his environment, or if he simply finds little to be satisfied with in life, his dreams will inevitably transcend the bleak reality of his everyday life and go beyond the limits of this world. One might describe this as an instance of compensation: to endure hardships and pains in this life one finds comfort and consolation in the prospect of a better and more just life after death. The dreams about a richer and more rewarding life, the belief in the spirit's capability of transcending all matter, are also of this world. In 'Beyond' we may have to do with a post-mortal flight of consciousness or a moment's fantasy in the Judge's brain, so that his visit in the realms beyond the gate takes place in the moment immediately preceding death. In 'Black Music' alcohol and a blow to his head account for the 'faun experience' of Midgleston, and his *interpretation* of this incident as something beyond the reach of ordinary humans is therefore what really matters in that story. In 'The Leg' sickness and madness accompany a dream of recapturing the pre-war idyll in England, and the dream turns nightmare. In 'Carcassonne' the dream is a dream of creation, so that the very text presenting the dream indicates the validity of this kind of experience as a way of coping with the world and at the same time contributing to an understanding of it.[55] That the dream of creation also feeds on more realistic and worldly experiences is shown in 'Artist at Home'. The desperate need to meet the demands of this dream is forcefully demonstrated in this story.

'Beyond' is a story about the dreams of immortality, about loss and grief, belief and non-belief, agnosticism and nihilism, but primarily about immortality. A Mississippi Judge pays a visit to Heaven to discover what immortality means in his special case, and when he returns he seems to be prepared for the final judgment. He knows what lies in store for him.

What the Judge experiences and discovers 'beyond' is largely dependent on what his former life has been like. His interest in immortality is a result of the loss of his only son who was to carry on his important family name – 'It had been a good name, you see' *(Doctor Martino,* p. 211). The Judge's dream for his boy and the pride he takes in the tradition he is to follow are both demonstrated in the lettering on the marble slab in the cemetery – 'Howard Allison II'. In the almost pathetic line of farewell, *'Auf Wiedersehen, Little Boy' (Doctor Martino,* p. 219) is implied a vague belief that the Judge hardly holds. The Judge's dream, his excessive pride, and his vain attempts to secure immortality for himself, are all instances of classical *hubris,* and one may well see the death of the boy as a symbolic act by some God-figure to prove that He alone rules over life and death and that no man should put any amount of faith in an unknown future.

On his journey through Heaven Judge Allison encounters spirits who have obvious allegorical functions. They represent blind hope, irrational dreams, and unwarranted beliefs. The dream seems to be an inseparable part of human nature, and it is not relinquished beyond the gate. The Judge is an agnostic, and he progresses as far into Heaven as possible in his quest for someone or something that his intelligence, if not his logic, can accept as Christ.[56] He does not find what he seeks, but he reaches a new kind of freedom because he knows where death will ultimately take him. His dreams have been replaced with a firm understanding of immortality and a new philosophy of life, both explicitly set forth in the story:

'You see, if I could believe that I should see and touch him [the son] again, I shall not have lost him. And if I have not lost him, I shall never have had a son. Because I am I through bereavement and because of it. I do not know what I was nor what I shall be. But because of death, I know that I am. And that is all the immortality of which intellect is capable and flesh should desire' *(Doctor Martino,* pp. 219–20)

The Judge also acquiesces that he does not require what the inscription on the slab implies; viz. 'Wiedersehen'. Instead his new insight tells him that:

'To lie beside him will be sufficient for me. There will be a wall of dust between us: that is true, and he is already dust these twenty years. But some day I shall be dust too. And –' he spoke now firmly, quietly, with a kind of triumph: 'who is he who will affirm that there must be a web of flesh to hold the shape of love?' *(Doctor Martino,* p. 220).

'Beyond' sets forth a belief that Faulkner often returns to: 'But he [the Judge] naturally and humanly prefers the sorrow with which he has lived so long that it not only does not hurt anymore, but is perhaps even a pleasure, to the uncertainty of change . . .'.[57] Between 'grief and nothing' Judge Allison chooses grief, knowing that the only thing you can have forever is what you have lost.

'Beyond' is a probing into the realms beyond the gate of death, a search for something to believe in, even if only the certainty of loss and bereavement, to replace the vague and logically untenable dreams of immortality.

146

An experience of something *beyond,* of transcendence, may be felt and described by a *living* person, and this is very important, since it may help readers to avoid misinterpretations of many a difficult Faulkner text. In 'Black Music' Faulkner describes the almost transcendental experience of a man who *in life* had 'been something outside the lot and plan for mortal human man to do and be' *(Doctor Martino,* p. 290), and 'The Leg' is close to being a story about the supernatural, also taking place this side of the grave.

'Black Music' and 'The Leg' deal with central ideas and themes in Faulkner's work, but their strangeness and apparent inaccessibility make it virtually impossible to give them satisfactory treatment. A brief note on some of the elements in these stories will have to suffice, even if they deal with the dream in a way hardly found elsewhere in Faulkner's short fiction.

'Black Music' relies to a considerable extent on ancient myths about fauns, sartyrs, Pan, and rebirth in Nature, but there is nevertheless a realistic situation at the centre of the story. It begins rather awkwardly: 'This is about Wilfred Midgleston, fortune's favorite, chosen of the Gods' *(Doctor Martino,* p. 263). Seen in the perspective of the whole story, it is difficult to agree that Midgleston in any fruitful way has freed himself of the old compulsions and the narrow circumscriptions which held him prisoner for fifty-six years. What is clear, although not unequivocally accepted by the narrator, is that to Midgleston himself the faun experience created something worthwhile to live on, it gave him a reason to escape, an excuse for quitting his former life with all its demands and restrictions. Only subconsciously does Midgleston acknowledge this, and he therefore believes firmly that he has once been chosen by the Gods to go their errands on earth as a faun in untouched nature. He cannot return to a normal life after this experience. That the choice to get away is very much Midgleston's own, is part of the narrator's final understanding of him.

Midgleston gives a series of clues to an understanding of his choice in the course of his long tale. He seems to accept that people are born into certain positions and that social equality is impossible and unwanted: 'the fellow that is born a tadpole, when he tries to be a salmon all he is going to be is a sucker' *(Doctor Martino,* p. 270). Yet he also feels that he is the double of the rich Mr. Van Dyming, and he shares his wife's belief that 'You're just as good as they are . . .' *(Doctor Martino,* p. 277). So his statement about social immobility is contradicted a number of times, which may help explain Midgleston's easy readiness to trust supernatural powers which can invert social roles, if only for a day.[58] Midgleston also believes in his own uniqueness, in his being *chosen,* and this may in part be explained by a reference in the text to his having been 'a powerful reader' *(Doctor Martino,* p. 286). Imprisoned in the city and dreaming about the ocean and the countryside he apparently came to think that 'living wouldn't play a trick on him like getting him alive and then. . . ' *(Doctor Martino,* p. 286). This implies that all through his fifty-six years of being nondescript he expected something to happen to prove life to be worth living. His *readiness,* based on his dreams, must therefore be seen as a very important motivating factor behind the chain of events, and may further serve to explain why he happily and carelessly accepts the sordid life in Rincon after the big event.

Wilfred Midgleston succumbs to the effects of a small injury and much drinking – to which he is unaccustomed – and plays his faun for a day role. He also does this because he believes that he is as good as anybody else, and because he has always expected life to be more than it has proved to be so far. Midgleston is well prepared for his threshold experience, and to him the incident proves that he *has* experienced 'something beyond the lot and plan for mortal human man' *(Doctor Martino,* p. 276). The faun experience proves that life can be more than an architect's job at $75 a week and the confinement of a monotonous city life. Midgleston is also prepared to act on behalf of nature to scare intruders away, believing as he does that Nature strikes back at those who interfere with it. Anyhow, Midgleston gets his excuse for leaving his job and his former life (including his wife), to go on to lead an inconsequential life somewhere where human beings leave their marks in the dusty streets. Basically, Midgleston has experienced something so special that other people do not mean much to him anymore: he is outside life, he is chosen, he has something to live on.

'The Leg' is one of Faulkner's most intricate and complex stories. It seems to resist any logical or coherent interpretation or explanation.[59] The story is enigmatic and mysterious beyond the grasp of the characters involved in it, and we shall only mention the possibility of interpreting this story on the basis of the dream-like idyll in the opening paragraphs of it. The attempts to keep this dream intact or to salvage elements of it through hard and bitter years of loss and pain during the war may account for the madness, insanity, and tragedy experienced by the characters involved. Supernatural powers seem to be at work, too, and even if stress and pain and delirium may account for some of the mysterious deaths, it is difficult to see how this story can be explained even if one resorts to abnormal psychology.[60]

'The Leg' is an uneven story in the sense that its subject transcends the normal boundaries of a short-story narrative and has to be violently compressed, even to the point where it becomes unintelligible. The shifts in setting, tone, and atomsphere are many and dramatic. The story opens on one of the most purely idyllic and innocent scenes in all Faulkner's writings, but moves quickly on to an army hospital frequently visited by a ghost and further to scenes of intolerable anxiety, fear, and insanity. The almost poetic experience of the two young Oxford students, Davy and George, in the 'peaceful land' *(Doctor Martino,* p. 298), England, in 1914 when they were twenty-one, seems to underlie most of the strange and inexplicable events later on.[61] George courts the Thames lock-keeper's daughter, Everbe Corinthia Rust, in an innocent fashion, and she is a nature's creature with a 'dairy-maid's complexion and her hair like mead poured in sunlight' *(Doctor Martino,* p. 292). The pastoral idyll is broken by a series of incidents which become significant in relation to what happens later: George falls into the water, and Davy in the skiff 'shot through the gates' *(Doctor Martino,* p. 293). George is pulled ashore by 'a long running shadow carrying the shadow of a boat hook' *(Doctor Martino,* p. 293), who proves to be Everbe's brother. Most significantly, George accuses Davy of envying him Corinthia, to which Davy, unnecessarily harshly, retorts 'You ghastly lunatic' *(Doctor Martino,* p. 295).

Despite these incidents, there is no doubt about the idyll of the scene, the innocence and peace and quiet in an Edwardian England before the war. When the battlefield and then the hospital replace the pastoral idyll, Everbe Corinthia and all she represents to the two boys fade into memory; a nostalgic dream of youthful passion and easy days, but the memory becomes stronger and may function as a kind of substitute for life during the hospitalization days. George is killed early in the war, and Davy has one of his legs amputated. George visits Davy in 'the corridor where the mother of dreams dwells' *(Doctor Martino,* p. 305),[62] and the spiritual conversation between the etherized patient and the spirit of his late friend inevitably centres on Everbe's tears on that idyllic day in 1914 when George fell into the dirty water of the Thames.

Recapturing the past somehow, reliving that idyll, is what Davy does in his delirium and dreams. He is unable to draw a line between verities and illusions, between truth and delirium. The lines seem to blur all the time, and in Davy's later experiences reality and dream are one and the same. Davy is almost beaten to death by Corinthia's brother, and it is then revealed that Corinthia has died after a day's insane screaming and her father has died within the same week. Jonathan Rust, the brother, has seen Corinthia with someone in a small punt, he has heard a strange laughter, and has found David to be the man with this laughter. Jonathan even has a picture of David, which was taken at the time when he lay in the hospital, if we are to believe David. David has been to the Observer's School for training, and may have had the opportunity to see Corinthia, but he seems to be subconsciously hiding information which might have given a clue to a consistent interpretation of his queer story. What David, and the story in itself, now suggest is that the amputated leg has been reincarnated and may be responsible for the strange deaths that occur. The hidden rivalry for the female, Everbe Corinthia, and the dream of a pre-war paradise are at the core of this story, and a final suggestion might be that David in his insanity and loss is blaming the outcast leg for something he is responsible for himself but is unwilling to admit. Under dense layers of sexual symbols and dreams, an explanation for some of the strange elements in 'The Leg' may be found, but even Freud cannot account for everything here. Yet it may be valid to maintain that under circumstances like those David experiences during the war, insanity may be a possible way of survival; and the only possible way to have some dreams come true may be through loss and bereavement, by sacrificing that which you love.

David is the name of the innocent and later insane protagonist of 'The Leg', and David is a name Faulkner has given to a number of characters with a few significant features in common: David is the youthful and spirited artist in 'Out of Nazareth', and the poet of 'Carcassonne', in the two typescript versions of the story, is also named David. In the published version he is nameless, and in 'Carcassonne' only one place-name is found so that the story may be located, viz. Rincon, a Latin-American port. Carcassonne is also a name of a place – a medieval

French city; and Rincon thus represents the actual, physical setting of the story while Carcassonne probably stands for the dream or fantasy world of the imagination.

There is thus immediately established a contrast in the story: between the 'real' world of a port where people own everything from oil and the air you breathe to other people, and an 'inner' world of a young poet's imagination.[63] This dream world may be seen as a way of coping with a too harsh reality, a means to survive, or as an escape by someone who does not want to adjust.

This contrast is continued in the opposition between the Standard Oil Company, Mrs. Widdrington, and Luis in the cantina on one side and *him of Bouillon and Tancred too'* – glorious figures from the early crusades – on the other side. These medieval heroes also fought for a young man whose Kingdom was not of this world, and the poet's 'kingdom' apparently lies in the transcendence of reality: in artistic creation. The final pair in the series of contrasts is a body-soul dichotomy: 'he himself' and 'his skeleton' are presented as if they were actually separate beings, even to the extent that they discuss and quarrel with each other. This dialogue is a part of the total conflict of the story: a conflict between a young man who wants to follow his dream and calling and an environment remaining hostile or at best indifferent.[64]

The poet dreams, and the whole short story has the quality of a dream. This is so because the poet of 'Carcassonne' repeatedly lapses into escapist dreams of the final quietude and solitude, as a result of the agony and despair artistic creation brings with it:

Bones might lie under seas, in the caverns of the sea, knocked together by the dying echoes of waves. Like bones of horses cursing the inferior riders who bestrode them, bragging to one another about what they would have done with a first-rate rider up *(These 13,* p. 355).

The poet dreams of a less barren soil to feed his imagination from, but his skeleton moans in dissatisfaction with the wooden floor. It also supplies the protagonist with 'bits of trivial information', and provides him with the wisdom that 'the end of life is lying still' *(These 13,* p. 357); a wisdom not agreed upon by the spiritual he. The conclusion of the dialogue shows that the poet accepts that somebody must give him advice, but he then qualifies his assent: 'At least it looks like it' *(These 13,* p. 358), implying that the trivial things the skeleton can feel and understand ought to be unnecessary. It does not look like it, however; the artist cannot live in his ivory tower, isolated and withdrawn. The skeleton is there, the outside world is there. The story is in itself proof that the poetic spirit may transcend all such matter, so that it can become possible to 'create out of the materials of the human spirit something which did not exist before'.[65] 'Carcassonne' is a poetic fable of the artist's plight, and it is an evocation of the imaginary realms the creative spirit can reach, in spite of the strange and hostile world surrounding it. In the last resort 'Carcassonne' negates that 'the end of life is lying still' by being one more scratch on the wall, and it implies that the artist's creation will, when genuine, work restlessly in ever-widening circles.[66]

'Carcassonne' is a dream-like story about an artist's struggle to create. The problematic nature of artistic creation is central in the story, but it is contemplated only in very general terms. In 'Artist at Home' there is, on the other hand, little doubt about what the artist uses as his raw material, and the painful and sacrificial nature of art is emphasized, although the writer *has to* sacrifice and suffer to get his story told and thereby gets some kind of vicarious satisfaction. The narrator of 'Artist at Home' insists on directing the reader's attention to certain facts and observations. He leaves no doubt as to what the story is about: the agony and sweat of artistic creation – not primarily about a bizarre love triangle.[67]

In 'Artist at Home' the narrator is consciously directing the narratee to what he considers important in his story, but also to what he finds strange or fears that his readers may find hard to believe. It is particularly important to keep the readers alert when the affair between the writer's wife, Anne, and the poet, Blair, is shown to *inspire* the artist and furnish him with material for a short story. The artist silently accepts his wife's affair and Blair's bad poems, even to the extent that he patiently waits for the further development of the affair so that he may continue his story. The strange triangle is in some instances reduced to a juxtaposition of the two artists, seen from the outside. The narrator even tries to include the reader in his spying on the tableaux of betrayer and betrayed, of youth and old age, of moral concerns which have to surrender to the urge to create, even when creation means to sacrifice one's own heart's blood.

And there they are: the bald husband with next week's flour and meat actually in sight, and the homewrecker that needs a haircut, . . . (*Collected Stories*, p. 637).

And here we are again: the bald husband, the rural plute, and this dashing blade, this home-wrecking poet. Both gentlemen, being artists: . . . (Collected Stories, p. 642).

The husband, Howes, is of course the 'artist at home' of the story's title, and although it has been pointed out that his place is no real 'home', the significance of the title and its ironic ambiguity lies in the adverbial phrase 'at home'. The narrator seems to think that the responsibilities and regulations of family life may imperil an artist's creative ability, and the love story further indicates that Howes is more at home when he, through his wife's affair, regains his creative powers; i.e., when he gets something to write about. The artist is thus *at home* only when he is actually in the creative process, when he labours in the agony of the human spirit.

One should not forget that the poet, the lover, also gets his poem written, but only when the affair is brought to an end and sickness and despair and his own gentlemanly foolishness lead to his death. Howes sells the poet's poem, and he also sells his own story:

And what was it he had been writing? Him, and Anne, and the poet. Word for word, between the waiting spells to find out what to write down next, with a few changes here and there, of course, because living people do not make good copy, the most interesting copy being gossip, since it mostly is not true (Collected Stories, p. 644).

This is, indeed, an unexpectedly candid expression of what literary art can be. The narrator of 'Artist at Home' emphasizes the extraordinarily private and sacrificial nature of artistic creation, and also the distance there is between *life* and *art*. The usurpation of the love affair in a literary text includes a kind of sacrifice of life on art's altar, but the story ends on a humorous and optimistic note on life's miraculous ability to prevail in the end, if only because it outlasts all bereavement, and loss. Despite the urgent need to get one's story told, summer will come and make life easier, and time will heal all wounds. 'Artist at Home' nevertheless demonstrates how important the dream is, and to what lengths an artist is willing to go to see it come true.[68]

The Yoknapatawpha stories discussed in this chapter seem to refer to a wider, more general, background story, about which a few hints are given in each narrative. A common experience of Yoknapatawpha past and present is evoked, very often at the outset of these stories, and thus the narratives become vaguely linked to one another in time and place if

153

not in theme. Technically the narratives often resemble one another through this implied reference to some arsenal of common knowledge. The reader, accordingly, will have to piece together information from each and every story and bring it with him to the next narrative, becoming, little by little, better prepared to enter the new narratives as he listens to 'the best of gossip'.

Many of the stories, as we have seen, start in medias res, only to turn to the past or to anticipated future events. Strict chronology is seldom found, but on the now-level the stories progress chronologically with a linear development through crises and solutions. Retrospective capsule stories are now and then given a numbered part of the narrative, so that in our reading we place this part of the story in its proper story-place and time, despite the anachrony of the narrative time-schedule. This technique is demonstrated in 'Miss Zilphia Gant' as well as in 'Dry September', and Faulkner's revisions of 'Dry September' prove that the start in the midst of events is an enormous advantage compared to a start in a slow-moving narrative about Minnie's dreary life in Jefferson.

Faulkner has come a long way from the New Orleans writings in most of the stories in this period, but we may as well postpone our evaluation of his achievement in the major period till the concluding pages of the following chapter, in which the remaining stories from the period will be discussed. A few additional remarks about Faulkner's story-telling techniques may be appropriate at this point, though.

Most of the stories deal with instances in the lives of Faulkner's townspeople, and many of them are told from the so-called 'community point of view'. One should not forget, however, that even though a 'we' is narrating, referring to 'our town', to 'they' and 'them', the narrative voice is not so easily pinned down to a group or an individual. Rather, it is a voice that we might place with the implied author, or describe as a more distanced and more knowing perspective on the story told in the narrative. This voice gives the impression of having much more sympathy for the characters, because of the greater understanding he possesses, and because he is outside the rigid conventions and expectations of the small town community. Also, one should remember that there is a first-person narrator hidden behind the 'we' in such stories, and although we should perhaps reserve covert narration for some other purpose, it seems to be an apt term for this kind of narrating, too. More often the narration is overt, and a first-person narrator steps forward to relate a

154

story to us or even to some listeners (narratees within the framework of the narrative).

Faulkner's use of language differs considerably from narrative to narrative. In parts of 'Dry September' and 'Ad Astra' language abounds with metaphors. Imagery of many types, and extended symbolic descriptions are used to emphasize the ensuing action or to prepare it. In 'Dry September' this is done very deftly, while the symbolism may become rather obscure in some of the 'Beyond' stories, even when it is Freudian symbolism ('The Leg', and also 'The Brooch'). One should not only blame extended or even exaggerated symbolism for the problems that such a story as 'The Leg' presents. Here, then, we may see the subject of a novel or a story of novel-length being reduced to a short narrative, with serious interpretive problems as the result. Faulkner avoids some of these difficulties in 'Beyond', and he does this by using a frame narrator who is omniscient. The narrator introduces the dying Judge, and the long journey to a Christian Heaven and back again, taking place in the Judge's mind while he lies dying, is seen completely from the Judge's point of view, although the narrator's presence in the frame leads us to think he has arranged all the smooth transitions from one sphere to another, and the detailed descriptions of Heaven and earth.

In many of the stories from a community point of view, where a narrator may use 'we' and 'our town', the narrator at the same time relies on other informants and on general gossip. In 'Death Drag', for instance, information is to be filled in about the background of the fliers and their circus, and since the narrator here has limited knowledge, he finds support from a more perceptive and knowledgeable townsman. Faulkner is not as careful all the time, so that narrators may easily go beyond that which they normally and realistically could possibly know. 'A Rose for Emily' has been discussed with this in mind; but perhaps we should not be so concerned with the limitations of the narrator according to his own definitions of himself and his position. His narrative is in (written) language, and his selection of material for presentation – what he decides to tell from the story in his narrative – may be responsible for the problems that limited narration often presents.

The use of extra-narrators, or first informants, is very cleverly done in 'Black Music', one of the most autonomous of the stories from this period. Most of the story is told by Midgleston to a narrator who then relates the whole story, by letting his protagonist speak directly, but also

155

by compressing parts of the story, and commenting on it as it slowly unfolds. The narrator likewise sets the tone of the story in an introduction. Since Midgleston is allowed to tell so much of his own story, the narrator includes newspaper clippings in the tale to add verisimilitude and to link the strange story to a reality outside Midgleston's mind. There is, moreover, a third party involved in the narrating of the story. This is a first informant, who tells the narrator his suspicions about Midgleston prior to the narrator's first encounter with his hero. All in all we thus get three interpretations of the same character and of his attitude to life. The narrator, who listens to two versions of the story and meets the actual character, attempts in the narrative as a totality to reconcile the opposing views and reach a more mature and 'true' understanding of Midgleston's experience and decision to quit his former life.

'Artist at Home', with its insistence that the narratee 'listens' and 'understands' is also a unique story in Faulkner's career, and it is hard to see that such a story in any meaningful way could he described as a novelist's short story; although it most certainly is an artist's short story about art, about creation. This story, as well as many others discussed in the preceding pages, are told in brief narratives because the story is brief in itself. In addition, the mode of narration – often a narrator limited in insight or completely omniscient and therefore free to select whatever he wishes to delete or include – makes it evident that the discourse-time becomes shorter than the story-time. Even when retrospection or anticipation (prolepsis/analepsis) are used, the narrative remains brief because only that which bears upon the significant elements of the story proper is included.

Faulkner wrote most of the stories in this period in times of relaxation and economic need between novels; some of the stories he only revised from unsold typescripts from 1926 and 1927 (probably). His concentration on the long narrative, and then on the short narrative, might be indicative of an attempt to keep the two related genres apart. And it is true that the short stories of the Major Period are more autonomous than those of any other period; despite his cyclical habit of mind, Faulkner was less eager to change the stories into longer narratives than was the case later on in his career.

5. Short Stories 1928–1932
Man's Nature and Man in Nature

I want to perform something bold and tragical and austere he repeated, shaping the soundless words in the pattering silence, *me on a buckskin pony with eyes like blue electricity and a mane like tangled fire, galloping up the hill and right off into the high heaven of the world*
– Faulkner, 'Caracassonne'

Faulkner's major concern in his short fiction is not with form and experimentation. His concern is not 'with manipulating his characters nor with documenting the stages in their development', as Olga W. Vickery puts it.[1] His chief interest is nonetheless in people. He assumes that people are capable of all things, yet he has given his people – 'flesh-and-blood people that will stand up and cast a shadow'[2] – their autonomy, and concentrates on exploring and understanding their behaviour. Some of Faulkner's recurrent patterns present conflicts between individual human beings or between an isolated individual and a group. Stories with such a conflict pattern may, indeed, be regarded as a formulaic construction where the author leans back and manipulates his characters. Yet the characters are 'quite real and quite constant ... the character I don't forget, and when the book is finished, that character is not done, he still is going on at some new devilment that sooner or later I will find out about and write about.'[3] Faulkner's life-long interest was in 'all man's behavior with no judgment whatever'.[4] To render man in his ageless struggle, to catch the fluidity of human life and arrest its motion for a moment, Faulkner explored the limits of story-telling techniques, but since the stories always had a solid kernel substance, he succeeded in keeping the precarious balance between substance and presentation.[5]

In the preceding chapter we have seen how in a number of Faulkner's short stories from the Major Period, people yield to the pressure of their environment or their troubled selves. They cannot solve their conflicts, and they are unable to endure their situation. Other characters, whether

157

they dream of a past that cannot be recaptured or about an immortality that cannot be reached, may be said to use their dreams as a means of survival, but hardly in order to *escape* from life and the problems they face. The various defence mechanisms applied by numerous Faulkner characters in many critical situations *could* be called an avoidance or escape from reality, but they could also be regarded as mechanisms necessary to help them endure and last through the critical phases of their lives.

It is thus obvious that what appears to be a pair of antithetical terms – endurance and escapism – are not exact opposites. Faulkner does not give examples of one positive attitude to life and its opposite. Endurance, despite the author's and his narrators' apparent admiration of it, may be escapism in disguise, and it may also well be that a little escapism is needed to make life endurable. Endurance and escapism are both terms heavily loaded with moral and philosophical significance, and it will to a great extent depend on the kind of context these qualities are displayed in whether any one of them should be regarded as admirable. As individual, personal qualities in the narrow circumscriptions of life within the family or some other small unit, there would probably be less doubt as to their relative value – especially since *escapism* normally is used as a pejorative term. The question remains, however, to whom endurance and/or escapism is a positive value, and their common definitions are definitely given by those in power at any given moment in time, and, not least significantly, by the myth-makers. Endurance is, for one thing, a quality to be admired in ordinary people, it is a quality assigned to the noble savage, to the poor and ignorant, to those who had better endure their various shortcomings and privations not to disrupt the order of society as it is. Even if it is admirable of the many black characters in Faulkner's fiction to endure and last through all kinds of hardship and humiliation, the time must come when they have endured long enough and when a different attitude takes over. So when *endurance* is used to describe the ability to survive under extreme social circumstances, the implications go beyond those normally found in the term. Used about people's stubborn resistance to pressure and hardship when the causes for their predicaments cannot easily be found, or about personal perseverance and ability to hold on in critical phases of one's life, the term may well be understood as a positive human quality.[6] If *endurance* is used to define man's positive and fruitful relationship to nature (in a wide

158

meaning) and understanding of his place in the great chain of being, in the ordering of nature, then the word becomes more useful and would be applicable to numerous Faulkner characters. To see endurance as Faulkner's ethic, or as his doctrine of nature,[7] is to remove Faulkner's characters from their social context, from their life, not in nature, but among men. Endurance and perseverance, escapism and cowardice, may all be used to describe man's nature, but Faulkner's own work proves beyond any possible doubt that man's nature is not something given *a priori,* once and for all. Man's nature is culture-relative, it is not anthropological, and it changes as history and society change. To hold that all 'non-endurance is rooted in cowardice', is, indeed, not to understand man and his motivations, and it is – which is worse – a critical misunderstanding of Faulkner and *his* view of man, change, history, society, humanity.[8] The term 'endurance' will here be used to refer to any Faulkner character's ability to balance his zest for life, his inherent greed and competitive spirit, with consideration and respect for his fellow beings. Endurance is also the quality that makes it possible for an individual to face indifferent nature, to survive hardships, without ever giving in to fatalism, without ever attempting to escape.

Escapism, on the other hand, is to avoid challenges, shy away from problems and conflicts, flee the hardships of everyday life and the burdens of critical situations, either by retreating into oneself or simply by leaving all problems for others to solve.

Closely related to the question of endurance is the theme of injustice, which also recurs in Faulkner's stories from this period. It is clearly linked to the author's outrage at seeing man waste his opportunities of having a good life. This outrage is especially strong in this period in Faulkner's career. The outrage finds an outlet in fiction that is critical of social institutions, accumulation of power and the misuse of it, and of traditions that limit man's possibilities of growth and development. This is demonstrated on many different levels in Faulkner's stories. The World War I stories and the stories located in the small town – often Jefferson itself – are prime examples of man's greed, envy, and evil. The village stories also show how respectability and the fear of what people may say, limit people's freedom. Conformity is responsible for many a crisis in the village short stories. The wide and ambiguous theme of 'man's injustice to man' may be made more specific if we talk about man's use of man for his own private and selfish ends. The apparent need to control other people, the reification of them, together with a constant struggle for material prosperity and personal gain are all elements of an incessant fight for power which is central in stories like 'Doctor Martino', 'Fox Hunt', 'Elly', and 'The Brooch'. Faulkner also describes power and misuse and corruption in a number of comic stories, and he thus cleverly reduces some of the brutality and murderous desire for power by introducing unbelievable bargains, incredible shrewdness and unlimited greed in a framework of light and good-humoured saturnalia. This is seen, for example, in 'Spotted Horses', and also in the World War I story, 'Thrift', and, less significantly, in 'Death Drag'. Bargains may involve lies and deceit, and be used to gain economic power, as in 'Lizards in Jamshyd's Courtyard' – and in 'Spotted Horses' for that matter. Even if it fails, the same kind of careful scheming and planning to gain personal profit is seen in 'Centaur in Brass'. The common denominator for all these stories is of course Flem Snopes, and one should accordingly not be surprised to see how money and profit at any cost are central in them. Rapacity and greed, almost invariably linked to a dream of improving one's social position, are typical characteristics of the Snopeses, and since they as a rule pay no attention to other people's miserable conditions (cf. Flem and Mrs. Armstid in 'Spotted Horses'), the consequences are tragic and may indeed be seen as man's deliberate use of man, through shrewd and secret bargains and through a clever exploitation of the weak points in one's fellow men. When pure power – power to rule and judge and decide and demand everything – is sought through violence, threats, deceptions and bribes, a much more bleak and pessimistic picture of man and man's nature is the result. Faulkner wrote a few stories where man's propensity for evil and his willingness to use it whenever he finds his position threatened are focused on. 'A Justice' is such a story about man's *Wille zur Macht,* and it is probably not incidental that Faulkner has placed this tale of misused power, of corruption and murder, in the past, and also has sifted the tale through the conscience of a child narrator who only later will understand what he was told because the grim and humorous tale eludes him. Neither is it incidental that the story is one of Faulkner's relatively few Indian stories; not only because governmental power could be observed and scrutinized within the limitations of a small tribe, but also because the evil acts and the desire for power seem to be by-products of a culture almost forced upon the 'natural' Indians by the white men.

'Red Leaves', another Indian story, seems to imply that man is doomed because he opposes some evident law of nature.

In 'Red Leaves' the juxtaposition of nature and culture is significant. The recurrent and obvious contrast between country and city, the South and the North, the wilderness and the wasteland in many Faulkner's stories must also be studied.[9] Changes in the social environment are shown to have influence on people's lives and attitudes, and in a few stories we may even see nature explicitly fighting culture, or culture destroying nature ('Black Music', 'The Hound', 'Crevasse', to mention a few). Nature is not only a positive element being destroyed by men because of their hunger for profit. Nature can be terrifying and drive people insane; and a little cultivation of nature is needed to create livable conditions for human beings. Parallel to Faulkner's many descriptions of man in nature are numerous descriptions of 'nature in man', or, rather, man's nature, which, indeed, could need a little culture and civilization. To destroy nature is also to overcome nature; i.e., to suppress the unsound and destructive forces in oneself to become more considerate and moderate. This duality of the term 'nature' is exploited very carefully and cleverly by Faulkner in a good many stories, and he has excellent material for an investigation of man's nature, morals, and culture, since he has as many as three different races at various stages in their development present within the borders of his imaginary kingdom.

Faulkner's two Indian stories from this period give examples of an old and more natural way of life corrupted little by little by white influence and by the institution of slavery. 'A Justice' contrasts the old life style and the old ways of life in the Indian community – beliefs, traditions, customs – with a modern understanding (Quentin's) and a modern world of the time of narration.[10] In 'Red Leaves' the historical development of the Indian tribe is given in a capsule story, while the rest of the short story is located in ancient days in Yoknapatawpha, even if the events of this story are later than those of 'A Justice'.

Many related themes are thus found in the stories from this period, and the narratives display a multiplicity of forms. Faulkner's themes – at least if set forth in general terms – remained stable over the years, but the variation on the level of narration is significant if not dramatic. He repeatedly stated that his primary aim was to get a story told; that his interest was not with form or technique in themselves. In 1956 Jean Stein

161

asked him what technique he used to arrive at his standard (of which he had just spoken in the interview). Faulkner answered:

Let the writer take up surgery or bricklaying if he is interested in technique. There is no mechanical way to get the writing done, no short cut. The young writer would be a fool to follow a theory.[11]

But he admits that 'sometimes technique charges in and takes command'.[12] We should be careful not to accept his statements about technique without serious qualifications. Albeit technique was not his first concern, he became one of the most accomplished craftsmen in the art of the American short story in the twentieth century.

For the most complex stories from the major period, e.g. 'A Justice' and 'That Evening Sun', extensive discussions of the narratives, with particular emphasis on the narrator's position and role, are required, whereas the more straightforward tales can be treated more lightly also in this respect. This principle is, basically, followed in the following presentation and discussion.

'Idyll in the Desert', a story of love and everlasting sacrifice, is saved from becoming melodramatic only by the skilful handling of the narrative. The narrative embroidery in this story is more elaborate than in most of Faulkner's stories, but it is needed to make the tale credible at all. The method is chosen in an attempt to achieve ironical effects and to arrive at some kind of detachment from the main narrative, so that the sentimentality that lies in the story can be avoided or at least played down considerably through the double narrative framework.

'Idyll in the Desert' is mostly told by the mail rider, Lucas Crump, who once got a telegram to send from a young man, Darrel Howes,[13] who had come to a cabin to recover from consumption or die from it. Five days after the telegram was sent, a woman arrives to take care of the young man. Looking after the sick man and doing all the chores in the place, she eventually catches the disease herself while the man gets well and suddenly leaves, without knowing that the woman is sick. The woman stays on in the cabin in order to recover herself. Her reason for not going away is also that she expects Darrel [Dorry] to come back. With a perseverance typical of some of Faulkner's female characters she waits faithfully and patiently as the years go by. Her firm belief in Dorry and her female endurance alone would have been sufficient to keep her waiting for the never-returning lover. Crump is nevertheless instrumental in giving her new hope and hence a reason for waiting so long. Crump telegraphs her *husband,* who then sends money to his consumptive wife on a regular basis, and Crump arranges it so that she believes the money comes from her escaped lover. Crump does more than this: he keeps the woman alive, and he gives her a lie to sustain her through her lonely days. All this points to more than a normal interest for the faithful woman on the part of the mail rider. His endurance is in some ways almost as remarkable as hers. To write letters to the husband of a woman who has been betrayed by her lover and who waits for him, seemingly forever, is in itself quite a unique feat. To write every week for more than seven years reveals a stubborn endurance which is hard to believe. The sick woman and her guardian, Crump, are not the only people who show unmitigated endurance in this story. The husband's attitude and sacrificial perseverance may even be said to surpass the other persons'. Loyal, apparently faithful, without hope of any reward or of ever getting his wife back, he sends the money asked for and never mentions her betrayal.[14] Yet the woman is the one who really gives all to love; she has risked everything on one card, she has sacrificed all in her pursuit of love, and, having lost and knowing it without admitting it to herself, she never breathes a word about her loss. In the eyes of the world, represented by the mail rider, she clings to her hope, admits no defeat, maintains her dream of love untarnished and unravished because her love never had to be tested against the strain and burdens of everyday life. Her relationship to Darrel may have been of the kind you cannot just forget and be done with; at least she may have seen and felt it that way. It seems likely, however, that Dorry fled from what he imagined would be the future of their relationship, when he saw how *reality* would intrude and eventually annihilate the unreality of this illegal liaison.[15]

Dorry not only flees from his responsibilities as a human being and as the woman's lover. Within the framework of the story he flees from the desert and even if he deserts someone by doing so, he escapes from death into life: from solitude and a static life to activity and motion and youth – as represented by his young bride and the rice in their hair in the scene where his former mistress accidentally meets them at the railway station.[16] The story suggests that the idyll in the desert as it existed between Dorry and the woman was unreal and could hardly be transplanted into the real world of cold facts, of money and respectability not the least. Accordingly, and by its very nature, the idyll could not last, and

163

was replaced by the long years of suffering and loneliness. It was also, in the last year of the woman's life, substituted by another idyll, which could last unto death because the relationship that made it possible asked for nothing, demanded nothing, and appeared to be a sublime and rare example of human kindness and of quiet and unobtrusive admiration and love. Crump's eight months of camping in a canyon in the vicinity of the cabin to stay close to the woman during her last days is such an act. Crump's credibility is seriously questioned by the frame narrator of the story, and also by his own inability to stay on the track of his own tale without the help of the narrator. Crump is apt to digress into funny tall tales so that his inquirer (the frame narrator) has to put him on the track again. Numerous humorous devices are also applied to put Crump in a comic light at the conclusion of the story, but even if we only have his own words for what he did to the woman, there is no reason to doubt his selfless behaviour.

'Idyll in the Desert' thus gives three versions of endurance related to romantic and to some degree sentimentalized love. The story is not only a salute to the faithful, self-forgetting soul who never relinquishes the hope of her lover's return and who *endures* till death, but this element is by far the most important one.

A kind of stubborn endurance chosen as the only possible way to cope with difficult circumstances is found in 'A Dangerous Man'. Endurance here is simply acceptance of one's apparent destiny, and it is made possible by regulated habits and self-deception on a large scale. This story about infidelity, gossip, insults, and fist fights changes from its overly dramatic beginning into a story about unsatisfied desires and a quiet acceptance of an inconsequential life. Apart from the opening incident with the 'drummer', the story is about Mr. Bowman[17] – the 'dangerous man', and his wife. Bowman holds a sinecure job as an express agent, and his wife runs the station office for him. She has at one time operated an eating place, but her husband has sold out because of some trouble with an engineer. Even if Bowman in most respects seems to treat his wife condescendingly, and reacts in what Faulkner ironically describes as 'a proper and thoroughly masculine way, co-ordinating to a certain simple masculine creed with a kind of violent promptitude' (*Uncollected Stories,* p. 575), he seems to have settled down to a life with few pleasures, small quarrels, and easy days. He washes the dogs and quarrels with his wife; every day he drinks coffee in the café, buys a magazine – preferably *The Ladies Home Journal*. He reads about how to raise children right, and he still dreams of having children of his own (a son, of course). The fact that the Bowmans have no children is explained by the narrator:

... the very heat of his desire for children perhaps consumed and sterilised the seed in that deep provision of nature's for frustrating them [sic] who would try to force nature beyond her own provisions... *(Uncollected Stories,* p. 580).

Mr. Bowman may have tried to force nature, but at the time of the incidents in the story, he seems to have relinquished whatever hopes he may have had and gets his pleasures from reading about children and child care! He has apparently also more or less given up his wife and their relationship. Despite the opening incident of the story where he helps another man to beat up a drummer who has insulted the wife of that man, Mr. Bowman's wife, 'fullbreasted, broad of hip, duck-legged' *(Uncollected Stories,* p. 578), is having an affair with one of the great womanizers around, and gossip seems to know that Mr. Bowman silently accepts this. This may well be so, since the leisurely, insignificant life Bowman seems to have settled down to, represents a choice on his part. He understands this as a choice not to fight Nature and endure whatever provisions Nature has for him. His endurance is not impressive or admirable, but it represents a decent and necessary way of coping with circumstances beyond his understanding. Mr. Bowman's apparent acceptance of the status quo, of leading an uneventful and inconsequential life within a closed circle of a small community, is reminiscent of Midgleston's life in Rincon. Aside from this, there is little of significance in Bowman's life, and his endurance is not extraordinarily strong, compared to many other characters in Faulkner's fiction. Compared to those who have a stronger motivation for their endurance, or who are better capable of explaining and understanding why they behave in such and such a way, Bowman simply has to find some kind of adjustment to make life endurable. He finds a solution that seems to fit him, especially if he can have a fist and skull fight now and then to break up the monotony of his days.

Some characters seem to be more persevering and patient than others, either because of what may seem to be an inborn or inherited trait, or because they have been conditioned by their upbringing and environment to react in such ways. Their individual situation may further account for the almost incredible stamina they show, and if their endurance has to yield to outside forces, this creates a human drama – at times tragic in its dimensions – that seems to suit the short-story form very well – or vice versa. 'The Hound' is in some ways such a drama, where stubborn endurance through hardships and toil and poverty suddenly yields to inhuman pressure, and a man is compelled to act contrary to his nature and, by implication, contrary to Nature.

The protagonist of 'The Hound', Ernest Cotton,[18] is one of the lowest among the low, poorest among the poor; a loner who can barely make ends meet, a man who has so far been successful in nothing except survival. Cotton is a bachelor,[19] and he lives in a log cabin, floored with clay. His body is underfed, and his only clothes appear to be the overalls he wears daily. He endures his barren, lonely life of hard work and little food and no pleasures because he knows of nothing else: he has an unconscious understanding of his place in the great chain of being, he accepts creaturehood and fights nature without much hope of ever getting more from it than to eke out enough to keep himself alive. If Cotton had been left alone, he would probably have led this same monotonous life of hard labour all his life; he would have endured as thousands of his fellow men have endured in deep poverty without complaints and without being aware of a different, better life. It they by chance became aware of it, which they were likely to do living in deep poverty in the land of plenty, they would more or less stoically accept their social position, their poverty, ignorance, and, in some cases, their being exploited by the rich landowners, as inevitable. They would not be the ones to question the ordering of Nature, nor the ordering of the society of men. Cotton would never have done this either, if he had not been treated inhumanly by his well-to-do neighbour, Houston. Through the conflict with Houston Cotton comes to understand the *injustice* there is in the world, man's great capacity for injustice to other men, especially those *below* him who are already down on their knees. Cotton even seems to think that his poverty is undeserved, since he knows that he works hard, asks for nothing, endures. Naturally and inevitably he comes to hate Houston's dog, which gives the story its title: 'A dog that eat better than me. I work, and eat worse than his dog. . .' (*Doctor Martino,* p. 60). 'The Hound' is in many respects a superb story, central in Faulkner's short-story career as well as in one of his major works in the novel genre, the Snopes trilogy.[20] 'The Hound' is a penetrating and perceptive psychological study of how a man under enormous pressure behaves, and it is also a study in jealousy, revenge, and guilt.

Cotton kills Houston, and the story opens on the very sound of the shot that kills. The omniscient narrator describes Houston as 'that prosperous and overbearing man', and the men who discuss his disappearance seems to agree that 'overbearing' is an accurate description of his behaviour (*Doctor Martino,* p. 60). He is also said to be a secret man, and 'well-fixed as ere man in the county' (*Doctor Martino,* p. 58). He has taken advantage of Cotton by letting a hog of his winter on Cotton's corn; then, when the case was taken to court, he got away with a one-dollar fee.[21] More than this measurable injustice, Cotton feels that Houston has done this on purpose, and he hates seeing the rich neighbour leisurely riding on horseback with his well-fed dog running alongside, while he struggles day in and day out to make ends meet. Cotton may, indeed, have felt that Houston encroached upon him and upon his self-respect.[22] Up to this time, Cotton has accepted his lot and gone about his work without any fuss: he is in the eyes of the local people and the narrator a mild man in worn overalls, but even to his patience and endurance there is a limit. One might argue that Cotton in anger and hatred lost his perspective and moral judgment, but in his undefined and limited set of clear-cut values he senses that there is no other solution to the problem with Houston than to kill him. All the injustice Cotton has ever experienced becomes embodied in Houston, and killing him is the only way Cotton can maintain his dignity and even restore some of his pride. Houston has disrupted and in a sense destroyed Cotton's world, and it would not be possible for him to go on doing what he had done up to this point without some kind of reaction. His patience and his endurance came to an end, but it would be wrong to think of his murder as a form of escape. Cotton will have to endure more hardships because of his crime.[23] Before detection, he does everything conceivable in a traumatic fight with nature to conceal what he has done.

'The Hound' centres more and more on Cotton's behaviour as the story progresses. His vain attempts to calm down after the murder, his symbolic washing of shoes and shotgun, his relentless and terrifying struggle with the decaying corpse, his own frailty, his guilt, and his human dignity are important and central elements in the story. Interwoven in the probing and penetrating psychological description and analysis of the mind of a common, hard-working man, forced to become a murderer through circumstance, is the background story, which seems to indicate that to any unprejudiced observer Cotton is a sympathetic character. This does not mean that murder is condoned or accepted in the story – the course of events is in itself proof of this as Cotton lives in Hell from the very moment when he hears his shot. Nor does the text leave any doubt about the premeditation of the act. Yet there are mitigating or extenuating circumstances in Cotton's background.

Cotton has a vague understanding of what he deserves, and what is just and unjust. He knows that he has done his best, kept within his limits and possibilities, and hence he cannot accept encroachment or intrusion by somebody else. The necessity for maintaining his pride and dignity and the need to ascertain that he was right in killing Houston come through a number of times; e.g. in his incoherent, almost insane and repetitious statements to his fellow prisoners. It becomes vitally important to Cotton to prove that he did succeed as a killer, and that he suffered defeat only when nature itself played a trick upon him and the corpse started falling into pieces. In the very last sentence of the story he is seen clinging to a last straw; his presumed superiority as a white man compared to the negro prisoners. Cotton fails in whatever he tries to do, or so it seems to him. Even his attempt at committing suicide is discovered and stopped, the hound is still alive, Houston's body is found, and prison waits. His sense of injustice and of his own worth is all the same intact.

The patient and unrewarding work as a farmer has taught Cotton to expect little, and it has taught him endurance. In the struggle to bury Houston's body, Cotton finds himself in what appears to be an inescapable trauma, a nightmare where even nature resists what he is doing. Despite his final failure, the lasting struggle, which is combined with a strong feeling of guilt, is another example of perseverance and single-mindedness. The problem of evil and guilt and the question about what it takes to make a man kill under a given environmental pressure, are both at stake in this story. 'The Hound' also demonstrates that normality is highly relative, and that a mild man who is talking quietly with his neighbours not only may be thinking about killing one of them, but potentially *is* a killer. Cotton may well be feeling guilt, and the hound itself takes on a symbolic quality to represent this guilt, but he nevertheless sticks to his personal understanding of right and wrong, just and unjust, and even when imprisoned he still thinks that Houston deserved what he got. So Cotton makes no attempt to escape his evil deed, and through the last scenes in the story a kind of stubborn persistence and patience are felt.

Technically 'The Hound' is a simple narrative. It is told by an omniscient narrator, who finds it useful and relevant to restrict his story to comprise almost exclusively the elements that can be observed from Cotton's point of view. In large parts of the story we are taken inside Cotton's mind and allowed to follow his thoughts and reactions, his excuses and justifications. The reader has to live along with Cotton, not only in the very act of committing murder, but also with his tortured, agonizing thoughts afterwards. But Cotton is also seen from the outside by the narrator, as a member of the gossiping group outside Varner's store or as a prioner at the end of the story. Yet we experience Cotton's incoherent thoughts now that he is on the brink of insanity, apparently as he lives through them, and the narrator thus manipulates the distance between the readers and the story he is narrating to enhance effectiveness of this story of self-torture and guilt. Moreover, he succeeds unusually well in the shifts between the outside world and Cotton's mind, and uses nature imagery very deftly, to create a dense and rich story that would later play such a prominent part in one of Faulkner's masterly works in the novel genre.

Endurance is often assigned to the white-trash population in Faulkner's stories, as an admirable part of their lives and social behaviour. Endurance in its most magnificent and admirable form seems likewise reserved for the least cultured and most oppressed races. In Faulkner's fiction this would mean the Negroes, and, in a few stories, the Indians. Proverbial Indian calm, patience and perseverance play minor parts, however. The prime example of endurance is, as Faulkner himself indicated in his Appendix to this novel, Dilsey in *The Sound and the Fury*. Dilsey's endurance and all her other qualities and her wide and deep understanding of life and eternity are too complex to be taken up here, but it might be worthwhile to mention that Faulkner wrote 'They endured', and not 'She endured' in the Appendix.

Some kinds of endurance may prove to be escapism in disguise upon closer scrutiny. Miss Jenny in 'There Was a Queen' is often regarded as an outstanding representative of traditional Southern womanhood – a lady who survived the war and brought with her the best of the old society into the modern world of this century. On first glance, the title of the story seems to fit the contents and to be actually true, taken at face value. 'Queen' is necessarily a positive attribute, but it need not be unqualifiedly so, and although admiration certainly is a part of the picture given of Miss Virginia Du Pre, she has after all become *was'*, and it would be strange if lamentation of a loss, resulting in cheap sentimental nostalgia, was the main emotional impact of the story, even if Miss Jenny had *endured* to become *was*. Things, persons, objects, and institutions which have become *was* and no longer *is* in Faulkner's use of these terms, had better be accepted as a necessary part of a world at change. Change, on the other hand, need not be for the better, and progress can be bought too dearly. Yet Faulkner's vision of human life proves in itself that some things had better change if a better world shall be possible, and fallen monuments of value should be used as materials for the building of the new society. Traditional values, when tested and found genuine, ought to be kept alive, but always under close surveillance not to hinder the positive values in the new and progressive development replacing them. Miss Jenny is a kind of embodiment of the best traditional values, and she is clearly celebrated because of this role and because she has endured all kinds of hardships and has become an anachronism without complaining.[24]

Miss Jenny changes over the years, especially if we look at her character as it develops in the novels where she appears, but she keeps her dignity and self-respect through all the sad events in the Sartoris family. In 'There Was a Queen' Jenny is compared to Narcissa, who has only been married to a Sartoris. The two women have their widowhood in common, and both have refused to re-marry; Narcissa in spite of Jenny's having urged her to do so. Narcissa hides behind her status as a widowed mother – her son protects her in various ways. She thus escapes or avoids the demands and hardships of the outside world, and when the old story with the infamous letters from Byron Snopes comes to the surface again, she chooses respectability before virtue and finds what appears to be the easiest way out of her dilemma.[25] Miss Jenny never could do such a thing: one might accuse her of being totally unaware of the more sordid aspects of life, but simply by being a Sartoris, a fixed code of behaviour is given her by tradition, and she never deviates from her assigned role. Miss Jenny endures her long, long years of widowhood and looking after the Sartorises who need looking after, sacrificing herself to the demands of her clan. Her endurance is thus partly a result of her being a Sartoris, and it has come to her through heritage as well as through environmental expectations and pressure. She has also had to endure because of the circumstances her mature life began under: she was widowed at the beginning of the Civil War at the age of 23, and she moved from Carolina to Mississippi in 1867, according to the short story.[26] The story deals with events leading up to and including the death of Miss Jenny,[27] and it gives in retrospect a description of how Miss Jenny came from Carolina a long time ago as well as the story of Narcissa toward the end of World War I, including the infamous letters which form the logical basis for the crucial and fatal confrontation between the two ladies in 'There Was a Queen'. These retrospective parts thus provide the background and past events which set the stage for the small-scale human drama witnessed in the story, but they also furnish sufficient information to form a judgment of Miss Jenny and her life. What we eventually get in the story is a final and admittedly dark picture of the end of a legendary family, the Sartorises, and not even Miss Jenny's endurance and sacrifice had thus been enough to save this family.

All the same, Miss Jenny is in many ways an unacknowledged perpetuator of a tradition, and she is this because she has given herself completely to the 'family and clan culture of the old South', as Melvin Bradford quite accurately puts it.[28] In such an interpretation Faulkner's ideal women become the 'natural keepers of community and of its vehicle, the family'.[29] Miss Jenny is, however, less of an ideal in this respect than critics have found her to be. She never remarried, and she has never been a mother. Her role as a keeper of the community has been far less important than it might have been, if the ideals had been different and her female role did not curtail her possibilities of choice so severely. Furthermore, Miss Jenny's understanding of herself as a Sartoris also puts certain limitations on her, and being fenced in by all these expectations and ideals, she has fared rather well after all. Miss Jenny obviously had a choice to break out of the sacrificial role as aunt and keeper of male Sartorises, and by not doing so she not only endures and lasts in a traditional role as conveyor of certain values from one generation to the next; she also avoids or escapes the changing, eventful, brutal yet beautiful life in a teeming outside world. Jenny lives within her limits and limitations, and her success is moderate if not great, but by doing so she avoids or misses all the challenges and valuable hardships and strains of living among people who may be inferior to her family and the values she believes in, but who actually are better off than a *Miss Sartoris* could ever be.

In 'Evangeline', probably the best of Faulkner's stories not published till *Uncollected Stories of William Faulkner,* different kinds of endurance with their basis in a traditional understanding of honour and pride and 'the Sutpen ways' are presented. Judith Sutpen [Bon] endures her long years of widowhood after her husband was killed by the last shot fired in the war, and her fate is possibly more tragic than that of Miss Jenny. Judith became 'a widow without having been a wife' (*Uncollected Stories,* p. 584), since her husband, Charles Bon, left immediately after their marriage to participate in the Civil War. Up to 1863, Judith's mother was alive, but from then on Judith was alone on the Sutpen plantation. Life was hard, but simple: they buried the silver and ate what they could get. Yet Judith did not worry or complain: she apparently felt that Charles would be back, together with her brother Henry, she hopes, with whom he rode off to fight for the Confederacy. Her father, Colonel Sutpen, is of course also fighting in the war.

... Judith stayed in the house, looking after the niggers and what crops they had, keeping the rooms fresh and ready for the three men, changing the bedlinen each week as long as there was linen to change with. Not standing on the porch, looking up the road. Gittin something to eat had got so simple by then that it took all your time .... All she had to do was to be ready and wait. And she was used to waiting by then *(Uncollected Stories,* p. 590).

Judith accepts the waiting, the shortage of food, and the solitude, because of her quiet faith and her almost fatalistic belief that Charles will return safe and sound from the war. Yet she is not surprised when Henry brings Charles' dead body home: the last shot fired in the war had killed him. She locks herself in a room with her dead husband; she is quiet and composed, and laughter or tears will no more be among Judith's emotions. This is not only a result of her widowhood, but rather of her discovery of Charles Bon's secret. Henry had discovered that Charles Bon lived a secret life in New Orleans before the war, and he had therefore broken with his friend. He was too much of a gentleman ever to divulge what he knew to his family, least of all to Judith, who was in love with Charles, and only reluctantly did he accept Judith's marriage to Charles, and rode off to the war with him. Henry had probably hoped

172

that the war would put an end to his and his family's problem, but Charles survived the war. Although Judith does not seem to suspect foul play, the narrator of the story thinks that Henry killed Charles – when he finally grasps the meaning of the buried truths that are revealed to him little by little as the story progresses.[30]

Judith discovered her husband's secret during the night she spent with his dead body in the room that she had kept ready for him while she waited during the long years of warfare and hardships; the narrator discovers the same secret some 60 years later in the ruins of the burned Sutpen house. Charles had carried Judith's picture with him in a metal case when he rode off, and Judith opened the case during the night that changed her completely, only to bang it shut, and later keeping it to herself. In the concluding paragraphs of the story, the narrator discovers that Judith found the picture of Charles's New Orleans wife, who is part Negro, in the frame. Judith suffers, but keeps the grief to herself. She behaves honourably and stoically. She gets in touch with Charles's New Orleans wife, sends her money, and invites her and her son to the plantation where Charles is buried. She does all this out of a strange understanding of her duty to her dead husband, despite his betrayal, and because she is a Sutpen.

Judith goes about her work and lives in decent poverty till she dies some twenty years after Henry brought Charles's body home. In the meantime she also buries her father, and when she feels that her time has come, she has a message sent for Henry. An old Negro woman, Raby, who is also a Sutpen, takes care of her in her last months, before Henry comes to live on the plantation. Judith had done her best to keep the secret about Charles hidden. She pulled herself together and showed no emotions when she discovered her husband's betrayal. She endures; she acts honourably and sees to it that the family name as well as the family place are kept in relatively good shape. As the years go by, she becomes terribly tired, and when she is gone, Henry takes over the Sutpen heritage. He endures on the plantation for forty more years, without anybody except his Negro half-sister knowing that he lives at the place. The business with Charles Bon and his bigamy is unbearable to 'a Henry Sutpen born, created by long time, with what he was and what he believed and thought' (*Uncollected Stories,* p. 609), and he had to put an end to Charles when the war failed to do so. Most unbearable is, of course, the fact that Bon's New Orleans wife is an octoroon. After this

173

discovery brother and sister had no choice but to endure and last. The shame could not be mentioned; they could not begin new lives. Being Sutpens they had to stick to what they considered to be Sutpen ways and act accordingly.

This strange story about the tragic lives of Judith Sutpen and her brother, shows a kind of stupid, remorseless, and inevitable endurance, which has its basis in what these persons consider to be their duty as Sutpens. Judith and Henry live by very strict and rigid codes. Being Sutpens, their expiation, suffering and endurance apparently cannot be avoided.

There is, however, one more person in the story who endures over a longer period of time than the two Sutpen children. This is the Negro woman, Raby, who is 'a regular empress, maybe because she is white' (*Uncollected Stories,* p. 585), as Don tells the narrator. Raby endures all hardships and helps Henry in his secret life, with the same loyalty and dedication that she gave to Judith when she was alive. When the narrator asks her why she has done all this for Henry Sutpen instead of living her own life, she answers quietly: 'Henry Sutpen is my brother' (*Uncollected Stories,* p. 604). To her, there had been no choice but to do her duty and endure.

Judith, Henry, and Raby – all Sutpens – come to life in 'Evangeline' through a narrator who desperately tries to piece together the bits of information he has, in order to understand the significance of his own story. Finally, he seems to grasp the significance of it all, and then he understands that Henry, Judith, and Raby had to act the way they did, given the time, the tradition, and the beliefs they had in common. The endless patience, the stoic endurance, and the sacrificial nature of what they had done, baffle the narrator. He understands that their reactions were 'normal' and inevitable because he senses what made and moulded these characters. He does not see clearly, however, that their endurance is a kind of avoidance or escapism: although he indicates that Raby could have acted differently and chosen a more rewarding way of life.

The Sutpen 'family secret' is too dark to be revealed to a misunderstanding outer world, because the Sutpen name must be kept bright and stainless. Instead of burying the past and setting their lives in order after the war, the remaining Sutpens choose withdrawal from life and a life lived in so complete secrecy that the surrounding world must think that they are dead. Raby's behaviour is a combination of an active life in the

174

changing and challenging world of the living, *and* a life in and with the past; a past that she hopes to bury before she dies herself.

In the raging fire that destroys the Sutpen house, one small piece of property is not destroyed: the picture case. It provides the missing link to the past, and it tells about miscegenation, racial prejudice, incredible pride and stubborn resistance to change. Personal endurance, even when the consequences are as tragic as in this story, may still be admirable, but all in all 'Evangeline' indicates that the motivating forces behind this endurance are destructive. The narrator indicates that in 1925 things have changed for the better, whereas the Sutpen attitude to life implies resistance to all change and therefore is a negation of life itself.

Miss Jenny in 'There Was a Queen' functions better in relation to her family tradition than any of the Sutpens, probably because the two traditions are different, but also because she becomes a part of a living tradition where new generations are born and must be taught the code, with the necessary adjustments because the society they live in has changed. Judith and Henry can only live down the shame they feel so strongly, and while Jenny does her best to perpetuate the family and clan culture of the South, the Sutpen characters can only sacrifice their lives to a lost and doomed variant of that culture. They escape the demands for change and adjustment. Thus they become dead while still being alive, and the qualities they exemplify – loyalty, pride, endurance – must definitely be used in the pursuit of other goals to become admirable.[31]

Faulkner's short stories from the village have much in common, although the narrative distance is varied from story to story, and the reliability of the narrators varies. In order to look more closely at Faulkner's story-telling strategies in these stories, 'Hair' may be used as an illustration. It is the most typical gossip story in Faulkner's career, and the conclusion of the story leaves no doubt about the first-person narrator's lack of insight and understanding. 'Hair' also indicates that first-person narration does not necessarily imply short distance to subject and character, but it also demonstrates the author's attempts to solve the problem of the limitations of point of view inherent in this kind of narrator. In point of fact, a different point of view (which even a first-person narrator could have been given) would have solved the problem of information and knowledge and created reliability and credibility.

The first-person narrator of 'Hair' is a travelling salesman in 'work-

175

shirts and overalls' (*These 13*, p. 216), who only in this respect, resembles the great Faulknerian story-teller Ratliff.[32] The narrator of 'Hair' is a married man, who has a daughter of his own; and this piece of information is important in the greater design of the story: the narrator's misunderstanding and faulty judgment is partly a result of his fear that his daughter might one day act and behave like Susan Reed.

This first-person narrator tells the story from beginning to end, and although he gets much of his information from other persons and from observation, he alone is the one who tells us what 'they' told him. The manner of narration, the personal idiom, the private moral deduced from the story about Hawkshaw, all belong to the first-person narrator. Only in the last part of the story, when the conversation with Judge Stevens is narrated, does the narrator allow the Judge's own words to become part of his story. Fragments of gossip in the barber's shop have also been presented in this fashion, but the point of view, the angle of vision, is the limited one of the first-person narrator. Because of his job and a propensity for gossip, combined with an inborn curiosity, he accumulates information but does not increase his understanding. The story about Hawkshaw and Susan Reed is the product of the narrator's rather limited total understanding, and yet there is more to it than this. The narrator reveals some of his prejudice, and the denouement shows that he has misinterpreted everything that he has watched and speculated upon. This does not come as a surprise to the reader, since the authorial silence has prepared him for such a conclusion. This is not paradoxical: authorial silence does not necessarily mean that the implied author's attitudes and judgments cannot be felt and seen between the lines, beneath and above the speculations of the narrator. One might call it irony, possibly dramatic irony, but Booth has found that 'secret communion' sometimes goes on between author and reader,[33] and 'Hair' may be seen as a rather direct and not very subtle use of this device, which Faulkner employs in a persuasive manner in Jason's section of *The Sound and the Fury*.

'Hair' indicates that the matter of first-person narration is not as simple as it may appear to be at first glance. The narrator of 'Hair' excuses himself towards the end of his story by saying that 'I guess maybe a talking man hasn't got time to ever learn much about anything except words' (*These 13*, p. 210). His curiosity and his interest in people should not be underrated, and his propensity for gossip and story-telling are not unequivocally useless, in spite of his lack of insight. In contrast to his narrator, Faulkner knew that the arrangement of a story, the control of perspective and atmosphere, the omission of detail and the expansion of important events, are very important. The fallible narrator of 'Hair' is too easy to condemn, the communion behind his back almost too obvious, and more complex and involved manners of narration had to be used, even in the presentation of the village people and their uneventful lives. The narrator's propensity for guesswork and approximations proves that he does not try hard to reach an understanding of the significance of his own story. Thus the narrative inconsistency underscores the theme of the story, which also proves the narrator's incapability to grasp the meaning of his own experience, observation, and narration.

Despite the misconceptions about Hawkshaw and the gossip about Susan Reed – whom he actually marries – the narrator reveals some inadvertent sympathy for the barber. This is mostly so because he half-heartedly admires his stamina. Yet Hawkshaw is capable of sacrifice, love, compassion, patience, and a stubborn endurance which the narrator cannot possibly grasp. Many a Faulkner character goes quietly about his work, adjusting his life in accordance with some kind of established design or plan which is worthy of sacrifice and painful endurance. These characters are all the same scarce, and when one appears in a small town like Jefferson, he is bound to be misjudged.

One might expect that 'Honor' would also include some reference to, or description of, endurance. It does so only in a very limited sense, as we have discussed earlier, and Monaghan's drifting about to maintain his personal integrity may be more of an escapist attitude than endurance in the normal meaning of the term. The many characters who break loose after defeat and yield to a fatalistic attitude could not possibly be described as enduring. Endurance implies an understanding of one's own place in the order of things – either one's significance as a human being in the great chain of being, or one's position in the society of men. Endurance also implies man's adaptability and adjustability; without being able to change and grow with the changing world while not obliterating oneself and one's beliefs, endurance is worth little. It may be remarkable and admirable simply by being endurance, but its value, both to the individual displaying it and to society may be disputed.

The power inherent in tradition and establishment and accepted conduct is very strong, and to resist this power is to resist the forces of

177

socialization.Defeat is almost inevitable, and this is in itself indicative of the enormous powers of conformism and respectability. Faulkner, or his narrators, rather, do not necessarily question the traditional pattern of social regulations, but the rigidity and self-importance with which grown-ups expect the younger generation to adjust are criticized. If the old ways of organizing one's life were the best, people should be allowed to find out for themselves, and there would be no danger in letting them do so. The reluctance to change and experiment found in the people of Jefferson thus indicates that they fear that freedom to choose and to look for oneself might endanger the stability of the traditional system, simply because young people might find it not to be the best of all possible worlds.

A part of this traditional system has to do with the place and function of women in society. Maternal power is highly valued, and for some women this power turns out to be their only power when faithless husbands leave them for 'liberty' or other women. In 'The Brooch' maternal power is misused from the time of birth to take complete command over the son, and it seems evident that this power is used, with tragic results, to make sure that the mother is never again left alone by a man. This power, when carefully used, seems stronger than the younger woman's power to beguile and lure men. 'The Brooch' is, one should keep in mind, a rather peculiar story in Faulkner's career, and one should not draw hasty conclusions on the basis of this story alone.

How social position can be used with devastating effect is seen in 'Dry September', where Minnie uses the power of her social prestige and of racial prejudice in a last desperate attempt to force people to take notice of her. As a white woman of good (though not the *best*) social standing, Minnie can exploit the respect which any white woman of a certain quality deserves, and she can rely on the racial hatred alive in the community to achieve the effect she wants. She reveals no concern whatever about the consequences of her lies; to her it is only important to prove her value and, for the final time, have someone react to her femininity. This female power, which is assigned to most women in the better social layers of these traditional communities without any reservations, is misused time and again – often simply because it is misunderstood by the women themselves. Miss Emily uses her power and the respect and privacy she is entitled to, to conceal a deadly crime and to keep a man forever; Mrs. Compson uses her position as *wife* and member of a rich family to get rid of Nancy, the reserve cook, even when she knows that Nancy is scared to death and has every right to be so. Mrs. Compson fakes illness and gives her husband to understand that he has to choose between taking care of his lawfully married wife properly and helping a 'nigger'.

Time and again the consequences of misused power are in shocking disproportion to the gain. By being less selfish and more considerate, much suffering and pain could have been avoided. This is implicitly stated in numerous Faulkner stories. The author demonstrates how the manipulators themselves become manipulated simply through their own manipulations, and that victory on such terms involves a loss of some sort.

'Fox Hunt' involves a struggle for power and control of a more basic kind. In this story the sexual and marital relationship between Mr. and Mrs. Blair is transformed into a mutually destructive relationship because sexual attraction time and again is used to gain power and control. If sex does not result in actual death, it is often seen as resulting in spiritual death in many Faulkner stories, and it serves to create hard and cruel people whose contributions to positive and meaningful human relations are utterly destructive. The struggle for personal profit involves inhumanity and objectification of human beings, and people are easily sacrificed and manipulated to serve the ends of one important character: oneself.

'Doctor Martino' is also a short story where human interrelations are portrayed and scrutinized. The many conflicting interests of the protagonists make all of them incapable of either love, understanding, pity, or compassion. Other people are seen as objects to be used, exploited, and usurped for private and selfish needs. The comedy originally staged, quickly turns into tragedy, and the most destructive character in the story is also the most victorious one. Dr. Martino uses Louise to stay alive. Mrs. King keeps and dominates her daughter and uses Hubert Jarrod for her own ends. Hubert plays around with his swamp angel, and uses both mother and daughter to satisfy his psychological needs. Louise, in a sense, uses Dr. Martino to prove her own fearlessness and importance, and she uses Hubert as an insurance in case Dr. Martino should die. The double conclusion of the story features *hysteria* and *death* and the final comment on the conduct described in the story could hardly be less ambiguous, although the story in itself seems full of unresolved tensions.

Dr. Martino gives the story its title, and yet he only remains a static centre about which everything seems to revolve. His power to control and lead the movements of other characters is nevertheless great, even if it is clearly on the decline. He cannot actively take any sort of action, and he therefore falls prey to the other characters, who both can and will use him and other people, and whose *Wille zur Macht* is just as dominant as his own, but less justified – if the conscious and selfish manipulation and usurpation of other people can indeed be forgivable.

Faulkner seems to take a particular interest in people who are seriously lacking in humanity. These characters seem to be so self-possessed and selfish that they are totally unaware of the existence of other people and unable to understand and treat other people as human beings, with all the implications this has. This means that such characters without regret or pity or a conscience that bothers them can treat other people as objects; simply because to them they exist as nothing but objects. Faulkner also makes it clear that this is a modern phenomenon, and that the preoccupation with money and success in materialistic terms is responsible for this. He also gives funny portraits of old-fashioned characters whose greed and rapacity can hardly be matched.

The proverbial Scotsman in 'Thrift' is such a character. MacWyrglinchbeath tries to make as much money as possible during the war, taking care at the same time to survive so that he can use the money where he belongs – in the Highlands. Contrary to later con-men and thrifty gamblers in Faulkner's fiction, Mac uses himself more than he uses other people in his pursuit of money. He is not only a gambler; he also does his best to make as much money as possible by earning higher wages. This means doing the more dangerous jobs, but he finds what he considers a reasonable proportion between the risk of a certain war-time profession and the payment he would receive, and his middle-way between riskiness and profit proves profitable: he makes a good profit, and he survives the war.

Mac's story demonstrates how thriftiness and greed may work without doing too much damage to other people, if and when the thrifty man is decent and honest and does not give in completely to rapacity. In most cases, money like power seems to corrupt over time, and MacWyrglinch-

180

beath is one of the few Faulkner characters who escape the money-making business without having been changed considerably. He may, in point of fact, be the only character who gives up the profitable business of lending and borrowing, betting and gambling, to settle for a quiet and uneventful life where money is very scarce. Flem Snopes would certainly not have been able to do so, even if he – as Mac had to do after the war – had to return to a less monied area than he had been in.

Before we turn our attention to Flem Snopes, a brief note on one of Faulkner's detective stories must be included. 'Smoke' is Faulkner's first story of detection, and it naturally involves a murder that has to be solved and a murderer who has to be proved guilty and sentenced.

'Smoke' presents a man who has married a single daughter and heiress with the sole purpose of gaining possession of some of the best land in the county. Misusing his wife till she dies, and misusing the land, which can never become his, justice finally catches up with him through a devious agent whose greed for the land, kept at bay but nourished for fifteen years, makes him kill to come into possession of it.[34]

The greed of the usurping outlander and the way he misuses what is only his through marriage and which therefore rightfully belongs to his twin sons, is only one of two different kinds of misuse of power in 'Smoke', although the other one is used to see justice done. Gavin Stevens applies rather doubtful methods in his longwinding attempt to make the murderer reveal himself, and his use of tricks and lies in order to enforce law and justice could only be done by someone thoroughly familiar with the law and with the proceedings in a courtroom. It is thus a mild type of misuse of power, and is of course accepted not only by the narrator (the community 'we' most of the time), but also by the audience, since not only is justice done but truth is also revealed.

The short stories about the Snopes clan form a special and very important part of William Faulkner's short-story achievement, even though these stories are very closely related to some of his novels. All Snopes stories belong in one way or other to the Snopes trilogy, and all of them, with the exception of 'Barn Burning', appear in one of the three novels. 'Barn Burning' was written as the opening chapter of *The Hamlet,* but was left out of the novel when it was published. A brief reference to the incidents in the short story is retained in the first chapter of the book. 'The Hound' forms one extreme here, since this originally non-Snopes story was included in a collection of short stories before it was extensively revised and used in *The Hamlet*. 'Barn Burning', as we have seen, forms the other extreme. Between these extremes are the other Snopes stories – 'Spotted Horses', 'Lizards in Jamshyd's Courtyard', 'Centaur in Brass', 'Mule in the Yard', 'Fool About a Horse', 'By the People' – which, extensively revised but basically unaltered, form chapters or scenes of *The Hamlet* (three stories), *The Town* (two stories), and *The Mansion* (one story).[35] It should thus be fairly evident that all of these stories stand in a closer and more obvious relationship to Faulkner's novels than do his stories in general and the stories of the 1928–1932 period in particular. Faulkner had been working with the Snopes material as early as in 1927, and it would only be natural if some of the attitudes and sentiments in these stories are similar to those expressed in other stories from around 1930. Since the first Snopes novel was not published till 1940, it is not surprising to find that Faulkner tried to publish scenes or complete incidents from the work in progress as short stories.

Three of the Snopes stories were written in what we have called the major short-story period; viz. 'Spotted Horses', 'Lizards in Jamshyd's Courtyard', and 'Centaur in Brass'.[36] All three contribute significantly to our understanding of Flem Snopes, as they relate central incidents on his way to wealth and social position. All the stories are furthermore the best examples of man's misuse of man and of one man's exploitation of all virtues and vices while he himself stands beyond and above anything faintly resembling virtue.

'Spotted Horses' is an almost tragic study in poverty, suffering and human frailty, exploited to the utmost by a shrewd and inhuman businessman whose only interest is profit. 'Spotted Horses' is certainly also one of the funniest stories Faulkner ever wrote, a classic in American humour, comparable to the best of Mark Twain's tall tales. The tone is kept unchanged and at the same pitch all through the story, so that comic and grotesque elements are juxtaposed with elements of suffering and tragedy. A deep understanding of human frailty and misery pervades this story, in which greed and stupidity, vanity and viciousness come quickly to the surface when the poor population of Frenchman's Bend is given the rare opportunity to buy new horses at a cheap price. There may be something in the strength and virility and wildness of the horses that speaks to something deep and hidden in the men and which compels them to forget everything in order to buy horses and afterwards to chase them about the countryside. The horses are also representative of many other things that would have set the men off hunting in a similar fashion: in their hard and relentless work on a soil that barely yields a living, the horses seem to be part of a better world, an easier life, a dream. Flem Snopes knows exactly what he does when he brings the Texas ponies to Frenchman's Bend, and he has not miscalculated his fellow men.

In the magazine story 'Spotted Horses', a group of listeners in Jefferson are introduced to Flem Snopes and his career so far, and in a few years they will get to know him better than most of them would like. From the long introduction about how Flem came to Frenchman's Bend and what he has achieved so far, a picture of a rapacious, money-obsessed, almost un-human person emerges from the broader outline of the Snopes clan. It appears that Flem in point of fact stands distinctly apart from his own kind, being much worse than any of the other Snopeses because he is much more shrewd and secretive and knows where to find people's weak spots. When the story about the horses is told in all its hilarious fun and outrageous exaggerations and metaphors, the final and very emphatic picture of Flem is one of the 'exploiter par excellence'. No profit is too small for him, and his vicious cunning and lust for money is rendered most dramatically in the story of how he embezzles Mrs. Armstid's five dollars, earned by weaving by night and desperately needed to support her children. Despite some scenes and numerous different and additional thematic implications found in the story, Flem's part in it and the interest vested in him by the narrator (and the author) cannot be emphasized too strongly. The story opens on a statement about Flem, it ends on another, and the whole exposition is devoted to the early phase of Flem's rise to money and power in this backwood area of Yoknapatawpha. Granted that Flem disappears from the scene time and again, but this is simply typical of Flem's shrewdness and secrecy in all affairs. He has to leave the scene of the horses and the auction so that his complicity in the deal is not too obvious.[37]

Flem's rapid rise to power in the countryside of Yoknapatawpha County, his merciless and relentless exploitation of his poor and illiterate fellow men, could only be possible in a permissive society where little social control – formal or informal – is present. The kind of human and social evil Flem represents can only find foothold where stupidity and gullibility join forces with some uncertain wish to ascertain and prove one's masculine strength and male supremacy. The endless struggle to eke out a living from the barren soil may to some extent be responsible for the dream of a better world, of which the horses appear to be representative, and this may help to explain why the men from French-man's Bend waste their money and undertake to catch the horses, putting both themselves and the more innocent bystanders in jeopardy. Part of the tragedy ultimately resulting from the horse sale is that pain is inflicted upon people who have done nothing to be so punished. The Tull episode in all its bizarre humour exemplifies this, as does Mrs. Armstid even more poignantly.

The narrator of the story[38] has been outsmarted twice by Flem Snopes, and among the group of characters not participating actively in the auction, Mrs. Littlejohn – who goes about her work as if nothing had happened – is the only one who can match the horses and, indirectly, not be harmed by Flem. Mrs. Littlejohn and the narrator are passive; they watch, but they do not interfere, and they resemble in many ways the uninvolved, 'innocent', men around the square in 'Dry September'. The passivity and non-interference of those not susceptible to Flem's and the Texan's deceit or the horses' enthralling power are a prerequisite for the success the businessmen have.

The auction, the pursuit of the runaway horses, the suffering but enduring Mrs. Armstid, the seriously wounded Tull and Armstid are all results of one man's wile and deliberate actions. Even if Flem stays away from the auction itself – which underscores his apartness – he is the central character in the story. Towards the end of 'Spotted Horses' he is watched eagerly by all people present, but it is not easy to find out what goes on in his mind. He always acts surreptitiously, and there is nothing showy or ostentatious about him. Everything he does is preposterous. The Texan is deliberately shown to have at least a minimum degree of pity, and this unexpected character trait in such a man is used to put Flem's total lack of any virtue in relief. As R.P. Warren has said, Flem 'stands beyond appetite, passion, pride, fidelity, exploiting all these things'.[39] Flem shows no signs of the normal weaknesses and shortcomings of man. He is in his unfathomed selfishness, in his undeviating course towards money and position and – finally – respectability, beyond good and evil. The inability and apparent unwillingness of society to halt the all-de-structive exploiter pave the road for Flem so that he may use French-man's Bend for his immediate goals, and then move on. The story's conclusion indicates that *he alone* could escape without punishment:

'You boys might just as well quit trying,' I.O. says. 'You can't git ahead of Flem. You can't touch him. Ain't he a sight, now?'

I be dog if he ain't. If I had brung a herd of wild cattymounts into town and sold them to my neigbors and kinfolks, they would have lynched me. Yes, sir (*Uncollected Stories,* p. 183).

During the horse auction and the ensuing pursuit of the 'ponies', Flem indirectly keeps the farmers away from their work on the land; work badly needed to support their families. This is a first, minor, illustration of what a force like Flem can do when it is let loose and *allowed* to function. Natural life becomes corrupted, and Flem is an avatar and a precursor of times to come which will change the whole system of agriculture and social life in general in Yoknapatawpha County, and, for that matter, in the non-fictional world of the South.

Suratt, the itinerant sewing-machine agent, who later was renamed Ratliff and is one of Faulkner's master story-tellers (if not *the* master teller), refers to his having been outsmarted twice by Flem Snopes. The two times this happened are both parts of 'Lizards in Jamshyd's Court-yard', and the events narrated in this story are thus earlier than the horse auction in 'Spotted Horses'. The first bargain in which Suratt was fooled by Flem functions as a kind of background for the second deal: Suratt has a vain hope of getting even with Flem, but he is fooled once more, and this time Flem's victory gives him the foothold in Jefferson which he has been waiting for. Flem's viciousness is less significant in this story, and his shrewdness and cleverness are almost admired. This is possible since the losers in the trade involving a salted gold mine are shown to be so greedy, gullible, and easily fooled as to deserve what they get – with some reservations.

Suratt had been fooled or as he puts it, outsmarted, by Flem Snopes in a goat deal, and he is very anxious to get even with Flem, not least in order to reinforce his own position as a businessman in the district. Suratt is a dedicated salesman, and the narrator, with all his sympathy for Suratt, nevertheless reveals this propensity for trading and bargaining:

He had a regular itinerary, selling perhaps three machines a year, and the rest of the time trading in land and livestock, in secondhand farm tools and musical instruments, or whatever came to his hand (*Uncollected Stories,* p. 138).

Suratt knows that Flem is a shrewd businessmann – he must be since he has beaten Suratt on his own terms – and he is looking for an opportunity to revenge himself on Snopes for the goat business. Flem is smarter than Suratt thinks; he is so smart that he knows that Suratt will try to get even with him, and that Suratt is likely to be interested in any deals Flem makes. Furthermore, Suratt will probably expect some secret reason behind whatever bargain Flem might consider, knowing that Flem does nothing if a profit is not somehow involved. On the basis of this understanding not only of human envy and greed in general but of the itinerant salesman Suratt in particular, Flem can set his trap. Suratt learns that Flem has bought the old Frenchman's Place from Will Varner,[40] and immediately suspects that there must be more to the Frechman's Place than what meets the eye. Suratt's knowledge of Flem's cunning and nose for a profit leads him to believe that a hidden treasure is Flem's reason for buying the place, and he is unable to see that his own reactions are exactly those Flem has planned. Flem leaves nothing to circumstance or luck; his plan includes a prospective buyer as well as the struggle of digging at the place, and the bait is well worth the time and effort it takes to arrange it. Suratt and two companions dig stealthily in the garden at the Frenchman's Place at night, and since Flem has 'salted' the ground, they find gold coins. Blinded by their own lust for money, and, in the case of Suratt, revenge, they find nothing suspicious about the coins or the solid sacks containing them. For the unheard of price of $ 3 000 the companions buy the place; Suratt giving a lien on his half share of a Jefferson restaurant – and Flem is on his way to Jefferson.

Flem is not presented as inhuman, vicious, or cruel in 'Lizards in Jamshyd's Courtyard'. Flem is mostly characterized by his shrewdness in this story, and this shrewdness relies in point of fact on a deep understanding of other men's weaknesses and desires. Flem can exploit these weaknesses, for he himself never succumbs to human feelings – even if *this* story does not make such implications possible. Suratt and Flem are both fond of trading; so they trade, and Flem wins. The very distance there is between Flem and Suratt in this text – it is even greater in *The Hamlet* – is probably chiefly a result of the choice of narrator. The gap between the two businessmen widens as a result of the two deals they have been involved in. Suratt grows in his understanding and in his humanity because of what he experiences with Flem. Perhaps the two losses in bargains with Flem have shown Suratt that one must either stay away from Flem – as he in fact does in 'Spotted Horses' – or take up arms against him and try to halt his corruption of everything and everybody around him. Suratt may well feel that his vanity and stupidity have been instrumental in providing Flem with a foothold in Jefferson, so that his later interest in Flem, as witnessed throughout the trilogy, also stems from a feeling of guilt and responsibility.

The third Flem Snopes story to be mentioned here renders an episode in Flem's early career in Jefferson, and is unique in the way it presents an intricate plot where other people whom Flem is using for his benefit are successful in fooling him. 'Centaur in Brass' is nevertheless another story about Flem's shrewd dealings, which this time are directly illegal and include the participation of other people whose suspicion little by little is aroused. So Flem for once comes out a loser, because the people involved in his stealth – albeit only two and only 'Negroes' – join forces and find out how Flem has played them off against each other for his own personal benefit. Flem is thus by no means invulnerable, and the story about the stolen brass proves this beyond doubt. If people cared and did something *together* instead of jealously guarding their own individual prides and prejudices, Flem and all he represents might have been checked if not exactly avoided. This would also have made it possible for the larger society to control and guide its own development. The revised version of 'Centaur in Brass' – in *The Town* – explicitly states that Flem's *loss,* the brass he never could make a profit from, became nothing but a *footprint,* saying '*This is where I was when I moved again.*'[41]

The deals narrated in 'Lizard in Jamshyd's Courtyard' provided Flem Snopes with a foothold in Jefferson. He could leave Frenchman's Bend, which he had exploited as far as he could hope to do, and which he had in point of fact outgrown. In 'Centaur in Brass' an anonymous person from Jefferson narrates the story, reiterating the little he knows about Flem's background and career and about how he came to own the Jefferson restaurant. The narrator uses the collective 'we' when he renders Jefferson's expectations of Flem and their reactions to his affairs, and – not least – to his wife. Eula Varner (unnamed in the story) is described as possessing 'something of that vast, serene, impervious beauty of a snowclad virgin mountain flank' (*Collected Stories,* p. 151), and it is supposed that she is the reason why Flem is given the job as superintendent at the municipal power plant by the new mayor, Major Hoxey.[42] The fact that Flem and the Major are on amicable terms outrages the town more than the alleged adultery behind Flem's position:

187

It seemed foreign, decadent, perverted: we could have accepted, if not condoned, the adultery had they only been natural and logical and enemies (*Collected Stories*, p. 151).

This reaction on the part of the town is important in the light of what goes on between the Negro characters in the story, and with regard to the almost good-humoured description of Turl, whose tom-catting knows no limits. The Negro husband and the wife's lover reach a kind of understanding and friendship, and this relationship is presented as admirable within the limits of the story. It is, indeed, admirable, even though the friendship results from a deadly fight, because Turl has visited the other Negro, Tom Tom's new wife for a long time, but this fight comes to an end when the two Negroes discover that they have both been used by Flem to pursue his plans. They join forces when they see through his devious plans, and Flem is licked, if not exactly 'killed off' as the *Scribner* editor said.[43] Flem even has to pay money to the city clerk twice, having been caught in the web of his own lies and deceits so that he cannot possibly risk charging Tom Tom and Turl with the disappearance of the brass.

The final brief section of 'Centaur in Brass' emphasizes Flem's defeat; he resigns from the plant and chooses to keep a low profile for some time, biding his time. Flem has to halt his progress for a moment, tending his wounds, before he can move on again. The interesting interpretive problem in 'Centaur in Brass' is whether Flem's defeat is simply a result of coincidence and a series of unfortunate events, or whether the story really demonstrates that there is a limit to exploitation, or that people can avoid him, or even beat him, by sticking together. When Tom Tom's and Turl's lethal fight has come to an end, the two men, exhausted, talk: 'Because there is a sanctuary beyond despair for any beast which has dared all, which even its mortal enemy respects. Or maybe it was just nigger nature' (*Collected Stories*, p. 165). The social conventions that the negroes live by, through inherited tradition and as members of a sub-culture in a predominantly white society, make it impossible for Flem to rely on the Negro characters' respect for 'white' respectability. All these important elements of what we might call social pressure work less effectively with Negroes than with white people, whom you can threaten or force to do various tasks simply by jeopardizing their social position. Owing to their place in the social hierarchy of Jefferson and to what Faulkner's narrator describes as 'nigger nature', Negroes do not pay

188

much attention to respectability. So perhaps Flem simply miscalculated or misjudged his own talents and the hold he assumed he had on Tom Tom and Turl, since he was their boss. Where white men might have succumbed to his threats and to his power, the Negroes finally break loose from him.

Flem Snopes stands above and beyond all human qualities that we normally find admirable. In the trilogy the use of his wife, Eula, and her daughter, Linda, is the ultimate proof of what Flem is willing to do in order to make money, reach a position, become powerful.[44] In other stories the struggle for power is easier to accept and justify, because these stories take place a long time ago when people presumably were less civilized and considerate than we believe ourselves to be today.

By writing his first Indian stories, Faulkner created some new people living within the borders of his fictional kingdom. When he felt the need to establish a chronology or a tradition in a work, the Indians were there ready at hand, simply by being the aboriginal inhabitants of Yoknapatawpha County. It is not till about 1940, with the composition of the stories later constituting *Go Down, Moses,* that Faulkner really sets the Indians in an overall relation to his whole creation and to the moral problems of ownership and slavery.

In 'A Justice', Quentin Compson tells a humorous story, clouded by the introduction of poison and non-hereditary ways of succession to power, and by the implied discovery of moral anarchy.[45] Much of the story centres round three phenomena: Doom's immediate rise to power upon his return from New Orleans; the quarrel and competition about a Negro woman between Craw-ford and the Negro husband, including the cock-fight and the fence-building; and the whole tribe's work to get the steamboat into the camp. Pervading the episodes where it is not predominant, the contest between an Indian and a Negro is the force behind both the humour and the horror found in 'A Justice', especially so since Doom has shown his strength and intends to have control over his subjects.

There is not much point in talking about how the outside, civilized world had corrupted Ikkemotubbe (Doom) and made him the murderous villain who does everything to secure his power and establish a kind of justice within these limits. While the decaying girandoles and the red slippers are effective and unequivocal symbols of corruption of the Indian culture in 'Red Leaves', we have a much more diluted picture of

Doom's return from the outside world in this later story: '. . . when Doom got off the steamboat that night, he wore a coat with gold all over it, and had three gold watches . . . ' (*These 13*, p. 186).

Ikkemotubbe brought six black people with him, including the woman who later gave birth to Sam Fathers, but he did not introduce slavery in the camp. There were already 'more black people in the Plantation than they could find use for' (*These 13*, p. 185); moreover, Ikkemotubbe seems to have been born evil or mischievous. The Man would look at Ikkemotubbe when he was just a boy, and say, 'O Sister's Son, your eye is a bad eye, like the eye of a bad horse' (*These 13*, p. 187). When Ikkemotubbe returns from New Orleans, Herman Basket says that Doom's eyes had not changed after seven years, thus clearly indicating some kind of hereditary psychological cause for his *Wille zur Macht*. The killing of a puppy and of the Man and the Man's son, scaring the Man's brother, Sometime-Wake-Up, to relinquish his position, can thus be given psychological motivation by referring to the inherently malevolent character of Ikkemotubbe. This is hardly the whole truth: the Indian community, life in the wilderness, the desperation over the Negroes, all seem to have led to a moral anarchy where the fittest (i. e., smartest, strongest, least sentimental) survive. Craw-ford has no scruples about killing three white men and sinking them in the river, and it is an Indian pastime to run the black men with dogs, 'like you would a fox or a cat or a coon' (*These 13*, p. 186). There are, however, indications in the story that the Negroes are questioning the way the Indians treat them, and although they hardly think of an uprising, when treated unjustly as individuals, they react. The Negro woman's husband stands up against Craw-ford, backed by his fellow men:

'This woman is my wife', one of the black men said. 'I want her to stay with me.'
'Do you want to be arranged in the river with rocks in your inside too?' pappy said to the black man.
'Do you want to be arranged in the river yourself?' the black man said to pappy. 'There are two of you, and nine of us' (*These 13*, p. 195).

The suggested reading of this conversation, viz. that the Negroes refuse to be treated as slaves, at least in some respects, should not deceive us into believing that this is the only significance of the encounter. The meeting is one instance in a long row of dramatic controversies where *pure power* (the poison, the number of men, the fence-building, or other

190

threats) is used by the strongest party to force their will and wish through. In such an analysis of 'A Justice', *power* becomes not only the way in which an authoritarian personality gains and keeps control of his 'people'; it becomes a treacherous and destructive road to survival. Faulkner's Indians in 'A Justice' are incapable of adjustment to new situations; this is exemplified by the use of genuinely evil persons like Doom, or by a destructive white influence (slavery, luxury, treachery, whiskey). Indian greatness passes away, and is lamented by some of the characters speaking in the stories or narrating them. Faulkner, in the disguise behind a dense layer of narrators, can hardly be accused of lamenting the lost Indians. There may have been a Southern Paradise once, but what Faulkner portrays is a group of people unable to change as the world around them changes, be it for the better or for the worse.

In the numerous episodes where Doom hands out justice in accordance with his own position and in order to secure it further, one should not forget that these episodes are extremely important to the combatants involved in them. The cock-fight and the long-lasting building of the fence, which Craw-ford, helped by Herman Basket, must work on to fence himself out, both reveal a racial Negro-Indian conflict without any whites involved, and although the black woman gives birth to a 'yellow' baby first, the Negro triumphs when he, over the high fence, can show Craw-ford a black baby.[46]

Quentin Compson, who listens to the old tale of power and corruption and strange justice and who narrates the complete story, does not understand the story fully. He knows that his half-knowledge, his suspended understanding, will be overcome later on: 'I was just twelve then, and I would have to wait until I had passed on and through and beyond the suspension of twilight. Then I knew that I would know' (*These 13*, p. 207).

What Quentin does not yet see or understand has more to do with Sam Fathers than with Doom or the rest of Sam's tale. The last paragraph of the story is devoted to Sam, and Quentin's assurance that he will come to understand the strange tale later is not quite satisfactory because Sam will be dead by then. The problem for Quentin involves, among other things, that he must figure out the relationship between Doom and Sam, and he is curious about this, since he senses a strong respect and even admiration for Doom running through Sam Fathers's narrative.

Quentin Compson is the narrator of two important short stories from this period, 'A Justice' and 'That Evening Sun', and in both stories there is a suggestion of initiation, since Quentin narrates stories he has either experienced long ago ('That Evening Sun') or has listened to when other people told them ('A Justice'). The serious problems of a narrative that is a reminiscence of a dream-like past, and the contemporary understanding of this past experience, are presented in 'That Evening Sun', and, to a lesser extent, in 'A Justice'. In the latter story, Faulkner employs the 'carry-over principle', so that Sam Fathers tells the bulk of the story, which Quentin then broods over, knowing that he will grasp the meaning of it only much later, when he has passed through and out of the twilight zone of innocent childhood.

There is more to the narrative strategy of 'A Justice' than this, however. Sam Fathers's story was largely told him by Herman Basket a long time ago, and accordingly the events narrated and the time of actual narration are very far apart. Nonetheless, the very fact that the Indian story is told by Sam Fathers to Quentin Compson, who is the oldest son in the family Sam belongs to, establishes an important link between time past and time present. Quentin's comment on what Sam's story signifies stresses this connection, and the partly ironic 'justice' in the title becomes a moral question seen from two distinctly different points of view. The narrative pattern includes the old man (a clever carpenter, which in Faulkner's language, is exactly what a good story-teller is) telling a tale, almost taking on the quality of a legend, to a young boy, and this tale was once told to him by an old man. The well-known pattern of oral story-telling is thus set up within the story, so that Quentin's parts of the narrative (the first and the last parts) become a kind of frame for the story proper. This is not the whole truth, however: Quentin establishes himself as the narrator in part I; he will tell the story as it was related to him when he was twelve years of age and visited the farm with his grandfather. In other words, an older Quentin tells the whole story, but the parts of it told earlier by others are rendered without intrusion from him. Such a technique allows the reader to mistrust both Quentin's and Sam Fathers's memory. The real events are sifted through three minds and memories for a hundred years. This distance in time makes it easier to accept uncommon and strange events or a different outlook on life, but it also paves the way for a critical understanding where the primary narrator becomes the character of principal interest. In a story where a secondary, 'take-over' narrator is allowed to tell three fourths of the real story, his importance cannot be overlooked, either. What the use of Herman Basket's story as told by Sam Fathers accomplishes, is, among other things, to reduce the unreliability and limitations of the child narrator. The child's limited point of view is also reduced by the very fact that the child narrator is a grown-up when he narrates this childhood reminiscence.

Faulkner wrote stories both in the comic vein and of a more tragic kind to give instances of man's injustice to man and to demonstrate how money, greed, and power corrupt. Flem Snopes is of course the grand character in this respect. Flem feels no solidarity with people of his own class or background, and if he had tried to improve their situation as he moved upwards himself, he would have lost his battle before he started. The very basis for Flem's success, what made it possible for him to become prosperous and wealthy, was in fact the exploitation of his people, of his own class. No deal was too small for Flem, and accordingly his hatred and egotism and inhumanity made him take advantage of everybody and everything.

Flem is the complete and systematical and completely unscrupulous version of a character type we have come across a number of times in Faulkner's short fiction. Flem Snopes and some other members of his clannish family surpass every other character in Faulkner's fiction in exploitation and heartless usurpation of even the weakest and poorest members of their own community. Even if Flem may be seen as an embodiment of much human vice and viciousness, other characters in Faulkner's stories are not much better than he: a number of characters manipulate and use other people for their own profit and benefit, even if Flem's inhumanity is larger, since money and power and social position are his aims and not more 'human' desires such as sexual gratification. But even if evil and greed and rapacity may be inherited and explained by individual psychology, there is little doubt that Faulkner in many of his stories gives descriptions of an environment – a social milieu – where such negative human qualities are given excellent conditions so that they may thrive and multiply.

'A Justice' may be said to portray a natural life, as opposed to the civilized world of a later time when the story is told and retold. The story is focused on power and corruption, and even if the young Quentin Compson reacts immaturely and cannot understand the tale, there is not much in the story to indicate that this is a result of his lack of contact with nature, his having become 'civilized'. On the contrary, the story seems to make Quentin uneasy and set him thinking, because the emotions and reactions displayed by the characters have not changed much over the years, so that Quentin accordingly feels strongly that the tale of the Indians of Yoknapatawpha has something to tell him. His lack of understanding has nevertheless something to do with his being a child of his time: the unguarded, direct, and natural reactions shown by the Indians – and even by the white men at that time – cannot be fully grasped by Quentin, not only because he is young and because he is the Quentin Compson we know from *The Sound and the Fury*; but because he has been conditioned by certain influences and attitudes that belong to his culture or class.

'Red Leaves' is probably the best example among Faulkner's short stories around 1930 of culture's influence on nature; and the story is also about the 'vanishing American',[47] about the declining wilderness, and the emerging of a modern civilization. That it is also possible to see in this story 'a terrifying existential confrontation with the reality of death',[48] does not reduce the significance of the nature-culture conflict which is at the base of 'Red Leaves'. The influence of the greedy white man upon the primitive and natural Indian is also shown, but most important is perhaps that three cultures are juxtaposed in this story. The themes of hunt and escape, of man's ultimate inability to accept death and his clinging to life however gloomy it is, are also parts of the story and may serve to indicate its existential dimensions.

'Red Leaves' is structured around a burial ritual, which builds a basis for the rest of the story to rely upon. It also sets forth that the body servant of the Chief, a Negro slave, must die simply because tradition requires it. This requirement is followed, quite logically, by the Negro's running away, and the need to hunt him before the Chief's corpse starts smelling too badly, and, eventually and inevitably, by the capture of the slave. The ritual is a human institution, in so far as the Indian tradition is concerned, but it may also be seen as more or less a law of nature that the slave must follow his master to the grave.[49] The Indians have had a very close relationship with nature, and their laws and traditions seem to have been made to enhance their possibilities of surviving in the wildner-ness by adhering to the laws of nature. Behind the tradition that requires the slave to follow his master to the grave lies the assumption that man is part of nature, and that all living things must die. The time you die is

194

nonetheless of some importance. It is more important to human beings than to any other among nature's creations, and most important to the civilized, cultured human beings for whom death appears to be one of those reprehensible things which cannot be controlled. Whether man lives in close contact with nature or has lost all such contact, he alone is capable of thought, of consciousness, and this may account for the human tragedy (the existential dilemma) played out in 'Red Leaves'.

The significance of the burial ritual to the meaning of the story is also evidenced by its title. 'Red Leaves' is clearly designated to mean the autumn leaves, *les feuilles mortes,* which, as a natural part of the cycle of the seasons, must wither and fall. Faulkner himself explained the title thus:

> Well, that was probably symbolism. The red leaves referred to the Indian. It was the deciduation of Nature which no one could stop that had suffocated, smothered, destroyed the Negro. That the red leaves had nothing against him when they suffocated and destroyed him. They had nothing against him, they probably liked him, but it was normal deciduation which the red leaves, whether they regretted it or not, had nothing more to say in.[50]

The narrative of 'Red Leaves' is handled so that the focus is divided between the Indians' pursuit and eventual capture of the Negro slave and the Negro's desperate hiding and running. Throughout the story we are thus offered two very different perspectives on what is going on: one shows us by way of satire, dialogue, and a capsule story, what the Indian culture has been and has become through white influence and interference; the other gives an existential discussion of a human being's struggle with his fate and the inevitability of death. This is, even if it may sound complex, an oversimplification. The Indians are not only satirized and the Negro is not simply a non-conformist to a natural ritual. Furthermore, the question of corruption is not explained only by the introduction of slaves in the Indian society; slavery is only the major symbol of the corruption and degeneracy the Indians are victims of. The background story of Doom[51] is in fact proof that the Indians are corrupted in other ways than by the institution of slavery. The bi-monthly whiskey delivery is another piece of evidence to the same effect.

It is tempting to suggest that the institution of slavery with its basis in actual history was another tool Faulkner used to get his story told, and that the story first and foremost is a 'compact and inevitable . . . fable of life',[52] an existential study. In such an argument slavery and the abuses of it would only foster a macabre humour and a vicarious comment upon an originally white institution. It may be more to the point, and also a more valid interpretation of the story, to see in it the effects of the white culture on the natural life of the Indians. This statement needs to be qualified somewhat, too, to avoid misunderstanding. It is possible, perhaps even probable, that Faulkner saw in the Indians an opportunity to find a 'middle' race in his treatment of racial problems in his South; likewise that he in the natural wilderness where the Indians had a stable society saw primitive qualities of a more lasting value than the more ephemeral and elusive qualities found in the white village culture. Moreover, Faulkner's Indians are often representative of a race treated unjustly, thus giving him ample opportunity for social criticism.[53] It is important to notice that this generalization is not limited to Faulkner's treatment of the Indians. In point of fact, the Indians are hardly treated more unjustly by white men than Negroes or other white men are in his fiction. In addition there is plenty of evidence in Faulkner's Indian stories of their own mistreatment of their own race.[54]

To see the clash of different worlds in 'Red Leaves' as a clash between nature and culture, one must draw attention to the fact that the story is abundant with symbols, most of which show what the white man has brought to the Indians and how useless and out of place these things are – at least until the Indians adjust to a new and different way of life, to a world where a natural life cannot be led.[55] In the Indians' repetitive nostalgic remarks about the old days when no Negroes forced them to organize work for the slaves, there is little more than a general misunderstanding of what old days were like and a lazy attitude towards life. The old-time Indian territory is of course pictured as a pre-capitalistic Eden, but we should not fail to remember that rituals requiring human sacrifice were parts of that Eden.

The part of 'Red Leaves' that we have described as a 'capsule story' (part II) testifies more than anything else on the contemporary scene to the corruption the Indians – not always too unwillingly – have been subject to. The red-heeled slippers, a symbol established as a kind of leitmotif in the story, carry the symbolic value of power, since they belong to the Man, but they are also deadly as a result of the envy they create. These slippers are totally useless, as are most objects from the civilized world and which are now in the steamboat-house. It is therefore important to notice that the slippers are bought for money earned by

196

selling slaves. Not knowing how to use the money, Issetibbeha went to Europe, wherefrom he brought home all the property which really serves to symbolize estrangement from nature:

... a year later Issetibbeha returned home with a gilt bed, a pair of girandoles by whose light it was said that Pompadour arranged her hair while Louis smirked at his mirrored face across her powdered shoulder, and a pair of slippers with red heels. They were too small for him, since he had not worn shoes at all until he reached New Orleans on his way abroad (*These 13*, p. 137).

Behind it all, as the ultimate reason for the unlucky situation the Indians find themselves in, lies the introduction of slavery and the encroachment upon nature by the cultured and civilized outside world whose hunger for more space to live in, larger profit and more power, combined with its limitless desire to bring the white man's civilization to the undeveloped people, seems insatiable.

Another symbol of Indian degeneracy and corruption is Moketubbe himself, who is 'already diseased with flesh, with a pale, broad, inert face and dropsical hands and feet' (*These 13*, p. 138). Moreover, in his inertness and almost mystical behaviour, Moketubbe's degeneracy is also shown on a moral plane. The suspicion and the struggle for power within the leading family of the Indian tribe change and become more refined as a result of the Chief's knowledge of the world of culture and civilization. The struggle itself and the very desire for power are not products of the modern world – even if power becomes more significant when it can procure manufactured goods, whiskey, and the luxuries of the white man's world.

How things change over the years in the Indian camp is demonstrated in an emotional speech rendered by an old Indian. The plight and burden of the Negroes on the Indians are central elements in the otherwise rather nostalgic outburst, which also serves to underline the estrangement from nature, which more recent development has led to:

'This world is going to the dogs', he said. 'It is being ruined by white men. We got along fine for years and years, before the white men foisted their Negroes upon us. In the old days the old men sat in the shade and ate stewed deer's flesh and corn and smoked tobacco and talked of honor and grave affairs; now what do we do? Even the old wear themselves into the grave taking care of them that like sweating' (*These 13*, p. 141).

This description of ancient days in the Indian territories of Yoknapatawpha Country compared to the life they are forced to live now almost ridicules ancient days and ways of the Indians. It is nonetheless obvious that as the white men have closed in on the Indians, cleared the forests, tilled the soil, killed the animals they hunted and depended on for a living, new ways of life had to take over and these are not necessarily better ways of living. A life in close contact with nature has been replaced with a life in which the Indians exploit and use other people to make a living, and the great profit they make enables them to buy useless things, which further threaten to disrupt and destroy natural life. Culture and the benefits of civilization seem to have come too quickly, and the Indians have not been given time to adjust their own culture to the demands of a new situation, and they have not been adaptable enough to change with the incessant changes of the world around them. Faulkner does not directly portray man in nature and the advantages of natural life; nor does he imply that civilization and culture necessarily are improvements. 'Red Leaves' is nevertheless a story about natural life corrupted, and there is little doubt that some of the values and qualities inherent in the old life style of the Indians would have been beneficial to a modern world. In 'Red Leaves' culture seems bound to destroy and rule out nature and a natural life, and even if criticism of this is modified by the descriptions of certain inhuman institutions and traditions among the Indians, the passing of a natural and traditional life style is lamented while the modern and progressive life is contemplated. 'Red Leaves' is also a story about life and death, and about man's attitude to death. Images of life and death mingle and contrast throughout the story, ultimately to give an impression of man's ability to reconcile to his fate.

'Red Leaves' gives vivid images of man in nature and of natural man, and in the old Indians' reminiscences of how it once was we get an impression of an easy, leisurely life in accord with nature. In the Negro's attempt to escape from his pursuers or hunters we see a human being who has never lived close to nature and who is terrified by nature itself and eventually caught by it, almost directly. Numerous Negro characters in Faulkner's fiction share an irrational fear of nature, believing that some hidden force in nature may strike and hurt. In some ways nature seems to embody all the oppression and fear they suffer in their daily lives and for which they cannot give the actual explanation or reason, since that would lead to more suffering. Nancy in 'That Evening Sun' suffers from such an irrational fear of what the darkness may have in store for her, and she is afraid to be left alone. The emotional gap between Nancy in her terrible anxiety and suffering and the cold, matter-of-fact Compsons can be measured by their cultural levels. Nancy is still something of the primitive, uneducated, uncultured 'noble savage', who has not yet reached a level where superstition has been overcome by information, knowledge and a hard-won security in the form of a large house, locked doors, servants, and so forth. The Compsons have reached a level of success, wealth, and self-assurance where nothing is allowed to interfere with their convictions and beliefs. It is significant that Nancy can persuade the Compson children to take her home and stay with her for a while, but that the grown-ups refuse to accept Nancy's excuses and explanations. One should be cautious, however, not to condemn a whole white culture because of the whining and moaning Mrs. Compson, who seems to find her own position in the household threatened and accordingly refuses to be left alone 'while you take home a frightened Negro' (*These 13*, p. 241).

'That Evening Sun' is also one of the Faulkner short stories in which memories of the past form the story proper. These recollections are often set in a frame that gives an indication of the distance in time between *then* and *now* and shows the most important changes that have taken place. This is to some extent the case with 'A Justice', and in the opening paragraph of 'That Evening Sun', Quentin Compson gives a sophisticated physical description of Jefferson now, contrasted with a more quiet and steady Jefferson only a decade or so ago.

In 'That Evening Sun', the ironic dimension between the use of a child narrator and a story about race relations, sex, fear, and death is possibly even more significant than in 'A Justice'. The discrepancy between the limited point of view of the child narrator and an experience beyond his comprehension is modified by the fact that the child has become an adult at the time of narration. Faulkner is extremely cautious not to let the grown-up interfere with the memories of a childhood experience by way of commentary, direct statements, or even by letting the narrator tell it in his adult language.

The established narrative pattern nonetheless makes it quite clear that the whole story is told by a twenty-four-year-old Quentin. All the words, even those uttered by other characters, are Quentin's words as he recollects them at the time of narration. This postponement of narration is extremely important. The obvious gain of it is an opportunity to analyse and comment upon the story proper, which may either be done directly,[56] or simply be an indivisible and indistinguishable part of the narrative. The adult narrator unconsciously but inevitably comes to put his mark on the child's story. The child's feelings, reactions, and impressions are remembered such a long time afterwards that memory has necessarily distorted some of the events he tells about.

This leads to another distinction between the *was* and the *is* of the story: *then* Quentin was the child character participating in the story; *now* he is the adult narrator looking back upon a past that is forever lost, except as dream and experience, except as a part of himself. What Quentin narrates is one peculiar moment from his childhood, but as he places it in an historical and social context, its meaning multiplies and increases.

The narrative pattern in 'That Evening Sun' is thus very similar to the pattern in 'A Justice'. The main difference is found in the position in the text of the grown-up narrator's description of the *now* moment. In 'A Justice', Quentin comments in the very last part of the story that he did not see where the story took him. In 'That Evening Sun' the story to come is defined in the opening paragraphs as a memory from a time that can never return, from a childhood that was secure and innocent, and into which death, sex, and fear were not allowed access. In 'A Justice' there is no internal evidence to refute the impression that Quentin tells his story as a grown-up, looking back with some nostalgia upon the Sundays of his childhood world.

By using representatives of other races – Negro and Indian – in these stories, Faulkner is able to fuse the meaning of legend and myth to Quentin's own life, and at the same time the significance of his 'initiation' is suspended and cannot be fully grasped neither by the narrator himself nor by the reader.

Irrational fear of nature, of something inexplicable and unmentionable which may come out of darkness and night and catch up with you for whatever sins you have committed, is not only irrational. It also has its basis in a traditional superstition and in general gossip and factual knowledge about members of the black race disappearing and vanishing without trace. When Faulkner places inexperienced and immature people in untouched nature he can demonstrate that fear comes easily and needs not have logical explanations. Such stories also prove how shallow and fragile and useless our thin layer of culture and civilized manners are when they are put to a test in what Faulkner in one of his stories calls

200

'natural exaggerated situation[s].'[57] A few examples of how Faulkner presents 'man in nature' will suffice to make this clear.

The two young men, 'Don and I'[58] who travel together in Italy in the short story 'Mistral', feel an ice-cold and vicious hostility in the elemental forces around them, and due to their immaturity and unreadiness they cannot cope with these forces. Reverberating through the story is the sigh "I wish it were summer" (*These 13*, pp. 301, 306, 313), and the mistral blows right to their bones. The descriptions of the two men, awestricken and afraid in a terrifying nature, also serve to underscore the emotional forces at work in this story. The young men feel that the mountains 'lean in toward' (*These 13*, p. 306) them, and the two Americans are outsiders to everything around then because of their upbringing, background, culture. The wind and the cold are real enough, and the men may have experienced them before. Yet there is a feeling of maliciousness in the very landscape and in the persons they encounter. Even the priest seems to belong to a pagan world where strange rituals are performed to the accompaniment of wind and rain, fire and ice. A desperate sense of frustration and helplessness overwhelms the young men, and the images used to create this frustration and despair are also related to the four elements:

It was like being at the bottom of a dead volcano filled with that lost savage green wind dead in its own motion and full of its own driving and unsleeping dust (*These 13*, p. 306).

This use of imagery is then twisted around and carried further to add significance to the story. The description of a hostile natural world is not used just to prepare for and then to emphasize the strange events taking place on the personal level where various characters are manipulated and where tragedies occur. The narrator voices the opinion that in critical situations man is always alone, but he does so by reference to 'natural exaggerated situation[s]', in a scene where the desperate priest, recently home after having buried the man he himself has killed, is heard talking behind a wall:

He was not talking to anyone there: you could tell that. In whatever place he was, he was alone: you could tell that. Or maybe it was the wind. Maybe in any natural exaggerated situation – wind, rain, drouth – man is always alone (*These 13*, p. 313).

Ernest Cotton of 'The Hound' is also a man trapped by nature, lost in nature, and terrified by nature; mostly because he has committed murder and has thus acted contrary to nature. Ernest is also in an exaggerated situation, and he is completely alone. Nature's resistance to what he is trying to do – bury the corpse, kill the dog – reflects a struggle within Cotton himself, and the vicious and undying dog may represent Cotton's guilt. Despite these psychological interpretations of the story, there is also a realistic level in it where Ernest Cotton fights nature and finally has to give in. Cotton stumbles for many a night in the impenetrable undergrowth and darkness of the woods where he has hidden the body of his neighbour, but nature will neither hide the body nor let Cotton remove it easily from where he first hid it. He is just as trapped in the darkness and mist of the woods as he is in a dark and inescapable trauma, and when he finally is taken prisoner, he even tries to commit suicide. Even then nature (his own body) resists, and it seems to Cotton that he must be the eternal loser, beaten by an invincible enemy: nature and his own nature (guilt, reproach).

Nature's spellbinding and terrifying forces are most clearly at work in early stories such as 'Yo Ho and Two Bottles of Rum', and in the published version of the two-part story, ' "Once Aboard the Lugger- - -".' This is a mosquito-ridden tale reminiscent of *Mosquitoes,* but as a sea-tale where the natural setting provides the mood and the atmosphere it is closer to 'Yo Ho and Two Bottles of Rum'.

' "Once Abroad the Lugger- - -" ' moves from a surface description of action and character to a deeper lyricism, presented in eloquent, rich language, often bordering on flatulence combined with a lasting vacillation between the narrator's toughness of speech and action and his acute sensitivity to nature and his own place in it. The narrator's cultured self is revealed through the abundance of literary similes and metaphors in the text, while the more natural side of him is revealed through his actions and rough speech. With twilight and approaching darkness, more and more of the story turns to descriptions of nature; of sights and sounds, stars and moon, pines and the hush of the sea, as these phenomena are interpreted or sensed by the narrator. Sand and heat, undergrowth and mosquitoes give the narrator 'a sense of hopeless enslavement to an obscure compulsion' (*Uncollected Stories,* p. 357), and the three workers on the island, digging out the illegal whiskey, are pictured 'like three figures in a ritualistic and illtimed dance against that background of ghostly incandescence and the deep breath of the sea stirring the unceasing pinetops overhead. . .' (*Uncollected Stories,* p. 356).

In the encounters between civilized man and untouched nature or even only man acting unnaturally in nature, nature seems to be victorious time and again. This is nevertheless only the fact in limited experiences where individuals try to impose their will on nature, or where they act contrary to their own nature. Little by little man 'gnaws' at the woods, and the wilderness disappears; rivers become polluted, fowl and fish and animals are decimated, nature becomes cultivated to provide man with more and better living space. Nature fights back, takes revenge, or this is at least what some of the protagonists in a few Faulkner stories from this period tend to believe. A man like Midgleston in 'Black Music' even acts on behalf of the virgin nature in 'the quiet mountains where never many lived' (*Doctor Martino,* p. 276). Midgleston believes that nature itself draws a line where the encroachment of human beings and culture must stop, and he is accordingly more than willing to act as a faun for a day to scare the intruders away. There is in Midgleston's opinion – and he is a city-dweller – something that man had better leave alone; otherwise it will strike back with disastrous consequences.

The fact that Faulkner's characters act, think, and behave according to whether they live in a city, town, or village or in more rural areas, may also be seen as a comment on the nature-culture dimension. In numerous stories, people from the big cities are presented as rootless, dishonest, and completely estranged from the traditional values and ways of the slow but stable and secure life of the less sophisticated country people. The two worlds are very effectively contrasted in 'Fox Hunt'. Here the contrast is also the one between North and South, which so many critics have found to be significant in Faulkner's fiction. This is not to say that culture and civilization cannot be for the better; Faulkner leaves no doubt that they indeed are, but he also shows how easily man dismisses positive values and ways of life for new and exciting ones, even if individual man often fights a losing battle against change of all kinds. It is rather the exaggerations, outgrowths, and abuses that inevitably accompany progress which Faulkner's narrators relate to and often are critical of. The heaviest criticism is of course found in the war stories, where technological innovations and man's unlimited ingenuity are used for killing other people, destroying whole cultures, and almost annihilating nature.

The opposition nature versus culture may also be seen as an opposition between the old and the new. The historical dimension is important in a number of Faulkner's short stories; for instance in the Indian stories in which ancient days in Yoknapatawpha are described. Other stories, such as 'A Mountain Victory', show that humanity and compassion and a deep understanding of the life and time of man are not only products of a modern conscience. In 'A Rose for Emily' successive generations in the small but expanding town of Jefferson are presented, giving the implied author an opportunity to emphasize the need for change and adjustment, since the conditions of life seem to change by some law of nature. In 'There Was a Queen' the moral qualities of the Southern *ladies* of the Civil War generation are compared to the younger and more sophisticated Narcissa Benbow Sartoris, who pays more heed to respectability and to her personal well-being than to some unwritten code of conduct. Generally speaking, Faulkner seems to suspect that man's nature is unchanging; it remains the same through the ages, while the conditions man lives in and is conditioned and moulded by, change. Since conditions and values and life styles and ways of behaviour, philosophy of life, outlook on the world and everything else are subject to the law of change, man has to change, no matter how unchanging his nature may be. Faulkner stresses man's refusal to change because any change involves uncertainties and unpredictable dangers; yet change is inevitable. In his preface to the third volume of the Snopes trilogy, *The Mansion* (1959), Faulkner wrote:

Since the author likes to believe, hopes that his entire life's work is a part of a living literature, and since 'living' is motion, and 'motion' is change and alteration and therefore the only alternative to motion is un-motion, stasis, death, there will be found discrepancies and contradictions in the thirty-four-year progress of this particular chronicle;...[9]

In our lives we have to solve the paradox of being afraid of change and alteration, yet being dependent on it for growth and motion, to make life endurable and worthwhile.

Most of the stories discussed in this chapter were collected in Faulkner's first two short-story collections, *These 13* and *Doctor Martino and Other Stories*. In the first of these collections, Faulkner chose stories and arranged them carefully to present a coherent vision of the world as a wasteland. Practically all the stories are sceptical in their *Weltanschauung*; they show a universe in which people lack understanding, kindness, and pity. Also those characters who do not waste their youth in a war and suffer a non-life after the war are trapped and lost and bewildered. It makes little difference in the world of *These 13* whether people are trapped in a cave filled with skeletons or whether they succeed in digging themselves out into the light of day to live a regular and boring life in a stable and static peace-time world. The entrapment and the non-life are nonetheless present, and Faulkner seems to offer no other alternative than to live as best one can in a tightly compressed universe, under ominous stars.

The situation is not radically different or better in the countryside and backwood areas of Yoknapatawpha County. Wasted lives and actual waste of people are central in these communities too, and it is indeed a severe criticism that the people and their social life in most parts of Yoknapatawpha compare neatly with the battlefields of World War I and the soldiers fighting for their lives there. Even the ancient primitive communities described in 'A Justice' and 'Red Leaves' prove to be as power- and money-ridden as the modern world of Jefferson with its paved sidewalks and gasoline pumps.

The stories collected in *Doctor Martino and Other Stories* indicate a clear shift from the focus on village and wilderness in the first collection of stories, to a preoccupation with uprootedness, sex, death, loss, and decay. The struggle for power, the exploitation of other people, and the violence that is used without much reluctance, since people are regarded as objects, are significant elements in these stories. Faulkner's narrators object violently to the lack of sincerity and compassion they find in their environment, and the implied author's attitudes are often very clear and strong. The outrage of a potential believer is discernible, despite the great variety in narrative handling we find in the stories from the major years.

The narrative control in Faulkner's stories from this period varies significantly from story to story, and it seems to a large extent to be dependent on the kind of material he is exploring and how familiar he is with setting and character. Thus it is quite clear that some of the village stories, set in Jefferson, are the most rigidly controlled ones. This is so because the narrators are well acquainted with the groups of characters and with those who fall outside the group: outsiders, outlanders, imbeciles, children, girls who do not want to adjust, men who despair over a life so remote from that which they dreamed about and almost grasped during the years of war and violence. In these stories Faulkner can rely on atmospheric detail, on metaphors from the teeming city life contrasted with nature imagery, to create a sense of irrevocable fate and tragedy, and of enclosure and entrapment. 'Dry September' is here perhaps the best example.

In the village stories there is frequently an isolated individual in opposition to a group. Since the individual is often an outsider, someone on the fringes of society, one would expect the narrative voice to sympathize with this outsider, and by doing so, reduce the distance to him both for Teller and Hearer. Yet what Faulkner does is to choose what has commonly been referred to as the community point of view; i.e. to let a spokesman for the town ('we', 'our town') narrate the story so that the isolated individual's reactions and actions can only be inferred from what the in-group's representative narrates, which is of course his interpretation of the events. Irony and the use of fallible or faulty narrators may reduce the confidence in the narrator severely, and the attitudes he expresses in the very telling about 'them' and us also serve to change the impact of the story in the end. The use of unreliable narrators is, of course, a common trick, and their use of hearsay and gossip does not make them more reliable. Faulkner's strength in these village stories lies in his complete control of the setting, his superb use of the typical small-town behaviour, his intimate knowledge of prejudice and foolishness, his insight into people's unlimited need for self-respect, all of which he uses to portray man in his ageless struggle for honour and dignity.

On the basis of these stories we may also describe the implied author; i.e. an anonymous voice in some stories, or a set of detectable attitudes and judgments interwoven into the texture of the story. Since Faulkner does not want to manipulate his characters to demonstrate something or to let them have an exemplary function, he cannot possibly define and describe his characters from a position of authorial authority. His people must be self-motivated, autonomous characters. Yet it would be wrong to see Faulkner's non-authorital stories as examples of impersonal narration. The authorial exclusion has been replaced by a narrative voice, which in the final analysis is the author himself, one more step removed from the scene, offering one more perspective on it. This perspective, this point of view, may not be the conclusive or final one on the scene, the events taking place, or the people involved; but to the reader this understanding

206

of the implied author may well be as far as he can possibly get in his interpretation of the text as it stands. Although Faulkner wanted to be inconclusive, because he always felt that his characters were on their way to some new kind of devilment, the literary critic ends his textual explanation and interpretation where the text ends. That the critic then may, and probably should, continue his investigations and speculations in order to relate the text to something beyond the text itself, is a different problem.

The different narrative strategies must be seen in relation to the use of a community point of view, or at least the use of a closely defined and rigidly structured in-group. Thus the narrative handling and the explicit or felt presence of a narrator differ from the village stories to those placed outside Jefferson or even outside Yoknapatawpha. In the non-Yoknapatawpha stories the narrative distance is often great, since the third-person narrator here does not often adopt the point of view of a character or a group, and only rarely does a first-person narrator tell about events outside Yoknapatawpha. The narrative voice can be heard, however, distributing sympathy in ways that may differ seriously from the opinions and attitudes of the narrator. In 'Idyll in the Desert' the narration is carried out by a double set of 'I' figures, and the story is very close to the oral storytelling tradition. In 'Mistral', also a story placed outside Faulkner's mythical kingdom, 'I' tells about his and Don's experiences while they were travelling in Europe. The first-person narrator's limitations here reflect the uncertainty of youth and inexperience, so that such stories become very personal attempts at the initiation story, which Faulkner would master completely later on – in particular in 'The Bear' and 'The Old People'.

The matter of narrative distance and of the implied author's understanding is not dependent only on whether first or third person narration is chosen. Indeed, the narrative may include no reference to a narrative persona, and the same feeling of distance and objectivity, or closeness and subjectivity, may still be felt. In the discussion of 'Miss Zilphia Gant', this narrative method was mentioned. Without any reference to a narrator, and without the narrator ever disclosing his presence, the narrative takes on the character of first-person, 'community' narration from the very opening of the story. On the other hand, the use of an 'I' narrator may indicate great sympathy and empathy, as in 'That Evening Sun', which Quentin Compson narrates. This story presents different problems for the author, since the grown-up Quentin narrates a memory from his childhood, as if he were a child, while his adult understanding, maturity, and humanity nonetheless pervade his retrospective tale.

The change from the collective consciousness and the use of 'the best of gossip' in some of the village stories, to individual consciousness and the use of legend and myth in 'That Evening Sun' and 'A Justice', is but one example of the wide range of story-telling techniques that Faulkner used during his major period. In other stories he would rely on the oral tradition and establish a frame and a take-over narrator with whom the frame narrator might discuss things in the course of the tale proper ('Idyll in the Desert'); in other stories atmospheric detail and colourful descriptive passages of landscape and people carry the whole story, as in ' "Once Aboard the Lugger - - -".' In a few stories, notably some of the 'Beyond' stories ('Carcassonne' and, to some extent, 'The Leg') Faulkner approximates poetry, and uses dream sequences to portray experiences beyond those of ordinary, mortal men. 'Carcassonne' is thus an almost static story, while 'Mistral' and 'Divorce in Naples' also have their lyrical passages, making a contrast to the struggle of everyday life, and indicating a longing for transcendental understanding and for values not normally cherished in the wasteland of post-war Europe.

The World War I stories are very different when narrative method is considered, but none of them are particularly interesting from this point of view. In 'Victory', the narrator manipulates his distance to the protagonist, and multiple points of view are used to give descriptions of war scenes, post-war Europe, the stable Scottish family, and the rapid decline of Alec Gray, who has become dehumanized and uprooted by the war. In 'Crevasse', an almost cold objectivity is chosen, but even here the voice of the outraged believer who has lost his faith is heard, especially in the final scenes. 'Ad Astra' is told by a first-person narrator, who is also one of the characters in the story. He narrates an episode from the war, thirteen years *after* the war, but immediacy and presence in the descriptions of the drinking and fighting are clearly sought, so the effect of the distance in time established in the first paragraph of the story is to some extent lost. 'All the Dead Pilots' is more of a reminiscence, a nostalgic memory from a period in life when the young men realized some of their dreams of glory. This memory is contrasted with the non-life of the post-war period. The narrator promises to give 'a series of brief glares' (*These 13*, p. 82); his narrative will be composite. From a secure position as spectator, thirteen years later, he sets up tableaux as he remembers them, freezes moments of action, but remains strangely unaffected and uninvolved. His apparent estrangement may be taken as another piece of evidence of the nothingness and irrevocable loss which are so typical of Faulkner's wasteland of war. In the last World War I story of this period, 'Turn About', Faulkner struggles to avoid melodrama and farce, and is not altogether successful in doing so. Only when the philosophical statements about 'all the dead pilots' are shown through metaphors and imagery – as in the opening paragraphs of 'Ad Astra' – do they become convincing.

Numerous stories from this period depend largely on plot complication and action, ending in some sort of resolution or in unresolved tension. 'Doctor Martino' and 'The Brooch' may be described in such terms, and both stories are outside the Yoknapatawpha fiction. One should be careful not to over-emphasize this point. The main division lines in Faulkner's short fiction are not between the Yoknapatawpha fiction and the non-Yoknapatawpha stories. In a study of Faulkner's narrative methods, such a division would, of course, not be very revealing. One should avoid the Saga fallacy and not consider the Yoknapatawpha fiction as one group of particular interest, while the other short stories are interesting only in so far as they indicate the 'possibility of alternative or additional sagas that were never developed'.[61] The short stories of this period exist as narrative units in their own right, and to emphasize their usefulness in interpretations of Faulkner's longer works, or in creating a grand design, a Saga, is in many ways to deny them their individuality and autonomy.

Faulkner once said that 'there are so few plots... the plot has not changed too much, only the people involved in it have changed....'.[62] If Faulkner's statement has any bearing upon his short fiction, some recurrent design should be found. There is no reason to go as far as some critics have done, and call this use of recurrent plots 'formulaic';[63] yet the fact remains that Faulkner often centred his stories around a *contest* or a *hunt*. 'Centaur in Brass', 'Spotted Horses', 'The Leg', and 'Red Leaves' are stories from this period which rely rather heavily on these patterns, although some of the stories, if not all, transcend the formula and the pattern to become much more than an artistic exercise in filling old bottles with new wine. As will become evident in the following sections of this study, these recurrent patterns are more frequent in later short stories; e.g., those used in *The Unvanquished* and in *Go Down, Moses,* with many qualifications.

Compared with the other periods in Faulkner's career, the major years produced very few comic stories. There are certainly comic incidents and humorous exaggerations in such stories as 'Spotted Horses', 'Centaur in Brass', and 'Thrift', yet the prevailing mood and atmosphere is sombre and serious. The young man who failed to become a hero in the war, the dedicated writer who reacts violently to injustice, inhumanity, and human folly, does not yet have the broad acceptance and the mild understanding the more mature writer possessed. The anonymous voice, or the implied author, is angry if not outraged, yet preaching and moralizing can hardly ever be found. Faulkner creates living characters, and shows them in frozen moments, in tableaux of arrested motion and emotion, before he lets them on to some new 'devilment'. Flat descriptive passages alternate with dramatized action, and outside presentation alternates with interior monologues. The distance from narrator to character varies from cold objectivity to heart-shattering closeness, and above and beneath it all is the controlling conscience of the craftsman and born story-teller, who was most interested in people, and whose voice can be heard in the midst of the brawling and desperate self-assertions of his characters.

The relationship between Faulkner's short stories and novels in this period is very different from the relationship that we will find in later years. It is a closer relationship than in the preceding years, but it becomes even closer as the years go by. In the major period a number of stories can be seen as germs for novels, as sequels to novels, as preliminary drafts of chapters for novels, while most of the stories are independent and autonomous, without any obvious relationship to any of the novels. With the broad exception of the Snopes stories and a few others, Faulkner the short-story writer seems to separate himself from the novelist in this period. A study of his short-story career also shows that he, basically, wrote short stories between novels, in periods of relaxation from novel writing and in periods of great financial need.

Yet the short stories that do not relate in any obvious or significant way to any of Faulkner's novels may still be a novelist's short stories in the sense that the author narrates a complex and long story in a relatively brief discourse. By the use of various narrators and often thereby a limited point of view, he can select representative bits and pieces from the wider story and show them on a contracted scale. The narrative concentration is usually very high, although characters may be studied from many angles and events interpreted from more than one point of view. Strict chronology is not followed, but often the use of capsule stories enables the narrator to give background information in concentrated form, before he moves on to relate the central elements of a story.

Faulkner's discovery of his postage stamp of native soil, of Yoknapatawpha County, also enabled him to rely on suggestive references to other parts of the story about his people and his landscape. His short stories profit from the rich associations readers may have from their familiarity with other works, stories as well as novels, placed in the imaginary kingdom. Thus discourse-time might be considerably shorter than story-time, also (but not only) because of the common background of so many characters from story to story, and because one story, almost imperceptibly, followed up what had been told before, or would be followed up in stories yet to be narrated. This being said, one should not be misled into thinking that the relationship among the stories is so close that an individual story cannot be read and appreciated alone. On the contrary, the stories from about 1930 are more individual than Faulkner's stories from any other period, yet the reader's experience may be enhanced if he has become acquainted with Faulkner's people and country also in the novels.

6. Short Stories 1933–1941
From Yoknapatawpha to the Golden Land

> It's my country, my native land and I love it. I'm
> not trying to satirize it, I'm trying – that is, I'm not
> expressing my own ideas in the stories I tell, I'm
> telling about people, and these people express ideas
> which sometimes are mine, sometimes are not mine,
> but I myself am not trying to satirize my country, I
> love it, and it has its faults and I will try to correct
> them, but I will not try to correct them when I am
> writing a story, because I'm talking about people
> then.
>
> – *Faulkner in the University*

While Faulkner's short stories between 1928 and 1932 may be described
as largely independent of his other works, many of the short stories after
1932 were revised and incorporated in books, which may either be
regarded as novels or as short-story cycles or composites.[1] In the period
from 1933 to 1941 Faulkner wrote the stories that came to form *The
Unvanquished*, he wrote most of the stories that much later would make
up *Knight's Gambit*,[2] and he wrote and re-wrote the stories that became
Go Down, Moses.[3] He also wrote a number of miscellaneous and autonomous short stories. Some of these stories are of high quality and among
Faulkner's major achievements in this genre: 'Uncle Willy' and 'Barn
Burning' are two such stories.[4] Most of the stories from this period have
close affinities with novels of the same period, or, in one case, a much
later novel.[5] 'Wash' was re-used in *Absalom, Absalom!*; 'This Kind of
Courage' was abandoned because the story it told was expanded into the
novel *Pylon*; 'The Wild Palms' never appeared as a short story but found
its final form in the novel, *The Wild Palms*; 'Fool About a Horse' was
reused in *The Hamlet* while 'Afternoon of a Cow' and 'Barn Burning' are
both closely related to this novel, without being directly used in it.[6]
Finally, 'Mule in the Yard' was incorporated in *The Town*, which was
published in 1957. Thus seven of the altogether thirteen individual short
stories from this period – the 1941 story, 'The Tall Men', is included in
this number[7] – relate significantly to novels, while the other six stories are

more autonomous in the sense that they were never reused in any form and that they accordingly live on as short stories in their own right: 'Lo!', 'A Bear Hunt', 'Golden Land', 'That Will Be Fine', 'Uncle Willy', and 'The Tall Men'. Basically one might also hold that 'Barn Burning', written as the opening chapter of *The Hamlet* but removed from the novel, is such a 'pure' short story, but its close link with the novel cannot be overlooked.

These statistical facts indicate a shift in Faulkner's literary activity after his great period of short-story writing. Moreover, most of his short stories from this period are independent yet interrelated texts in the sense that they group together in series of stories and finally become published as novels: *The Unvanquished,* and *Go Down, Moses.* This is not to say that 'Ambuscade', 'Raid', 'The Old People', 'Gold Is Not Always' and all the other stories that make up these two books are not short stories in their own right. Most of them were, in point of fact, published separately as short stories in magazines and were rather extensively revised before their inclusion in the respective books. Such publication criteria are not conclusive evidence, however; but for all practical purposes here, it must suffice to emphasize the different intention Faulkner obviously had with these stories from the very time of composition,[8] and that his practice during these years represents a turning away from the writing of individual short stories which would remain short stories also in the readers' minds because they were collected in his various short-story collections, to the writing of stories that belonged within a larger, pre-established design and framework.

More than half of the short stories written between 1933 and 1941 are in the humorous vein: Faulkner is rarely closer to the tall tale than in 'Mule in the Yard', 'Lo!' and – to a certain extent – 'That Will Be Fine'. The strange story by Mr. Ernest V. Trueblood, 'Afternoon of a Cow', is also hilariously funny; not only because of its subject-matter, but also because of the laconic and dry narrative, which in no way reflects the events that take place. The discrepancy between the lofty narration and its apparent seriousness and refinement, and the rather unlikely and inconsequential events of the story, allows for the comedy in it. 'A Bear Hunt' is also a humorous story, as is 'Fool About a Horse'. We have seen how Faulkner earlier has used the comic tale to present bargains and deceits and lies, and we have seen how humour has to give way to seriousness when the bargains come to involve people and destinies.

Accordingly, beneath the surface of these tall tales more serious problems are present, and in all the stories mentioned above, save for the inconsequential 'Afternoon of a Cow', there is a search for revenge at the centre, often with disastrous consequences for the people involved. The protagonists of most of the stories between 1933 and 1941 suffer from some kind of injustice, which they either have been aware of for a long time or suddenly discover in a moment of insight and revelation. This injustice often originates in greed and corruption on somebody's part, and may thus be explained as the result of individual shortcomings and failures. Yet in stories like 'Lo!' and 'A Bear Hunt' the injustice may be described as racial or cultural, and the wrongs in 'Lo!' are done by a whole nation, represented by its President and Government. In 'Wash', on the other hand, Wash Jones suffers from his own illusions about Sutpen and from what Sutpen apparently understands as his aristocratic right to own and use other people.

The injustice and the many conflicting interests that lead to plans of revenge and retaliation may well be seen as a result of a society where everyone is left to fend for himself and where ownership of property and money becomes increasingly important as time goes by. When money and position are valued as highly as in Faulkner's Jefferson in its modern age, people seem to be more than willing to cheat and steal and fight to secure their position, or to make it to the top in this money-ridden world. Even though the Snopeses are the prime examples of this attitude, the short stories from the mid-thirties prove that this is a common feature of life in modern Yoknapatawpha. As we shall see, Faulkner's one and only Hollywood-based story, 'Golden Land', implies that things are even worse elsewhere, but it also indicates, since the distance from Yoknapatawpha to the Golden Land is rather short, that even small-town and rural America may soon catch up with the decadent, inhuman and shallow life style exposed in 'Golden Land'.

The conflicts in these stories are less dramatic and violent than in many of the earlier stories, especially those collected in the 'Middle Ground' section of *Collected Stories*. In stories such as 'Doctor Martino', 'There Was a Queen', 'The Brooch', and others, violent deaths were the result of strong emotional conflicts. Of the stories discussed in this chapter, only 'Wash' includes violent death, but the horror of this story is unparalleled in Faulkner's short fiction. The conflicts of the other stories are not so much on a personal, emotional level where love and sex and family ties are important motivational forces behind people's actions. Even when the conflicts seem to be between individuals, these individuals must also be understood as representatives of a class, a race, or a culture, and the conflicting interests must be viewed in this broader perspective. The traditional opposition between nature and culture may also be found in these stories. In 'Uncle Willy' the old drug addict and the boy-narrator represent a natural life where freedom and love of one's fellow man are important elements, while Jeffersonians in general represent a well-regulated, civilized, 'normal' life where non-conformity is a deadly sin. In 'That Will Be Fine' all the characters seem to be preoccupied with money and prestige and respectability, paying no attention to human values, and another set of values is detectable only by inference and through the workings of the story's strong irony. This irony may be described as dramatic irony; the narrator does not by any means grasp the significance of his own story, whereas the readers conspire with the author to discover what really goes on and hence also to judge the values and attitudes of the characters involved.

The opposition between 'nature' and 'culture' is by no means as simple as this may indicate. In a story such as 'Barn Burning', Sarty Snopes may well be found to have some in-born human qualities – a sense of justice, a feeling of what is right and wrong – but he is contrasted with his father, Ab Snopes, whose animal-like character and brutal behaviour might also be described as natural. On the other hand, De Spain and his mansion represent not only negative qualities in the civilized, cultured, world; they are also positive attributes of tempered, cultivated nature. The implied author's attitude in these stories cannot, in point of fact, be described in simple oppositions of this kind.[9] There is no doubt a norm to be found in these texts which implies a heavy criticism of the new, because of its shallowness and hollowness, because most values seem to be centred around money and property, and because human beings seem to matter less and less in the modern world. People seem to have forgotten about people in Faulkner's fictional world of these stories, and they have done so in a frantic attempt to adjust and conform to the mainstream of American life, by adopting middle-class values without questioning their usefulness or appropriateness. Uncle Willy is the victim of such a conformist system, where the belief is that everyone who does not share our convictions and values and attitudes should be saved. The boy-narrator who tells about Uncle Willy, insisting that he was the finest man he ever knew, seems to be rather close to the implied author whom we may detect in these stories.

In the heading of this chapter there is implied a kind of development or movement from Yoknapatawpha to the 'Golden Land'; and this movement is along an axis of greed, corruption, and conformity. The picture is more complex than this might indicate, but there is nonetheless such a growth in inhumanity, greed, selfishness, from a story like 'Mule in the Yard' at one end of the scale through, e.g., 'Uncle Willy' and 'That Will Be Fine', to 'Golden Land'. As mentioned above, this also shows that it is not very far, after all, from Jefferson to L.A.

In such a line of argument 'Wash' and 'Barn Burning' fall more or less outside the established thematic framework. 'Wash' is one of Faulkner's taut and forceful short narratives; self-contained and complete in itself despite its close relationship to *Absalom, Absalom!* The story has a couple of retrospective flashbacks or memories on the part of Wash Jones, but it is mostly a story about a *situation* which develops into tragic, apocalyptic drama when Wash suddenly *sees* and understand what Sutpen *is* and *does.* It is thus a story where illusion has to give way to reality or disillusionment, and where violence is Wash Jones's only means to preserve some of the pride he has vainly and falsely asserted all his life by apotheosizing Sutpen. Despite the story's apocalyptic horror, Faulkner refuses to describe the violence directly, and the omniscient narrator moves aside and looks in another direction when Wash lifts the scythe, and, later, the butcher's knife. In its slow development from apparent friendship and admiration to revealing insight and conflict, 'Wash' may be seen as a 'concentrated parable of Southern degeneracy in the aftermath of the Civil War', as Jack F. Stewart has said.[10]

Presumably because 'Wash' is a very short story, it is not divided into parts, yet there are some easily discernible phases of it. The first scene is one of Faulkner's marvellous frozen tableaux, and it is important in so far as it sets the stage for the violent action which is then retarded till the relationship between Wash and Sutpen in the past is described. The effectiveness of the narrative rests in part on the many foreshadowings or anticipations in the introductory paragraphs: Sutpen's arrogance and cynicism; the rank weeds and the scythe acquire additional meaning and importance, since they point to the later action during the same day, a day when the sun rises and sets over the Sutpen plantation and the people living there, in more than one sense.

216

The central portions of the story fall between the narration about the early dawn of the Sunday in 1870 and about the tragedy just before sunset of the same day, and can be said to fall roughly into two parts. The first one deals with Wash Jones's life and thoughts in the years when the 'Kernel' was away fighting the Yankees. This part is important, since it conveys the impression that Wash looks upon Sutpen as God. He virtually fuses his image of Sutpen on the black stallion with his conceptions of God: 'If God himself was to come down and ride the natural earth, that's what He would aim to look like' (*Doctor Martino*, pp. 227–8). Wash has to rely on his own misinterpretations of the Bible to feel superior to the Negroes, too. Building up a false picture of his own importance, he also distorts the relationship he has with Sutpen so that his master, God-like on his black horse, strong and arrogant with his whip in hand, becomes a good, trustworthy and reliable man:

'I ain't afraid. Because your air brave. It ain't that you were a brave man one minute or day of your life and got a paper to show hit from General Lee. But you air brave, the same as you air alive and breathing. That's where hit's different. Hit don't need no ticket from nobody to tell me that. And I know that whatever you handle or tech, whether hit's a regiment of men or an ignorant gal or· just a hound dog, that you will make hit right' (*Doctor Martino*, p. 231).

This paragraph is immediately followed by the narrative's return to the now-level, where Milly, seventeen now, gives birth to a girl baby. The change is not so abrupt as this might seem to indicate, however: although the flashbacks give information about Wash Jones's life back to 1850 when he was first allowed to become a squatter on Sutpen's place, the central portions of the narrative render a chronological movement of the story up to the last recorded conversation between Sutpen and Wash, taking place when Milly is fifteen. The two years' jump in time is thus less than many other such jumps within the retrospective parts themselves. Yet it is a significant change in the narrative, since the penultimate scene of the story, which is the opening scene in the narrative, now is brought to its terrifying climax. Outside the flashback, the narrative presents Jones before dawn on the crucial day, and then moves rapidly into dawn, and further on chronologically till sunset.

While the opening scene focuses on Sutpen as he comes to see Milly and their daughter at dawn, the last scenes are basically seen from Wash's point of view. The cyclical movement of the day from sunrise to sunset is used very deftly by Faulkner, primarily to give an additional symbolic touch to the scenes in which descriptions of the sun are found. Dawn not only represents the beginning of a new day, it is also the time when a new life begins, and it is the time of dawn – understanding, insight – in Wash's mind. So when he suddenly grasps the meaning and the intention of Sutpen's remarks, the sun is said to be up. He kills Sutpen in broad daylight, and his vigil for the law-enforcers lasts through a 'long, bright, sunny forenoon' (*Doctor Martino,* p. 236). When the long waiting comes to an end, sunset is there, and in 'Wash' the evening sun really goes down, more so than in the short story of that title. Wash kills his granddaughter, probably also the baby, with a butcher's knife, and he sets fire to the shed. He has been forced to give up Sutpen as his God, and now that he has set out upon his tragical path, he acts as if he were not only jury and judge but actually God himself.

Wash Jones's horrible actions are not only a result of his rage and despair when he discovers that he has misjudged Sutpen completely. Wash also reacts against the whole code of conduct which Sutpen represents, against a whole social order where he himself is placed at the bottom, even though he insists that the Negroes are inferior to him in all respects. After Wash has killed Sutpen and awakens from the trance he has been in, he has a vision in which he sees Sutpen, Milly, himself, and the whole society they are a part of as a result of men who are nothing more than 'bragging and evil shadows' (*Doctor Martino,* p. 238) who have been allowed to 'set the order and the rule of living' (*Doctor Martino,* p. 238). These men populate the whole earth as far as Wash knows it, and there is no place for him to go. His chief concern is not with the dead Sutpen; his problem is all the *living* Sutpens from whom men like Wash Jones can never escape. After Wash has had his epiphanic insight he knows what life has in store for him, and he therefore refuses to remain in the world of the living.

Ab Snopes's problem in 'Barn Burning' is in some ways also all the living Sutpens, in this story represented by Major de Spain. The story, which is much later in historical time than 'Wash', proves that the Sutpens are still alive and vital, and that the situation has not changed much for the Wash Joneses of this world. This is, however, only a minor element in 'Barn Burning', since the story centres on Sarty Snopes and his refusal to act out his father's wishes or to become like his father. Sarty is torn between conflicting loyalties, to his family on the one side and to his sense of justice and righteousness on the other side. When his loyalties are put to a test, his 'good' nature wins, but Sarty has no other option than to leave his family and escape into what he already knows to be a hostile world.

The 'Snopesism' which infests virtually all members of the clan is what Sarty escapes when he runs away, but 'Snopesism' can be found outside the clan, too. There are also some members of the family who suffer from it in a more diluted form. I.O. Snopes of 'Mule in the Yard' is such a Snopes, but his illegal activities are clear enough as they are. The fact that the Snopeses have such a hard time making it in the world of Yoknapatawpha and Jefferson is not only a result of some good and decent people's attempts to oppose them and prevent them from destroying everything around them. It is just as much a result of other, ordinary Jeffersonians whose capacity for shrewd deals is not small and who defend their accumulated money, property, and position with admirable endurance. The Snopeses have to fight hard simply because people around them are apt to fight on their terms; they have also become greedy money-makers and the responsibility they show for other people also seems to be on the decline, although it may never reach the level of usurpation and malice where a man like Flem Snopes enjoys himself.

If we use the model of growing greed, rapacity and corruption from old Yoknapatawpha via modern Yoknapatawpha to Californian life as depicted in 'Golden Land', 'Mule in the Yard' occupies a position very low on the ladder. 'Mule in the Yard' is an extravagantly humorous tale about Mannie Hait's revenge for her dead husband. She beats a Snopes on his own terms, and even if I.O. is so impossible a Snopes that Flem finds it problematic to use him, Mannie Hait's victory is important in so far as it proves that justice is still possible, if no attention is paid to the losses involved in the fight for it.

'Mule in the Yard' is told by an omniscient narrator in a straightforward way; a mode of narration which Faulkner may have found appropriate and useful, since he had to give considerable background information to get the story proper told. The story moves quickly and easily forward, save for a few passages where the narrator has to dwell on a character or has to explain connections with the past. Besides the Snopes material in the story, its detailed and varied portrait of Old Het provides most of the humour present in it. Old Het is the town beggar, whose childish nonsense puts the other characters' stupidity and rapacity in relief. 'Mule in the Yard' as a short story is in many ways saved by Het, despite the story's many macabre elements and unusually grim humour. Old Het's presence and exclamatory nonsense, her zest for life, and her indomitable endurance through all tragic events make this a representative Faulkner story of this period, where the stoic, often elderly person, who shows endurance and who by the community at large is forced to live on the fringes of society, is the real hero. It is thus consonant with the tone of the story and with the author's special concerns in this period that Old Het ends the story 'with weary and happy relaxation. "Gentlemen, hush! Ain't we had a day!" '[11]

While Mannie Hait gets her long-sought revenge due to a series of almost incredible events, the revenge is more calculated in 'A Bear Hunt', even if it still remains on a level of good-humoured jokes and friendly retributions. Behind the farcical plot of 'A Bear Hunt' lies the problem of human interrelations and interdependence, and once more the failure to understand and communicate is demonstrated. At the very centre of the story is Old Man Ash's stolid and long-nourished lust for revenge, because the Provine Gang burnt the celluloid collars belonging to him and some other Negroes twenty years ago. This incident is one of three prerequisites for the story in 'A Bear Hunt', the second being Suratt's propensity for practical jokes, and the third Luke Provine's incredible stupidity, gluttony, and superstition.

As John L. Longley, Jr., has shown, 'A Bear Hunt' is also a social comedy,[12] and although there is little need to resort to theories of comedy to explain this story, the social classes or layers in Jefferson and its immediate surroundings are described, discussed, and given representation in the action of this story. Luke Provine is

a tall, apparently strong and healthy man who loafs in a brooding, saturnine fashion wherever he will be allowed, never exactly accepted by any group, and who makes no effort whatever to support his wife and three children (Collected Stories, p. 64).

He has been a wild youth, but there is no doubt as to the frame narrator's attitude to Luke. Twenty years ago, Luke had had 'some driving, inarticulate zest for breathing which has long since burned out of him' (Collected Stories, p. 64). Jeffersonians in general adjust and conform; money and respectability, and the normal concentration round the traditional role as breadwinner and provider tie men down just as much as the rigid female roles seriously limit women's possibilities. The conflicts and contrasts in 'A Bear Hunt' never get really serious, and the

220

chief interest of the story lies in its intricate use of the induction's *raconteur*.[13]

Justice and revenge, bargains and deceits are also elements in 'Fool About a Horse', but here the events are largely kept inside one small family and are told by the young son in the family, whose evaluations and understanding are somewhat misleading, but nevertheless revealing. Poverty and shortcomings on all levels are presented in this text, but a mild irony and a deep understanding of some of the forces which shape these people's lives soften the impact of the small-scale human tragedy evidenced here. When the narrator uses *destiny* to explain why his father was a fool about a horse if ever there was one, Faulkner might well have explained this destiny in sociological terms. He does not do so explicitly, but his story demonstrates convincingly how human dignity and a deep sense of justice are also parts of these poverty-ridden people and shape their lives and account for some of their strange actions. The effects of poverty and of an inarticulate but nonetheless strongly felt class hatred are elements shared by 'Fool About a Horse' and 'Barn Burning', and it is therefore somewhat telling that both stories have strong connections with *The Hamlet*.

While all these stories may be said to be rather mild and moderate in their descriptions of injustice and revenge, with little being said about the greed and corruption and the inhuman treatment of other fellow beings, 'Lo!' is a unique example of a story that is wildly and exaggeratedly humourous yet strong and serious in its use of cultural and federal injustice and corruption.

Through its chief character, Chief Weddel, 'Lo!' is loosely related to 'A Mountain Victory',[14] and through a brief note in the Chief's letter to the President it hints upon the very important question of ownership of land which later is more fully exploited and more seriously treated in *Go Down, Moses*. In the Secretary's explanation of what had taken place at the ford where the white man established his toll gate, one can vaguely discover a hard and deadly struggle for power, although Francis Weddel in his inscrutability and mocking timidity deliberately plays this aspect of the case down. Yet however serious some of the negotiations and the killing are, 'Lo!' is first and foremost a very comic story; a situation comedy which at times borders on wild farce.[15] The situation comedy is handled with virtuosity and the use of comic suspense is a brilliant performance. One should be careful not to forget that the story is intended to be comic, yet the story points to important elements in an understanding of how the Indians came to lose their land. Shrewd white men have tried to cheat the Indians out of their property, and the Indians are more than willing to set up a wager so that they may regain what they have lost simply by not understanding the white men's thinking. Enormous values are at stake in gambling, swimming, horse racing and the like. In 'Lo!' the necessity to kill the white man who had established himself with a tollgate at the ford forms the basis of the controversy between the Indian chief and the President of the United States.

The Indian Chief, who has brought his tribe to camp on the White House lawn to the President's despair, controls the whole incredible situation. The President wrings his hands in helpless gestures, saying 'I'm just the President', and Weddel in his inflectionless voice retorts 'We are but Indians: remembered yesterday and forgotten tomorrow' (*Collected Stories*, p. 396). In one way this demonstrates the patience and perseverance his people are capable of; in another sense it shows the subtle and intelligent way Weddel plays his cards in this power game, which all the same he is bound to lose in the long run.

In 'Mule in the Yard', 'A Bear Hunt', 'Fool About a Horse', 'Lo!' and – in a different sense – 'Afternoon of a Cow' Faulkner excels in comic effects, in exaggerations and incredible situation comedy. It would thus not be fair to over-emphasize the serious elements in these stories; to do this would in fact be a misinterpretation in itself. Yet the events and conflicts which form the bases of these tall tales seem to be structured around the same conception of certain trends or tendencies in human behaviour: the sense of injustice, the search for revenge when you feel mistreated, the need for preservation of one's dignity and honour as a human being, especially in relation to one's fellow men. One might say that these human qualities are presented as unchanging, almost anthropological verities. Closer scrutiny of the individual stories seems to indicate that this is not quite so simple. Man's need for self-assertion, for emphasizing his importance, is also a result of changing social conditions, of the tougher climate he has to survive in now that modern times have reached Yoknapatawpha County. In the remaining short stories from these years this is seen very clearly, and the implied criticism of a way of life cannot be overlooked, even if more universal themes and narrative techniques are given particular attention. A general impression is that while more philosophical and fundamental problems pervaded much of

Faulkner's shorter fiction up to 1932 – often resulting in brave experimentation in form – his later stories are more concerned with individual and not always very representative destinies, even if they are related to certain specific environments and environmental pressures.

'Uncle Willy' and 'That Will Be Fine' are the Faulkner stories that best demonstrate how the half-way agrarian county of Yoknapatawpha loses most of the positive traditional values it its pursuit of happiness and some elusive American dream. Both stories would be rated high in a comparison of Faulkner's stories in this period on the basis of their treatment of injustice, revenge, lack of understanding, corruption, greed, conformity, and, in short, a perversion of all values. The negative qualities displayed in these stories are only surpassed by those in 'Golden Land'. The significance of 'Uncle Willy', 'That Will Be Fine', and 'Golden Land' necessitates a somewhat broader discussion of them, compared to the stories that have been discussed above.

'Uncle Willy' is narrated by a fourteen-year-old boy as an apology and defence for his running away from home, for which he has been reprimanded by his father. He also narrates the story about Uncle Willy as a tribute, a kind of homage, to 'the finest man I ever knew' (*Collected Stories,* p. 225), who had become a father figure to many boys in Jefferson because he met them on their level and paid no attention to the rules and regulations of the non-permissive and very narrow-minded society he lived in. Faulkner hardly ever painted Jefferson in so bleak colours as in this story, and the well-meaning, Christian woman, Mrs. Merridew, is pitilessly exposed in all her malicious and self-sufficient lack of understanding. She is, indeed, 'the super-ego in female form',[16] who decides to take Uncle Willy away from what in her eyes is a sordid, drug-ridden life. She aims to give him 'a complete rebirth' (*Collected Stories,* p. 232), and, hiding behind some arbitrary standard of conformity and believing that it is best for everybody to conform and adjust to her way of life, she treats the old man viciously and brutally. The ends justify the means in her case, and she has the full support of the church. Uncle Willy can do little but show stubborn defiance and break away for his cherished freedom to be himself. Now, much of what Willy does is a rebellion without any particular goal. Yet the reaction is started by the good women of Jefferson, and before their insistence on reforming Willy, he harmed nobody but himself and demanded nothing save to be left alone in his dark and dirty drugstore with his morphine needle. Willy is

223

not presented as any sort of ideal, but Faulkner (or the implied author, rather) seems to suggest that those who know best and feel that they have a normal supremacy have no right to meddle with other people when no wrongs are performed. The new clerk in the drug store, with 'letters to the church' (*Collected Stories*, p. 232), takes advantage of his job, and criminal activities on his part are strongly suggested in the story. Thus the moral issue at stake in the black and white portraits of protagonist (Willy) and antagonist (Mrs. Merridew and her supporters) is not so simple as some critics have found it. It is further complicated if we take into consideration the fact that the story about Uncle Willy is a four-teen-year-old boy's story, filled with his reactions and childish outbursts, yet less governed by preconceived ideas about good and bad than a grown-up's story probably would be.

The boy explains why he ran away to accompany Willy in his final attempt to get away and start a new life:

I went because Uncle Willy was the finest man I ever knew, because even women couldn't beat him, because in spite of them he wound up his life getting fun out of being alive and he died doing the thing that was the most fun of all because I was there to help him. And that's something that most men and even most women too don't get to do, not even the women that call meddling with other folks' lives fun (*Collected Stories*, p. 225).

When Mrs. Merridew and her colleagues do their best to save Willy, the boy feels that Uncle Willy is 'like one of those sheep they would sacrifice back in the Bible' (*Collected Stories*, p. 231). The good women of Jefferson take great pride in their reform work, and refuse to be thwarted by the old dope addict. When Willy seems to yield to the pressure, this is so only because a new plan to defy his would-be saviours has been formed. The final offence to the decent people in his home town is that he marries a whore in Memphis and brings her with him to town. Mrs. Merridew, in a fit of hysterics, gets the wife to leave (with $ 1000 and the car Willy's sister has given him), and then she leaves with Willy herself. The boy narrator does not get word from or about Willy until he suddenly receives a letter, instructing him to come to Memphis to meet him. He leaves, refusing to accept that Uncle Willy was crazy and had a strange hold on the boy which he should try to free himself from:

I went because I wanted to, because he was the finest man I ever knew, because he had fun all his life in spite of what they had tried to do to him or with him, and I hoped that maybe if I could stay with him a while I could learn how to, so I could still have fun too when I had to get old. Or maybe I knew more than that, without knowing it, . . .(*Collected Stories*, p. 239).

The boy also understands that Uncle Willy has not escaped Jefferson; he has merely dodged it; and that rebellion and defiance do not necessarily and in themselves solve any problems. Uncle Willy's final act is suicidal, and the boy knows this, and still he lends him a helping hand. He alone understands the urge and the deep need to be left alone that Uncle Willy feels.

The kind of reciprocal respect, of mutual friendship, of understanding and not demanding love between two people as we see it in 'Uncle Willy' is very rare, and it is therefore difficult to understand or to accept:

And now they will never understand, not even Papa, and there is only me to try to tell them and how can I ever tell them, and make them understand? How can I? (*Collected Stories*, p. 247).

'Uncle Willy' is a story about a friendship lasting beyond death – the boy narrator is grown-up and looking back at his childhood memories[17] – fragile yet strong enough to last through all hardships. In its emphasis on Willy as an outsider whom society puts pressure on in order to make him adjust, the story is also a harsh criticism of a trend in modern life towards uniformity and conformity. The boy who tells the story hopes to discover some secret about the good life, about a meaningful existence, and the only lesson he may have learnt is that it must be sought in himself and that it ultimately depends on his strength to withstand the pressure to conform and accept the rigid rules and regulations of life in a modern, urbanized world. 'Uncle Willy' is an entertaining and important short story. Its manner of narration, heaping episode upon episode in a surprising array of strange events, its suspended and yet partly revealed conclusion, its assurance that the story's deepest motivation and the real reasons for the boy's actions lie in love and understanding and human commitment, all contribute to a vivid, dramatic and extremely entertaining story. In a world where most of us show the outside 'for comfort and convenience', the story assures us that deeper fellings may still exist. When these are abandoned for comfort and decorum, human beings have become a lot poorer. If they are abandoned for other reasons – money, property, personal well-being – we are in the worlds of 'That Will Be Fine' and 'Golden Land'.

'That Will Be Fine' is also a story told by a child-narrator, Georgie, who is only seven, and who appears to be 'telling' the story immediately *after* the events described have ended. His family is preoccupied with the family honour; their only thoughts are what other people will think about this and that, and they are willing to go far to preserve the family's respectability and good name.

Told consistently in the first person and from the limited point of view of the child, whose rapacious greed is reminiscent of the young Jason Compson in *The Sound and the Fury,* the story remains comic even through its tragic end. This is so because the boy's greed is so single-minded and so much exceeds our expectations that human tragedy and death cannot do away with the exuberant comic tone of the story. Like Sut Lovingood, who believed that everybody does at least one good deed in life and goes on to say that his father put off *his* for a long time, but then he died, Georgie cannot be sidetracked by any events, possibly also because he does not grasp what really happens.

Georgie's incredible greed is explained and motivated through the conversations between the grown-up members of his family. The making of money and the possession of it is all-important to them, and family pride, honour, and a strong dose of self-indulgence (based upon money and property) in its most insincere, shallow form are greatly appreciated. Georgie's mercenary nature, his obsession with money, is thus the older generation's responsibility. The boy's greed is his defining vice, while the lecherous Uncle Rodney is defined by his vice, which in turn leads to his death. The killing of Uncle Rodney and the macabre twist in the story of calling the corpse a gift from 'all the husbands in Mottstown' (*Collected Stories,* p. 286) illustrate Georgie's limited understanding. Thus the most important narrative device in this text is the dramatic irony, resulting from this lack of understanding and the reader's perfect insight. Faulkner has had a lucky hand in rendering this prodigious child with consistency and credibility, and he has avoided the risk of becoming banal by not letting George change at all. True to his creation, Georgie does not change during the events of the story.

Debasement of human character as a function of new and easy ways of life, and of social change in general is shown in 'That Will Be Fine', and there is nothing of the stubborn pride and human honour detectable in Uncle Willy and his friend in 'Uncle Willy'. 'That Will Be Fine' only opens to a tragedy, beyond the events of the story, but as far as Georgie lets us in on this Christmas story, it remains one of the Faulkner texts most clearly in the tradition of dark Southwestern humour.

The last Faulkner short story to be discussed in this chapter and with emphasis on the theme of corruption and greed is 'Golden Land'. This is an unusual Faulkner story, to say the least. It is unusual mainly because of the choice of locale, and because of the ultra-modern, urbanized Beverly Hills life style it describes. In a different sense, 'Golden Land' also introduces the theme of *endurance* explicitly. A scrutiny of Faulkner's earlier stories will, of course, reveal this theme and also that the narrators often set great store by people's ability to endure, but as a rule this is to be inferred from the texts, whereas 'Golden Land' almost preaches *endurance* as a kind of gospel.[18] Nebraska frontier life a generation back is contrasted with the corrupt and decadent Hollywood life of the thirties, and a clash between preferences, values and morals occurs. The Southern writer, depressed and dissatisfied in his Hollywood exile, inevitably sided with the old, traditional values, a catalogue of which would include fidelity, honour, pride, compassion, and endurance. In some of Faulkner's 1942 stories, written in a period between stays in Hollywood and in an attempt to avoid going back there, the same values are stressed; so much, in point of fact, that some of the stories are more or less ruined as short stories. They tend to become banal and vague declarations about what life has become compared to what it once was. Here Faulkner preaches a gospel and forgets to create more convincing narratives about people and their lives, which might, more forcefully, bring the same message.

The implied author of 'Golden Land' reveals a norm for behaviour and decency, a norm that is not found in the easy Californian life but in the old frontier life in Nebraska. The story about the Ewing family, centring chiefly on the second and third generation living in affluent luxury and moral anarchy in California, moves back and forth in time to give precise and normative descriptions of Nebraska frontier and pioneer life and to give exact and condemning descriptions of the disgraceful, escapist life led by the modern Ewings under the 'soft – almost nebulous California haze' with its 'treacherous unbrightness' (*Collected Stories*, p. 706).

By giving few but carefully selected descriptions of the frontier life of Ira Ewing's parents and by devoting all of part III of the story to Ira's mother, Samantha, Faulkner underscores the difference between the two ways of life; and through an outline of how Ira Ewing has climbed upwards in society only to lose any and all decency he may have had, while letting his children grow up without anything to believe in or care for, Faulkner shows the complete corruption of what might be termed 'natural life'. Even if the praise of the wheat-farmer's agrarian ways and days may be judged old-fashioned and impossible to transfer to an industrialized, urbanized modern society, the story seems to deliver the message that some values should be 'learned through hardship and endurance of honor and courage and pride' (*Collected Stories*, p. 722).

In the glib and glittering world of Hollywood – in many ways a celluloid, pseudo-world – Ira Ewing is at home. Here everything has its price but nobody knows its value. Yet Ira has some unsevered roots in his Nebraska boyhood and a father who has grown 'into the proportions of a giant' (*Collected Stories*, p. 712) as he now remembers him. Ira is equipped with the capacity and stubborn unweariness that might save hime, but he seems to have come too far. The fact that he visits his mother daily indicates some of the old type of respect and piety, but in his conversations with his wife, Ira indirectly states what is needed by telling about a childhood episode. On the moral plane, especially with regard to the children, things have become so bad that Ira's solution seems the only possible one:

'. . .The question is, what to do about it. My father would have known. He did it once.' . . .'I remember. I was about ten. We had rats in the barn. We tried everything. Terriers. Poison. Then one day father said, 'Come'. We went to the barn and stopped all the cracks, the holes. Then we set fire to it. What do you think of that?' (*Collected Stories*, pp. 709—10).

Yet under the California sun life is good and easy – too easy perhaps for the Ewing family but hence also impossible to surrender. The artificiality and the hollowness of life as seen in the Ewing family is apparently representative of life in California in general, if the narrator's comments and descriptions of Beverly Hills, Los Angeles, Hollywood, etc. are accepted. 'Golden Land' may thus well be seen as a fictional comment on 'America in mid-passage',[19] where the author by implication gives unequivocal suggestions about which direction to go in the future. To endure and to prevail man simply cannot escape all hardships and responsibilities.

One critic has found 'Golden Land' to be an almost puritanical protest against the easy life in California,[20] and this critic also finds that sociological commentary overpowers the literary art in the story. Another critic finds that the story illuminates by comparison Faulkner's other works which insist that man must endure if he is to prevail.[21] Both conclusions seem a bit unfair to the story. The social criticism is evident;

228

the criticism of life in California is clear, and a moral norm is detectable. The story does not say that the easy and good life is impossible or that it cannot be accepted, however. What the story demonstrates is the lack of involvement and the total lack of human care and interest in a society where mammon and personal, private gratification are the only goals worth striving for. Where success is gauged in non-human terms, some law of Nature is broken. The final image in the ironically titled 'Golden Land' is of a landscape where Nature is exiled:

The sun was high; she could see the water from the sprinkler flashing and glinting in it as she went to the window. It was still high, still afternoon; the mountains stood serene and drab against it; the city, the land, lay sprawled and myriad beneath it – the land, the earth which spawned a thousand new faiths, nostrums and cures each year but no disease to even disprove them on – beneath the golden days unmarred by rain or weather, the changeless monotonous beautiful days without end countless out of the halcyon past and endless into the halcyon future (*Collected Stories*, pp. 725–26).

This land is perhaps 'golden' and sunny and promising, but it is the sort of land and life that takes the backbone out of man, as the Marshal in 'The Tall Men' puts it.[22] Things were different out on the Nebraska frontier where husband and wife 'stood side by side in an irrevocable loneliness' as 'blood brother and sister, even twins, of the same travail because they had gained a strange peace *through fortitude and the will and strength to endure*' (*Collected Stories*, p. 712, my emphasis).

Without a detailed study of Faulkner's autonomous short stories from 1933 to 1941 (of narrative concentration and variation, language and style), little can be said about their being a novelist's short stories. In theme and subject-matter they are closely related to Faulkner's novels of the same period – 'Wash' becomes part of a novel even. On the other hand, most of these stories are independent in the sense that they do not rely on support from the larger 'saga' of Yoknapatawpha or gain added significance because they are reiterated attempts to tell the same story as in earlier novels or short stories. 'Lo!' is vaguely linked to 'A Mountain Victory' and to Faulkner's other Indian stories, whereas 'Uncle Willy', 'That Will Be Fine', and 'Golden Land' are autonomous short stories, complete in themselves. With the exception of 'Golden Land' which is placed in Hollywood, these stories are located in well-known areas of Yoknapatawpha County, and this makes it possible for the author to avoid detailed descriptions of background, history, etc. He can select the most pertinent and most telling elements of his story for the narrative, and leave the others out also because his kingdom is established before-hand. In this sense also the stories discussed in this chapter are a novelist's short stories: broad and dense stories about people and events in Yoknapatawpha can be narrated within the relatively limited length of the short story because concentration is possible now that the author (if not all his readers) know the environment of his characters. The use of a limited point of view, e.g. the child narrator, also makes it permissible, but not necessary, for the author to keep within the limitations of the narrator's vision, perspective and understanding. In all these relatively brief narratives, stories of a wide expanse, including both analepsis and paralepsis and with reiterative forms as a common trait, can be narrated because the artist deliberately has left out, summed up, hinted and indicated, instead of telling it all in chronological order. Discourse-time is, of course, much shorter than story-time in all these narratives, and although not all of them carry in them the material of which novels are made, it is fair to say that they show that Faulkner's short stories are a novelist's short stories, also when the obvious and superficial relation-ships with novels are not present. The other short stories from this period are, on the other hand, very close to his novels, as will be seen in the following chapter.

7. Short Stories 1933–1941
Cycles of Stories, or Novels?

> And as he talked about those old times and those
> dead and vanished men of another race from either
> that the boy knew, gradually to the boy those old
> times would cease to be old times and would become
> a part of the boy's present, not only as if they had
> happened yesterday but as if they were still happen-
> ing, the men who had walked through them actually
> walking in breath and air and casting an actual
> shadow on the earth they had not quitted.
> – Faulkner, *Go Down, Moses*

In the years between 1933 and 1941 Faulkner wrote a number of short
stories that were later revised and included in books. The revisions gave
the stories an overall unity that the individual stories did not originally
have, or they served to link the stories more closely together in a
narrative that finally came to look very much like a novel. This is true for
the stories about Bayard and Ringo that became *The Unvanquished,* and
for the stories about race and wilderness, love and death, in Yoknapatawpha of yesterday and today, collected in *Go Down, Moses*. To a lesser
extent the detective stories that were later collected in *Knight's Gambit*
form a unified and linear story, although it is probably fair to describe
this as a collection of short stories despite similarities in theme, character
and setting. Obviously many of these stories, if not all, are a novelist's
short stories in the sense that the author could fairly easily revise
previously published and a few unpublished stories and join them
together in books that deserve to be called novels. We may have to say
that they are loosely joined novels, but they are certainly not 'mere'
collections of short stories.

Faulkner did not evaluate his stories about Bayard and Ringo and the
Civil War very highly. He felt that he sacrificed more important work by
writing short stories with the single purpose of bringing in badly needed
money. As a short-story writer Faulkner here exploited material that in
a sense belonged more to his novels than to his short stories: the Sartoris
clan, a Snopes figure, the carpetbaggers following in the wake of the

Civil War, to write humorous, light-hearted, and entertaining stories which he thought would be appreciated by the editors of the *Saturday Evening Post*.[1] Some of Faulkner's more genuine concerns about race, family-ties, decency, and honour nevertheless slipped into these stories; in particular in the later stories and also in his revisions of the earlier ones.[2] Yet for the most part the seven stories must be deemed 'romanticised "tall tales" of heroic Southern resistance to the North', as Michael Millgate puts it.[3] Every attempt made to understand this book or to rank it with the major works in Faulkner's canon, should not forget to take into account the fact that all seven stories[4] were created with an eye on the *Post,* and that Faulkner's craftsmanship enabled him to write light and amusing stories, without the serious and solemn overtones which the subject-matter inevitably invites. *The Unvanquished* stories are professional work on a high level, but they are definitely geared to the needs of a particular market, where Faulkner's normal heaviness and seriousness would be a disadvantage. The very fact that Hollywood bought the movie rights for the book indicates something to the same effect; if Faulkner's 'pulp writings' are better than the average writing so termed, it still remains pulp, and *The Unvanquished* is undoubtedly a minor work among Faulkner's novels, if it is regarded as such.[5] Critics have been very cautious in their evaluations of *The Unvanquished,* in part because their opinions have been influenced by the fact that six of the seven stories appeared in popular magazines, and in part because they have not been sufficiently aware of the significant change that most of the stories underwent before being included in the book. Recent scholarship has tried to set this right, and in its reaction to earlier criticism, this new trend may well have gone too far in its celebration of *The Unvanquished* as a first rate work of fiction and a superb example of what some critics find to be a modern form of fiction and which they term short-story cycle or short-story composite. Joanna Creighton and Forrest L. Ingram most strongly advocate such a new genre concept, and defend *The Unvanquished* on a new set of criteria compared to what Cleanth Brooks used when he, as one of the few, praised this book relatively early. Brooks as well as Creighton plead their cases convincingly; Brooks by showing that structural elements of great significance, also with relation to the theme of the novel, serve to link the chapters together and form a loosely structured novel out of the seven original stories. Creighton makes extensive use of Faulkner's revisions to show how carefully and conscientiously he introduced an older and more mature narrator into the revised version and thereby established a more clearly retrospective view of the incidents and cruelties of war. She also demonstrates how Faulkner through the same revisions underlined certain structural elements and gave added significance to the issue of *race*.

The significance of Faulkner's revisions had been overlooked by most critics for a long time, with the notable exception of James B. Meriwether, who paid close attention to the revisions in his 1958 doctoral dissertation and thereby could demonstrate the closer unity of the work as a whole.[6] Brooks, Ingram, Creighton, and Holmes[7] thus differ from most critics in their insistence that *The Unvanquished* must be taken as a serious work of art and in stressing the quality of Faulkner's writing in this book.[8] Yet Ingram and Creighton hold that the book is not a novel, even though they do not dismiss it as merely a collection of individual stories.

Cleanth Brooks suggests that a more useful, though more prosaic, title for *Go Down, Moses* would be *The McCaslins,* 'for the book has to do with the varying fortunes of that family and only one story, "Pantaloon in Black", does not deal with it directly'.[9] Although Faulkner's title is functional and relates directly to the theme of the book, Brooks's suggestion indicates one important element of *Go Down, Moses* which should be emphasized: the book's overall unity, despite the fact that it consists of as many as nine stories, most of which were published separately as short stories in periodicals.[10] One might argue that the unifying elements that can be found in all the stories only serve to give the book the character of a loosely structured novel,[11] and then go on to show how Faulkner carefully revised the original short stories to achieve this unifying effect. The overall impression of *Go Down, Moses,* which a study of recurrent phrases, memories, names, events, thoughts, as well as of symbols and images, supports, is one of a strangely unitary composition, in which the individual short stories function not as separate narratives but rather as variations and concretizations of a complex and at times rather abstract theme. The fire on the hearth in Lucas Beauchamp's cottage is such a unifying element, which also carries important symbolic connotations; the pursuit or, rather, a kind of ritual hunt, provides a frame for most of the stories, and all of them – including 'Pantaloon in Black' – are related to the McCaslin plantation, the very centre of the novel if we regard it as such.

233

Faulkner's detective stories are less interesting in relation to a discussion of short-story cycles and loosely joined novels, since *Knight's Gambit* should first and foremost be seen as a collection of individual stories, with detection and the same detective-lawyer as unifying elements. The stories appear in the book in the chronological order of their appearance in magazines, with a revised and expanded version of an unpublished story to finish the volume.

In public appearances Faulkner was evasive and cautious when asked about detective books. Interviews were a part of Faulkner's late years when he was an established, almost canonized writer, and it may well be that his evasive answers to such questions were attempts to defend the image of the serious and inscrutable sage. To Jean Stein's question in 1956 whether he 'ever read mystery stories', Faulkner answered that he 'read Simenon because he reminds me of Chekhov'[12] and the year before he had used the same technique of dodging the questions when Cynthia Grenier asked a similar question about his reading habits. *The Brothers Karamazov* was the one 'good' detective story he mentioned in his answer.[13] The twenty-five volumes of detective books in his library, including John Dickson Carr, Dashiell Hammett, Ellery Queen, and Rex Stout – all among the top-notchers of American crime writers – alone negate or reduce the validity of Faulkner's interview replies. Even though there is every reason to stress the significance and formative aspect of Faulkner's very selective reading of classical literature, there is no reason to conceal his lasting interest in detective fiction. Being an avid reader, and showing a great variety in taste, he simply had to come across writers like Chandler and Hammett. Furthermore, Faulkner in early novels such as *As I Lay Dying* and *Sanctuary* – as well as in numerous stories from the early thirties – showed a particular – some critics said morbid – interest in violence and cruelty, in uncontrolled passions and murder. It was only natural that he would also try to present these elements of human life from the point of the investigator where justice or truth was sought.

The fact that his only collection of detective stories was called *Knight's Gambit* is also an indication of this element of the tales of ratiocination: Gavin Stevens is the modern Knight who helps the underdogs in seeing justice done, even if justice and truth are not always the same.[14]

The composition of the volume covers a time span of almost two decades, and the stories demonstrate Faulkner's experimentation and preliminary concepts of Gavin Stevens, who would mature and become an extremely important character in the last two books in the Snopes trilogy: *The Town* and *The Mansion*. 'Smoke' is one of Faulkner's first Gavin Stevens stories, if not indeed the very first. 'Smoke' is chosen as the opening story of the volume, and Michael Millgate finds this to be one of the most serious flaws of the book, which he all in all only grants minor importance.[15] Millgate finds the story to be the weakest of the six stories in the volume, and he speculates that Faulkner's reason for including it at all may have been that he needed every one of the Gavin Stevens stories to fill the book. That 'Smoke' fails as a detective story because vital information is withheld from the reader is not the most serious accusation; more important is that the tone set by this opening story is false. What follows in the volume is superior to the limited expectations the opening story creates, and hence the reader's understanding of the subsequent stories may be seriously harmed. Millgate's criticism is understandable, but nonetheless a bit unfair. Admittedly, 'Smoke' is a weak story, but its chief weakness lies in the ratiocinative parts and the incredible denouement in the courtroom. Yet the introductory part presents an area of Yoknapatawpha where almost primitive and uncivilized, uncultured, people live and love and breed and die. This setting is almost identical to the settings of all the other stories. Moreover, the usurping outlander, Anselm Holland, is presented here. The outlander – and the 'outlandish' things he can do – is at the core of all the stories. The strangers come to remote areas of Yoknapatawpha County and appropriate parts of the land or other wealth which they have no claim on. They do not communicate with anybody in particular or with the community in general; some of them because they simply lack the ability (Monk), others because they are loners whose affairs had better be concealed ('An Error in Chemistry', 'Knight's Gambit'), and others again because they have absolutely nothing in common with the community they live in. A rigidly structured society with codified expectations and demands does not easily accept strangers, of course, and the good citizens of Jefferson are not without blame for the total lack of communication with the outlanders. This theme, pointed out and demonstrated most thoroughly by Jerome F. Klinkowitz,[16] is an important unifying factor in the book, which nevertheless is very loosely held together by this theme and the two characters of Chick and Gavin

235

Stevens who appear in all the stories. The fact that Chick is the narrator of the first five stories might have added to the unity of the work, but this is hardly the case. Even if *Knight's Gambit* is consistent in narration, scene, tone, and, to some extent, character and theme, it remains a collection of six stories and has never been intended to be more unified than this by the author. Klinkowitz quotes Faulkner's statement about a short-story collection's 'form' and 'integration' towards 'one end, one finale',[17] arguing that the author would never allow a publisher to assemble at random what he had written since the last collection. Faulkner *was* particular about his collections of short stories, and he always did some if not most of the work on them himself, but this does not imply that the unity of *Knight's Gambit* necessarily is very strong. What Faulkner actually did with this collection was to rewrite the title-story (by vastly expanding it); otherwise he collected the Gavin Stevens stories according to chronology of composition and publication.

* * *

The revisions that Faulkner had to undertake for *The Unvanquished* and *Go Down, Moses,* and also for 'Knight's Gambit', follow a familiar pattern for many of the author's revisions of short-story texts in the major period, albeit he then revised the stories for magazine publication and not to become parts of a larger unified whole. Additional background and motivation for the characters' conduct is given; anecdotes are told to broaden the perspective or to place the central characters in a more clearly defined social environment. In *The Unvanquished* there is also a movement away from simplicity of language towards a structure where much more complex and complicated relationships and patterns of reaction may be detected. This movement is closely related to the change in narrative perspective, because the more mature narrator in the novel contemplates and speculates and broods over many problems which escape the mind of the playful young boy as we see him in, e.g., 'Ambuscade' in the *Post* version.

What the revisions as a whole do is to interject a more serious view of character and war-time experiences, without abandoning the wildly exaggerated humour which is central in the magazine pieces. The heaviness and seriousness is not allowed to replace the boyish joy and excitement, yet it inadvertently modifies and softens it now that it is seen in retrospect. As mentioned above, the alteration of perspective necessarily also changes the language and the tone of the narrator, and it also

236

subtly redistributes emphasis in the book so that certain themes become more important there than they appear to be in the series of short stories. This is not only due to the change of perspective and the consistent use of a more detached, yet involved, narrator; it is also a result of the author's interpolation of new scenes and episodes where the problem of black-white relations is focal. The sketch of Uncle Buck and Uncle Buddy functions in this way.

Despite the paramount importance of the racial questions in the book-version of the stories, one should not forget that Bayard Sartoris devotes considerable thought to a re-evaluation of his father, or rather, of his own childhood image of his father. This is in particular true of the first story in the book, 'Ambuscade', and seen in relation to Bayard's later struggle to live up to and yet break loose from the Sartoris code ('An Odor of Verbena'), this is very important. The opening paragraphs of the two versions of 'Ambuscade' show how substantial Faulkner's revisions were. These paragraphs include none of the revisions concerning Bayard's reactions to his father, yet it is quite evident that the rather sophisticated language and the intricate use of parenthetical comments together with the massing of minute details all belong to an adult awareness of things that happened in his past. From being a more or less nostalgic picture of his childhood experiences during the time of war, 'Ambuscade' in its revised form has become a more critical and analytical portrait of past events. Thus an important gap between the actor Bayard and the narrator Bayard arises. This gap may also be described as a double perspective: we are told how Bayard perceived events as a boy and also how he interprets them now that he has matured. There is little doubt that the writing of 'An Odor of Verbena' – which unquestionably is the very keystone of the book –[18] necessitated some of the changes and led to additional alterations when the author had set about doing this work.

Even though numerous critics have pointed to this double perspective,[19] they have not all made satisfactory use of the interpretive help and the deeper significance it offers. The discrepancy between the boys' world and what they see and react to in it, and the adult narrator's interpretation of these past observations and perceptions, becomes in the final analysis a scrutiny of how our memory works and of how far our understanding really goes. Bayard examines in great detail, with numerous speculations and assumptions, the *facts* that must lie beneath his understanding of them. He has to disentangle his imagination and childhood exaggerations from what really must have gone on, and he has to rely on his own retrospective analysis to do this. Bayard is desperately in need of some of these facts; e.g. with regard to his own father, who loomed so large in his childhood fantasy, because he has to build his future life on his past experiences. He has to come to grips with the Sartoris code, and he has to break with it. Without digging beneath the picture he has more or less conjured up in his fantasy of the Colonel and seeing that this image of his father has been both romanticized and idealized, Bayard would probably not have been able to free himself from the claims which simply *being* a Sartoris put upon him. Bayard, together with many a Faulkner character who has to look to the past to understand the present, draws a lesson from his war-time experience. As a Southerner, he may well regard the war as a lost cause and regret it; yet if he – and the South – were to prosper and grow in the future, they would have to build their lives on the hard-won lesson which defeat has taught them. Faulkner, as we have seen many times, seemed to believe strongly that defeat was good for a people.

The seven short stories and the seven book chapters cover a period of about twelve years beginning in 1863,[20] when Bayard is twelve years old. The first five stories are set in the war-ridden South, and the events narrated in these stories reach a culmination in the gruesome revenge carried out by Uncle Buck, Ringo and Bayard in 'Vendée'. Although episodic and apparently loosely linked together by character and scene, one can also find causal connections between the short stories. The revenge in 'Vendée' is a direct result of the murder of Granny (Rosa Millard) in 'Riposte in Tertio', while the business with the silver, the mules, and the Negroes which is so vastly exaggerated in the same story, has its basis in earlier stories ('Retreat' and 'Raid' in particular). Textual evidence also shows that these five stories originally fitted less well in with the more serious direction of the two later stories. They had therefore to be considerably revised, while the Drusilla-story ('Skirmish at Sartoris') called for only slight revision and 'An Odor of Verbena' was, of course, written as the concluding chapter of the *book*.

The first three short stories have wildly exaggerated plots, and the stories are in fact centred around these plots, which become their most important structural units. The plots are kept almost unaltered in the revised versions, even though the framework around them (including the narrator's interpretation of them) changes significantly. In 'Ambuscade' the two boys fire at a Yankee soldier, shooting his horse, but since the officer turns out to be a Gentleman with due respect for an old Southern lady, he lets Rosa Millard get away with her lies when she hides the boys under her wide skirts. In 'Retreat' Colonel Sartoris and the two boys capture a small group of Yankee soldiers; in 'Raid' Rosa and the boys recover not only their own confiscated silver and mules but further ten chests of silver, 110 mules and 110 Negroes; all due to an incredible misunderstanding on the part of the Yankee officer. Even Cleanth Brooks, otherwise a strong defender of The Unvanquished, thinks that Faulkner should have played down this part of the story.[21] In 'Riposte in Tertio' the invincible grandmother forges official letters in order to requisition still more mules from the Yankee army, only to sell them back to other regiments in the same army. She plays the role of a Southern Robin Hood, giving her profits to the poor in her county, but keeping accurate accounts of what she has given away. Ab Snopes aids her in the mule business but he is nonetheless indirectly responsible for her death, since he talks her into dealing with Grumby's band of raiders. 'Vendée' shows Bayard, Ringo, and Uncle Buck McCaslin tracking down and killing Rosa's murderer. They take his right hand home with them and fasten it on the headboard of Granny's grave. Bayard has lived up to the demands of his name and the code implied in the very name Sartoris; and accordingly he feels no regrets, although the strain on him has been enormous.

The Drusilla-story tells about Drusilla Hawk, who has fought with Colonel Sartoris's troop and who now that the war has come to an end is still wearing men's clothes, living in the Sartoris house after she returned from the war with the Colonel. The good ladies of Jefferson – finally also with the help of Mrs. Hawk – force Drusilla into a dress and demand that Colonel Sartoris marry her. Some Northerners meanwhile try to give the Negroes voting rights and they even try to get a Negro elected U.S. Marshal. Faithful to his code and to the tradition of the Southern Gentleman and plantation owner, the Colonel stops the election, appoints Drusilla commissioner, and moves the election to the Sartoris place. To achieve all this he has to kill the two Northerners, so it is no wonder that he and Drusilla forget to get married! 'Skirmish at Sartoris' thus demonstrates how little war has changed Colonel Sartoris, and how his traditional role as ruler of other people's lives is intact. In many ways he acts as the proverbial Southern gentleman and plantation owner and in the post-war period he uses his position and influence and ingenuity to build a railroad and thus lay the foundations of a new prosperity and a new society.

In 'An Odor of Verbena' the almost inevitable has happened: Colonel Sartoris has pressed a man too far, and this man – his one-time partner – has shot and killed him. Sartoris has met his adversary unarmed, and he had informed Bayard that he would do this. This knowledge is vital to Bayard, since he has to resist the pressure from men in his father's troop who expect him to avenge his father's death. Moreover, Drusilla is the one who most passionately and desperately urges Bayard to kill, believing that vengeance is his duty and mission.[22] Bayard faces his adversary unarmed and Redmond[23] fires and misses twice on purpose, and flees to leave Jefferson for good. The verbena of the title is important: it is said to have the only scent that can be smelled above the smell of horses and courage, and Drusilla leaves a sprig of it behind as a token for Bayard. Thereby she quietly acknowledges that his decision not to kill also shows great courage, if not of the physical kind that she was apt to admire, but yet possibly a greater courage than a gun fight would require.

Bayard's final decision is the end-product of a lasting conflict which pervades every page of the book, and which is also present – if not very explicitly – in the magazine stories. The conflict may be analysed and interpreted as an individual dilemma or as the conflict between a given set of norms (a *code*) and a personal morality with its basis in Christianity. The conflict is also a different one, however: a conflict between an absolute law upon which society rests and the need for more immediate and drastic measures in time of war. Robert E. Knoll gives this description of what he calls 'two modes of behavior', and which he finds side by side in each section of the book:

The mode which Granny preaches is one-dimensional: lying is bad, sharpness in business is bad, and cursing must be followed with a soaped mouth. The system of rules which she teaches her boys is proper to a settled society. It is the codified result of multiple, not individual, experience. Few persons can learn from their own observation that blasphemy, even such blasphemy as Ringo's occasional 'damn', undercuts the bulwarks of society, but Granny knows it is wrong. She knows it on principle. She knows it as part of her traditional faith. It is her insistence on civilizing Law that sets her apart and above in a world collapsing into chaos about her.

But beside the traditional system of conduct which Granny teaches the boys, and gives her allegiance to, the stories propose a new pattern of behavior. The characters in the stories must live by it. It is primitive. It makes no reference to a set of absolute principles, to the accumulated wisdom of generations. According to this new code, an action is justified by its consequences.[24]

When Bayard and Ringo and Uncle Buck killed Grumby this was a right and necessarry thing to do, not only because of a Jungle Law and some 'an eye for an eye' principle, but also because Grumby deserved it and the war itself required this kind of expediency. When Bayard later decided not to seek vengeance on Redmond, this is an even more admirable action not because killing is bad and revenge only calls for new revenge; it was also the right thing to do, since the time of expediency and vengeance and primitive law had passed. The time for civilized life, for Law, had come. Thus the apparent inconsistency in Bayard's actions can be explained not only with reference to his greater understanding and his maturation which make him avoid bloodshed; his refusal to meet Redmond on the old system's terms must also be judged against the contemporary scene. As Knoll puts it, 'the times had turned around', and he maintains that the central theme of the novel is that all action must be judged within the context of its happening.[25]

Bayard's growth and maturation through hardships and struggle during the war is an important element in *The Unvanquished,* particularly so since Bayard is *the* central character in the story he himself narrates. He is finally the one who must break out of the vicious circle of hatred and revenge and retaliation, and his repudiation of the code of vengeance is also of great significance to the rest of the community around him. One may agree with Andrew Lytle that *The Unvanquished* shows the disintegration of a particular society,[26] even though it is difficult to accept that the book functions as a 'parable of the way in which any society goes to pieces'.[27] For one thing, the element of social comedy and light and warm-hearted humour is too strong in this book to allow us to invest the characters and their actions with too much symbolic significance. Even though order and stability and rigid standards (codified conduct) give way to new ways of life in the South after the war, disruption is by no means total and chaos is not inevitably the result. The South's defeat could not be a defeat in this sense; in Faulkner's philosophy it seems that the victorious lose what the defeated gain, and that one cannot help but profit as a people – in understanding, humanity, love of mankind – if one is defeated. This would also explain the book's title: characters like the ones we meet in this novel could lose a war and see the tragedy of their lost cause, but they could never be vanquished, never really be beaten.

If one insists that *Go Down, Moses* is about Ike McCaslin and his repudiation, one is bound to be troubled by the apparent inconsistencies in narrative tone and by the fact that Ike is missing from large parts of the book. If, on the other hand, one holds that the theme of the book is black-white relations, one may be seriously troubled by the hunting stories and the wilderness theme. Furthermore, if one sees the book as the story of the tainted family of the McCaslins, 'Pantaloon in Black' does not necessarily belong in such a book. Yet the fact remains that Faulkner included the story there, and this can only be understood if emphasis is put both on the theme of racial injustice and on what might be described as the world or society of a Southern plantation. *Go Down, Moses* centres significantly around the McCaslin place[28] – all the characters in the book of any importance relate to this place in some way or other, and even in the book's present time (early 1940's), this place seems to form the stable and unchanging centre of a society in miniature.

The apparent singularity of 'Pantaloon in Black' has led critics to argue that it is not integrated in *Go Down, Moses,* and hence does not belong there. This is a wrong approach to the short story, and to the book as a whole. There is reason to think that the author placed the short story here with serious intentions and because he felt that it contributed to the volume as a whole. Accordingly one should look for those elements of 'Pantaloon in Black' that correspond to or broaden the themes and relationships found in the other parts of the book, and there cannot be any doubt that the primary effect of 'Pantaloon in Black' is to demonstrate how a simple and primitive man is capable of grief and sorrow which none of the educated and cultivated men around him could possibly match.[29] In other words, the hard, tough, apparently untouched Negro, who has lost his wife, displays an intense and desperate grief which tears him apart, although he is not able to articulate his loss – at least not so that the white people would grasp it. That the strong, hardworking Negro, Rider, works at a saw-mill links the story vaguely to the wilderness theme, which will become central in the next sections of the book, while his poverty implies exploitation by the white employers. Usurpation and foul play are also present in this story; the man whom Rider slays has been cheating all the Negro hands at the mill out of most of their incomes for years.

This preliminary presentation of one of the chapters – the most problematic one in relation to the book's structure – indicates that the double theme of exploitation – of the black man and of the wilderness – must be taken into account if we are to explain some of the peculiarities of the structure of *Go Down, Moses*. These themes are very broad and can only be deemed valid if the book is seen at a great distance. If we look more closely at it, the themes become much more explicit, and multiple and varied manifestations of them can be found in all parts of the book. I have chosen to concentrate on what I consider to be two main groups of stories in the book – each might be termed a 'novella' – and on the thematic subtleties of individual stories as well as of the volume in general.

Go Down, Moses opens with a description of Uncle Ike, 'past seventy and nearer eighty than he ever corroborated any more, a widower now and uncle to half a county and father to no one' (*Go Down, Moses*, p. 3). This introduction has troubled many critics, since Isaac McCaslin is not participating in the events of the story 'Was', in point of fact he was not yet born then. Yet Ike had to have a place in the opening story, if only because he is the central character of the book as a whole, and because the things that once existed, which were part of 'was', are parts of his heritage and had to be told somehow, as Faulkner himself put it in Virginia when asked about the title 'Was'.[30] The outrageously comic story about various hunts and numerous almost-captures[31] was revised substantially from the unpublished typescript Faulkner had, and the most important addition is, of course, the lengthy addition of part I – which could not possibly work with the short story alone, even though Faulkner readers now may find that it functions well as an introductory frame to this story alone as well as to the volume as a whole. 'Was' is thus given the significance of a romanticized legend which probably has a core of truth in it, and the 'was' of the story may be compared to the 'was' as it is now remembered as 'is' in the mind and consciousness of people like Isaac McCaslin. Faulkner may be right when he asserts that there is no such thing as was 'because the past is. It is a part of every man, every woman, and every moment. . . . And so a man, a character in a story at any moment of action is not just himself as he is then, he is all that made him. . . . '[32] Faulkner's fictional representation of the relationship between things past and things present is not as simple as this may indicate, and this has to do with the distorting effect of memory and with the conscious or unconscious modifications which time and memory and pride and prejudice and all kinds of attitudes and expectations have at 'was'. What really 'was' seldom corresponds to what memory has made out of it, and few characters have the power and the will to search beyond the veils of time to come to grips with the real events of the past. The use of Ike in the opening paragraphs of 'Was' may be seen in relation to this: he is here to lend credulity and verisimilitude to the story; he is outside the story, and to some extent outside and exempt of time too, since he outlived all his contemporaries.

The fragmentary and almost unintelligible introductory section of 'Was' presents numerous expectations, and it promises by implication more information, not only concerning the central character of Uncle Ike, but also pertaining to the broader themes and involving genealogical and miscegenetic considerations which are linked with Ike's heritage and even with his repudiation of his inheritance. Faulkner's revision of the original story, especially the change from first-person narration by the boy Bayard to a third-person narrative through the broader perspective of Cass Edmonds, was clearly done with the structure and unity of the *book* in mind.[33] The wildly funny story opens on Uncle Buck's and Uncle Buddy's hunt for Tomey's Turl, who constantly escapes from under their very noses, and gives the author an opportunity to place Uncle Buck in the bed of the spinster Sophonsiba, which in its turn sets the scene for the final poker games where Buck's bachelorhood and Tomey's Turl's freedom and Tomey's Turl's girl are at stake. It is subtly in tone with the atmosphere of the story that Buck's escape from marriage to Sophonsiba depends on one single card in the game. It should not be overlooked that much of the humour of the story stems from the fact that Uncle Buck and Uncle Buddy are stereotypes: the proverbial bachelors, one of whom – the better poker player – has to help the other when he is unable to extricate himself from the web the determined Sophonsiba had laid out for him.[34] Yet the story also supplies the information about how Buck and Buddy abolished slavery on their own plantation, a point which is very important to Ike and which is retold in greater depth and detail in 'The Bear'. Since Ike is introduced in 'Was', it is important to note that Buck's and Buddy's action comes to represent an ideal attitude and also a promise for the future. Their unselfish deed is partly responsible for Ike's repudiation of *his* inheritance when he is twenty-one. As we shall see, there is much more to it than that, and it may well be that Ike's ideal

244

crumbles somewhat under closer scrutiny, so that even his own convictions and his attempts at expiation may be judged as escapism or defeatism.[35]

'Was' may be discussed as a short story in its own right – which it has been, albeit critics in general treat it condescendingly. Yet not only its first section but the story as a whole may be seen as an introduction to the novel; not because it sets the tone or the atmosphere for the book, but because the most important thematic implications of *Go Down, Moses* are intermingled with the humorous tale about the various hunts and the poker game. Seen from this point of view, part I of 'Was' (together with section 4 of 'The Bear') may be regarded as 'key unifying devices of the composite', to use Creighton's words.[36] Despite Ike's significance as the central character of the book, we do not meet him again in person till much later, in the almost mythical, sombre, and quiet ritual of 'The Old People'. There are numerous references to him in the three-part story, 'The Fire and The Hearth', which follows 'Was' in *Go Down, Moses,* and which continues much of the fun and comic adventures of the former story. Serious comments on life on the McCaslin plantation and recurrent memories of how it once was to be both a plantation owner and a slave take over and replace the humour and incredible cunning which Lucas demonstrates and in fact embodies. Without the serious and at times grave overtones, 'The Fire and the Hearth' would easily become another instance of Negro-White comedy, where the fun stems from the old Negro's outwitting all white people, and thus gaining a brief victory over his masters. The inversion of the positions assigned to certain people, races, or classes by their prescribed roles or by a society's order, almost invariably calls forth comic effects. Lucas, in all his gluttony, rapacity, and unbelievable smartness and endurance, is a figure with certain pathethic if not tragic dimensions. He is a McCaslin himself, more so than Roth Edmonds, and he has fought hard for his pride and integrity. The retrospective parts of the story which tell about the flood and Lucas's role in fetching a doctor to save the child of the plantation owner, and the ensuing sacrifices his wife, Molly, and he himself had to endure, portray not a comic villain but a human being doing what is right and what must be done, but who is nonetheless uncertain about what he has done. His wife, feeding their child as well as the white proprietor's, lives in the white man's house; Lucas has to get her back without losing face, without losing any of his personal integrity. Lucas has been moonshining for over 20 years on the plantation, he is crazy about money, and believes strongly that hidden treasures can be found and almost kills himself hunting for them. Yet Lucas has money in the bank,[37] probably more money than the white plantation owner. Lucas is scheming and cheating, or so it seems, whenever he has the opportunity; yet the only code he lives by is definitely a code of strict and old-fashioned honour. Lucas wants to fend for himself, he does not scrape or crawl for the white men, he never calls Roth Mister until his wife has decided to leave him. His giving in and promising to stay at home and stay 'sane' are all implied in his use of Mister Roth Edmonds.

'The Fire and the Hearth' is made up of two published and one unpublished short story, so that the section of the book when viewed as an entity might possibly be described as a novella. At any rate, 'The Fire and the Hearth' is undoubtedly one of Faulkner's finest long stories. Some of the strength of the story lies in its avoidance of melancholy or pathos – even though it has touches of both in its moving and heart-shattering descriptions of Molly's plight (section 3). It is important not to forget Molly's central position in this story (and in the concluding, title-story of the volume). This may somehow reduce what seems to be a very neat balance between Lucas in one main part of the novel and Isaac in the other main section; especially since these two men – black and white – are the two most important characters in the book and because they both contradict and to some extent complement one another. Molly is nonetheless the prototype of Faulkner's admirable and beloved old Negro woman – a fictional portrait of Mammy Barr, whom he dedicated the book to – and she is in many respects the embodiment of all the virtues which are cherished in this particular society and which may be regarded as key-stones in most decent, civilized communities.

This tiny Negro woman, who has been married to Lucas for more than forty years, wants a divorce and almost gets it before Lucas gives in and decides that he has so little left of the three score years and ten which the Lord provides for that it is too late for him to find the fortune he has been hunting for. On the day of their marriage, a fire was lit on the hearth and through all these years, in summer and winter, spring and fall, in happiness and in sorrow and pain, the fire has been burning. It becames a symbol of endurance and faith, of love and forgiving, and it is one of the few stable and unchanging signs at the plantation where so much has happened over the years. Lucas is an old man – only Isaac is older but he lives in Jefferson now – and his memories of the past are interpolated into the narrative about the events of 1941, so that the story broadens and diversifies and takes on additional sociological implications. Ike's repudiation of his inheritance and Lucas's violent reactions to this act, which he considers an act of weakness and of giving in to pressure from the Edmonds branch of the family, is also a part of this story. We thus have a certain basis on which to begin an evaluation and appreciation of Ike McCaslin before 'his' part of the book. Before the story of Ike begins, 'Pantaloon in Black' intervenes to slow down the pace of the narrative and to add drama and tragedy in a very concrete way where tragedy has only been remembered and hinted at before. We have discussed this story briefly above; suffice it therefore here to mention only that this story, in which grief and loss and murder come in close succession and cause a man to go mad, greatly underscores and emphasizes the incredible stamina, endurance, and other admirable human qualities that must have been necessary for many of the black people simply in order to survive. 'Pantaloon in Black' adds to the world of the plantation, but with its looser connection to the McCaslin world it also prepares us for the sojourns in a somewhat larger world, a world that is not limited by the boundaries of the plantation and where people's lives are not bound to it forever by the frail but everlasting threads of kinship, blood-relations, debts, work, sympathies or whatever. 'Pantaloon in Black' thus prepares us to enter a world where 'The Bear' can take place, and where the wildnerness can be gnawed at till its ultimate destruction is achieved.

Warren Beck, who has written what is probably the most thorough and detailed analysis of *Go Down, Moses,* describes Isaac McCaslin's life story as 'one of the most impressive novellas in modern fiction'[38] and this novella is not only 'The Bear'. Beck includes 'The Old People' and 'Delta Autumn' in it, so that the central text, 'The Bear', is framed by the other two stories. It seems valid to discuss these three short stories as a unit, even though a serious examination would have to include a consideration of the relation between the various parts of 'The Bear' and of the relation between the frame stories and the parts of 'The Bear'. Section IV of 'The Bear' is particularly problematic; as Faulkner explained it this section belongs to the book-chapter while it does not belong to 'The Bear' as a short story, which explains why it was printed without part IV in *Big Woods*. Despite the uniqueness of part IV, there is no doubt that the incidents and decisions in Ike's life relayed in this part are closely and subtly connected with his experiences as a hunter, beginning in 'The Old People' and continuing throughout 'The Bear', one of the greatest hunting stories in world literature. Ike's priest-like purity, his initiation to the wildnerness, and his growing understanding of what it takes to compound a man, may in part serve to explain his radical decision, which can be judged in many ways. In 'The Old People' young Ike is initiated into manhood by Sam Fathers, through a ritualistic hunt and through the ceremonial washing of his face in the blood of the animal. The initiation also has a second part, where Sam and Ike see an enormous buck, which the other members of the hunting party do not discover. Cass Edmonds reveals that Sam had taken him to see the same buck when he had killed his first deer, many years ago. 'The Old People' also gives a sustained description of Sam Fathers's background; he is an unacknowledged son of Ikkemotubbe, the Chickasaw chief, whose rise to power through murder and terror is also described in Faulkner's early Indian stories, especially 'A Justice'. Sam has red, black, and white blood in him, and he is in many respects given exemption from the duties and toils of the McCaslin place; which in part is the result of his being primarily a hunter. Each November he joins the hunting party on its annual expedition to the Big Bottom, until one day he leaves the plantation to take up permanent residence in the camp.

In the ritual of the hunt strong primitive and pagan elements have a decisive influence on young Ike; and all through the story of his life this influence can be detected. In 'The Old People' as well as in 'The Bear' much space is given to the early and formative stages in Ike's development, and the central position of Sam Fathers as Ike's substitute-father and mentor is frequently mentioned. Knowledge of the 'old people' comes to Ike through Sam Fathers, but it serves to give Ike a deeper understanding of the natural world and hence almost a deeply felt piety and respect for the untamed wilderness and for the game running there. Sam teaches Ike something which nobody in the McCaslin family could possibly teach him, and Sam's tales of the old days create a dream world, untainted and unspoiled, where reciprocal respect is needed if man and nature shall exist together in peace.

Warren Beck describes Isaac's dream in this way:

For the entranced child it is as if Eden were still to be and his innocence in it yet to be known; it is a type of the Arcadian dream some men in every age have come upon, in deep consciousness of existing within nature, and with a related humanistic faith in natural law.[39]

The author's description of how Isaac reacted to Sam's tales and how he later related these tales to his own situation as heir to the McCaslin plantation, also includes a preliminary presentation of Isaac's philosophy and understanding of Southern history. By hearing about the old people, those who originally lived on the land and lived in peace with it, Isaac feels that he 'was the guest here and Sam Father's [sic] voice the mouthpiece of the host' (*Go Down, Moses,* p. 171). In 'The Bear', especially in the fourth section, Isaac's understanding of property rights and the curse laid upon the land by a just but punishing God is part of his reasoning which finally makes him repudiate his inheritance and his heritage.

'The Bear' without section four makes a marvellous hunting story, and even as it stands in the book with the added significance and moral depth of the fourth section, the first parts of the story are first and foremost a hunting story: the story of the hunting party's repeated but unsuccessful attempts to track Old Ben, who is the very apotheosis of the wilderness, and who is therefore also a thing of immense beauty and strength, so that Isaac stands awed in front of it, accepting its position as ruler of the wilderness and symbol of an era and a way of life that he understands must come to an end. Ike knows that the dog that Sam has trapped and Boon Hogganbeck raises will be instrumental in the killing of Old Ben, and he knows that he should have hated and feared the dog, Lion, yet he does not do it. This is so because Ike refused to shoot Old Ben when he had the chance; not because he is against killing, but because he has been witnessing a grand drama unfold over many years and does not want to see it end. Yet at the same time, he knows that end it must, and he prepares for it:

It seemed to him that there was a fatality in it. It seemed to him that something, he didn't know what, was beginning: had already begun. It was like the last act on a set stage. It was the beginning of the end of something, he didn't know what except that he would not grieve. He would be humble and proud that he had been found worthy to be a part of it too or even just to see it too (*Go Down, Moses,* p. 226).

He has been a part of it for many years now that he is sixteen, and the great drama is coming to its final act: Old Ben is bayed by the mongrel dog and Boon kills him with his knife in a deadly embrace. Lion is fatally wounded, and Sam has collapsed; now that the spirit of the wilderness is killed it seems that his time and the time of people of his kind has finally reached its end. Boon and Ike remain in the camp, which is broken up after the killing of the enormous bear, to watch the deaths of their close friends, Sam and Lion, and to pay them and the wilderness the respect they deserve.

The story is concluded and rounded up in the last section, which takes place two years after the killing of Old Ben. Here Isaac is revisiting the 'stage', the scene of the killing. A new planing mill has been erected after a lumber company bought the land, and the wilderness is dwindling and slowly disappearing. Sam Fathers and Lion are still in untouched, unspoiled land, but the traces of the graves are almost gone after only two winters. The knowledge and the attitudes of Sam Fathers will linger on in Isaac McCaslin for more than half a century, and he will act upon this knowledge in many situations, but he cannot pass his understanding on: also in this respect he remains childless. In the future world where the wilderness is either destroyed or tamed, where roads and railroads are built where only hunters found the paths before, there seems to be little use for the 'old people', and their wisdom and Old Ben can live on only in legend – but this legend has no bearing upon people's lives. The apparent futility of Ike's learning and maturation thus becomes an important aspect of his future life: he becomes inactive, a passive looker-on in a world of constant change.

Isaac had learnt much from Sam Fathers, from the hunting expeditions themselves, and from Old Ben, the very symbol of the great myriad wilderness itself. *What* he has learnt is adequately summed up by Cleanth Brooks:

What Isaac learns from his experience with Old Ben is something that is quite universal: it has to do with a perennial problem and with a problem made more and not less relevant in these days of man's conquest of nature. Man's attitude toward nature is a function of the health of his own nature. . . . But when man loses his awe of nature through a purely efficient utilization of it, or when he ceases to love it and to carry on his contention with it in terms of some sort of code, then he not only risks destroying nature but risks bestializing his own nature.[40]

We must return to section IV of 'The Bear' for a brief discussion of it. It is vitally important and in keeping with the understanding of nature discussed above, to be aware that the experience with Sam Fathers in the wilderness – from the ritualistic initiation when he killed his first buck to his digging of Sam Fathers's grave and burying him in the woods he loved so much – relates directly to Isaac's renunciation of his heritage at the age of 21. In the woods he had learnt that to be permitted to meet the famous old bear he had to divest himself of everything which made him tainted and impure, all the signs of civilization had to be left behind, before he could be free so that the spirit of the wilderness could materialize before his eyes. Sam Fathers himself had also proved to Isaac that freedom is valuable and important, and in Ike's case this means freedom from the burdens of property, responsibility for a subject race, family, kin and so on. It also includes an attempt to exempt himself of the burden of Southern history, as well as of the curse of slavery, miscegenation, exploitation of the black people and of the wilderness, love for money and property, inability to share with one's fellow beings the good life which God has made possible in this New World. He repudiates his inheritance, and he does not even consider the possibility of returning to the plantation and taking over from Edmonds, which his wife tries to persuade him to do later on. She has, in point of fact, married him because of his birth-right to the land; now that Isaac refuses to be tainted with the McCaslin curse of miscegenation and incest and wrong ownership of land and people, she denies him her body, and Isaac takes up carpentering, finding it suitable, since the Nazarean once found it sufficient for his needs.

Most of part IV consists of long conversations between Ike and Cass Edmonds, but the part also includes the past history of the McCaslin family as well as glimpses into Ike's future. The part is almost Biblical in tone, and God and providence are important parts of Isaac's long argument in defence of his decision. The plans God had with old Carothers McCaslin and which were continued through his sons, Uncle Buck and Uncle Buddy (Ike's father and uncle), who set their slaves free, were not sufficient to cure the curse of slavery. There would never be enough Buck's and Buddy's to set God's lowly people free, so God used the Civil War as a stronger medicine. The South lost the war, because people there could *'learn nothing save through suffering,'* only in defeat would victory be possible.[41]

Ike's interpretation of history is strange, to say the least and the logic of his arguments is not always convincing. His main point is that since the very moment the Indian chief first sold the land to his forefathers, the land ceased to be his, since by the very act of selling it, the Indian forfeited his claim upon the land. Isaac cannot inherit the land, because the land has never really belonged to his family. Cass argues that if the Indian chief could not sell the land, then it probably would be Sam Fathers's, and who would be the closest to inherit from Sam than just Isaac? Isaac reluctantly admits that his grandfather had title to the land, yet he himself is free. He will not have the land, he will not participate in the chain of McCaslins and thereby implicitly carry on the curse.

Isaac sets himself free, but by this very act he also gives up his responsibilities as a human being and as the head of the plantation and of a family that could indeed need qualified leadership or stewardship. A closer examination of Ike's decision and its consequences will be postponed till the final chapter of Ike's story is discussed, and this is the nostalgic, warm, and in many respects magnificent short story, 'Delta Autumn'. Here a last view of Ike is given; the year is 1940 and old Ike is once more on the annual hunt, now far away from Jefferson, since the wilderness has been destroyed in vast areas.

Ike is lying awake on his mattress – as he always does now the first night in the woods – and he listens to the talk of the other men in the party. Their reference to Roth Edmonds and his hunting does, but this time does on two legs, introduces the most important element in the story. Roth has apparently met a young girl near the camp-area a year ago, he has met her once since then, and now she has waited for him and seen him arrive in camp. He does not want to meet her, and leaves an envelope with Isaac to give to the girl if or when she appears in camp.

The girl turns up; she speaks to Ike and calls him Uncle, and their conversation reveals that she is the granddaughter of Tennie's Jim (James Beauchamp). Roth Edmonds is the father of the baby she brings with her, but he does not know who she is. She hopes to find a message from Roth in the envelope, but finds only money. Isaac sees the old McCaslin curse has reappeared: once again one of the black descendants of Carothers McCaslin has been mistreated by a white descendant of the same patriarch. History repeats itself, and the evil in the family seems to be perpetual. When Isaac first discovers that the girl is a Negro – when he sees 'the pale lips, the skin pallid and dead-looking yet not ill, the dark and tragic and foreknowing eyes' (*Go Down, Moses,* p. 361), he thinks to himself, 'Maybe in a thousand or two thousand years in America,. . . But not now! Not now!' (*Go Down, Moses,* p. 361), and he later advises the girl to go back North and marry within her race, because 'We will have

252

to wait' (*Go Down, Moses,* p. 363). The girl accuses Isaac of having spoiled Roth Edmonds, because he gave 'to his grandfather that land which didn't belong to him, not even half of it by will or even law' (*Go Down, Moses,* p. 360). She is almost in line with Lucas in 'The Fire and the Hearth', who cannot see what possible reason other than weakness Ike could have had for relinquishing his patrimony.

The girl's answer to Isaac leaves him behind with a new kind of despair. This is the result not so much of having been charged with having spoiled the Edmondses but it is rather the sudden insight that Isaac may have had that even in the wilderness where he had learned so much about piety, truth, courage, and honour, he was not free of the curse. A simple child of the oppressed race could give him a lesson and show him not only that he had failed but possibly also where and how he had failed:

'Old man', she said, 'have you lived so long and forgotten so much that you dont remember anything you ever knew or felt or even heard about love?' (*Go Down, Moses,* p. 363).

Readers and critics may disagree on whether Isaac's renunciation of his inheritance and his subsequent behaviour are acts of sacrifice and expiation or rather acts of weakness and escape. One may nevertheless support the girl in her bitter criticism of Isaac; he is a great failure when it comes to love, and in this respect the implied author's criticism coincides with the girl's bitterness and despair. This should also prepare the readers not to read Isaac's many remarks, clear or cryptic, on segregation policy as a tract. Isaac's response to the girl – giving her his only valuable possession, the hunting horn – is a personal and private response, and even when read as a symbolic act, it can only be seen in the perspective of Isaac's own earlier decisions: the renunciation and the ascetic life Isaac has led since then.

Whichever way we view Isaac, he is more than anything else a believable fictional character, compounded of many and varied influences; the McCaslin heritage, Sam Fathers's tutorship, the history of the South in the years of reconstruction, the burden of slavery, his marital problems, the diminishing wilderness, the annual hunting parties. In Andrew Lytle's words Isaac is just this kind of believable individual, 'of a certain heritage, in a certain time and place, acting among individuals who perform out of the mores of a society'.[42]

From the first almost unintelligible portrait of Uncle Ike in the opening pages of 'Was' and of *Go Down, Moses,* till we take leave of him in 'Delta Autumn', Ike is a strange character, evoking sympathy yet always open to severe criticism because of his apologetic nature and what must be regarded as an escape from responsibilities and from accepting the challenge which his position provides. His lasting passivity is futile and egotistic; it cannot possibly solve any problems, except – on the surface – Isaac's own. Yet Isaac remains one of Faulkner's most authentic characters, touching in his desperate search for solutions to serious and tormenting problems, pathetic in his inability to solve them even on a personal level.

With 'Delta Autumn' the story of Ike McCaslin is concluded, but the story of the McCaslins is not quite finished yet. Undoubtedly, 'Delta Autumn' would have been a proper ending for *Go Down, Moses* – in particular if the book was only or mainly Isaac McCaslin's story. With the long novella on Lucas Beauchamp and the frame-like stories in 'Was' and 'Pantaloon', it seems only fitting that the book should be rounded off and concluded with a more autonomous story, which the title story 'Go Down, Moses' in some respects may be said to be. This story may in point of fact be seen as a kind of coda to the work as a whole.

In 'Go Down, Moses' Molly Beauchamp, whom we have met as a very pitiable and sympathetic character in 'The Fire and the Hearth', appeals to Gavin Stevens for help because the son of her eldest daughter has killed a policeman and is now about to be executed for his crime. She is helped by Miss Worsham, and even though there is nothing that can be done to save the convict, Miss Worsham insists that Molly's grandson must come home to be buried there. The circumstances behind the boy's death are not revealed to Molly, and Stevens and the newspaper editor agree that nothing about the execution is to be printed in the paper. Then they collect money around the square to add to Miss Worsham's twenty dollars, to which they have to add substantial amounts themselves to pay for the railway fare, the coffin, flowers, and a hearse to take the body to the graveyard.

The body of Molly's grandson is taken out into the country towards the Edmonds plantation, and Molly's wish, that he 'come home right' is acted upon and carried out by the community of Jefferson, Yoknapatawpha County. Two old women – white and black – have joined forces so that honour and decency and a stronger sense of community may prevail in a book where racial injustice and the crumbling of old mores and ways are central themes.

'Go Down, Moses' opens onto a larger world than the other parts of *Go Down, Moses,* and at the same time it is directly related to the plantation world of the book as a whole. Molly's reiterated intonation, 'Sold him in Egypt' (*Go Down, Moses,* pp. 380, 381) shows this.[43] The old Negro woman refers to the Bible to stress the severe mistake Mr. Edmonds made when he sent Butch off the plantation after he had broken into the commissary store. Indirectly Molly may be just in her judgment, but to her there is no doubt that her grandson's fate was determined the day he was chased out of the relatively stable and secure world of the plantation. Butch made the mistake that Lucas almost made in a very old age, namely trying to get rich quickly and easily, and this should also be mentioned, since it is another link between the final, slightly comic but mostly pathetic, story in *Go Down, Moses* and the book's more central parts.

For readers familiar with Faulkner's novels of this period, notably *The Hamlet,* many of the stories in *Knight's Gambit* are likely to be regarded as by-products of the process which created characters such as Mink Snopes, Flem Snopes, and a whole population of strange characters in the backwood areas of Yoknapatawpha. It is tempting to speculate that Faulkner merely re-used stock-characters, phrases, attitudes, and events that he had either treated in a different way in his longer works, or which he had discarded from works where he used his whole creative potential. The ability to accept all kinds of hardship and pain, to suffer and endure through the most incredible injustice, poverty, and ignorance, is central in most of these stories. Stoic acceptance of one's fate is presented as an admirable virtue even when pure ignorance or simplicity of mind is responsible for this attitude. Yet somewhere deep beneath the surface of events, a lasting and invincible quality guides some of the characters to act surprisingly and do things which seem inexplicable and strange to the world of sense and order. This quality seems to have become a part of even the least civilized characters – Monk, Jackson Fentry – and it might be described as love, pity, and compassion. None of the characters would be able to express his feelings, or even give them a name; yet they act according to them and thus they tend to become human in spite of their strange, if not murderous, activities. Compared to the modern, matter-of-fact world of Jefferson, the implied narrator seems to indicate that these people have still maintained a core of admirable virtues which the more civilized people lack.

The protagonists of the Gavin Stevens stories are not outlanders and outsiders because they come from other places and settle in Yoknapatawpha County; they are outsiders because they live by different norms, because their standards of behaviour are different from those in Jefferson. This is easily seen in 'Monk'.

Stonewall Jackson 'Monk' Odlethrop belongs in an isolated section of Yoknapatawpha, an area of the county where nobody ever goes, and which is populated by clannish people who 'made whiskey and shot at all strangers from behind log barns and snake fences' (*Knight's Gambit*, p. 41). Monk is an outsider to Jefferson – the narrator's environment – not only because he comes from this remote and secluded area, but also because he is mentally isolated. In the first part of the story Monk's childhood and arrival in Jefferson are outlined. The crime that he allegedly commits and for which he is sent to the state penitentiary to serve a life sentence, is described here. In the second part of the story, Gavin Stevens's ratiocinative work is at the centre, yet the story is Monk's from beginning to end. Gavin learns from a drunkard that Monk had been framed for the killing in Jefferson, but Monk refuses the pardon that Gavin arranges. Inexplicably Monk a little later kills the warden in the jail to whom he has given his dog-like devotion, and there is thus every reason to suspect that he has been framed by someone again, someone smart enough to use Monk's mental weakness. Only Monk's final words on the gallows lead Gavin to uncover the truth about another convict who had convinced Monk that he ought to be 'walking out into the free world and farm it', and to achieve this, he had to kill the warden. Stevens's detective work is successful in so far as he reaches the truth, yet Monk's child-like devotion and misunderstood attempts at communication with his fellow men are at the heart of it. Monk remains the outsider in a double sense, and the interest of the story is with him from beginning to end. In 'Hand Upon the Waters' Gavin functions much more successfully as a detective, and the structure of the story is more in accordance with Gavin's role; i.e. more than the two former stories in the volume, 'Hand Upon the Waters' is a detective story where the ratiocination – the solving of the crime – is more important than the crime or its ramifications.

When Gavin Stevens is given such a central role in this story compared to the other stories, this is so because he shares something central with the victim, Louis Grenier [Lonnie Grinnup]. What Gavin has in common with the outcast Lonnie Grinnup, who lives in a hut and makes a living by fishing, is that they are the only survivors of the three original founding families of Yoknapatawpha County. Lonnie has his hut and fishtrap in the exact centre of the enormous area of land his family once owned, and even if he lives on the outskirts of society in more than one sense, he is by implication the very centre of it, despite his exile from society at large. Gavin may be said to solve the crime for personal reasons, as he is said to look at the dead man's face 'for a sentimental reason', and his participation in this story is of a different kind than in the other stories. Here he is not only *the* County Attorney; he is also involved and interested in seeing justice done for personal reasons. His work as a detective is more than simple detection: it becomes a vital part of the central theme of the story and adds to its meaning.

Gavin may be seriously involved and engaged in a crime for other reasons than those at work in 'Hand Upon the Waters'. In 'Tomorrow' he not only shows greater understanding than ever before; he also tries to teach Chick a moral lesson. 'Tomorrow' deals with the killing of a man namned Buck Thorpe by a Mr. Bookwright, who seems to have had every reason to kill the brawler and gambler who had seduced Bookwright's daugher, a minor. Everybody accordingly expects the jury to vote the killer free, but one man on the jury, Jackson Fentry, refuses to acquit Bookwright. Through Gavin Stevens's detection we get to know that Fentry had once sheltered a pregnant girl who died in childbirth. He then took care of her baby, until her relatives fetched him. The victim of Bookwright's killing is this boy, so the poor, ignorant and pathetic Fentry felt that *his* son had been killed. Chick nonetheless maintains that he would have freed Bookwright, because Buck Thorpe was bad. In a passionate and strong speech Stevens tells Chick that life is more complicated than this:

'It wasn't Buck Thorpe, the adult, the man. He would have shot that man as quick as Bookwright did, if he had been in Bookwright's place. It was because somewhere in that debased and brutalized flesh which Bookwright slew there still remained, not the spirit maybe, but at least the memory, of that little boy, that Jackson and Longstreet Fentry, even though the man the boy had become didn't know it, and only Fentry did. And you wouldn't have freed him either. Don't ever forget that. Never' (*Knight's Gambit*, p. 105).

More than the other stories, 'Tomorrow' functions as an episode in the education of Chick Mallison, while at the same time it demonstrates Gavin's great understanding, his wide range of human compassion. The story laments the loss of Fentry, the lonely and isolated outsider, while at the same time it shows how the outlander who tries to abduct a member of the community must die for it, and deserves to die. Expectedly, Bookwright finally goes free, and balance is restored within the community of Yoknapatawpha.

The final two stories in the volume, 'An Error in Chemistry' and 'Knight's Gambit', both centre on the theme of the outlander, the foreigner, who comes to Yoknapatawpha mostly to reap a profit and who has no intention of becoming a real member of the community he lives in. In 'An Error in Chemistry' the outlander is Joel Flint, who by the end of the story is revealed to be Signor Canova, a circus illusionist, and who has killed his wife and father-in-law to come into possession of the farm and sell it for his own gain. His father-in-law, Pritchel, is known for drinking whiskey by mixing sugar and water with it, and when Canova impersonates Pritchel after having killed him, he makes the serious mistake of pouring whiskey first into the tumbler and then adding sugar. This is the story's 'error in chemistry', and it is difficult to see how the editors of *Ellery Queen's Mystery Magazine* could describe this story as 'almost pure detection'. In point of fact, the mistake is so obvious and the detection so simple that everybody present, including the narrator, Chick, discovers the mistake and draws the inevitable conclusion; viz. that Joel Flint has killed his father-in-law and is now disguised as him.

The point of the story lies somewhere else, though. Signor Canova might easily have slipped away from detection and from Yoknapatawpha if he had not felt the need to play a final act as illusionist. His vanity is indeed what reveals his terrible deeds, and Stevens interprets this as a 'supreme contempt for mankind', which he finds to be only natural for a man of Canova's gifts. The moral lesson one may draw from this story, and which may give the story a significant place in the long line of development which Gavin goes through, is voiced by the Sheriff, who quotes, 'Man, fear thyself, thine arrogance and vanity and pride', asking Gavin what book this is in. Gavin's answer is revealing, also when seen in relation to the volume as a whole: ' "It's in all of them", Uncle Gavin said. "The good ones, I mean. It's said in a lot of different ways, but it's there".' (*Knight's Gambit,* p. 131).

The title story, 'Knight's Gambit', was the first of the many short stories which Faulkner wrote in the early months of 1942. This statement requires modification, however, since the story Faulkner wrote in 1942 was 23 pages long, and even though Faulkner may have thought of revising and expanding it relatively shortly after 1942, there is no proof that he really wrote the very long final story of *Knight's Gambit* before his publishers had agreed on publishing such a volume, which would place it late in 1948. The basic events of the two versions are almost identical, but in many respects the versions differ significantly. The most important change has to do with the narrator: in the early version he is called Chuck and is even given the family name of Weddel, yet he is still Gavin's nephew.[44] One can only speculate why Faulkner had chosen to re-name the nephew in this last of the Gavin Stevens detective stories, which he most certainly intended to publish in its original version. It is likewise easy to guess that Faulkner felt the need to make the names of his characters accord with those used in the preceding stories of the volume when he rewrote 'Knight's Gambit'. But the two names of Chuck/Chick are not the most interesting thing about the narrative mode here: much more important is it that while Chuck is a first-person narrator (as Chick is in the five former stories) in the short version, there is a unidentified third-person narrator in the long version, so that Chick Mallison and Gavin Stevens become 'he and his uncle', as compared to the 'My uncle and I' of the earlier stories.[45]

Other changes from the early version to the book-version include a slight change in the name of the Argentine captain, from Gualdes to Captain Gualdres, and numerous changes in detail and characterization. Gavin Stevens of the early version seems much more in keeping with the other stories; in the short novel he is much more garrulous and talkative, and his romanticism is played upon to an unusual degree. As Millgate has pointed out, Gavin Stevens in this story is reminiscent of the Gavin we meet in *Intruder in the Dust* and may also be seen as an early sketch of Gavin Stevens as he appears in *The Town* and *The Mansion*.[46] Yet the story may – in both versions – be seen as the final stage in the development of Gavin Stevens as we have watched it in *Knight's Gambit:* here he succeeds for the first time in preventing a crime,[47] and the story also offers a conclusion to Gavin's personal affairs. With the recurrent references to his secret bethrotal to Melisandre Backus and the letters which got mixed up so that she married somebody else named Harriss

259

(even though additional reasons – money – should also be mentioned) the early beginning of Stevens's personal career and development is set forth in this story. If the other stories in the volume give descriptions of central events in Gavin's life, then we may indeed have both the original motivational forces behind his search for justice and truth, examples of how he solved crimes and added to his understanding of human behaviour and reactions, which finally would help him to solve his personal problems so that he might save his Queen.

The theme of alienation is strongly felt in this story, too. The outlanders are many in this story: Harriss, who is a stranger to all Mississippi and who marries a girl of an old Jefferson family; later his two children have the same function on the now-level of the story, a function they share with the Cavalry Captain from Argentina. They are all accused by the community because they are different, and because they take over property and wealth which do not rightfully belong to them. That they also bring in money and spend it in the county is not mentioned: the very fact that Harriss spends so much money alienates him even more definitely from the rest of the community. Stevens's personal participation in this story and his final act of marrying Melisandre may also be interpreted in relation to this theme. Melisandre has been removed from the community she by birth and heritage rightfully belongs in, and when Stevens marries her, she is brought back into it.

The outside world is more important in this story than in any of the other stories in the volume, not only because Harriss and Gualdres are complete strangers to Yoknapatawpha, but because one of them is a stranger even to the United States and because their lives are totally outlandish to the good people of Jefferson. In other stories the strangers might live in the more remote and isolated area of the county; in 'Knight's Gambit' the characters come and go by aeroplanes or automobiles; they travel in Europe, and soon some of them will have to go off to a war that will have the whole globe as its scene. The story ends on a Saturday, and 'The next day was December seventh' – the day of Pearl Harbor. Even though the earliest version of 'Knight's Gambit' was written shortly after Pearl Harbor, it is obvious that the events of the second World War and the larger perspective on it that the author had in 1948, account for many of the changes in emphasis in the late version. Yet it is fair to say that basically the two stories are very close to one another: the vast expansions added to the late version bring significant

260

background information and add to our understanding of Gavin Stevens and of the events surrounding the Harriss family. They do not, however, change the basic tone and impact of the story.

In the presentation of Faulkner's many stories that were combined into unified cycles of stories or novels, it should be rather obvious that these stories occupy a middle position with respect to the question of their being a novelist's short stories. They are a novelist's short stories in the very direct sense that he used them, in revised form, as book chapters, in books that must be regarded as novels. As individual stories there may hence be less of the narrative concentration that we have mentioned for Faulkner's stories of the major years and before, since these stories to an even greater degree than usual can rely on previously written material and leave out parts of the larger story that will appear in stories to be written later on. Still, the stories open on to a wider scene, a different perspective, more destinies, and in this sense the brief narratives in each short story do not only tell parts of a long story – a novelist's story; they indicate and reflect this larger story through the workings of foreshadowing and retrospection, through omissions and ellipsis that reveal much in themselves.

Whether *The Unvanquished* is seen as a cycle of short stories, with the linear unity apparently typical of this genre, or whether it is seen as a novel, is not very important. The original Bayard-Ringo stories are short stories in their own right, now easily available in their magazine form in *Uncollected Stories of William Faulkner*. *The Unvanquished* is an important, but not too successful, book in Faulkner's career. Even if this is a study primarily of Faulkner's short stories as such, one has to admit that *The Unvanquished* as a novel is much more than the sum of the original magazine stories; possibly also more than the sum of its chapters viewed as individual units. Faulkner must have been pleased with his revisions, and had proved once again that revisions could 'save' a book.[48] He had also proved to himself that a number of stories might well be rewritten into a unified novel. So even if the short stories that came to form *Go Down, Moses* were not conceived as a series, the author had experience to rely on when he joined ten published and unpublished stories together in a book, which he later insisted was to be looked upon as a novel.

Go Down, Moses is a unique work in Faulkner's fiction. Here he succeeded in re-using individual short stories to make a unified and well-structured novel. The short-story writer Faulkner proves that he is the great novelist by the very quality of his revisions: the addition of minor details, the change of names, a shift in stress, together with more substantial alterations, linked the stories to one another on the thematic level while symbols and images were also chosen with deliberate care to add to the structural unity of the volume as a whole. The book has two major parts, which I have taken the liberty of calling 'novellas'. The first is the chapter called 'The Fire and the Hearth', which, as we have seen, was made up from two published and one unpublished short story, and which basically is the story of Lucas Beauchamp and his atrocious greed. The story is nonetheless linked to Ike's story by numerous references to the McCaslin legacy to the black McCaslins and by recurrent comments on Ike's renunciation. The second novella is the three-part story of Isaac McCaslin's life, 'The Old People', 'The Bear', and 'Delta Autumn'. This story is introduced already on the first page of the book, in a brief part which has been described as an important unifying device in the book's structure. The two main parts of the book are framed by the opening story 'Was' and the concluding story, 'Go Down, Moses', while they are separated by the least integrated story in the volume, 'Pantaloon in Black'. All through these separate parts there is a cluster of images that bind the parts together, while the theme of usurpation and exploitation of the black race and of the wilderness also has this structuring effect. Human virtues and human vices mix and mingle in this book; there is no model villain here, nor is there a model saint. The curse of ownership and of slavery is contrasted to the blessings and virtues of unspoiled nature and the abundant and free wilderness, represented most magnificently by Old Ben. Despite discussions of original sin and of God's curse upon the land, despite philosophical and personal interpretations of Providence and Fate and of American history, despite expiation and incapacity either for love or for grief, the thematic and philosophical content and significance of *Go Down, Moses* is perhaps not the most impressive aspect of the book. Its rich and profound respect for and insight into human nature and the magnificent narration of the stories about racial problems, love and loss, hunt and destruction, are qualities that make *Go Down, Moses* 'one of the most subtly imaginative of creations within the modern novel's ongoing originative trends', to let Warren Beck have the last word.[49]

On the basis of publication information one might be tempted to regard *Knight's Gambit* as a by-product of the process which led to the publication of *Collected Stories,* but as I have tried to show in this chapter, the collection of detective stories is more than that. One may venture the guess that Faulkner's long fascination with detective fiction and his reiterated studies into the character of the murderer had drawn him to this genre. It is similarly more than likely that Faulkner saw in these stories an opportunity to experiment with his characters, especially with Gavin Stevens, for whom he had a much more significant fictional role in books to come.

The unity of the collection, which may be established on the basis of the outlander-community relation, should not be over-emphasized. The theme adds significance to the stories, but mostly so if the outsider and his problems of adjustment in a rigidly codified society are contemplated. Nor should the stories be taken mostly or primarily as left-hand exercises in the presentation and characterization of Gavin Stevens. No matter what our principal interests are, *Knight's Gambit* consists of six detective stories, and the stories deserve to be taken seriously, also because they have as a rule been disregarded and scorned for their quality as detective stories.

Some of the tone and atmosphere of the backwood areas of Yoknapatawpha rings very true in these stories: here are the poorest among the poor, people whose lives are lived on the lowest possible level in all respects, but who nevertheless are invincible because they will 'endure and endure and then endure, tomorrow and tomorrow and tomorrow' (*Knight's Gambit,* p. 104). Faulkner's biding interest in people is demonstrated in these stories, where his principal character, Gavin Stevens, despite his profession, is more interested in justice and human beings than in truth. Thus *Knight's Gambit* is a book that could only have been written by William Faulkner of the middle years.

8. Short Stories 1942–1962
Yoknapatawpha and the World

> ...the men and women who did the deeds, who
> lasted and endured and fought the battles and lost
> them and fought again because they didn't know they
> had been whipped, and tamed the wilderness and
> overpassed the mountains and deserts and still went
> on as the shape of the United States grew and went
> on.
>
> –Faulkner, 'Shall Not Perish'

A dramatic change on the national and international scene, combined
with pressing need for money and a wish to stay home from Hollywood,
made Faulkner make a new and last effort to write and market short
stories in the early months of 1942. In these stories, Yoknapatawpha and
some of its people face problems of the greater, outside world. Yet
Faulkner also here locates his stories in Yoknapatawpha, and demonstrates how dramatic and violent changes in the outside world must
influence and change Yoknapatawpha and life there too. It seems almost
as if Faulkner's writing by this time is so deeply immersed in his native
region that he feels that any subject-matter, any theme, can be treated
or described with Yoknapatawpha as a point of departure. In his local
milieu there is a stable and slow-changing society. This society, urbanized or still rural, follows certain fixed codes of behaviour, laid down by
tradition, inherited through the ages, and proved to be worthwhile to live
by. Against such a society may be measured any other society; against
these people and their code, may be measured any other people. Faulkner's plain people of Yoknapatawpha are not necessarily model people,
their society is not necessarily an ideal society. Yet in some respects they
undoubtedly represent some of Faulkner's ideals: endurance, love, pity,
compassion, honour, and decency. In his early 1942 stories some of these
qualities are demonstrated almost in pure form, and when properly
understood, they also include love for one's country: patriotism.

In the final story of *Knight's Gambit* – the title story – the last events
take place on a Saturday; on the following Sunday the Japanese bomb

264

Pearl Harbor. 'Knight's Gambit' in its earliest version was written in January 1942, but even before this time, Faulkner had written his first patriotic short story, 'The Tall Men'.[1] He wrote this story in the days before America entered the Second World War, and it became a story of patriotism and optimistic hope. 'The Tall Men' must be grouped with 'Two Soldiers' and 'Shall Not Perish' as strongly patriotic and rather sentimental reactions to the new war. Faulkner had written short stories from the Civil War and numerous ones from and about the First World War, but then he was a young man whose dreams had failed to come true, and who was outraged with the injustice and cruelty he observed about him. In 1941 and 1942 he was an established, if not accepted and popular, writer of novels and stories, he was a family man with a strong sense of responsibility, and he probably felt that he had a right to comment, in fictional form, upon the war that America would have to fight and win. The stories are written by a man who believes in America and in America's strength, and who is capable of giving fictional probability to his beliefs by showing some of his low and poor people reacting to the demands of their country.

In 'The Tall Men' a state draft investigator goes with the local marshal out to the McCallum farm with a warrant because the two McCallum boys have failed to register for the draft. He is angry with the Sheriff, who had phoned McCallum to tell him that he and the investigator would be coming, and he fears that the boys may have escaped by now. The marshal – himself one of 'these people' (*Collected Stories*, p. 46) – understands that he cannot get through to the investigator to inform him about the people he is going to meet. The investigator lives in a different world, but the marshal feels confident that the city-dweller will receive a good lesson from seeing the McCallum place and the people living there. The lesson is likely to be extraordinarily dramatic and effective, since Buddy McCallum had had one of his legs almost cut off and the doctor is there now, ready to amputate it.

The McCallums are representatives of a group of characters in Faulkner's Yoknapatawpha fiction which alone or as a group may teach any outsider a lesson in 'humility and pride', endurance, and natural loyalty. They are independent, proud, and strong, and even though they may be clannish and self-sufficient to a degree where their behaviour seems selfish, these people are undoubtedly admired by the implied author of 'The Tall Men' as well as by William Faulkner himself.[2]

Most of the lesson in loyalty and perseverance may have come to the investigator directly, simply through his watching the reactions and talk in the farm-house. Faulkner does nonetheless stress his points time and time again in this text, by letting the marshal tell, in very conservative and at times sadly exaggerated and misunderstood statements about 'modern life', what the McCallums stand for and why it is important that some basic qualities are passed on to new generations. At any rate, within the development of the story, it does not take long before the investigator discovers how totally wrong he has been. The men he meets are not cowards by any standards, they are not draft-evaders by any deliberate choice; these men are not curious or uncivilized. The marshal's long and insistent speech in which he gives the background history of the family also serves to change the investigator's understanding of the McCallums and of 'these here curious folks'. It takes courage simply to live as they do, and it requires a strong sense of self-sufficiency and a love of their almost unlimited freedom to resist and resent government regulations and relief money.

Honour and pride and discipline[3] are the qualities which the marshal ascribes to the McCallums, and these are qualities which together make them 'the tall men' of the story's title. The free, independent farmers want to be left in peace, but they feel a strong sense of duty and loyalty to their community and to their country. Their goals are not to buy more land and grow big and rich and important – they share no dreams with a Sutpen or a Snopes. They simply want to make a living where God has placed them. They are not well off, nor are they very poor. They belong to a class of free, yeoman farmers, and in Faulkner's fiction they play an important part as avatars of some of the qualities he admires most – qualities which become increasingly rare and hence even more remarkable in a world of 'pretty neon lights. . . .and easy quick money':

'Yes, sir. We done forgot about folks. Life has done got cheap, and life ain't cheap. Life's a pretty durn valuable thing. I don't mean just getting along from one WPA relief check to the next one, but honor and pride and discipline that make a man worth preserving, make him of any value. That's what we got to learn again. Maybe it takes trouble, bad trouble, to teach it back to us;. . . .' (*Collected Stories*, p. 60).

M.E. Bradford is certainly right when he writes that these 'yeomen farmers' live 'almost unaffected in the mid-twentieth century by the coming of industrialism and the new capitalism to the South – indeed live beyond the reach of these powers and resist their influence.'⁴ Despite the significance of these characters in much of Faulkner's fiction, they become central only in his late fiction, and nowhere do they attain such a stature as in 'The Tall Men', and to some extent in the other patriotic stories from 1942. Usually, however, these people remain in the background of Faulkner's novels and short stories, but it may be fair to note that such characters as the Griers ('Two Soldiers', 'Shall Not Perish'), Jackson Fentry in 'Tomorrow', and possibly even Byron Bunch of *Light in August* all belong to this class. Unfortunately these characters play only minor if not totally inconsequential roles in their societies, so that their influence is less felt and seen then what we could expect and want. Independence and self-reliance also call for egotism and egocentricity; the McCallums accept responsibility for their own fate and refuse to accept government help when it is offered to them, yet they also rid themselves of some of the responsibility that they have as human beings living in a community with others, by maintaining their self-sufficiency.

'The Tall Men' shows self-sufficient and courageous people, who live by strict standards for decent conduct and honourable behaviour: these people may seem curious and out-of-date in a modern world, yet in a critical situation their attitudes and their beliefs combine with an unflagging love for the land and an undeviating patriotism to make them ideal defenders in time of war. In 'Two Soldiers' and 'Shall Not Perish' Faulkner describes the more immediate repercussions of World War II upon such people and on the community of Frenchman's Bend and Yoknapatawpha County in general.

These three short stories were all collected in the first section of *Collected Stories,* 'The Country', together with 'Barn Burning', 'A Bear Hunt', and 'Shingles for the Lord'. It is remarkable that four of the short stories in the opening section of this major short-story collection were written as late as 1941 and 1942, and that the major short-story period produced no short story of this type or set in this environment.⁵

There is little reason to speculate why these stories and the beliefs they convey came so late in Faulkner's career; their place in *Collected Stories* may indeed reflect Faulkner's satisfaction with them and his own beliefs in what they show of lasting and valuable human qualities. Yet the stories are by no means among Faulkner's best; they are overwritten, slightly sentimental without being moving, and at times they are rather pathetic in their insistent demonstrations of admirable behaviour. In

'Two Soldiers' and 'Shall Not Perish' Faulkner walks a tightrope between cheap sentimentalism and dramatized grief and despair. He slips too often, so that the stories' chief interest is not their thematic implications, or the glory of being allowed to die for one's country.[6] The country scene and the boy narrator are more significant elements of these stories, which, of course, were also written during the war and are influenced by this fact.

'Two Soldiers' is a story about loyalty and patriotism, and Faulkner chose the familiar setting of Frenchman's Bend – with its many associations with just family loyalty.[7] He created new characters for this commercially successful story about two boys, nineteen and nearly nine, and their unlimited patriotism. The principal family of the story, the Griers, farms seventy acres and the father is always behind with his work. When Pete, the older brother, unexpectedly comes home and tells them he has to go and join the army after Pearl Harbor, the father resents his decision, mostly for selfish reasons. His mother understands how Pete feels. Without knowing why he must go, she knows that he must do his duty:

... 'I don't want him to go. I would rather go myself in his place, if I could. I don't want to save the country. Them Japanese could take it and keep it, so long as they left me and my family and my children alone. But I remember my brother Marsh in that other war. He had to go to that one when he wasn't but nineteen, and our mother couldn't understand it then any more than I can now. But she told Marsh if he had to go, he had to go. And so, if Pete's got to go to this one, he's got to go to it. Jest don't ask me to understand why' (*Collected Stories*, pp.84—85).

Pete's decision to go to Mephis to enlist is not only accepted by his younger brother; the brother insists that he will go there too, to help his brother, and to 'whup the little uns' (*Collected Stories*, p. 83). No power on earth could get him from trying to join his brother in Memphis, not even Pete's attempts to invest him with mature responsibility by saying that he will be badly needed at home now that he is gone. So the boy sets out to Memphis,[8] fighting with those who try to stop him from joining the army, even using his pocket knife when he is forced to. The boy is persuaded by his older brother to return home, but his affection and his foreboding of what will happen to Pete, make the less than nine-year-old boy say that 'I would pure cut a throat if it would bring you back to stay' (*Collected Stories*, p. 96).

268

In his violent attempts to join his brother in Memphis, the unnamed narrator of the story echoes his mother's words about having 'got to go', but only after he has met Pete does he understand that where he has 'got to go' is back home to take over some of the jobs that Pete cannot do now that he is fighting in the war. The young boy's patriotic sentiments and his violent actions on the way to Memphis make it hard to believe in him; he is a larger-than-life character, and he is created this way to serve certain deliberate purposes the author had when telling this story. The boy is also the narrator of this episode, and he is an unreliable narrator. His reliability is one problem, since he not only describes what 'Me and Pete' did, but also comments on what the other characters say and do. He is at times the author's mouthpiece; as when he describes his father's remarks as being foolish; and he does not seem mature enough to be capable of expressing the sentiments which the author invests in him. Yet by using this kind of weak and – to some extent – innocent narrator, immediate and unqualified comments on loyalty, fidelity, and responsibility are given. The boy narrator does not have to be trusted; his story does not have to deliver a message that may be logically defended or explained: his story is a tale of the human heart. 'Two Soldiers' is a competent story, written to make money and to meet the wishes of the average *Post* reader, and despite its easy sentimentalism and exaggerated patriotism, it remains mildly entertaining.

Stronger in some respects but also more overwritten and sentimental, is the sequel to 'Two Soldiers', 'Shall Not Perish'. This is one of Faulkner's most emotional stories, which is not surprising since the story involves the deaths of two young men in the Second World War, Pete Grier and Major de Spain's son. In addition to the grief in both families, the effects on the parents of the two boys are opposed and contrasted so that the personal tragedies gain deeper significance.

The unnamed younger brother of Pete Grier is also the narrator of this story, and in the beginning his description of the message about Pete's death, and the reaction to it are poetic and eloquent:

And that was all. One day there was Pearl Harbor. And the next week Pete went to Memphis, ...and one morning Mother stood at the field fence with a little scrap of paper. . .saying, *A ship was. Now it is not. Your son was one of them (Collected Stories,* pp. 101—2).

The Griers allowed themselves 'one day to grieve', because the message came in the hardest push of the planting time, but this does not mean that their grief was not deep and strong. Even in time of grief, the family must carry on with their duties. They are responsible to the land they love, and life must go on. The boy's vision of death wanders away from the strictly emotional grief for a dead brother to the abiding land, which has to be planted. War and heroic acts in a war are ephemeral; the land itself seems eternal and demands dedicated work in ever-lasting repetitions of the changing seasons.

The same duty to life and the living is seen when the father breaks the news about Major De Spain's son: the mother goes on churning, and only when she has finished does she ask her husband to read the news for her. The understanding on the boy's part, shared by his mother, too, that 'it happened again' and will happen again and again, that young men die in the war, seems to indicate a sense of equality within the greater community of Yoknapatawpha County. So the death of Major De Spain's son affects the Griers deeply; they have already felt this kind of loss, and the mother makes up her mind to pay de Spain a visit to share in his grief and thereby possibly lessen his burden.

Mrs. Grier and her son – who narrates all the events of their trip – enter a totally different world when they pay de Spain their visit. De Spain apparently does not welcome any visitors; he has planned to cope with his grief through self-destruction, which Mrs. Grier prevents by wrestling his gun from him. De Spain is very much a Southerner, in the sense that he does not accept that he, or his son, has a country to fight for. 'His country and mine both was ravaged and polluted and destroyed eighty years ago, before even I was born' (*Collected Stories,* p. 108). His parlour is decorated with a Confederate flag, and his ties to the past are not only exaggerated and foolish; they prevent him from adjusting to the needs of the present day and time. Since his son had gone to the war, it is very likely that he did not quite share his father's beliefs. De Spain lives in the past, while the Griers have to live in the present, even though the past is a living tradition to them, since other Griers have fought in other wars and even more so, since other Griers have tilled the soil and have been outlasted by it because they did right to it.

The story reaches its peak in the conversations with de Spain, and emotion slowly recedes when Mrs. Grier takes her son to the Museum, where paintings from all over America are shown. This has not only the function of relief, as the pictures in the museum combine in the boy's mind with the memory of his grandfather who had participated in the

Civil War, and who had a vivid memory of the men he knew when he was a young soldier. The memory of the grandfather adds comic relief to the story, but it also adds to our understanding of the young boy's education and maturation, as well as serving to explain some of the beliefs laid down by tradition in the older brother, who gave his life in defending his country. The boy suddenly seems to grasp that he and his family are parts of a larger community, and that other people love their regions of the land so much that they are allowed not only to perpetuate it through pictures, but also to die for it and to grieve for the loss of someone dear. The plain people of Yoknapatawpha seldom see beyond the boundaries of their own area, and they are distrustful of anything new and strange from the larger outside world. Young Grier's experience is therefore extremely important. His brother seems to have had the same experience of the vastness of his country and his right and duty to defend it. Some of the awareness may possibly stem from listening to the radio during the first days and weeks of the war.

While the Griers are used for serious purposes in 'Shall Not Perish', Faulkner's third story involving this family, 'Shingles for the Lord', is a humorous work, relating a hilarious and almost ubelievable adventure. 'Shingles for the Lord' is also located in Frenchman's Bend, although no specific mention of the place is given. Res Grier,⁹ the principal character of the story, is not necessarily identical with the father of the two earlier stories, and if he is, it is probably the older brother, Pete, who narrates this story rather than the young narrator of the two former Grier stories.

The story deals with the poor but honourable people in a rural community where the church occupies a central position, in the lives of the people as well as in their minds. Res Grier is, however, an exceptional character in this respect: he is willing to do his part of the job to put shingles on the roof of the Lord's house, but his bad planning and lack of any foresight whatsoever make him a bad worker in the Lord's vineyard. Res is not lazy; he is an average hard-working farmer trying to do the best he can, but he does not even own the tools needed for the repair job. Instead of working steadily and patiently to improve his situation, Res hopes to improve it quickly and substantially. The result is almost a foregone conclusion: he loses in all his affairs and, trying to make up for his losses, he is unfortunate enough to set fire to the church so that it burns down. The narrator – and the implied author – may pity him, but there is no doubt that Res Grier's hard luck is a result of his bad

271

planning, his lack of discipline, and his impatience. In the end, when the preacher decides to have the church rebuilt, he will not let Res participate in the work on the new church. The church and the preacher represent an ideal of permanence and indestructibility, and this is possible only because the men in the community are willing to work to rebuild the church. In the men's willingness to contribute their time is inherent an element of permanence and indestructibility, too, and the young narrator who has a father who lacks these qualities, is very much aware of them as he narrates the story.

During a period of international crisis, in which loyalty and personal integrity came to be tested on many levels, Faulkner found the best human qualities in the remote areas of his imaginary kingdom. But he also went back to the few ideas and fragments he had left unused from the major short-story period, and this produced one story, 'Snow'. It belongs in every respect in the main short-story period, and has absolutely nothing to do with the 'country' or with Yoknapatawpha. 'Snow' is a frame story, with an introductory part placed in the early days of the Second World War, while the real story takes place in the inter-war period before 'all the people in it [Europe] started to hate and fear Germans' (*Uncollected Stories,* p. 665).

The story proper is a remembrance of the past, told in the first person by a young man who is travelling with Don in Europe, and who watches what may be a murder among mountain climbers. As in 'Mistral', 'I' and Don can only watch and react to the dramatic events, while they as outsiders cannot influence them. The murder is elaborately planned and calculated, and the frame story deals with what may be the very much delayed revenge of a Swiss woman who lost her husband during the mountain climbing episode that the first-person narrator now recalls. The story deals with initiation into evil and with the inability to grasp the full meaning of a strange and traumatic experience. The boys are too young and too inexperienced to be seriously influenced by what they hear and see, but the frame of the story and the very fact that the narrator thinks back to this minor episode of his past, indicate that the mystical events have lingered in the boy's mind for many years.

The serious theme of 'Snow' and its being related to the events of the Second World War in the opening paragraphs of the introductory frame are elements which place it with stories such as 'The Tall Men' and 'Shall Not Perish'. In 'Shingles for the Lord' humour and comedy seem to replace the tragedy inherent in the other stories, and in 'A Courtship', and 'My Grandmother Millard and General Bedford Forrest and the Battle of Harrykin Creek', humour and farcical comedy are at the core, although more serious themes can easily be found in these two stories about Indians and Whites; Yankees and Confederates, respectively.

'My Grandmother Millard...' is a long story told by an unnamed narrator, who is nonetheless recognized as Bayard Sartoris because of the story's close relationships with central episodes in *The Unvanquished,* and because of his relatives who are named in the text (John Sartoris, Rosa Millard). The story is in point of fact another Bayard-Ringo story, and the narrator describes the appearance of the first Yankee troops at the Sartoris place. The unexpected arrival interferes with grandmother Millard's plans for having the family treasure buried. The sudden appearance of a young Confederate Lieutenant, who drives away the enemy single-handed, saves Cousin Melisandre, who had hidden in the outhouse with the valuables. The Lieutenant, whose name is Backhouse, is infatuated by 'that beautiful girl', but his name is very embarrassing to her, since he first met her just in – the backhouse. General Forrest and Grandmother Millard therefore have to join forces and persuade the young officer to change his name to Backus so that the young couple may get together and finally even get married.

It may be tempting to speculate that Faulkner had originally written 'My Grandmother Millard. . .' as part of his series of Civil War stories in the mid-thirties. There is no evidence to corroborate such an assumption, and he may simply have turned to familiar material to create what he obviously thought of as a story the better-paying magazines would accept. Apart from the broad similarities in setting and character, most connections between 'My Grandmother Millard . . .' and *The Unvanquished* are contrasts rather than similarities, and none of the serious concerns that slipped into the book-version of the Bayard-Ringo stories are present in the 1942 story. 'My Grandmother Millard. . .' is void of any deeper significance; it is a very simple story, broad in its outlines, based on outrageous events, and deliberately intended to evoke laughter.

'A Courtship' is also in the humorous vein, and the events of this story of a long-lasting Indian-White competition are possibly more outrageous than the amusing incidents of 'My Grandmother Millard. . . .'. The fact that Ikkemotubbe – who later is known as Doom, and whom we are familiar with from 'A Justice' – is one of the competitors and suitors in

'A Courtship' adds seriousness to this story. Any Indian story somehow includes elements of the 'vanishing American' and is thus by implication more serious in tone, than a humorous-heroic Sartoris story from the Civil War, although one may talk about 'a lost cause' even in this connection.

At the centre of 'A Courtship' is, of course, a courtship. The Indian maid is Herman Basket's sister, and she 'walked in beauty. Or she sat in it, that is, because she did not walk at all unless she had to' (*Collected Stories,* p. 362). Faulkner's use of Byron[10] is direct and free, as is his use of qualities and characteristics he had given to Eula Varner. The similarity between the Indian girl and Eula Varner in *The Hamlet* further makes the reader think of Helen of Troy, to whom Faulkner alludes more than once in his description of Eula. This is in keeping with the heroic figures of Ikkemotubbe and David Hogganbeck and their athletic contests, which are reminiscent of *The Odyssey.* Moreover, the final running competition is 'of more than marathon proportions'.[11]

No winner can possibly gain a complete victory in the contest because his opponent must be present and watch his victory. Therefore the two men help each other in all situations, and no one is allowed to gain an edge, factual or psychological, over the other. This competition between two men from different worlds and races creates friendship and respect. Hogganbeck and Ikkemotubbe were considered to be the best of all men on the Indian plantation even before the race, and that is why both the contestants and most of the other men cannot think it possible that anyone else would try to win Herman Basket's sister. Their self-security and a good portion of male arrogance prevent them from even considering the possibility that the girl may have a say in this matter. In the masculine world where power, skill, and fighting ability count so much, the two men cannot even imagine that other qualities in a man might be important. Log-in-the-Creek may be a lazy good-for-nothing, but he is a persistent suitor who blows his harmonica on the girl's gallery – and marries her while the heroes compete violently for her. Ikkemotubbe is reminded of a sage of his tribe who knew more about women than the two heroes; and David Hogganbeck refers to Solomon in his answers:

'There was a wise man of ours who said once how a woman's fancy is like a butterfly which, hovering from flower to flower, pauses at the last as like as not where a horse has stood.'
'There was a wise man of ours named Solomon who often said something of that nature

too,' David Hogganbeck said. 'Perhaps there is just one wisdom for all men, no matter who speaks it' (*Collected Stories*, pp 379–80).

The fantastic competition and the growing respect and admiration between the two men are central elements in this complex but amusing story. Basically, 'A Courtship' is a humorous story about the contest between two strong men, followed by more serious considerations in the description of their disappointment when they see that the race has been for nothing. Especially Ikkemotubbe is, of course, disappointed, and in his failure to win the beautiful maiden lies the germ of serious conflicts in the tribe and murderous actions, which eventually make Ikkemotubbe Chief of the tribe under the name Doom. 'A Courtship' is thus a story with many comic and tragic aspects. The tragedy inherent in this story is seen clearly in 'A Justice'. In this much earlier story Doom comes back from New Orleans and seizes complete power in the tribe. In 'A Courtship' his motives for the murderous actions are provided. His use of poison to gain power is gruesome and cruel, and cannot be excused in any way. On the basis of Faulkner's last Indian Story his actions become understandable: Ikkemotubbe seeks revenge because of his failure to win Herman Basket's sister, and only to look at 'the Herman Basket's sisters of this world' (*Collected Stories*, p. 362) may be reason enough for the man who is taken in.

To conclude this chapter, two more works of short fiction by William Faulkner in the 1940's will be discussed very briefly. Both of them are what must be considered borderline cases, as to whether they really deserve being called short stories. Texts such as 'Appendix: Compson, 1699 – 1945' and 'Notes on a Horsethief' do not have to be included in a discussion of Faulkner's short fiction, and even though I have tried to be rather inclusive, I see no reason to discuss these texts at length.

The Compson Appendix was written for Cowley's *Portable Faulkner* so that the composition of it has nothing to do with the novel it is an appendix to: *The Sound and the Fury.* Yet Faulkner says that he 'failed to finish' this novel in 1928, and also that the 1946 appendix is a necessary 'key' to it.[12] The Appendix may be read as a short story without reference to any other Faulkner work, but it is doubtful whether anybody except the very seasoned Faulkner reader would find the Appendix interesting and worthwhile except in the context of *The Sound and the Fury.* In Faulkner's long career as a short-fiction writer, the Compson

Appendix does not deserve a central place, however. It is, of course, another instance of Faulkner's ability to use characters and material from earlier novels in new and different contexts, but in this case the context is indeed the original novel.[13] The last story to be mentioned in this chapter, 'Notes on a Horsethief', also occupies an intermediate position between being a long short story and what Faulkner called 'A Dangling Participle from Work in Progress'.[14]

One may argue that 'Notes on a Horsethief' is not a short story but a short novel, simply because it is close to 25,000 words long. Furthermore, 'Notes on a Horsethief' may be regarded as an early draft of a part of the novel *A Fable,* and hence not as a work complete unto itself. Yet it is at least as much of a work with a separate identity as the stories that were later used in *The Hamlet,* so that only the length and its being published as a book might be used to prove that it is not a short story. 'Idyll in the Desert' and 'Miss Zilphia Gant' were also published as books, so this would leave us with only the question of length, which is rather uninteresting here.

'Notes on a Horsethief' centres around two symbols: the race horse and a court house. The story is so organized that the first part of it deals with the theft of the horse and the thieves' success in evading the law and running the horse at small tracks all over the South, till they are finally cornered in Mississippi and shoot the horse rather than see him go to the stud farm to 'reproduce'. The second part of the story concerns the failure of law enforcement to capture the thieves and bring justice about. This failure is very important. Since there is a reward for the thieves' capture, one would suppose that someone told on them rather quickly. The horse evidently represents some kind of natural freedom, and this freedom is cherished by the citizens of small towns all over the South who believe in individual freedom and oppose the more formal and strictly enforced laws of the big cities.

The distinction between a sense of natural freedom and the rights of the individual on the one side, and civil law and justice in defence of the larger community on the other, is not as simple as it may appear above. The horse is not a symbol of anything to the groom who stole it and races it, and few people involved in the pursuit, one way or the other, attach any mythical dimensions to the horse. Only the deputy-poet of the story is capable of intellectualizing and mythicizing the horse and the theft to give it added significance. The mob that frees the preacher is not

276

necessarily opposing justice or trying to halt progress; they simply set the prisoner free because they think that the thieves have won a large sum of money, and they should accordingly not be punished for being successful or for making their version of the American dream come true.

'Notes on a Horsethief' is a story about progress, motion, freedom, and justice. It is a story in which freedom seems to be controlled and regulated because progress requires it, but Faulkner does not condone or defend the actions of either side in the conflict. He tells a long story, almost in one breath, although the story was finally published in 'normal language' with punctuation and regular sentences. The fabulous race horse in 'Notes on a Horsethief', being simply a good horse or a symbol of freedom, has to run on small and unimportant tracks, yet he is allowed to do what he is good at. On the other hand, his qualities will not be passed on to new generations of horses, since he finally pays with his life – with his genetic line – for the freedom to run.[15] In the conflicting understandings of this story one should also remember that the horse is not really free, since he is a piece of property, owned by men, whether legally or illegally.

'Notes on a Horsethief' is not an important or central story in Faulkner's short-story career, whereas it is far more important if seen in relation to the novel it became an integrated part of, *A Fable,* and even in relation to his last novel, *The Reivers.*

Faulkner's 1942 short stories are stories in their own right, independent of earlier stories, and with only the Yoknapatawpha setting as an almost inevitable common background with other stories and novels. The stories about the Second World War are clearly products of their time, and in their high-strung sentimentality they are among the weakest stories Faulkner ever wrote. 'Two Soldiers' and 'Shall Not Perish' are not much of a novelist's short stories either, and even though short stories always involve some kind of narrative concentration, with summaries, parts that are only hinted at, etc., in these stories the gap between the pseudo-time of the discourse and the story-time is not unusually wide. The other stories from the 1940's are, on the other hand, either of the same kind as the individual stories in the previous period, or they are in many ways related to novels in progress or novels that have already been published. This is true for 'Notes on a Horsethief' as well as 'Appendix: Compson', whereas 'My Grandmother Millard . . .' reminds one of the Bayard-Ringo series.

277

In a sense the short stories that Faulkner wrote in 1942 are similar to those he wrote in the early thirties. He took time off from other duties – among them novel writing – and concentrated on the writing of short stories. He could not quite forget his novels, and his people were with him all the time. Still it may be correct to maintain that for the second time in his career, short-story writing came first. The stories themselves do not therefore differ much from the stories he wrote in other periods or from stories that relate very closely to novels. Yet they are not so clearly a novelist's short stories in any of the meanings I have discussed earlier, although this is true only of a few of the stories while the remaining ones definitely are a novelist's stories in all respects ('Notes on a Horsethief', 'Appendix: Compson', etc.).

As Faulkner tired of short-story writing, and as success slowly came his way, his short narratives came to rely even more heavily on his novels than before. Also, his short narratives would tend to become even more strongly condensed versions of what appears to be material for novels. In the 1950's his stories, almost without exceptions, are by-products of his novels, and in this respect as well as with regard to the narrative concentration, they are a novelist's short stories – more so perhaps than ever before.

9. Short Stories 1942–1962
Echoes and Reminiscences

> Loving all of it even while he had to hate some of
> it because he knows now that you dont love because:
> you love despite; not for the virtues, but despite the
> faults.
>
> – Faulkner, 'Mississippi'

There is a strong tendency in much of Faulkner's later fiction to rely rather heavily on echoes and reminiscences of previous works, and he seems even more inclined to do this in the short fictional pieces than in the longer works. Apparently he was so familiar with his characters and episodes in their lives, which had been told in novels or earlier short stories, that it was natural for him to use this as a background in new stories. In 'Sepulture South: Gaslight' there are thus references to Uncle Rodney and the affairs narrated in 'That Will Be Fine', in 'Mississippi' obvious references to 'Ambuscade' and *Sartoris/Flags in the Dust* are found, and in 'By the People' there is a direct reference to the dog-swapping business in 'Shingles for the Lord'. These are only a few examples: the other stories of the fifties also echo previous works, and some of them are so closely related to novels that they hardly acquire an identity of their own.

Faulkner published four novel excerpts during the fifties and early sixties, before the publication of the novels themselves. 'The Jail', excerpted from the forthcoming *Requiem for a Nun,* was published in 1951; 'The Waifs', the concluding episode of *The Town,* was published in 1957; 'Mink Snopes', the opening chapter of *The Mansion,* was published in 1959; and 'The Education of Lucius Priest', excerpted from chapters 5,6, and 7 of *The Reivers,* was published in 1962. These texts are of course not included in our discussion here, since they cannot be judged to be short stories by any criteria. One must be aware, on the other hand, that a couple of the short stories in the fifties are very close to being excerpts from novels, without much that could be called a separate identity: this is in particular the case with 'Hell Creek Crossing', which will be briefly mentioned at the end of this chapter.

Strangely enough, Faulkner also wrote and submitted to his agent a short story that did not sell, despite his fame and popularity at that time. This is 'Hog Pawn', – now available in *Uncollected Stories of William Faulkner,* an early version of the Meadowfill episode of *The Mansion,* which Faulkner's agent received in 1955. The story must be considered a part of Faulkner's novel, and I see little reason to discuss it here.

The decline in Faulkner's short-story production in the fifties may not only be explained by a reference to his improved economic situation or his consistent and hard work on *A Fable, The Mansion,* and *The Town.* The rich short-story market of the 1930's no longer existed, and following the decline in this market, there was a sharp rise in the demand for essays and articles.[1] Thus Faulkner wrote numerous essays during the fifties – 'Mississippi', 'An Innocent at Rinkside', 'On Privacy', 'On Fear: Deep South in Labor: Mississippi', to mention only a few.[2] Some of these were commissioned by magazines, and were accordingly submitted and printed as essays. Yet it is possible to consider at least two of the pieces published as essays to be short stories. Because of their fictional elements, and because of the fictional techniques employed in them, 'Mississippi' and 'Sepulture South; Gaslight' may be regarded as short stories.[3] 'Sepulture South; Gaslight' may well be the finest short story of Faulkner's later years, and his last short story to be published, notwithstanding the 1962 publication of 'Hell Creek Crossing', which more than anything else is an excerpted episode from *The Reivers.*

The first short story by Faulkner to arrive at Harold Ober's office in the 1950's was 'A Name for the City', which Faulkner called a by-product of his play.[4] The story is a long-winding and slow narrative about the naming of Jefferson, and although Jefferson seems to have been a favourite among map-makers everywhere in America, because of President Jefferson and the ideas he represented, Faulkner here gives a new and unexpected explanation of how *his* Jefferson got its name. Faulkner had of course named the city decades earlier in his fiction, and it may well be – as Elmo Howell suspects – that Faulkner gave his new account of the naming of Jefferson in an attempt to distance himself from some of the Jeffersonian ideals which he did not share.[5] The story about the naming is nonetheless mostly amusing and entertaining, as it relates episodes from the early frontier days in Mississippi, and involves a number of stubborn but self-reliant men.

'A Name for the City' is a strange story in which an enormous

15-pound lock plays an important part. The lock, which originally came from Carolina, has been used on the U.S. mail bag, until it is used to secure the prison door and disappears after an outbreak from the jail. The mail rider, Thomas Jefferson Pettigrew, considers the lock Federal property, and will not accept the other characters' attempts to forget about the missing lock. They finally come up with a solution to the problem, which is to name their little settlement after the mail rider, deciding to build a courthouse, and later see to it that the place becomes a town and eventually a city.

'A Name for the City' is narrated by an unnamed nephew of Gavin Stevens, apparently Chick Mallison. He and his uncle are present only in the introductory part of the story, and he opens it by quoting his uncle's statement about experience: 'Experience', Uncle Gavin said, 'is not in the senses, but in the heart'.[6] It is difficult to see how Gavin's speech as narrated here has important bearings upon the story told, although the story may have something to do with the question of whether knowledge through experience is reached 'in the senses' or 'in the heart'. More likely the introductory part would fit better if it was used in the version of this story which formed the narrative prologue to Act I of *Requiem for a Nun.*[7]

Familiar settings and familiar characters are found in all other stories in the fifties, with one notable exception; 'Mr. Acarius'. This story is unique in Faulkner's short-story career in almost all respects.

'Mr. Acarius' (or 'Weekend Revisited') has a metropolitan setting, and most of the time the story is limited to an alcoholics' hospital. Mr. Acarius has begged his doctor to let him get to this place, since he is not capable of going all the way to skid-row, which he would have preferred. Mr. Acarius, middle-aged and well-off with serious problems,[8] wants to experience mankind. More than that: he wants to enter mankind, feel some sort of communion, and he will have to do it through baseness and debauchery. Mr. Acarius is well aware that he cannot really get down to the lowest level of human anguish and suffering, but at least he can try. Perhaps he will come to terms with his human condition by establishing links with other suffering people:

'... But at least we will be together in having failed to escape and in knowing that in the last analysis there is no escape, that you can never escape and, whether you will or not, you must reenter the world and bear yourself in it and its lacerations and all its anguish of

281

breathing, to support and comfort one another in that knowledge and that attempt' (*Uncollected Stories,* p. 438).

Mr. Acarius is no alcoholic, and W. Cantrell may well be right when he says that 'he undertakes his experiment in debauchery in an attempt to eliminate a sense of vacuity in his own life'.[9] Mr. Acarius feels isolated, he is getting old, and he has a feeling that nothing has ever happened to him. But, expectedly, his experiment does not work out at all. He finds the atmosphere unbearable and the patients inhuman. He breaks out of the clinic, and fights the police, before his doctor picks him up. The story thus ends in a conversation between Mr. Acarius and his doctor, parts of which are so cryptical as to be inexplicable.[10] Nonetheless, Mr. Acarius has proved to himself how alienated he is, and that there is no short-cut to 'brotherhood' and community. At any rate, man has to divest himself of some of his selfish concerns, if such brotherhood shall have any significance. Blotner's comment on the story when it was published in the *Post* in 1965 is pertinent, although it says little about the story itself:

> Here the protagonist enters on a kind of Dostoevskian quest to give his life meaning through suffering. He plans to descend deep into debauchery in an effort to link himself with other suffering men and to come to terms with the intolerable human condition. The failure of his attempt only increases the poignancy of Faulkner's story.[11]

The reason why 'Mr. Acarius' was not published till 1965 is probably the fear that Faulkner's publishers and magazine editors had, that people would read this as some sort of autobiographical account about one of Faulkner's drunken bouts; his heavy drinking being, as it was, public knowledge.

James B. Meriwether has argued convincingly that 'Mississippi' had better be regarded a short story and read as such.[12] *Holiday,* which had commissioned the story and printed it in April 1954, calls it 'a memorable article about his native state',[13] but the amount of fictional elements and possibly also the narrative technique employed, make it reasonable to include a note on 'Mississippi' here.

'Mississippi' is a 'moving tribute by one who has loved his land'.[14] 'Loving all of it even while he had to hate some of it because he knows now that you don't love because: you love despite; not for the virtues, but despite the faults.'[15] Faulkner's tour of his native state takes us 'through space and history and his own life story', as Malcolm Cowley puts it.[16] Faulkner blends facts with fiction, the state's official growth and coming

282

of age with his personal life story, augmented by some incidents that appear to be more fictional than autobiographical. The fictional essay is beautifully structured, beginning with the land itself, then moving on to its history and to the personal life of the author. In addition, the history of the state and the personal history alternate and support one another. What makes this more than an article on the state of Mississippi is just the personal history, or rather, the series of incidents in the narrator's life which he relates, and which build up to the concluding assertion about 'Loving all of it'. In these episodes from the narrator's life – whether true or not – the narrative technique is different from the more realistic and straightforward descriptions of the land and its history. When writing about the sailing trip on the Sardis reservoir, the narrator moves away from the scene he is participating in, and watches himself and his friends from the outside:

> . . . suddenly it seemed to the middle-aging that part of him was no longer in the sloop but about ten feet away, looking at what he saw: a Harvard undergraduate, a taxi driver, the son of an absconded banker and a village clown and a middle-aged novelist sailing a home-made boat on an artificial lake in the depths of the north Mississippi hills: and he thought that that was something which did not happen to you more than once in your life.[17]

The sweeping view and the generous and unrelenting love proffered by Faulkner in this text are typical of the mature and middle-aged author who had once dreamt about becoming a vagabond, but who was born of this land and is pleased to know that 'his bones will sleep in it'.[18]

Faulkner's last hunting story, 'Race at Morning', is also a tribute to the land he knows and loves. Here is the wilderness and the two weeks of hunting each November, which we have become familiar with in the story of Ike McCaslin, and which we have seen shrink and diminish year by year. The river bottom is still full of game, but the combination of being a farmer and a hunter is not enough any longer, according to the boy's mentor in this story, Mister Ernest. Apparently he understands what will eventually happen to the beloved wilderness, and he also senses that it will no longer be enough to 'belong to the farming business and the hunting business'; you have to 'belong to the business of mankind' (*Uncollected Stories,* p. 309).

The narrator of this story is a twelve-year-old boy whose mother has run off with a Vicksburg roadhouse jack, and whose father left him immediately after. He is now living with Mister Ernest, a deaf widower, who is a farmer and a skilled hunter. The boy tells the story in the first person, but one of the members in the hunting party, Willy Legate, describes the boy thus: '. . . He knows every cuss word in the dictionary, every poker hand in the deck and every whisky label in the distillery, but he can't even write his name. . .' (*Uncollected Stories*, p. 296). The boy is thus not totally innocent,[19] although he lacks both a formal education and to some extent even the education life in the woods among the hunters could give him. During the race narrated in 'Race at Morning' he seems to pass into manhood and is initiated into an adult world with regulations and demands of which he has hitherto been unaware. The boy and Mister Ernest hunt for a big buck, which escapes them as well as the other hunters, even though Mister Ernest had his opportunity to shoot it. By not shooting, Ernest has made certain that next November will also bring two weeks of good hunting:

'Which would you rather have? His bloody head and hide on the kitchen floor yonder and half his meat in a pickup truck on the way to Yoknapatawpha County, or him with his head and hide and meat still together over yonder in that brake, waiting for next November for us to run him again?' (*Uncollected Stories*, p. 310).

The young boy depends on Mister Ernest, and he relies on him. At the same time he is rather independent in his thoughts and attitudes, although most of his thoughts may come from other members of the hunting party or be extensions of thoughts and remarks Mister Ernest has uttered earlier. Anyhow, the boy has made up his mind to become a farmer and a hunter; farming three hundred and fifty-one days of the year and hunting for the remaining fourteen. He has discovered that hunting and farming are not different things at all – 'they was jest the other side of each other' (*Uncollected Stories*, p. 309). Mister Ernest has other plans for the boy, however. He wants him to get an education, because being a hunter and a farmer is no longer enough:

'. . . So you're going to school. . . . You can belong to the farming and hunting business and you can learn the difference between what's wrong, and do right. And that used to be enough – just to do right. But not now. You got to know why it's right and why it's wrong, and be able to tell the folks that never had no chance to learn it; teach them how to do what's right, not just because they know it's right, but because they know now why it's right because you just showed them, told them, taught them why. So you're going to school' (*Uncollected Stories*, pp. 309–10).

284

Mister Ernest is a wise man who has acquired his wisdom in the big woods and in the long years of steady farming. He knows that the future is bearable only because it is uncertain; because in his understanding 'maybe' is the best word in the language. It promises opportunity if you can use it, and it is 'what mankind keeps going on'. In other words: you must accept the risks and chances of change and alteration; you may do best by letting the buck run so you, maybe, can get him next November, or else life may lose meaning and little can sustain and comfort you.

The lessons taught by 'Race at Morning' are not as convincing or effective as those in 'The Old People' or 'The Bear'. The description of the race itself, of the various stages of the hunt, is done with Faulkner's usual mastery of this kind of material, and the revised version of this story, incorporated in *Big Woods* together with such marvellous hunting stories as 'The Bear' and 'The Old People', shows no diminution of Faulkner's creative power.

The hunting party in 'Race at Morning' is another example of Faulkner's use of well-known characters in his late fiction, and the next short story in this decade, 'By the People', shows the same practice. This must obviously be so, since it is a Snopes story, later incorporated into *The Mansion*. This story is about Senator Clarence Eggleston Snopes and his rise to political power before Ratliff finally beats him, so that Uncle Billy Varner forces him to withdraw from the congressional election. Ratliff's method is worthy of this great story-teller and shrewd sewing-machine agent: Ratliff arranges it so that the candidate's trouser legs are switched with wet saplings from a dog thicket (a place where every dog in the County has been at least once). The dogs then, as planned, use Snopes's trouser legs as they would have used the thicket and he is soon wet all through. The embarrassment caused by this is what finally makes Willy Varner decide to withdraw Snopes from all future political life, and is in point of fact another example of how little it takes either to win or lose support in the 'politicking' system of the South and of the United States in general.[20] Much criticism of the elective system and the vulnerability of it to the kind of cheap demagoguery Snopes represents is found in 'By the People', but since Ratliff defeats Snopes, the story ends in an assertion of 'government by the people' as its title indicated from the beginning.

'By the People' is told by an unnamed nephew of Gavin Stevens; again he is obviously Chick Mallison, but since he does not have the first-hand knowledge of the crucial public meeting where Snopes was beaten, he sets the stage for Ratliff, who, although reluctantly, tells what happened. In the course of his story, it becomes quite clear that Ratliff himself has been instrumental in planning the ingenious dog trick. Accordingly, Gavin Stevens, who had told his nephew that none of his generation could possibly stand up against Snopes, was wrong: Ratliff has done it successfully.

'By the People' is a central story about the Snopeses and their growth to power, wealth, and position in the Yoknapatawpha of the twentieth century. In 'Centaur in Brass' we have seen how Flem Snopes's rapid progress was halted for some time, but could not be stopped dead. In 'By the People', Snopesism faces another defeat, but despite the story's positive conclusion, the Snopeses would certainly regain political positions even on the national level later on. 'By the People' works better as an episode in *The Mansion* than it does as a short story. The short story is amusing, but the significance of it becomes clear only in the light of the longer work. This is especially true of Gavin's inadequacy to cope with Snopes: in the Snopes trilogy his deficiency is part of the very complex story of Gavin Stevens.

Faulkner's article or essay, 'Sepulture South: Gaslight', is one of his finest short fictional pieces in the last decade of his career. J.B. Meriwether has found the essay to be 'a short story, perhaps as much a short story as anything Faulkner ever wrote'.[21] He reaches this conclusion on the basis of his intimate knowledge of Faulkner's life, saying that it is certain that the author in this text was not drawing on his own family background more than he did in half a dozen of his novels. Meriwether also says that 'Mississippi' and 'Sepulture South; Gaslight' use fictional techniques, and warns against 'the dangers that attend to place unruly and original works of art in regular, neat academic pigeonholes',[22] which is, indeed, an apt reminder.

In 'Sepulture South: Gaslight' the first-person narrator sends the servant Arthur around to notify people in the town that his Grandfather is dead. The servant performs a rite, and assumes mythical stature: 'he was not even an envoy from us but rather a messenger from Death itself, saying to our town: 'Pause, mortal; remember Me' (*Uncollected Stories,* p. 450).

With the exception of 'Hell Creek Crossing', which is really an excerpt from *The Reivers* with a few paragraphs of introductory material supplied by the author,[23] 'Sepulture South: Gaslight' is Faulkner's last short story. It is therefore also an apt reminder to the readers of his short stories that we are taken to visit the sepulture and watch the marble 'effegies of the actual people themselves as they had been in life' in this cedar-bemused Southern cemetery:

And three or four times a year I would come back. I would not know why, alone to look at them, not just at Grandfather and Grandmother but all of them looming among the lush green of summer and the regal blaze of fall and the rain and ruin of winter before spring would bloom again, stained now, a little darkened by time and weather and endurance but still serene, impervious, remote, gazing at nothing, not like sentinels, not defending the living from the dead by means of their vast ton-measured weight and mass, but rather the dead from the living; shielding instead the vacant and dissolving bones, the harmless and defenseless dust, from the anguish and grief and inhumanity of mankind (*Uncollected Stories*, p. 455).

Here the mortals can pause, remembering, and thereby also contemplating their own lives, their own predicament, their toil and anguish and hopes and dreams; the human condition. The grandparents in 'Sepulture South: Gaslight' sleep in the earth which bore William Faulkner. In the soil of his native land he was perhaps the most fertile of all seeds, and it is more than fitting that most of the short fiction of the later part of his career is deeply rooted in this soil, in Yoknapatawpha County, Mississippi.

Faulkner's short-story production declined sharply in the two last decades of his life. The short stories written after 1942 may be described as chips from the novelist's bench, implying that a great many of the stories are significantly related to his novels. The relationships are of several kinds, and as we have seen, many stories are by-products of novels, while other use characters who are familiar from previous works. The recurrent use of characters and incidents from earlier works in Faulkner's late fiction also gives an indication of how most of the short stories in the late forties and all through the fifties appear to be echoes and reminiscences of earlier days. Yet it should not be overlooked that some of the better stories from this period have an identity of their own and are relatively independent of any of the author's novels or other short stories: 'Shingles for the Lord', 'A Courtship', 'Sepulture South: Gaslight', to mention only a few. Basically, however, Faulkner was drawing on the fictional world he had created up to 1942 in the short fiction he produced after this year.

If 'Sepulture South: Gaslight' is allowed to end Faulkner's short-story career, our discussion will end on a note of afterthought and calm despair. If, however, 'Hell Creek Crossing' is included in our discussion, the short-story career ends on a note of hilarious fun and shrewd cunning, in an encounter with some of Faulkner's characters we have known for a long time, and who make their final appearance on the stage. The grave as well as the funny mood would both be fitting; Faulkner's short-story production covers the comic as well as the tragic aspects of life, and in the 120 odd stories over a period of more than 40 years, all shades between these extremes are also represented.

10. The Novelist as Short Story Writer?

> ... literature ... is the record of those elusive
> moments at which life is alone fully itself, fulfilled in
> consciousness and form.
>
> – Leslie A. Fiedler

A series of good little tales may indeed prove to be ample work for a lifetime, to paraphrase Henry James.[1] William Faulkner did far more than write a series of short stories. His achievement in the short-story genre is not of the same scope and magnitude as his accomplishment in the novel genre, where he was innovative, originative, experimental, and influential. Yet one would do Faulkner's short stories a serious injustice if they were regarded as minor or inferior. Their interest is not primarily in their helpfulness when it comes to the question of solving difficult interpretive problems related to his novels, nor is their value found in the additional information they may shed on his mythical kingdom and those who live there. I refuse to consider the stories as 'adjunctive, projective, and parodic', which is Olga Vickery's classification of the Yoknapatawpha stories.[2] By this classification she implicitly defines the stories on the basis of their relationship to the Yoknapatawpha Saga. Either they 'add more information about certain characters, situations, or the history of Yoknapatawpha County', or they 'examine a new aspect of characters already established and so project new demands of action on the characters and new demands of understanding on the readers'. The third function is to 'parody the white man's follies and ways so as to counterpoint the design of the primary saga itself'.[3] Such a classification may serve as a useful tool, if information and insights about the *novels* are one's primary goals; it does, however, lead the critic astray if applied to the body of short stories itself, since it divests the stories of their autonomy and fails to consider them as separate works of art.

One's starting point should be that Faulkner's short stories are self-contained and unified works of fiction, and their autonomy does not have to be reduced because many of the stories are related to his longer works. It may sound as a paradox, yet Faulkner's stories and novels are simultaneously autonomous and interdependent. This study indicates that although the short stories may be described as a novelist's short stories, the interdependence, or rather the dependence of short stories on novels, has been vastly exaggerated by most critics. Thus, most of Faulkner's stories do not rely on any of his novels in any significant way, and among these stories we can include many of his finest: 'A Mountain Victory', 'A Justice', 'Red Leaves', 'Dry September', 'Uncle Willy', and several others. Accordingly one should not over-emphasize the closeness of the relationship between Faulkner's novels and stories. Faulkner wrote his stories for a market, the influence of which could not be avoided, however little he mixed with the literary circles of his time. Moreover, the demands of the short-story market – the magazines – made him write self-contained, autonomous short stories which do not need any support from his other works to function as good short stories. This is particularly true of the major short-story period, which is the period when Faulkner wrote most of his non-Yoknapatawpha short stories. These stories, obviously, have less to do with his other fiction and are less closely related to his novels than any other short stories. The fact still remains that even these stories are of the second type, according to Friedman's distinctions: they more often than not are broad in their outlook and perspective and cover episodes and incidents of large compass. The need that Faulkner apparently felt for supplying background information and adding atmosphere, history, and a past for many of his stories accounts for the length of them. He pauses in his narration, not to relax, but to provide capsule stories with abundant information, and thus he also creates suspense.

That the novelist William Faulkner put his mark on most of the short stories he wrote, is of course a truth with many modifications, as all such generalizations are. Short stories such as the *Knight's Gambit* stories tell about particular incidents and their ramifications; other Yoknapatawpha stories such as 'That Will Be Fine' and 'Uncle Willy' cover only brief periods in time and a limited experience in a young boy's life; the 'Beyond' stories are complete unto themselves, and the material they encompass is brief in itself, not only or chiefly because Faulkner has condensed or cut to maximize the artistic effect, but mainly because of the brevity of the material.

Faulkner's short-story achievement is remarkable, but seen in relation to the genre and in relation to the tradition of the American short story, it is less remarkable than his achievement in the novel genre. Yet even if his short-story accomplishment is less important than his novels, it stands comparison with all other American writers of his generation: Anderson, Hemingway, Fitzgerald, to mention the best ones, whose works in the shorter form often surpass their novels.[4] Faulkner, who is said not to have contributed significantly to the short-story genre, is one of the many gifted American writers in the 1920's and 1930's who carry on the great tradition of Poe, Hawthorne, and James, and participate in a new development of the short story, which gives it new life and greater freedom.[5] The judge of the O. Henry Awards for many years, Herschel Brickell, describes the development of the short story in America from Anderson's time onwards:

To put it as simply as possible, the short story of the middle period was a story of doing, with action as its theme. Then it gradually moved inward, and in the hands of many people, almost all of whom had first written poetry – and this includes both Hemingway and Faulkner – it became 'a slice of life', as we used to say of Maupassant, but a slice of the mind and the spirit rather than the body.[6]

Brickell finds that the short story has renewed itself because it has been drawn nearer to poetry, 'so that no story of the present is without its overtones'.[7] This trend is so strong that Brickell finds that the contemporary short-story (1951) 'owes more to Hawthorne than to any other one person'.[8]

This new development of the short story which Faulkner almost inadvertently participated in simply because he produced short stories for a market and worked within a given national literature, and adhered (subconsciously at least) to the conventions of a loosely defined genre, is aptly described by Austin McGiffert Wright, who, by the way, includes Faulkner's *These 13* in his discussion of the American short story in the 1920's:

The beginning of the new development of the twenties is commonly associated with the publication of Anderson's *Winesburg, Ohio* in 1919. It was acclaimed immediately and was followed swiftly by the eruption upon the scene of a whole cluster of brilliant writers writing brilliant stories: there was F. Scott Fitzgerald, whose first collection (not up to later ones) came out in 1920, to be followed by *Tales of the Jazz Age* in 1922 and *All the Sad Young Men* in 1926; Ernest Hemingway, with *In Our Time* in 1925 and *Men Without Women* in

1927; and a host of excellent lesser writers ... Toward the end of the period, William Faulkner and Katherine Anne Porter began to appear as short story writers; Miss Porter's *Flowering Judas* was published in 1930 and Faulkner's *These 13* in 1931.[9]

That this new development in its later phase may also be associated with the movement commonly known as the Southern Literary Renaissance is, indeed, possible. Not only Faulkner and Porter wrote short stories from the South; to their names could be added a long list of names, some of which have an international reputation, others which are well known in the national literature. In a postscript to an anthology of Southern writing, the editors write that 'In novels, stories, and poems of unprecedented vitality and richness they [the young Southern writers] gave renewed literary image to the experience of an American region that for more than two centuries has provided the nurture for important artistic accomplishment.'[10] And Faulkner was one of those who emerged from what, in H. L. Mencken's famous words, was 'the Sahara of the Bozart',[11] and he alone could fill the 'vast vacuity'[12] which was Southern literature in the 1920's.

He started out in the twenties with the searching and probing sketches and stories that gave him good practice in the portrayal of character and in the handling of narrative structure. The uncertain apprentice wrote more or less static stories in artificial prose, where he showed a propensity for frozen tableaux and interior monologues uttered by tormented souls. Little if anything of the master novelist and short-story writer can be found in the early sketches, although Faulkner's cyclical habit of mind, and his need for a varied cast of characters and a story of broader expanse than an average short story can normally contain, are detectable as early as in the New Orleans period.

In the New Orleans sketches alienation and loneliness are central themes. The characters often find themselves in an urban wasteland, and they feel that they are governed by some indifferent fate or destiny. The more complete stories from this period, 'The Liar' and 'Yo Ho and Two Bottles of Rum', are of two distinctly different types; the former placed in a rural setting and closely related to an oral story-telling tradition, the latter a non-Yoknapatawpha story with an international cast of characters and with an unusual reliance on mood and atmosphere. In the years following this period, Faulkner would pursue both kinds of stories. Although most of his stories are rooted deeply within his imaginary kingdom of Yoknapatawpha, he also wrote a number of stories without a realistic setting or stories that were placed in Europe (the Don and I stories, the First World War stories, etc.). The young author in search of a form, found his form when he found his material – when he discovered his postage stamp of native soil, and his desperate urge to create helped him perfect his story-telling techniques. Experimentation and search are typical of the artist in this period, and this is reflected in the stories themselves; not the least in the few allegorical tales that he wrote.

In the major short-story period Faulkner concentrated on short-story writing between novels, and he sold so many stories that it enabled him to take care of his growing responsibilities as a family man, to buy Rowan Oak and repair it. Short-story writing thus brought in more money than the novels so far had done, and although he had to go to Hollywood in 1932 to earn a living, his short-story writing in the early thirties must be deemed a success also in financial terms. Artistically this is by far Faulkner's most important period for short-story production, but one should keep in mind that a great many of the stories he sold in 1930 and 1931 were originally written before 1930; some of them perhaps as early as 1926.[13]

In the more than forty stories from this period, certain recurrent patterns can be found, on the basis of the reactions characters show when they try to adjust to the changing world or cope with a situation that has become untenable. In my interpretations of these stories I often referred to various antithetical terms: protection/rebellion, endurance/escapism, nature/culture, to mention only a few pairs of contrasts. The implied author, or the voice of someone who stands behind and above his story and communicates secretly with his readers, can be heard in these stories, and he invariably, although not uncritically, sides with the losers and loners against a rigid, non-permissive society that threatens to break down the human values in an ongoing progression towards greater prosperity and material well-being. Man's misuse of man for selfish ends is part of the recurrent pattern in these stories, as is man's destruction of nature; nature understood as physical nature as well as the natural qualities in man that Faulkner came to believe in more and more as the years went by: man's capacity for endurance, love, compassion, and sharing.

Faulkner's narratives indicate that he used all conceivable approaches to get a story told, and that he easily manoeuvred first or third person narration so that the distance from characters and events became more a question of attitude and language than of technical skill. His use of the first-person plural narrator, representing a community conscience or evaluation, is typical, especially since so many stories are located in Jefferson, where the social control seems rather rigid. Social control, group pressure, and role expectations seem likewise to be stronger in Jefferson than in the countryside. The demands of conformity, and the well-defined expectations of the society, are also stronger in the better families and among people from the middle class than they are shown to be among the poor people – especially the poor farmers who live in closer contact with nature than the urbanized city dwellers of Jefferson. Faulkner's perceptive analysis and compassionate understanding of women and children, are also elements which have been emphasized. Faulkner's women have been more misunderstood and unjustly treated than most other characters in his fiction – short stories and novels alike.

In some of the stories written between 1933 and 1941, a clash between different worlds and values can be found. In these stories we find a varying degree of corruption, greed, and inhumanity, which can be measured against a set of traditional values that a few characters, all of them with roots in an agrarian society, share. The country setting plays an increasingly important role in the last part of the 1930's and this development continues in the 1940's. The 'good country people' in these stories represent traditional and lasting values, and the stories may teach us a moral lesson in humility and pride. Moreover, endurance and loyalty are important qualities which these people not only talk about, but actually live by. They live almost untroubled by the changing times, and they refuse to adjust to the demands of modern life with its regulations and control.

Faulkner's short stories from the last period of his career echo earlier works; in the 1950's almost all stories rely heavily on echoes and reminiscences from previous stories and novels. Allusions to characters, incidents, and episodes from many texts in his career abound, not only to enrich the short stories but also to reduce their autonomy. Faulkner's best stories from the late years are probably two fictional essays, 'Mississippi' and 'Sepulture South: Gaslight'.

The late stories may thus be described as 'chips from the novelist's bench', although one should not exaggerate the decline in Faulkner's short-story activity. It cannot be questioned, however, that such a decline can be found. Faulkner had behind him 'a life's work in the agony and sweat of the human spirit', and he apparently saw no reason why he should anguish and sweat over short stories now that he needed and deserved relaxation and peace.

All in all Faulkner's short-story achievement is remarkable, albeit uneven and heterogeneous. His best stories are very good, and his worst stories are indeed very bad. He experimented little in the short-story form, being satisfied as he claimed himself, to get a story told. But his interest in people and their actions made it impossible for him simply to tell a story the easiest way he could find. Events and incidents were not the most important, but rather what these led to or how people reacted to them, interpreted them, and went on living after them. Accordingly, he would have to get under the skin of his characters, either by letting them narrate the stories they participated in, or by various techniques; he would have to structure the narratives so that an event was seen from many angles, often with conflicting results. The Yoknapatawpha stories demonstrate Faulkner's complete command of his material and people. In many of the non-Yoknapatawpha stories, links with Yoknapatawpha can be found, and the memory of the demands of the stable and closely-knit community remains with the characters and often explains their attitude and behaviour in war and peace.

For each chapter, and more generally for each period, I have tried to sum up some of the relationships between Faulkner's novels and short stories that seem important. As could be expected, the relationship differs in quantity and quality from period to period, being of no significance in the early years and becoming very close in the late years when Faulkner hardly wrote a single story that did not somehow relate to a longer work.

The question of the novelist's influence upon the short-story writer has thus received a number of partial and preliminary answers, and it is now time to look back upon the whole short-story career with this question in mind. In the 'Preface' I defined this hypothesis more precisely, maintaining that the more obvious connections between Faulkner's stories and novels were of little interest in such an investigation. Re-use of short stories in later novels, revised novel-excerpts published as short stories, numerous stories linked together (after revisions) to form a unified book, are all well-known in Faulkner's career. More interesting than the obvious and superficial relationships that exist between stories and novels, is the question of the type of material and its narrative handling in story or novel. A story may be narrated in a discourse of short-story length and type even if its material is so wide that it might well be viewed as sufficient for the longer narrative, for the novel. On the other hand, a short story may be narrated in the brief discourse because the story inherent in it is in itself brief, covering few and small events, introducing few characters, being short in time. If, in Faulkner's stories, the normal tendency is to have a material (story) of wide compass, and then through the narrative strategy compress and condense it to suit the requirements of the short-story narrative (discourse-time becoming much shorter than story-time), my assumption about Faulkner's stories as a novelist's short stories would be valid. One should not expect to find that all the 120 odd stories Faulkner ever wrote are of this type, and a first basic distinction may hence be made. The Yoknapatawpha stories have, with few exceptions, many superficial and obvious relationships with Faulkner's Yoknaptawpha novels, and they also seem to be of the kind where a wide and rich material is condensed through various technical devices to meet the demands of the short-story form and the magazine market. The non-Yoknapatawpha stories, perhaps especially the 'Beyond' stories, are of the second type; their story being insignificant and brief and almost static, so that discourse-time approaches story-time (if the term should be used for these stories) or is the only time we can grasp in these strange stories.

Faulkner had a number of valid reasons for using what I have called material for novels in short stories and not in longer works. He could not possibly write all the novels he had stories for, and he made very little money on his first novels. Also, he had experimented within the short-story form in the early part of his career, and knew that money could be made on the rich short-story market in the early 1930's. Moreover, narrating his stories about the Snopeses, the Bundrens, the Compsons, Sutpen, Joe Christmas and many others, he had to leave out episodes and anecdotes, and he opened up a treasure chamber of situations and characters and conflicts that could, and deserved to be re-interpreted by being presented, disguised perhaps, under new names, in slightly different circumstances, in narratives of short-story length. There can be little doubt that most of the material behind the short stories, despite the autonomy of some of them, may be seen as almost too abundant and too complex for a short story. The author's (or perhaps the narrative's own) capability to select which elements to present and describe and which ones only to imply or hint at, is one of the important principles of literary narrative that makes it possible to write the kind of stories Faulkner very often did.

An author can select, freely, which events and episodes he wants to present in a short story, and he can likewise leave out or imply all other elements that belong to the 'complete story'. To do this without serious problems for the readers, the order of presentation must be given particular consideration. The use of a narrator, whether overt or covert, first or third person, much and strongly present or only vaguely felt, seems to be one choice on Faulkner's part, made specifically to give credibility and verisimilitude to the arrangement of the material. The narrator may explain why things are left out; e.g. when a child narrator's limited understanding prohibits a deeper understanding; and only the narrative voice (in the discourse, not in the story) may communicate the wider implications of the story to us. But this is done, significantly, without expanding the discourse much.

In the early 1930's, when Faulkner wrote and revised more stories than in any other period, he had a habit of dividing his stories into parts, assigning Roman or Arabic numerals to them. Now and then he might move the parts about, adding an additional one, removing material from one part, etc. 'Dry September', 'That Evening Sun', 'A Rose for Emily' and 'A Mountain Victory' give good examples of this practice.[14] As to the structure of the narrative and the principle of selection, this indicates a method where the author pauses (tells nothing) in between key episodes. Instead of summaries, pauses (ellipsis) are used to indicate the passing of time, a new development of a crisis, and so on. But the method is also employed for other benefits: the different parts do not always follow each other chronologically, and commonly at least one of them is used for a retrospective story. As a rule this is not the first part, because Faulkner quickly discovered that he would improve the dramatic effect if he started in the midst of action in an opening section, and gave the background story in a later section. By giving a sustained presentation, e.g. of Minnie's upbringing and meaningless existence, the author had enabled himself to leave out much material of an explanatory nature that would otherwise have been needed later on in the short story. The 'capsule stories' that I have often referred to in previous chapters as a rule have this effect; they are flashbacks to render plausible the current events on the now-level of the narrative.

Faulkner's use of flashbacks and flashforwards (analepsis and prolepsis in Genette's terms) and his tendency to arrange his stories anachronically might on first thought indicate the opposite of narrative concentration. If 'was' is a part of 'is' and one also looks into the future, anticipating future events or insights, discourse-time might expand considerably, one should think. As I have tried to show, this is not the case, and Faulkner's use of flashback as well as flashforward serves the concentration since it enables him to leave out other segments of the 'story', and since the narrator's comments can be reduced and judgment or insight revealed through the voice of the narrative and not necessarily and always from the point of view of the narrator or some other focal person.

Faulkner's short stories show man in his ageless struggle, and may be described as universal in their thematic implications, despite their Southern setting. Man must adjust to the present situation, he must change with an ever-changing world. To record the minute changes that take place, and that add up to real changes only over the years, Faulkner might have chosen a few key-moments and episodes, minimal stories with great impact and significance, instead of telling what amounts to a Saga of his kingdom. But Faulkner's interest was with people, and he loved a good story, and only in a few and rare cases would he write the kind of short story in which almost nothing happens but in which the passing of a world and an age is still felt, stories of the kind that John Cheever is the great master of. Faulkner also recorded these minimal and almost invisible changes in a social group and succeeded in making them reflect the passing of a way of life, an era. His was a rich heritage of a heroic past, a sense of history which included defeat and defiance, a strong sense of belonging to a stable, well-ordered albeit somewhat rigid community. What he had inherited could not be changed quickly, but he saw the changes, and he became the chronicler of them, in stories and novels of lasting importance. Normally he would sweep 'wide to try to include everything',[15] even in the short stories, and it may be fair to say that they often contain material 'too big for the mold to which stories are fitted'.[16] He is a novelist first, and then a short-story writer, and his short stories are greatly influenced by this fact. On the other hand, his short stories (when they came first, as they often did) influenced or even made up some of his novels, so perhaps one should end this discussion by stating that Faulkner is novelist *and* short-story writer, and very often the two forms of fiction influence and enrich one another.

* * *

The principal goal of this book has been to give a composite but structured presentation of Faulkner's short-story universe, trying at the same time to demonstrate the importance of the short stories in the author's total production. Even a conclusion seems inconclusive when the material is so abundant, when the possibilities of interpretations are multiple, and when 'inexhaustibility' seems to be an adequate description of Faulkner's short-story achievement.

Notes

Notes to Chapter 1

1. See, e.g., Warren Beck, 'Art and Formula in the Short Story', *College English,* 5 (1943), 55–62.
2. Faulkner, in the famous *Paris Review* Interview with Jean Stein, said that he rated himself and his contemporaries 'on the basis of our splendid failure to do the impossible', and he was well aware that some of them (Hemingway for one) never tried for the impossible.
3. Malcom Cowley, *-And I Worked at the Writer's Trade: Chapters of Literary History, 1918–1978* (New York: Viking Press, 1978), p. 127. Cowley compares Faulkner and Caldwell.
4. Gregory H. Hemingway, *Papa: A Personal Memoir* (New York: Pocket Books, 1977), pp. 137, 138.
5. 'Wash' was revised and used in *Absalom, Absalom!,* but Faulkner nevertheless chose to include it in *Collected Stories.* 'Evangeline' remained unpublished till 1979, and Faulkner could thus have felt free to make whatever use he wanted of this story.
6. *Selected letters of William Faulkner,* edited by Joseph Blotner (New York: Random House, 1976), p. 84. Later referred to as *Selected Letters.*
7. There is no doubt that Faulkner submitted the story, 'An Odor of Verbena', to his agent and that he tried to sell it as a short story, even though he wrote it to complete the planned book. See my book *William Faulkner: The Short Story Career* (Oslo: Universitetsforlaget, 1981), ch. 4. This book is later referred to as *Short Story Career.*
8. '. . .*and Other Stories'* used for the first publication of this book is the responsibility of the publisher, not of Faulkner.
9. For a discussion of Faulkner's opinion of his own short stories and a description of how often he despaired of short-story writing, see *Short Story Career,* ch. 1.
10. Modern genre theory is mostly descriptive. According to Wellek and Warren, 'it doesn't limit the number of possible kinds and doesn't prescribe rules to authors'. See René Wellek and Austin Warren, *Theory of Literature* (3rd edn; New York: Harcourt, Brace, and World, Inc., [c.1956]), pp. 234–35. Normative definitions have nonetheless flourished. Alfred Weber describes 'die normative Poetik' thus: 'Die normative Poetik sind eine zeitgebundene und wertende Theorie. Sie wird vor allem von den Dichtern selbst und von den Kritikern formuliert, denen es nicht um wissenschaftliche und historische Objektivität, sondern um die Ausbildung und Durchsetzung literarischer Wertungskriterien und Idealvorstellungen gehen muss.' See Weber's article 'Amerikanische Theorien der Kurtzgeschichte' in Paul Goetsch, *Studien und Materialen zur Short Story* (Frankfurt–Berlin–Munich: Diesterweg, 1971), p. 8.
11. Paul Hernadi, *Beyond Genre: New Directions in Literary Classification* (Ithaca & London: Cornell University Press, 1972), p. 184.
12. 'Popular or general consent' is of course not a good enough criterion to use in any discussion of genre. Yet this popular consent may well parallel the practice that critics often seem to follow: the critical or analytical studies of the short-story genre seldom base their theories or typologies on empiric material, while the critics who work on the basis of a selective but presumably representative body of material, find that it is

almost impossible to structure this material so that generalizations or conclusions may be reached with at least a little plausibility and authority.

13. Cf. Hans H. Malmede, *Wege Zur Novelle* (Stuttgart, 1966).
14. Quoted from Seymour Chatman, *Story and Discourse: Narrative Structure in Fiction and Film* (Ithaca & London: Cornell University Press, 1978), p. 21.
15. Poe's definition of the short story was presented in his review of Hawthorne's *Twice-Told Tales* in *Graham's Magazine* in May 1842, and it can be found in many textbooks and anthologies of short-story criticism. See e.g. Hollis Summers, ed., *Discussions of the Short Story* (Boston: Heath & Co., 1963), p. 12.
16. See the discussion of this in Robert Scholes, *Structuralism in Literature: An Introduction* (New Haven and London: Yale University Press, 1974), pp. 85–6.
17. Norman Friedman, 'What Makes a Short Story Short?' *Modern Fiction Studies,* 4 (1958/59) 103–17. Quoted from p. 105.
18. Ibid., p. 114.
19. This does not imply that I regard Faulkner's Yoknapatawpha fiction as a saga or a legend so that everything he wrote (except the non-Yoknapatawpha writings) has its place within this legend. The legend is a construction by critics who have been misled by the apparent interrelationship of most of Faulkner's work.
20. Cf. Michael Millgate, *The Achievement of William Faulkner* (New York: Vintage Books, 1971), pp. 260–4. This book was originally published in 1966. Later referred to as *Achievement.*
21. This is particularly true of the last stories for *The Unvanquished,* especially, perhaps, the Drusilla story, 'Skirmish at Sartoris'.
22. The concept is introduced and defined by Forrest L. Ingram in his study, *Representative Short Story Cycles of the Twentieth Century: Studies in a Literary Genre* (The Hague, Paris: Mouton, 1971).
23. Ingram's study, p. 18.
24. Ingram's study, p. 19.
25. They would only satisfy some of the requirements of Ingram's definition, which is, after all, prescriptive or normative.
26. Ingram's study, p. 25.
27. This narrative dichotomy is emphasized and analysed in great detail by Seymour Chatman in his *Story and Discourse: Narrative Structure in Fiction and Film.* Since my original dissertation was finished in its first versions before the publication of Chatman's book – as well as before the English translation of Genette's *Narrative Discourse,* it has not been possible to use these theories as extensively as I would have preferred. I have made use of some of the new insights that these books and others have given, but I have not rewritten my book.
28. Gérard Genette, *Narrative Discourse: An Essay in Method* (Ithaca, N.Y., 1980). This book is a portion of the author's *Figures III,* originally published in French in 1972.
29. Genette's study, p. 29.
30. We may talk about 'narrative as discourse' and 'narrative as story', in Todorov's terminology, or we may follow Chatman's advice and stress the narrative dichotomy, saying that all narratives have a content plane (story) and an expression plane (discourse). Furthermore, considering the rather uncertain use of the term 'narrative', we may use it in its most widespread meaning, which would probably be 'narrative discourse', i.e. the narrative text, and then go on to analyse the relationships among the many parts it takes to create a narrative. Genette assigns 'narrative' as his term for 'discourse' plane; i.e., the signifier, statement, narrative text itself, stating that this is 'the only instrument of examination at our disposal in the field of literary narrative, and

particularly, fictional narrative' (p. 27). In the course of this study, I use 'narrative' in its wide meaning, and rely on Chatman's dichotomy to show the relationship between the story (content plane) and the discourse plane.

Notes to Chapter 2

1. The conflict between the individual and society is, of course, central in much fiction of this century; also in American fiction of the 1920's and 1930's. To reduce Faulkner's short fiction to the quest for communal ties is to do it an injustice, however. P. Momberger's dissertation, 'A Critical Study of Faulkner's Early Sketches and *Collected Stories',* is centred around this quest.
2. Michel Gresset, 'Faulkner's "The Hill",' *Southern Literary Journal,* 6 (1974), p. 13. Philip Momberger has also published an article on 'The Hill': 'A Reading of Faulkner's "The Hill",' *Southern Literary Journal,* 9 (1977), 16–29.
3. The story is described as 'lightly amusing' by Joseph Blotner in his *Faulkner: A Biography* (New York: Random House, 1974), I, 252–3. This important source-book is later referred to as *Biography.* Millgate (*Achievement,* p. 6) describes the story in similar terms, as does André Bleikasten in *The Most Splendid Failure: Faulkner's The Sound and the Fury* (Bloomington/London: Indiana University Press, 1976), p. 11.
4. I also rate 'The Hill' much higher than 'Landing in Luck', but in a study of Faulkner's development, the *first* prose sketch is nonetheless significant.
5. Faulkner attempted to be realistic in 'Landing in Luck', even to the extent that he tries to capture the clipped, British speech of the instructor, while he of course also excels in his knowledge of planes, instruments, flying terms, etc.
6. I would not, however, introduce a 'genius' theory to explain Faulkner's startling growth as a writer of prose fiction. He worked very hard at his metier, and he read all the good authors from whom he expected to learn something. His sojourn in New Orleans is of great importance in this respect, in particular because he became well acquainted with Sherwood Anderson while living there.
7. Faulkner in an interview in 1958 told James. B. Meriwether that 'Moonlight' was 'about the first story I ever wrote' and dated it to around 1919, 1920, or 1921. See 'The Short Fiction of William Faulkner: A Bibliography', p. 315. See also Blother's comments in *Uncollected Stories of William Faulkner,* p. 706.
8. Carbon typescript, University of Virginia Library, 16 pp., p. 13.
9. Ibid., p. 5.
10. Ibid., p. 5.
11. In answering questions at the University of Virginia in 1957, Faulkner explained that in Mississippi in August there is 'a luminous quality to the light', and that his observation of this quality gave him the title for the book. This special light is also central in 'Moonlight', despite its being placed at the nightly hours. Cf. *Faulkner in the University: Class Conferences at the University of Virginia 1957–58,* eds. Frederick L. Gwynn and Joseph Blotner (Charlottesville, Va.: University Press of Virginia, 1959), p. 199. Later referred to as *Faulkner in the University.*
12. This conflict is of course traditionally a conflict of adolescent years, of growing up and accepting some of the rules one does not understand the significance of at an earlier age. Faulkner uses a particular background and a specific social environment to depict this conflict, which makes it less of a private, individual problem.
13. TS., 47 pp., p. 1. An almost similar description is given in a marginal note on. p. 7. *Uncollected Stories* does not include any of the extant versions of 'Love'.

14. The Beth-Jeyfus plot incorporates an aeroplane accident in 1916, which made Jeyfus lose his nerve. At the now-level of the story this makes it impossible for him to pass the test Beth puts him to; viz. to fly a plane.
15. TS., 47 pp., p. 1.
16. Ibid., p. 1.
17. TS., 47 pp., p. 40.
18. 'Manservant' is in fact the title Faulkner used for a version of this story which he made in Hollywood, but which never came to anything. Cf. James B. Meriwether, *The Literary Career of William Faulkner: A Bibliographical Study* (Authorized Re-issue: Columbia, S.C.: University of South Carolina Press, 1971), p. 160. Meriwether's study was originally published in 1961, and this book is later referred to as *Literary Career*.
19. TS., 47 pp., p. 15.
20. Millgate calls 'Love' 'the least distinguished' among Faulkner's unpublished early stories, See *Achievement,* p. 11. Faulkner's later attempts to salvage some of the material from this story were by no means successful. Faulkner's propensity for the melodramatic and for the overworked plots was not allowed to spoil many stories; but time and again he wrote very poor stories. 'Two Dollar Wife', published in 1936, is one example from a period when his short-story accomplishment reached a summit.
21. TS., 47 pp., p. 14.
22. Revised versions of 'Love' as well as of 'Moonlight' were submitted to various magazines in 1928 and even in the early thirties, but they were never accepted for publication.
23. Gresset, 'Faulkner's "The Hill"', p. 4.
24. 'Epiphany' is one of the favourite terms of James Joyce, as when Joyce talks about 'the gropings of a spiritual eye which seeks to adjust its vision to an exact focus', and calls it epiphany when the focus is reached. Gresset finds that 'The Hill' demonstrates an epiphany manquée (p. 16 of his article), because the insight implied in the term 'epiphany' is lacking in this text.
25. *The Marble Faun,* Faulkner's first book, was published in 1924. It was re-issued together with *A Green Bough* in 1965. (New York: Random House.)
26. Philip Momberger, 'Faulkner's Early Sketches and *Collected Stories'*, Dissertation Johns Hopkins 1972, p. 29 emphasizes this point, since it is important to his thesis. But in *The Mississippian* this word was capitalized, and even though this may be a printer's error, it is barely possible that Faulkner wanted to give this word spesical emphasis, although it is not very likely.
27. Sally R. Page, *Faulkner's Women: Characterization and Meaning* (Deland, Fla.: Everett/Edwards, 1977), p. 32.
28. Gresset, 'Faulkner's "The Hill"', p. 14. These sexual overtones are stronger in other early stories; e.g. 'Adolescence', and, in particular, 'Nympholepsy'.
29. For a discussion of this, see e.g. Bleikasten, *The Most Splendid Failure*, p. 13.
30. The book is, of course, Hyatt H. Waggoner's *William Faulkner: From Jefferson to the World.*
31. *As I Lay Dying,* p. 217.
32. Ibid., p. 217.
33. *The Town,* p. 314.
34. Faulkner could not let his narrative rely so heavily on metaphor in the future, and a development towards a more discursive language may be discovered. See for instance Richard P. Adams, 'The Apprenticeship of William Faulkner', *Tulane Studies in English,* 12 (1962), 113–56, and Joseph Gold, *William Faulkner: A Study in Humanism from Metaphor to Discourse* (Norman: University of Oklahoma Press, 1966).

35. Notably, of course, in *The Sound and the Fury*, but also in some of Faulkner's best short stories, e.g. 'A Mountain Victory'.
36. We will meet her in various disguises in stories like 'Miss Zilphia Gant', 'Elly', 'The Brooch', and others.

Notes to Chapter 3

1. Faulkner's sketches were printed in the New Orleans *Times-Picayune*, with the exception of 'New Orleans', which appeared in the *Double Dealer*. The title 'New Orleans Sketches' seems to have been used for the first time when Ichiro Nishizaki edited *New Orleans Sketches* (Tokyo: Hokuseido, 1955). This book was, rather unfortunately, based on *Mirrors of Chartres Street* and *Jealousy and Episode: Two Stories*, published by *Faulkner Studies* in Minneapolis in 1953 and 1955, respectively. The two latter texts had been published in the journal *Faulkner Studies*, 3 (Winter 1954) before their book publication. Carvel Collins was instrumental in the discovery of these texts and it was only fitting when he published his edition of *New Orleans Sketches* in 1958 (New Brunswick: Rutgers University Press). Collins added 'New Orleans' from the *Double Dealer*, 7 (January–February 1925) to the sketches in the Japanese volume, and he also included 'The Liar', 'Country Mice' and 'Yo Ho and Two Bottles of Rum' – which are not really New Orleans sketches in any other way than that they probably were written at the same time as the New Orleans pieces and printed in the same New Orleans paper. A revised edition was published in 1968, incorporating textual corrections from Faulkner typescripts then available. Cf. *Literary Career*, p. 46 and Linton R. Massey, '*Man Working', 1919–1962: William Faulkner* (Charlottesville, Va.: University Press of Virginia, 1968), pp. 55–6.
2. *A Green Bough* (New York: Harrison Smith and Robert Hass, 1933).
3. *The Marble Faun* (Boston: Four Seas Company, 1924).
4. A good survey and evaluation of Faulkner's apprenticeship is given by Richard P. Adams, 'The Apprenticeship of William Faulkner', *Tulane Studies in English*, 12 (1962), 113–56.
5. This cycle of 19 poems was published shortly before Faulkner went to New Orleans. The favourable review by the book editor of the New Orleans *Times Picayune*, John McClure, certainly had a promotional effect and helped Faulkner get in touch with this paper and with other writers in New Orleans.
6. See Keen Butterworth, 'A Census of Manuscripts and Typescripts of William Faulkner's Poetry', *Mississippi Quarterly*, 26 (Summer 1973), 333–59.
7. He worked with poetry, he had published a book of poems, and accordingly he had little reason to think otherwise. In interviews and the like Faulkner refers to himself as a 'failed poet': '. ... maybe I think of myself as a poet, and I failed at that, I couldn't write poetry, so I did the next best thing'. *Faulkner in the University*, p. 4. Similar statement on p. 22.
8. The transition is discussed by Richard P. Adams (cf. n. 4), and also by Bleikasten in *The Most Splendid Failure* in the chapter called 'Faulkner before Faulkner'.
9. In *The Mississippian*, November 19, 1920, p. 5: 'Books & Things' - a review of W.A. Percy's *In April Once*. See *Early Prose and Poetry*, pp. 71–3. George Garrett in his 'Faulkner's Early Literary Criticism', *Texas Studies in Literature and Language*, 1

(1959), 3–10, is not aware of this review, since he uses Meriwether's 1957 checklist on Faulkner where this review is not listed.

10. See Faulkner's review of Joseph Hergesheimer's *Linda Condon, Cytherea, The Bright Shawl* in *The Mississippian*, 15 December 1922, p. 5, reprinted in *Early Prose and Poetry*, pp. 101–3.

11. See the review of Hergesheimer's novels in *Early Prose and Poetry*, pp. 103–3. Quoted from pp. 101–2.

12. Ibid., pp. 102–3.

13. Reprinted in *Early Prose and Poetry*, pp. 86–9. Original appearance in *The Mississippian*, 3 February 1922.

14. Ibid., pp. 93–7. Published originally in two parts in consecutive issues of *The Mississippian* (17 & 24 March 1922).

15. Ibid., p. 89.

16. *Early Prose and Poetry*, pp. 95 and 96.

17. Ibid., p. 94.

18. Some of these have been pointed out by Richard Adams in his 'The Apprenticeship of William Faulkner', and a few others by Cleanth Brooks in 'A Note on Faulkner's Early Attempts at the Short Story', *Studies in Short Fiction*, 10 (1973), 381–8. In his book, *William Faulkner: Toward Yoknapatawpha and Beyond* (New Haven and London: Yale University Press, 1978), Brooks discusses Faulkner's New Orleans sketches more extensively. See especially chapter 4, 'Sketches, Early Stories, and an Abortive Novel', pp. 100–28. André Bleikasten also points to a number of possible influences in his first chapter of *The Most Splendid Failure*, and so does Joseph Blotner in his *Biography*. Carvel Collins's 'Introduction' to *New Orleans Sketches* (esp. pp. xxviii ff.) should be mentioned.

19. See J.B. Meriwether, 'Early Notices of Faulkner by Phil Stone and Louis Cochran', *Mississippi Quarterly*, 16 (1964), 136–4. Cited from p. 141.

20. See especially *Biography*, I, 320–2. See also F.B. O'Brien, 'Faulkner and Wright, Alias S.S. Van Dine', *Mississippi Quarterly*, 14 (1961), 101–7.

21. Brooks, 'A Note on Faulkner's Early Attempt at the Short Story', p. 381.

22. Ibid., p. 381.

23. Brooks's attitude to the New Orleans sketches is unexpectedly negative, and it must be fair to maintain that they are interesting in their own right, and deserve treatment as works of fiction, not as documents showing a later master at an early stage.

24. Carvel Collins, 'Introduction' to *New Orleans Sketches* (New York: Random House, 1968; reissued in Great Britain by Chatto & Windus the same year).

25. Momberger's dissertation, 'A Critical Study of Faulkner's Early Sketches and *Collected Stories*' deals extensively with Faulkner's early fiction. An anecdotal account of Faulkner's acquaintance with New Orleans is given by Elmo Howell in 'William Faulkner's New Orleans', *Louisiana History*, 7 (1966) pp. 229–40.

26. Momberger, p. 45.

27. For a general discussion of the implications of this title, consult 'SINBAD IN NEW ORLEANS', by Leland H. Cox, (Diss., South California 1977). Quotation from p. xxix.

28. Lee Cox refutes all implications of social criticism in the New Orleans sketches, while Momberger both in his dissertation and in his article 'Faulkner's "Country" as Ideal Community' stresses the significance of the social ties, of man's environment. The article is found in Baldwin and Kirby, eds., *Individual and Community: Variations on a Theme in American Fiction* (Durham, N.C.: Duke U.P. 1975), pp. 112–36.

American critics have been reluctant to see the implied social criticism in some of the texts of the young William Faulkner, and even though I would not rate this criticism as very important in his fiction, it is nevertheless present and must be dealt with.

29. The conception of a series does not necessarily and inevitably mean coherence and unity; the individual pieces may be unified simply through the use of the same setting (New Orleans) or through the same kind of fictional handling (often a first-person narrator, describing character and scene and thereby also revealing his own thoughts). It does not imply a sameness of theme or subject-matter, even if some similarity between *some of* the sketches may be detectable.

30. There is no reason to go very far in one's speculations about how much of himself Faulkner brought directly into these sketches, but the first-person narrator and his painter friend, Spratling, indicate that Faulkner felt free to expose himself rather overtly in some of the sketches.

31. See Millgate, *Achievement,* p. 56.

32. See Wayne C. Booth, *The Rhetoric of Fiction* (Chicago: University of Chicago Press, 1969 (c. 1961), especially pp. 149 ff.

33. See for instance Carvel Collins, 'The Interior Monologues of *The Sound and the Fury',* *English Institute Essay,* 1952 (New York: Columbia University Press, 1954), pp. 29–56.

34. Faulkner made one more version of this text, where a new sub-narrative, 'Hong Li', replaced 'The Tourist', so all in all there are extant twelve sub-narratives which all are of the same type. See *Short Story Career,* p. 24.

35. Despite the 'authorial silence' (Booth's term) in such texts, the implied author conspires with the reader to reveal the bigotry of the speaker.

36. The transition from one speaker to another is far less marked in Faulkner's own text for this sketch, and since their individuality is of less significance than the composite pictures of lives and destinies in New Orleans which they give, the narrative is less fragmented than one might otherwise think.

37. Adams is searching for Faulkner *the artist* and tries to discover when his apprenticeship may be said to have been terminated. Accordingly, his otherwise interesting source-studies only add to Collins's pointing out of influences and prefigurations. See Adams, *Myth and Motion,* p. 32.

38. The monologues are of course the rendered speech or thoughts of a character, without intrusion from the author or an outside world. The quotation mark would then be used to distinguish between thoughts and direct speech, where there is someone to speak to, or where the thoughts are phrased in words, even if nobody listens to them.

39. This is not to indicate any borrowing or influence, but only to mention that the rural idyll in 'The Cobbler' is a common element of many a dream about a lost past which cannot be recaptured.

40. The story was probably not printed by the *Times-Picayune* due to editorial caution, since it deals rather directly with the sexual fantasies of a priest on the eve of his confirmation. The story was first printed in *Mississippi Quarterly,* 29 (1976), 445–50.

41. Interior monologues are of great importance in some of Faulkner's novels, most significantly perhaps in *The Sound and the Fury,* especially in the Quentin section. Faulkner's practice with this difficult and demanding form of narrative in the New Orleans period is thus very important, if not for his later short stories, then at least for his novels.

42. Charles D. Peavy, 'An Early Casting of Benjy: Faulkner's "The Kingdom of God",' *Studies in short Fiction,* 3 (Spring 1966), 347–8, and 'The Eyes of Innocence:

Faulkner's "The Kingdom of God",' *Papers on Language and Literature*, 2 (Spring 1966), 178–82. See also Collins, 'Introduction' to *New Orleans Sketches*, p. xxviii.

43. See Adams, *Myth and Motion*, p. 33: 'In "The Hill" this typical young man is almost made to think; now, like Faulkner, he has begun to write.' Since Faulkner may have invested David with some of his own dreams and thoughts about being an artist, a double portrait may be found in this story.

44. Adams, *Myth and Motion*, p. 34.

45. There is much talk about a plane accident in a test that involves taking up a plane, in one of the versions of 'Love', but apart from this rather unimportant use of aeroplanes, 'Country Mice' is the first story since 'Landing in Luck' to exploit this element which Faulkner knew well.

46. Destiny is, by definition, inescapable; but destiny will not invariably lead to defeatism. It may, rather, lead to stoicism and acceptance of one's fate, and thus to active participation in the working out of this fate. The Icelandic sagas often demonstrate this kind of destiny at work.

47. Momberger's dissertation, p. 77.

48. Published in the *Mississippi Quarterly*, 31 (Summer 1978). The subnarrative from 'New Orleans' is re-used, with minor revisions, in the longer text.

49. The narrator and his friend are both taken in by the innocent and good-looking David, and since the narrator in addition may have spotted some similarity between himself and the young would-be artist, he is even more likely to misrepresent David.

50. Momberger maintains this; cf. p. 60 of his dissertation.

51. 'Don Giovanni' was published for the first time in *Uncollected Stories*. Versions of it are extant in the Berg Collection at the New York Public Library. Don Giovanni makes numerous vain attempts as a seducer, but he is awkward and stupid in whatever he does.

52. This is, of course, almost a quotation of Faulkner's own statements about the artist's attempts to do the impossible. Failing to do so, he would have to try over and over again, so that now and then one of them would make a splendid failure. See e.g. the *Paris Review* Interview and *Faulkner in the University*, passim.

53. See Collins, 'Introduction' to *New Orleans Sketches*, p. xxxii.

54. Blotner, *Biography*, I, 445.

55. Blotner, *Biography*, I. 455.

56. Libby, 'Chronicles of Children', p. 89.

57. Blotner, *Biography*, I, 457.

58. *Selected Letters*, pp. 34–5.

59. *Early Prose and Poetry*, p. 94.

60. 'A Portrait of Elmer', probably an attempt to salvage some of the material from the abandoned novel about Elmer, is a portrait of the artist as a young man, and 'Christmas Tree' in its many and varied versions draws on contemporary slick magazine pieces.

61. See Carvel Collins, 'Faulkner's *Mayday*', published as a separate booklet accompanying the facsimile publication of *Mayday* (University of Notre Dame Press, 1977) in 125 copies. See also his comments in *Helen: A Courtship and Mississippi Poems* (Oxford: Yoknapatawpha Press, 1982).

62. This date is according to an entry in the diary of her father, Dr. Calvin Brown. This information is from an unpublished essay on 'The Wishing Tree' by Edwin T. Arnold III, originally delivered at a short story conference at the Southern Studies Program at the University of South Carolina in 1974.

63. Blotner, *Biography*, II, 1719.

64. The text for the abandoned *novel Elmer* was published for the first time in the *Mississippi Quarterly*, 36 (Summer 1983), pp. 337–451.

65. Expectedly, the young artist striving to learn his metier and to find the best possible way of giving expressions to his thoughts, feelings, and insights, would project much of himself into his writings. More so than later in his career, Faulkner's early short stories – and some of the novels – seem to be strongly self-reflective.

66. *Mississippi Quarterly*, 26 (Summer 1973), p. 401. Not in *Uncollected Stories*.

67. Statements by James B. Meriwether, quoted from *The New York Times*, June 1, 1983. This version of the early Snopes material was, unfortunately, not studied during my original research for this book, since I then considered it one of Faulkner's many early attempts with the Snopes material for *book* purposes. A presentation and discussion of early short-story attempts using Father Abraham and early mentions of the Snopeses are found in *William Faulkner: The Short Story Career*.

68. An attempt to trace some of these foreshadowings and to establish some of the relationships between 'Mayday' and *The Sound and the Fury* has been made by Gail M. Morrison in her 'Time, Tide, and Twilight': *Mayday* and Faulkner's Quest Toward *The Sound and the Fury (Mississippi Quarterly*, 31 [Summer 1978], 337–57).

69. Carvel Collins, 'Introduction' to *New Orleans Sketches*, p. xxx; Blotner, *Biography*, I, 511–12, and, most significantly, Gail Morrison's article referred to in n. 68.

70. *The Saturday Evening Post*, 240 (8 April 1967), p. 63 (p. 9 in the book version).

71. Michel Gresset has noted some of these similarities. See 'Un Faulkner Féerique', *La Nouvelle Revue Française*, 17 (September 1969), 437–40.

72. Edwin Arnold III (cf. n. 62) has searched for the source of the word 'mellomax' without finding any identifiable source for it, and hence he suggests that the tree seems to be entirely Faulkner's own invention.

73. The *Post* printing, p. 63, col. 1 (p. 77 in the book version).

74. *Mayday* (South Bend, Indiana: University of Notre Dame Press, 1977), p. 6.

75. Ibid., p. 7.

76. Ibid., p. 7. Similar expression on p. 3.

77. *Mayday*, p. 14.

78. Ibid., p. 43, and various other places in the text.

79. Ibid., p. 27. The quotation mark missing before 'that it is', is left out in Faulkner's handwritten version.

80. Ibid., pp. 35–6.

81. Ibid., p. 43.

82. To submerge oneself in water, to enter a relationship with Little Sister Death, has distinctly sexual overtones, and this is a recurrent image in Faulkner's fiction. 'Nympholepsy' and *The Sound and the Fury* are good examples of Faulkner's use of this image.

83. Quoted from the three page manuscript of 'The Devil Beats His Wife' in the Faulkner collection at the University of Virginia. Faulkner's friend, Ben Wasson, used this title for a novel after Faulkner had decided not to finish his own work with the rather awkward title.

Notes to Chapter 4

1. Approximately half the stories from this period are located in Jefferson, in French-man's Bend, or in other neighbouring areas of Yoknapatawpha County. The relatively

high number of World War I stories and 'Beyond' stories explain why the percentage of Yoknapatawpha stories is not even higher.

2. This is, in point of fact, what H. Simpson more or less does in his dissertation, 'The Short Stories of William Faulkner' (Florida State 1962).

3. This is the thematic division used by Philip Momberger in his dissertation, 'A Critical Study of Faulkner's Early Sketches and *Collected Stories*'.

4. See e.g. *Faulkner in the University*, passim, and the Nobel Prize Adress (*Essays, Speeches, and Public Letters*, pp. 119–21).

5. 'The Wilderness' section in *Collected Stories* contains only four stories, two of which were written after the major short-story period. It is fair to maintain that Faulkner was basically occupied with the contemporary scene in this period, and also that he only rarely went outside his 'postage stamp of native soil' in the stories.

6. In retrospective capsule stories, glimpses from more ancient days are given, and in works such as *Go Down, Moses* and *Requiem for a Nun* Faulkner traces the lines backwards through the history of his community.

7. Michael Millgate writes that the stories in Faulkner's first collection, *These 13*, show 'a commitment to an ultimately tragic vision of life'. See *Achievement*, p. 261.

8. See e.g. Melvin E. A. Bradford, 'Faulkner's' "Elly": An Exposé,' *Mississippi Quarterly*, 21 (Summer 1968), 179–87, and the same critic's 'Certain Ladies of Quality: Faulkner's View of Women and the Evidence of "There Was a Queen",' *Arlington Quarterly*, 1, (Winter 1968), 106–39.

9. These functions would be to bear and raise children, keep families together, and thus secure the continuation of the race. Bradford (cf. n. 8) maintains that some aspects of the female role must be kept unchanged at all times because of these functions, and he thus necessarily condemns Elly for her justifiable if exaggerated protest against the plans that have been made for her.

10. Giliane Morell 'Prisoners of the Inner World: Mother and Daughter in "Miss Zilphia Gant",' *Mississippi Quarterly*, 28 (Summer 1975), 299–305, discusses the imprisonment and the symbolic use of the *window* on pp. 304–5 of her essay.

11. This is, of course, a direct parallel to a similar scene in 'Adolescence'. Both stories have in common important scenes where children of different sexes are discovered by grown-ups who attach much more importance to what they see than what really goes on. Faulkner mentions sexual play between the two youths in the first version of 'Miss Zilphia Gant', while the second version rather places stress on the tenderness and warmth the youths search for in each other's company.

12. Genette, *Narrative Discourse*, p. 40.

13. For a discussion of this, see François Pitavy, 'A Forgotten Faulkner Story: "Miss Zilphia Gant",' *Studies in Short Fiction*, 9 (1972), 131–42.
   There is a 'me' in the Book Club version, p. 7, but this is not in the Texas typescript (p. 5). Although Pitavy thus incorrectly argues for a narrative persona on the basis of this 'me', it turns out that his interpretation is largely correct since there, on p. 29 of the published text and p. 23 of the typescript, can be found 'our' town.

14. Melvin E.A. Bradford discusses Elly as a flapper (he finds her to be one, and he also finds that Faulker has intended to portray her as one and hence condemn her conduct) in his 'Faulkner's "Elly": An Exposé' (Cf. n. 8).

15. For an elaboration of this point, see Helen E. Nebeker, 'Emily's Rose of Love: Thematic Implications of Point of View in Faulkner's "A Rose for Emily",' BRMMLA, 24, (1970), 3–13.

16. Cleanth Brooks has tried to establish a chronology for 'A Rose for Emily', and has shown impatience with typical misreadings which have led to impossible chronologies,

where, among other things, Emily's death takes place long after the year when the story was published. See *William Faulkner: Toward Yoknapatawpha and Beyond*, pp. 284–8, and pp. 382–4.

17. Olga W. Vickery, *The Novels of William Faulkner: A Critical Appraisal* (1959: revised edition: Baton Rouge: Louisiana State University Press, 1964), p. 299.
18. Ibid., p. 299.
19. *Selected Letters*, p. 34.
20. 'He wrote about events that were expected but never actually happened' according to John B. Cullen (in collaboration with Floyd C. Watkins) in *Old Times in the Faulkner Country* (Baton Rouge: Louisiana State University Press, 1975 [reprint of 1961-ed.]), p. 71.
21. *Faulkner in the University*, p. 185.
22. Joseph W. Reed, Jr., *Faulkner's Narrative* (New Haven: Yale University Press, 1973), p. 55.
23. Faulkner understood clearly that even if he tried for the impossible, he would be better off if or when he used the near and familiar as the subject and theme of his writings. Thus it is no surprise that many of the characters we encounter in non-Southern or undefined settings have Southern roots. This is in no way a limitation; it rather adds strength and credibility to many a weak story. Mrs. Blair in 'Fox Hunt' is from the Carolinas; the summer resort in 'Doctor Martino' is clearly located in the South.
24. Hubert Jarrod listens to his instructor in psychology at Yale and finds why young girls behave so unpredictably and strangely: 'The instructor was talking about women, about young girls in particular, about that strange, mysterious phase in which they live for a while. "A blind spot, like that which racing aviators enter when making a fast turn. When what they see is neither good nor evil, and so what they do is likely to be either one. Probably more likely to be evil, since the very evilness of evil stems from its own fact, while good is an absence of fact. A time, an hour, in which they themselves are victims of that by means of which they victimize".' *Doctor Martino*, p. 5.
25. The expression is used by Charles C. Clark in '"Mistral": A Study in Human Tempering', *Mississippi Quarterly*, 21 (Summer 1968), 195–204.
26. The description of Miss Emily's house among the new garages, cotton gins, and gasoline pumps is symbolic of the isolation she comes to live in, which in its turn may lessen the implied criticism of the society she lives in for living with a dead and unburied past. Critics have found that 'the necrophilia of an entire society that lived with a dead and unburied past' is implied in the story. See e.g. Magalaner and Volpe, *Teacher's Manual to Accompany Twelve Short Stories* (New York: MacMillian Company, 1961), p. 17.
27. Miss Emily's resistance to normal behaviour includes a resistance to change. Accordingly she wanted to keep her past alive and to keep her lover even if he had to be dead to remain hers. In R. B. West's words she has undertaken 'to regulate the natural time-universe' ('Atmosphere and Theme in Faulkner's "A Rose for Emily"', *Perspective*, 2 (Summer 1949), 239–45). In more general terms, 'A Rose for Emily' states that man must cope with his time, past and present, and that he cannot ignore the present and make time stand still or otherwise yield to his demands.
28. John. B. Vickery in 'Ritual and Theme in Faulkner's "Dry September"' (*Arizona Quarterly*, 18 [Spring 1962], 5–14) writes that 'one of the most tenaciously held dogmas of Plunkett [McLendon] and his like is that of the irrevocable inferiority of the Negro's culture and mentality.' Quoted from p. 14.
29. Wolfe and Daniels, 'Beneath the Dust of "Dry September",' *Studies in Short Fiction* 1 (1964), 158–9 write that the actuall lynching is not a community action.

30. 'Hair' is a good example; here the choice of narrator is decisive as to what impression of the girl the reader is given. 'Mistral' is another story where girls are seen as strange beings with inborn capacities for evil. In a few stories, *women* have the same propensity for evil, as in 'Divorce in Naples', 'Fox Hunt', and 'Honor'.

31. Faulkner's narrators have a certain tendency to look at women in this way. Faulkner himself apparently felt that there were too many almost similar, unwarranted and unmotivated negative descriptions of female characters in his manuscripts, and he accordingly left some of them out when revising some of the stories. Abstractions about female evil, or at least a propensity for it, were left out in the final version of 'A Mountain Victory', and in the final version of 'Beyond'. Only in stories such as 'Mistral' and 'Divorce in Naples' do these abstractions seem to have so close affinities with the central elements of the stories that their inclusion is inevitable and necessary.

32. Irving Malin makes this kind of generalization. See his *William Faulkner: An Interpretation* (Stanford: Stanford University Press, 1957), p. 31.

33. This may have something to do with the rather strange title of Faulkner's first collection of short stories, *These 13*. Other explanations are possible, however. I discuss some of these in my article, 'William Faulkner's Short Story Sending Shedule and His First Short Story Collection, *These 13*: Some Ideas'. *Notes on Mississippi Writers,* 11 (Winter 1979), 64–72.

34. A useful and interesting article on Faulkner's World War I fiction appeared in *Mississippi Quarterly,* 36 (Summer 1983), pp. 242–62, written by Melvin E. Bradford: 'The Anomaly of Faulkner's World War I Stories'.

35. The discrepancy between the plot action and the significance vested in it by the narrator is striking. The narrator misinterprets his own story, possibly because he intended it to be something different.

36. See Raleigh W. Smith, Jr., 'Faulkner's "Victory": The Plain People of Clydebank', *Mississippi Quarterly,* 23 (Summer 1970), 241–9. Towards the end of his article, Smith quotes from Bradford's article on 'The Tall Men' (M.E. Bradford, 'Faulkner's "Tall Men",' *South Atlantic Quarterly,* 61 (Winter 1962), 29–39), and concludes: 'Faulkner's plain people are normative because they almost invariably hold to this standard of endurance in *humility* and pride. This aspect of the endurance theme in Faulkner, the endurance of one's personal heritage, Alec Gray rejects. He is therefore damned' (p. 249).

37. War is pictured as destructive on all levels, but a weak hope of renewal and healing of the scars of war may be detected in some 'wheatspears. . . .[which] cling stubbornly in the churned soil' (*These 13,* p. 110).

38. The last sentence reads, 'Above his voice the wounded man's gibberish rises, meaningless and unemphatic and sustained' (*These 13,* p. 123). This may be compared to the last paragraph in *The Sound and the Fury.* Faulkner apparently liked this kind of ending, and it is indeed very effective.

39. Virginia TS., 47 pp., p. 31. The marks ([. . . .]) indicate that Faulkner has crossed out a number of words in his typescript.

40. Manuscript evidence suggests that this was no afterthought but clearly a part of the story. See also Faulkner's comments on 'Turn About' in *Faulkner at West Point,* pp. 72–3. Douglas Day finds that the ideas in the concluding paragraph are exceptional to the rest of the story. Cf. 'The War Stories of William Faulkner', *Georgia Review,* 15 (Winter 1961), 385–94.

41. *Faulkner at West Point,* pp 101–2.

42. This expression was used by Faulkner at West Point. See *Faulkner at West Point,* p. 101.

43. MacWyrglinchbeath is the proverbial Scotsman, and he fights in somebody else's war. The only other short story where exaggerated national characteristics are used as the most important motivating force behind a character is 'Death Drag', where Ginsfarb figures as the proverbial Jew.

44. Monaghan is one of the characters in 'Ad Astra', and there are references to the other characters in that story in 'Honor'. The relationship with 'All the Dead Pilots' and its love triangle is also obvious. It may well be that these two stories were written at about the same time.

45. 'Death Drag' may also be seen as an early attempt with material later exploited more fully in *Pylon* (which grew out of another short story, 'This Kind of Courage').

46. The plane flies in 'violation of both city and government ordinance' (*Doctor Martino*, p. 72) and is described by words such as 'empty and dead', 'dead black', and 'apparition' (*Doctor Martino*, pp. 72–3).

47. For the relations between these two unpublished versions of the same story, cf. *Short Story Career*, pp. 53–4.

48. In 'Dull Tale' this is changed to an art gallery.

49. He was actually killed on the night when Grant's stores at Holly Springs were burned by Van Dorn, by someone with a shot gun, during the raiding of a chickenroost. See also Blotner, *Biography*, I, 671, and Millgate, *Achievement*, p. 130.

50. Virginia MS., 'Rose of Lebanon', p. 2.

51. Ibid., p. 2.

52. Ibid., p. 3. Also quoted by Millgate, *Achievement*, p. 130.

53. Ibid., p. 4. My transcription differs in minor details from Millgate's. Cf. *Achievement*, p. 130. Similar description in 'A Return', *Uncollected Stories*, p. 569.

54. *Achievement*, p. 130.

55. In 'Carcassonne' the very text is proof that the dream is valid: it produces the literary text, in spite of the bareness of the surrounding world.

56. This is Faulkner's own explanation of parts of this story, in a letter to Ben Wasson, quoted in part in *Biography, I*, 809, and printed in *Selected Letters*, pp. 71–2.

57. See *Selected Letters*, p. 72 (letter to Ben Wasson).

58. Many of Midgleston's statements seem not to be representative of his genuine opinions or attitudes. His belief in them, in hindsight, should nevertheless not be doubted. The faun-for-a-day business may also be seen in relation to the old tradition of Saturnalia and the rather common use of the King-for-a-Day motif in much literature.

59. Despite the need for interpretation and analysis of this story, no critics have yet approached it seriously. The only discussion of more than just a few passing remarks is the one given by W.K. Everett in his handbook on Faulkner, *Faulkner's Art and Characters*, pp. 150–2.
The re-incarnation of a limb – the leg – and a series of strange deaths cannot be explained, and the lack of logical explanation almost forces a character like David to be seriously troubled in his mind.

60. W.K. Everett does this in his note on 'The Leg' (cf. n. 59). Despite Everett's over-zealous attempt at explaining the story in terms of abnormal psychology, it is admirable that he does try to explain this extremely difficult story at all.

61. The characters remind one of the protagonists in 'Mistral', despite changes of names and characteristics. The pre-war setting combined with the male protagonists' innocence (pre-adult age: 21) make the probing and confused study of the 'fall from innocence' very effective. Housman's poem 'When I Was One-And-Twenty' also deals with the loss of innocence between the ages of twenty-one and twenty-two, and Faulkner certainly knew this poem.

62. A similar expression is used in 'Carcassonne'.
63. The two 'worlds' do not exist alone and without influencing one another. On the contrary, the outside world is very much responsible for what goes on in the inner world, while the fantasy world of the imagination also determines the artist's perception of the outer world.
64. It is important to notice that the dialogue covers only about half a page of the story, and its significance should not be over-emphasized. The story is not a body-soul dialogue: the dialogue is but a part of the total conflict in the story.
65. 'Address Upon Receiving the Nobel Prize for Literature', *Essays, Speeches and Public Letters*, pp. 119–20. Quoted from p. 119.
66. Faulkner himself said something to the same effect about his art in the introduction he wrote for *The Faulkner Reader* (New York: Random House, 1965). See also my article on 'Carcassonne' (in Norwegian) in *Edda*, (1978), No. 4, pp. 207–12.
67. The narrator insists that the story is about this or that; he guides the narrator's attention in a specific direction, and what he wants us to pay heed to is the struggle and pain it takes to write a saleable story, while the love story is less important.
68. See also Melvin E. Bradford, 'An Aesthetic Parable: Faulkner's "Artist at Home",' *Georgia Review*, 27 (1973), 175–81, and Tony J. Owens, 'Faulkner, Anderson, and "Artist at Home".' *Mississippi Quarterly*, 32 (Summer 1979), 393–412.

Notes to Chapter 5

1. Vickery, *The Novels of William Faulkner*, p. 296.
2. *Faulkner in the University*, p. 47.
3. *Faulkner in the University*, p. 78.
4. Ibid., p. 267.
5. Joseph W. Reed, *Faulkner's Narrative*, p. 55, discusses this 'balance' at some length. Reed uses a terminology that differs from the one used by Chatman and Genette, as it differs from the terminology used in this study.
6. This is, for instance, the way the term is used about Dilsey, the Negro cook in *The Sound and the Fury*, in 'Appendix: Compson: 1699–1945'.
7. See Melvin E.A. Bradford, 'Faulkner's Doctrine of Nature: A Study of the Endurance Theme in the Yoknapatawpha Fiction'. Dissertation Vanderbilt 1968.
8. See Bradford's dissertation, pp. 8 ff.
9. One should be cautious not to over-emphasize these contrasts and search for them everywhere. The fact that Homer Barron in 'A Rose for Emily' is a Northerner is not the single most important fact about this story, while there is more reason to stress the South-North contrast in 'Fox Hunt'.
10. It is significant that Quentin Compson is the narrator of this story about sexual misconduct treated rather lightly, especially if we think of him as the Quentin Compson of *The Sound and the Fury*.
11. Meriwether and Millgate, eds., *Lion in the Garden: Interviews with William Faulkner 1926–1962*, p. 244.
12. Ibid., p. 244.
13. It is not clear whether his name is Howes or House. He is called Dorry for the most part, however.
14. Other loyal husbands in Faulkner's fiction are found in 'Artist at Home', 'Honor', 'The Brooch', but most significantly perhaps in *The Wild Palms*. These, then, are husbands who stoically accept their wives' affairs or elopements. That numerous loyal and loving

husbands in more stable and steady marriages are found in Faulkner's fiction is obvious.

15. A brief excerpt from the story may give an indication of how this story points forward to similar expressions in *The Wild Palms:* 'That would have been all right. They could have borne unreality. It was the reality they never had the courage to deny...'. (*Uncollected Stories*, p. 407). In this story as well as in the later novel, a woman finds death in her sacrificial pursuit of love. See also Blotner, *Biography*, Note-section, p. 93, col. 1.

16. Dorry does not recognize her, but she seems to recognize him – the narrator (Crump here) leaves some doubt about this.

17. A man comes to Mr. Bowman at the opening of the story to get help because a drummer has insulted his wife. Mr. Bowman's name is corrected from Mr. Gallup, which Faulkner originally used.

18. When the story was revised and reused in *The Hamlet*, Mink Snopes replaced Cotton as the murderer.

19. In *The Hamlet* Mink is a married man, and his strange – to say the least – relationship to his wife adds important dimensions to his character and to his behaviour within the frame of the story.

20. The story about Mink's murder of Houston is indeed at the very centre of the Snopes trilogy: it leads to Mink's being sentenced to 25 years in the State penitentiary, and when he comes out, he is bent on one thing: to revenge himself on Flem who did not help him when he could.

21. This is elaborated and vastly expanded in *The Hamlet* to motivate Mink's reactions better. He, more than Cotton, has obvious reasons for wishing Houston dead. Cotton's reasons seem to be much more subtle.

22. Cf. L.M. Jones, 'Faulkner's "The Hound",' *Explicator*, 15 (1957), item 37.

23. Most of the story is indeed a description of the hardships following the murder, and the very fact that the hound (Houston's) is impossible to kill may indicate that it is used as a symbol for Cotton's conscience. L.M. Jones sees it this way. Cf. n. 22.

24. Melvin Bradford finds Jenny to be a Lady of Quality, and thinks that she represents the most admirable kind of women in all Faulkner's fiction and that Faulkner shares this opinion. See 'Certain Ladies of Quality: Faulkner's View of Women and the Evidence of "There Was a Queen",' *Arlington Quarterly*, 1 (Winter 1967/68), 106–39. See especially Bradford's footnotes 1 and 3 on pp. 107–9.

25. These letters were received by Narcissa thirteen years earlier, before her marriage to Bayard. Byron Snopes stole the letters back when he robbed the bank and disappeared. The connection between the bank robbery and the theft of the letters makes the logical basis for the crucial confrontation in 'There Was a Queen'. A Federal agent investigating the robbery has got hold of the letters, and Narcissa buys them back with her body.

26. Faulkner's lasting interest in the characters of this story is demonstrated in books as different as *Flags in the Dust, Sanctuary,* and *The Unvanquished.* The inconsistencies one may find between the various appearances of Miss Jenny are not taken up here.

27. The story ends with her death, but one should be careful not to over-emphasize the causal connections between Narcissia's trip to Memphis and Jenny's death. She is, after all, very old and fragile.

28. Bradford, 'Certain Ladies of Quality', p. 108.

29. Ibid., p. 110. Bradford refers to Brooks's *William Faulkner: The Yoknapatawpha Country* as support for Faulkner's attachment to the ideas of community.

30. The narrator does not only discover the secrets of the Sutpen past by asking questions.

314

He also participates actively in the last acts of the Sutpen tragedy, and to some extent he is instrumental in bringing the story to its violent climax in fire and destruction.

31. The central elements of 'Evangeline' are, of course, used in *Absalom, Absalom!* The relationship between the story and the novel is not discussed here. For a brief discussion of it, see Estella Schoenberg, *Old Tales and Talking*, (Jackson, Miss.: University Press of Mississippi, 1977) esp. pp. 30–49.

32. W.K. Everett calls the narrator 'a V.K. Ratliff-type salesman'. Cf. *Faulkner's Art and Characters*, p. 144.

33. Wayne C. Booth, *The Rhetoric of Fiction*, pp. 300 ff.

34. The problem of 'Smoke' from a reader's point of view is the withholding of crucial information and the deliberate attempts to give wrong leads. Probability is not something absolute and definitive, but the background of the events in this story is so broad that the reader is only furnished with a very limited knowledge of the characters.

35. If we include 'Hog Pawn', published for the first time in *Uncollected Stories*, two stories were used also in *The Mansion* ('Hog Pawn' and 'By the People').

36. 'The Hound' is not regarded as a Snopes story here, since no Snopeses figure prominently in it.

37. His participation and responsibility is not doubted by any of the buyers or any other people present at the auction; yet the fact that Flem keeps out of sight for some time provides him with an excuse when those who feel cheated come to claim their money back.

38. This is Suratt (later to become Ratliff), and Flem fools him in a deal concerning goats and will fool him again when he sells the old Frenchman's place to Suratt and two of his companions. The last episode is rendered more completely in 'Lizards in Jamshyd's Courtyard'.

39. Quoted from James L. Sanderson, '"Spotted Horses" and the Theme of Social Evil', *English Journal*, 62 (May 1968), 700–4. (Quotation from footnote on p. 704).

40. In *The Hamlet* the Old Frenchman's Place is a part of the dowry, so that it comes to belong to Flem when he marries Will Varner's daughter, Eula.

41. *The Town* (New York: Vintage Books, 1961), p. 29.

42. He has, of course, become Major de Spain in *The Town*.

43. 'Faulkner's Correspondence with *Scribner's Magazine*', p. 270.

44. His abuse of the two women, perhaps the wife in particular, combined with the long-awaited revenge carried out by Mink Snopes, are the forces which lead to Flem's final downfall. He has not misjudged human nature or somebody's character, but he has not been able to calculate the long-range effects of his doings.

45. Quentin Compson, who narrates the story, is not aware of this moral anarchy; the story eludes him, but he expects to grasp some hidden implications later on. The humour vested in the story reduces the seriousness a little, while the choice of point of view functions in much the same way.

46. There may be some evidence to support the suspicion that Doom is father of the yellow baby, as he is the father of Sam Fathers in *Go Down, Moses*. Elmo Howell notes that not seeing or accepting that Doom is Sam's father is 'to overlook the moral meaning that Faulkner was trying to establish' ('Sam Fathers: A Note on Faulkner's "A Justice"', *Tennessee Studies in Literature*, 12 (1967), 149–53. Quoted from p. 149. I do not think one should infer from *Go Down, Moses* in one's interpretation of 'A Justice'.

47. See G.W. Sutton, 'Primitivism in the Fiction of William Faulkner', Dissertation Mississippi 1967, p. 122. The term is of course also used by numerous other critics.

48. Edmond L. Volpe, 'Faulkner's "Red Leaves": The Deciduation of Nature', *Studies in American Fiction*, 3(Autumn 1975), 121–31. The quotation is found on p. 130. Other critics make similar points.

49. For the relation of Faulkner's Indian tales to historical and sociological facts, see Lewis M. Dabney, *The Indians of Yoknapatawpha* (Baton Rouge; Lousiana State University Press, 1974).

50. *Faulkner in the University*, p. 39.

51. Doom or Ikkemotubbe is the oldest of the three Chickasaw chiefs we encounter in Faulkner's Indian stories; then follow Issetibbeha, and Moketubbe. The genealogy is not clear, however, and while Issetibbeha is the son of Doom in 'Red Leaves', he is the uncle of Doom in 'A Justice', where Doom is the son of Issetibbeha's sister.

52. Irving Howe, *William Faulkner: A Critical Study*, p. 267.

53. See Duane Gage, 'William Faulkner's Indians', *American Indian Quarterly*, 1 (Spring 1974), 27–33. See in particular the last paragraph.

54. See Noel Polk's review of two book-length studies of Faulkner's Indians – Lewis M. Dabney's book and Nigliazzo, 'Faulkner's Indians', (Dissertation New Mexico 1973) – in *Mississippi Quarterly*, 28 (Summer 1975) 387–92.

55. G.H. Muller, 'The Descent of the Gods: Faulkner's "Red Leaves" and the Garden of the South', *Studies in Short Fiction*, 11 (Summer 1974), 243–9, finds that the community in 'Red Leaves' must restore 'an ecumenical function in life' (p. 249). The entrapment he finds in the story he interprets as symbolic of 'man's fall from grace. Man has lost sight of the holy Garden and this failure of vision estranges him from the possibility of salvation' (p. 248).

56. An example of direct statement, instead of implicit commentary, is found in the paragraph left out from the *Mercury* version when the story was printed in *These 13*. Norman H. Pearson, 'Faulkner's Three Evening Suns', *Yale University Library Gazette*, 29 (October 1954), comments on what he considers the appropriateness of removing this paragraph. See pp. 66–7 of his essay.

57. The story is 'Mistral'. See *These 13*, p. 313.

58. This indicates that Faulkner makes extensive use of experiences he and Spratling had when walking in Europe in 1925. For an account of Faulkner's trip to and in Europe, see Blotner, *Biography, I*, chapter 25 (pp. 443 ff.).

59. *The Mansion* (New York: Vintage Books, 1965).

60. Vickery, *The Novels of William Faulkner*, p. 299, describes 'the anonymous voice' in such terms.

61. Vickery, *The Novels of William Faulkner*, p. 300.

62. *Faulkner in the University*, p. 117.

63. Vickery, *The Novels of William Faulkner*, p. 301.

Notes to Chapter 6

1. The term 'short-story cycle' has been used by many critics, but Forrest L. Ingram's study, *Representative Short Story Cycles of the Twentieth Century* (The Hague, Paris: Mouton, 1971) is the most recent substantial contribution to a discussion of this sub-genre. Ingram calls his book 'Studies in a Literary Genre', and even though the novelty of his study may be disputed, the book is interesting in a study of Faulkner also because it treats *The Unvanquished* at some length. Joanne V. Creighton *Faulkner's Craft of Revision* (Detroit: Wayne State University Press, 1977) prefers to use the term 'short story composite'.

2. The only short story in *Knight's Gambit* written after 1941 is the title story, 'Knight's Gambit'. Its short, early version was written early in 1942, while the long novella that is printed in the book may have been begun before 1948 but was definitely not written in its final version before Faulkner's plan for a collection of these stories in a volume of their own had been accepted by his publisher.

3. The earliest story for *Go Down, Moses* is 'Lion', published in 1935, while the final version of 'The Bear', incorporating material from 'Lion', probably is the latest of the stories. Faulkner revised all these stories considerably, mostly to add unity to the longer work, but also to improve style, diction, etc.

4. 'Barn Burning' is generally accepted as one of Faulkner's small-scale masterpieces, while no critics so far have paid serious attention to the masterly 'Uncle Willy'. The British edition of Faulkner's collected short stories, published by Chatto and Windus, has implicitly given special credit to 'Uncle Willy' by the very fact that the last of their three-volume edition is entitled *Uncle Willy and Other Stories*. (The first two are *These Thirteen* and *Doctor Martino and Other Stories*)

5. This is of course 'Mule in the Yard' which was incorporated in *The Town* (1957).

6. 'Barn Burning' was originally written as the opening chapter of *The Hamlet* (1940), while the relationship between 'Afternoon of a Cow' and this novel is limited to the cow-business in both (in *The Hamlet* this is in the section 'The Long Summer' where the idiot Snopes, Ike, and a heifer play the central parts).

7. 'The Tall Men' is included in the number thirteen, of course not among the seven that relate to novels. 'The Tall Men' is discussed in chapter 8, since this story has obvious relationships with the other World War II stories Faulkner wrote in 1942.

8. For *Go Down, Moses* there is no indication that Faulkner thought of his Negro-White stories as a series, or as material for a book. As for the Bayard-Ringo stories: he conceived of them as a series from the very beginning. At any rate, Faulkner always seems to have had the possibility of re-use and of a larger design in mind, and his craftsmanship enabled him to superimpose a unifying structure on formerly disparate material.

9. The implied author's attitude does not have to be absolutely consistent within a literary text, or it may be difficult to ascertain what his attitude is and hence what the significance of a story in the final analysis is. In the stories discussed here one should, of course, not expect to find an opposition between absolute opposites; only in Faulkner's worst stories do we have 'model villains' and 'model saints'.

10. Jack F. Stewart, 'Apotheosis and Apocalypse in Faulkner's "Wash",' *Studies in Short Fiction*, 6 (Fall 1969), 586–600. Quoted from p. 588.

11. *Scribner's Magazine*, 46 (August 1934), p. 70, col. 2. See also *Collected Stories*, p. 264.

12. John L. Longley, Jr., *The Tragic Mask; A Study of Faulkner's Heroes* (Chapel Hill: University of North Carolina Press, 1957), pp. 116–20.

13. The setting of the story in Major De Spain's hunting camp and the implied criticism of some ways of modern life add interest and seriousness to the story, especially since there is reason to believe that the frame narrator is Quentin Compson – as he is in the *Big Woods* version of this comic tale. The introductory description of life in Jefferson now is similar to the picture of life in Jefferson which Quentin gives in the opening paragraphs of 'That Evening Sun'.

14. Major Saucier Weddel of 'A Mountain Victory' is the son of Chief Weddel, whom we meet in 'Lo!', and in the former story, the Major gives a brief and slightly different account of the visit to Washington.

15. Lewis M. Dabney writes of 'Lo!' that it 'is a tall tale of how you can "fight City Hall",

written with a southerner's appreciation of the discomfiture of Washington power'. It is a situation comedy with broad elements of farce, which anticipates the confrontation politics of our time. See Dabney, *The Indians of Yoknapatawpha* (Baton Rouge: LSU Press, 1974), p. 43.

16. A.P. Libby, 'Chronicles of Children', p. 192. Libby has borrowed the expression from Leslie A. Fiedler's *Love and Death in the American Novel* (1960; rev.ed.: New York: Stein & Day, 1975).

17. This statement is disputable. In the opening paragraphs, the story seems to be a reminiscence, told in the past tense ('I know what they said'), while the concluding lines are in the present tense and directly related to the events of Uncle Willy's recent death. Here the boy despairs of the problem of telling about his understanding of Willy, and is clearly troubled by having to excuse himself even to his father. Some of the insights or more general views in the opening paragraphs indicate a more grown-up mind, while the story about 'I' and Uncle Willy of course is told by the child narrator and in his idiom.

18. M.E. Bradford says that 'Golden Land' 'is a most important story, for it contains Mr. Faulkner's most searching critique of the unnatural and escapist aspects of life in modern America'. See Bradford, 'Escaping Westward: Faulkner's "Golden Land",' *Georgia Review,* 19 (Spring 1965), pp. 72–6. Quoted from p. 72.

19. Bradford, 'Escaping Westward; Faulkner's "Golden Land",' p. 76.

20. Walter K. Everett, *Faulkner's Art and Character* (New York: Barron's Educational Series, 1969), pp. 143–4.

21. This is Bradford's statement, outlined in the article mentioned above in notes 18 and 19. A much broader discussion of Faulkner's use of the 'endurance theme' is found in Bradford's doctoral dissertation, 'Faulkner's Doctrine of Nature', Vanderbilt 1968.

22. See 'The Tall Men', *The Saturday Evening Post,* 213 (31 May 1941), pp. 14–15, 95, 96, 98, 99, or *Collected Stories,* pp. 45–61.

Notes to Chapter 7

1. Faulkner was very optimistic about the Bayard-Ringo stories and the *Post* when he submitted the first of these stories to Morton Goldman in 1934. See e.g. *Selected Letters of William Faulkner,* pp. 80–1.

2. In the composition of these stories, Faulkner came to a halt after he had finished the first three, which may explain some of the differences in tone and seriousness between the earliest stories and the later ones. The fact that the later stories deal with the reconstruction period may be another explanation. Bringing some unity into the volume comprising these stories, Faulkner had to revise the earliest ones to make them fit in with the most novel of his stories: the one he was writing for the volume, 'An Odor of Verbena', which is the most accomplished story in the book and also the most serious one in tone.

3. Millgate, *Achievement,* p. 170.

4. This is not quite true, since 'An Odor of Verbena' was written to finish the volume. On the other hand, Faulkner sent the story to the *Post* himself. Cf. letter to Goldman, 24 July 1937. *Selected Letters,* p. 100.

5. Forrest L. Ingram regards *The Unvanquished* as a superb example of the modern short-story cycle and discusses the book at length in his *Representative Short Story Cycles of the Twentieth Century* (The Hague, Paris: Mouton, 1971), pp. 106–42.

Joanne V. Creighton uses the term 'short story composite', and is more concerned with Faulkner's mastery of revision than with the book's overall structure. See *Faulkner's Craft of Revision* (Detroit: Wayne State University Press, 1977), pp. 73–84. Other critics have either described the book as a mere collection of stories or a loosely structured novel, while a few critics have made out cases for regarding the book as a novel.

6. Cleanth Brooks, Hyatt H. Waggoner, Carvel Collins, and James B. Meriwether are among the critics who have made out convincing cases for regarding the book as a novel (cf. Millgate, *Achievement,* p. 167). Brooks does this in *The Hidden God* (New Haven and London: Yale UP, 1963, pp. 30–4; Waggoner in *From Jefferson to the World,* pp. 170–83; Collins in 'Foreword' to a 1959 issue of the book (New York: New American Library); while Meriwether's detailed documentation is found in his 'The Place of *The Unvanquished* in William Faulkner's Yoknapatawpha Series' (Diss. Princeton 1958).

7. I am thinking here of Brooks's chapter on *The Unvanquished* in his *William Faulkner: The Yoknapatawpha Country* (New Haven and London: Yale UP., 1963). Ingram and Creighton are both referred to above, while Edward M. Holmes has studied Faulkner's re-use of his material and published *Faulkner's Twice-Told Tales* (The Hague & Paris: Mouton, 1966) where *The Unvanquished* is discussed on pp. 46–57.

8. In spite of Faulkner's use of stock situations and sterotyped characters and the uneven quality of the narrative in this book, there are also passages of brilliant writing, in the early as well as in the later among the stories.

9. Cleanth Brooks, *William Faulkner: The Yoknapatawpha Country,* p. 244.

10. The book does in fact draw on as many as ten short stories; of the seven chapters in the book, chapter 2, 'The Fire and the Hearth', includes three separate stories, while 'The Bear' makes use of material from the 1935 story, 'Lion', while a later version of 'The Bear', was published in 1942.

11. This is the term used by Olga W. Vickery in her discussion of *Go Down, Moses.* See her *The Novels of William Faulkner: A Critical Interpretation* p. 124.

12. *Lion in the Garden: Interviews with William Faulkner 1926–1962,* p. 251.

13. Ibid., p. 217.

14. See Albert Gerard, 'Justice in Yoknapatawpha County: Some Symbolic Motifs in Faulkner's Later Writing', *Faulkner Studies,* 2 (Winter 1954), 49–57.

15. Millgate, *Achievement,* p. 265.

16. Jerome F. Klinkowitz, 'The Thematic Unity of *Knight's Gambit*', *Critique,* II (1969), 81–100. An important article on Faulkner's detective fiction is also Mick Gidley, 'Elements of the Detective Story in William Faulkner's Fiction', *Journal of Popular Culture,* 7 (Summer 1973), 97–123.

17. Klinkowitz, 'The Thematic Unity of *Knight's Gambit*', p. 81. See also Faulkner's letter to Malcolm Cowley where he expressed his opinion of a short-story collection (*Selected Letters,* p. 278).

18. Edward M. Holmes calls 'An Odor of Verbena' 'that very keystone in the arch of *The Unvanquished*'. See *Faulkner's Twice-Told Tales,* p. 46.

19. Millgate (*Achievement,* p. 167) writes about the 'revaluation' of Colonel Sartoris's actions on the basis of 'An Odor of Verbena'. See also Robert E. Knoll, '*The Unvanquished* for a Start', *College English,* 19 (1958), 228–43.

20. For a dating of the opening episode, on the basis of references to events in the Civil War, see e.g. Edmond L. Volpe, *A Reader's Guide to William Faulkner,* pp. 78 ff.

21. Brooks, *William Faulkner: The Yoknapatawpha Country,* pp. 96–7.

22. See William E. Walker, '*The Unvanquished* – The Restoration of a Tradition', in

Reality and Myth: Essays in American Literature in Memory of Richard Croom Beatty (Nashville: Vanderbilt UP, 1964), pp. 275–97. A discussion of Drusilla's priestess-like quality is found on p. 292.

23. In *Flags in the Dust/Sartoris* he is called Redlaw.

24. Robert E. Knoll, '*The Unvanquished* for a Start', p. 342.

25. Ibid., p. 343.

26. Andrew Lytle, 'The Son of Man: He will Prevail', *Sewanee Review*, 63 (1955), 114–37. See also Brooks's discussion of this essay-review in *William Faulkner: The Yoknapatawpha Country*, pp. 382–3.

27. Brooks (referring to Lytle), p. 382.

28. Olga Vickery makes this point, finding that the stories are related through their connection with the plantation. This is then one of the unifying elements that makes *Go Down, Moses* a 'loosely connected novel' in her opinion. See Vickery, p. 125.

29. On the basis of a similar interpretation of 'Pantaloon in Black', Brooks calls the story 'Wordsworthian'. Cf. Brooks, *William Faulkner: The Yoknapatawpha Country*, pp. 254–5.

30. *Faulkner in the University*, p. 38.

31. An early title of this story was 'Almost', and this title may indeed refer to the narrow escapes described in the text.

32. *Faulkner in the University*, p. 84.

33. Cf. Joanne Creighton's discussion of this in *Faulkner's Craft of Revision*, pp. 88–9.

34. Later on Uncle Buck and Sophonsiba were nevertheless married, and Ike is the result of this marriage. When asked about how this could happen, Faulkner suggested that 'probably Uncle Buck finally just gave up. That was his fate and he might just as well quit struggling.' See *Faulkner in the University*, p. 46.

35. The critic who most strongly has advocated such a view of Isaac McCaslin is probably David H. Stewart in his article, 'The Purpose of Faulkner's Ike', *Criticism*, 3 (Fall 1961) 333–42. Stewart finds that 'Isaac is in many ways an unattractive creature' (p. 340).

36. Creighton, p. 87.

37. Old Carothers McCaslin had provided a legacy of one thousand dollars to be given to his part-Negro son when he came of age. The money was never requested by this son, so that the legacy was to be divided among this son's three children. The legacy was increased to one thousand dollars each for the children; Tennie's Jim, Fonsiba, and Lucas. This legacy explains Lucas's money, and the episode when he requested the money and put it in the bank is included in 'The Fire and the Hearth'.

38. Warren Beck, *Faulkner: Essays* (Madison: University of Wisconsin Press, 1976), p. 335.

39. Warren Beck, *Faulkner: Essays*, p. 378.

40. Brooks, *William Faulkner: The Yoknapatawpha Country*, p. 270.

41. *Go Down, Moses*, p. 286. As we have seen, this thought is central in *The Unvanquished* too, as well as in some of Faulkner's stories about World War I.

42. Quoted by Brooks in *William Faulkner: The Yoknapatawpha Country*, p. 274.

43. Notice that Molly is wrong in her memory of the story from the Bible: Joseph, not Benjamin, was sold into Egypt.

44. This does not appear to be simply a slip of the pen; the form Chuck is used throughout the typescript, and the name Weddel is given in the very last sentences of the story, which is the address of Charles Weddel, now on his way to participate in the Second World War.

45. Klinkowitz is aware of this important distinction between 'Knight's Gambit' and the

other stories of the volume. See 'The Thematic Unity of Knight's Gambit', p. 94. Millgate is in error on this point, as is also (apparently, since he does not discuss this point), Cantrell in his study of Faulkner's late short fiction.

46. Millgate, *Achievement*, p. 270.
47. In his letter to Commins (*Selected Letters*, p. 280) Faulkner himself states the different characteristics of this story: 'It is a love story, in which Stevens prevents a crime (murder) not for justice but to gain (he is now fifty plus) the childhood sweetheart which he lost 20 years ago.'
48. The first time he did prove it, and that time beyond any doubt, was in his revision of the galleys for *Sanctuary*. See Faulkner's introduction in the 1932 Modern Library re-issue of the novel: *Sanctuary* (New York: Modern Library, 1932).
49. Warren Beck, *Faulkner: Essays,* p. 334.

Notes to Chapter 8

1. Articles on 'The Tall Men' include Elmo Howell's 'William Faulkner and the New Deal', *Midwest Quarterly,* 5 (1964), 323-32 and 'William Faulkner and the Plain People of Yoknapatawpha County', *Journal of Mississippi History,* 24 (1962), 73-87; and M.E. Bradford's 'Faulkner's "Tall Men",' *South Atlantic Quarterly,* 41 (1962), 29-39.
2. Bradford says that 'No group of characters in the Yoknapatawpha Cycle offers more insight into the human qualities which Faulkner most admires than do his yeoman farmers.' See 'Faulkner's "Tall Men",' p. 29.
3. Honour and pride are familiar words in many Faulkner stories: 'discipline' is on the other hand, a quality becoming increasingly important in the country stories from 1942 and later.
4. Bradford, 'Faulkner's "Tall Men",' p. 29.
5. Faulkner's purchase of a farm early in 1938 probably made him better acquainted with country people and country life, and this may be one of the reasons why more 'country' stories came to be written now.
6. See Elmo Howell, 'William Faulkner and *Pro Patria Mori*', *Louisiana Studies,* 5 (1966), 89-96, which discusses 'Two Soldiers' and 'Shall Not Perish' on a very general level.
7. W.F. Cantrell discusses this point at some length in his 'Faulkner's Late Short Fiction', Diss. South Carolina, 1970, pp. 28-9.
8. Bradford calls the road to Memphis 'Faulkner's favorite highroad to self-discovery', which is an adequate description of it. See M.E. Bradford, 'Faulkner and the Jeffersonian Dream: Nationalism in "Two Soldiers" and "Shall Not Perish",' *Mississippi Quarterly,* 18 (1965), 94-100. Quoted from p. 96.
9. In 'By the People' (1955) there is a reference to this story, but here Res is called Eck and other inconsistencies may simply be accounted for by faulty memory on the author's part.
10. Faulkner's reference to Byron's 'She Walks in Beauty' is, of course, intentional, while his rather immodest use of the great Romantic poet is very much in keeping with the tone of 'A Courtship', if not with Byron's poem.
11. See Frank Cantrell, 'Faulkner's "A Courtship",' *Mississippi Quarterly,* 24 (1971), 289-95. Quoted from p. 289.
12. Cf. Faulkner's own note for the Compson Appendix, published by J.B. Meriwether: 'A Prefatory Note by Faulkner for the Compson Appendix', *American Literature,* 43 (1971/72), 281-4.

13. The use of this Appendix as an introduction is hardly correct (cf. The Modern Library edition of *The Sound and the Fury/As I Lay Dying* [New York, 1946]). It is an appendix, and should be placed at the end of the book, as it is in the Modern Library edition of *The Sound and the Fury* (New York, 1965). Here the Appendix is found on pp. 403-27.
14. Millgate, *Achievement*, p. 230.
15. This point is also made by Adrienne Bond in 'Eneas Africanus and Faulkner's Fabulous Racehorse,' *Southern Literary Journal*, 9 (Spring 1977), 3-15.

Notes to Chapter 9

1. For a discussion of this, see James B. Meriwether, 'Two Unknown Faulkner Short Stories', RANAM, 4 (1971), 23-30; especially p. 29.
2. Faulkner's essays are collected in Meriwether, ed., *William Faulkner: Essays, Speeches, and Public Letters* (New York: Random House, 1965).
3. 'Two Unkown Faulkner Short Stories', pp. 28-9.
4. *Selected Letters*, p. 306.
5. Elmo Howell, 'A Name for Faulkner's City', *Names*, 16 (1968), 415-21. Howell most likely exaggerates Faulkner's motives here.
6. 'A Name for the City', *Harper's Magazine*, 201 (October 1950), p. 200.
7. According to Cantrell, Dr. Noel Polk's work on *Requiem for a Nun* indicates that the introduction 'has far more to do with the novel than with the story, though Gavin Stevens' remark is deleted from the published version of *Requiem'*. Cf. Cantrell's diss., p. 99, footnote 4.
8. Michel Gresset, 'Weekend, Lost and Revisited', *Mississippi Quarterly*, 21 (Summer 1968), 173-8, finds Mr. Acarius to be 'an invcterate alcoholic' (p. 274). The story does not bear out such an assumption, as it is said that Mr. Acarius let himself go into alcohol completely again for the first time since his college days' (*The Saturday Evening Post*, 238 (9 October 1965), p. 27, column 3).
9. Cantrell's dissertation, p. 114.
10. The concluding lines of the story are discussed and interpreted by Gresset (p. 176). Cantrell disagrees with Gresset's interpretation (pp. 119-20); and I find it probable that 'him' in the final conversation refers to 'mankind' and not to one of the alcoholics in the clinic, as Gresset thinks it does.
11. *The Saturday Evening Post*, 138, (9 October 1965), p. 26.
12. 'Two Unknown Faulkner Short Stories', pp. 28-9.
13. *Holiday*, 15 (April 1954), p. 33. A better text of this story is found in *Essays, Speeches, and Public Letters*, pp. 11-43.
14. 'Mississippi' (the *Holiday* text), p. 33).
15. Ibid., p. 46, col. 3.
16. 'An Introduction' to the *Holiday* printing of 'Mississippi', p. 33.
17. Ibid., p. 44, col. 2.
18. Ibid., p. 44, col. 3.
19. Cf. M.E. Bradford, 'The Winding Horn: Hunting and the Making of Men in Faulkner's "Race at Morning",' *Papers on English Language and Literature*, 1 (Summer 1965), 272-8. Bradford sees the story as the education of the nameless waif narrator.
20. Faulkner's criticism of this system is of course only implied, since it is sifted through his characters. Gavin Stevens is very direct and harsh in his criticism of the elective system, where the most stupid and least suitable men seem to be most likely to be

elected to higher and higher offices. See in particular p. 134 of *Mademoiselle*, 41 (October 1955).

21. 'Two Unknown Faulkner Short Stories', p. 30.
22. Ibid., p. 29.
23. Cf. 'The Short Fiction of William Faulkner: A Bibliography,' p. 302. Ober's records reveal that Faulkner wrote a two and a half page introduction to go with the excerpt from the novel.

Notes to Chapter 10

1. 'To write a series of good little tales I deem ample work for a lifetime'. Quoted from Ray B. West, Jr., *The Short Story in America 1900–1950*, p. [v].
2. Vickery, *The Novels of William Faulkner*, p. 300.
3. Ibid., pp. 300–1.
4. Hemingway and Faulkner are often compared, since they are generally considered 'the two most significant (American) writers of fiction in the first half of the twentieth century', to quote Ray B. West, Jr., in *The Short Story in America, 1900–1950* (Chicago: Regnery, 1952), p. 85. While Faulkner's reputation has increased in the last couple of decades, Hemingway's seems to have been on the decline, so that Faulkner often is regarded as being the better short-story writer of the two.
5. Ray B. West, Jr., (cf.n. 4) even holds that 'it is probably in the realm of the short story that the supremacy of these two authors is least in question' (p. 85). He also thinks that Hemingway and Faulkner are the only writers in the first half of the twentieth century whose short-story accomplishment can stand comparison with James's short stories.
6. 'What Happened to the Short Story', (*Atlantic Monthly*, 188 (1951), p. 74, col. 2).
7. Ibid., p. 74, col. 2.
8. Ibid., p. 74, col. 1.
9. *The American Short Story in the Twenties*, pp. 4–5.
10. Davis, Holman, Rubin, Jr., *Southern Writing, 1585–1920* (New York: Odyssey, 1970), p. 987.
11. Henry Louis Mencken, 'The Sahara of the Bozart', in *Southern Writing, 1585–1920* (cf. n. 10), pp. 971–79. Originally published in 1917.
12. Ibid., p. 971.
13. This is discussed at some length in *Short Story Career*, ch. 3.
14. Ibid., ch. 3.
15. Waggoner, *William Faulkner: From Jefferson to the World*, p. 194.
16. Kazin, *Contemporaries*, (Boston: Little, Brown, 1902), p. 158.

Index of Names and Titles

The index does not include names of fictional characters; nor does it include titles of works of criticism, since these are referred to by the names of their authors. It includes references to the Notes section.

325

327

Publications of The American Institute, University of Oslo

Halvdan Koht: *The American Spirit in Europe. Survey of Transatlantic Influences,* ix, 289 pp. (Philadelphia, Pa., 1949). Reprinted 1970.

Einar Haugen: *The Norwegian Language in America. A Study in Bilingual Behavior.*
   Vol. I: The Bilingual Community, xiv, 317 pp.
   Vol. II: The American Dialects of Norwegian, vii, 377 pp. (Philadelphia, Pa., 1953). 2nd edition, in one volume, xxvii, 699 pp. (Bloomington, Ind., 1970).

Sigmund Skard: *American Studies in Europe. Their History and Present Organization.*
   Vol. I: The General Background, The United Kingdom, France, and Germany. pp. 1–358.
   Vol. II: The Smaller Western Countries, The Scandinavian Countries, The Mediterranean Nations, Eastern Countries, International Organization, and Conclusion. pp. 359–736 (Philadelphia, Pa.,1958).

Americana Norvegica. Norwegian Contributions to American Studies.
   Vol. I. Editors: Sigmund Skard and Henry H. Wasser. 340 pp. (Philadelphia, Pa., 1966).
   Vol II. Editor: Sigmund Skard. Editorial Committee: Ingvald Raknem, Georg Roppen, Ingrid Semmingsen. 357 pp. (Philadelphia, Pa., 1968).
   Vol. III. Studies in Scandinavian-American Interrelations Dedicated to Einar Haugen. Editors: Harald S. Naess and Sigmund Skard. Editorial Committee: Ingvald Raknem, Ingrid Semmingsen, Orm Överland. 390 pp. (Oslo, 1971).
   Vol. IV: Norwegian Contributions to American Studies Dedicated to Sigmund Skard. Editor: Brita Seyersted. Editorial Committee: Helge Normann Nilsen, Orm Överland, Ingrid Semmingsen, xiv, 442 pp. (Oslo, 1973).

Jan W. Dietrichson: *The Image of Money in the American Novel of the Gilded Age,* 417 pp. (Oslo and New York, 1969).

Per Seyersted: *Kate Chopin. A Critical Biography.* 247 pp. (Oslo and Baton Rouge. La., 1969). Reprinted 1980, paper (Baton Rouge), hardcover (New York).

Per Sveino: *Orests A. Brownson's Road to Catholicism.* 340 pp. (Oslo and New York, 1970).

Orm Överland: *The Making and Meaning of an American Classic. James Fenimore Cooper's* The Prairie. 207 pp. (Oslo and New York, 1973).

Dorothy Burton Skårdal: *The Divided Heart. Scandinavian Immigrant Experience through Literary Sources.* 394 pp. (Oslo and Lincoln, 1974).

Sigmund Skard: *The United States in Norwegian History.* 218 pp. (Oslo and Westport, Conn., 1976).

Sigmund Skard: *Transatlantica. Memoirs of a Norwegian Americanist.* 218 pp. (Oslo and New York, 1978). Reprinted 1980.

Per Seyersted, editor, with Emily Toth, assistant editor: *A Kate Chopin Miscellany.* 296 pp. (Oslo and Natchitoches, La., 1979).

Ingrid Semmingsen and Per Seyersted, editors: *Scando-Americana: Papers on Scandinavian Emigration to the United States.* 213 pp. (Oslo, 1980).

Hans H. Skei: *William Faulkner: The Short Story Career.* 164 pp. (Oslo and New York, 1981). Reprinted 1984.

Per Seyersted: *From Norwegian Romantic to American Realist: Studies in the Life and Writings of Hjalmar Hjorth Boyesen.* 208 pp. (Oslo and Atlantic Highlands, N.J., 1984).

Hans H. Skei: *William Faulkner: The Novelist as Short Story Writer.* (Oslo and New York, 1985).